STATE OF THE
WORLD
1995

Other Norton/Worldwatch Books

Lester R. Brown et al.

State of the World 1984	*State of the World 1991*
State of the World 1985	*State of the World 1992*
State of the World 1986	*State of the World 1993*
State of the World 1987	*State of the World 1994*
State of the World 1988	*Vital Signs 1992*
State of the World 1989	*Vital Signs 1993*
State of the World 1990	*Vital Signs 1994*

ENVIRONMENTAL ALERT SERIES

Lester R. Brown et al.

Saving the Planet

Alan Thein Durning

How Much Is Enough?

Sandra Postel

Last Oasis

Lester R. Brown
Hal Kane

Full House

Christopher Flavin
Nicholas Lenssen

Power Surge

STATE OF THE WORLD

1995

*A Worldwatch Institute Report on
Progress Toward a Sustainable Society*

PROJECT DIRECTOR
Lester R. Brown

ASSOCIATE PROJECT
DIRECTORS
Christopher Flavin
Hilary F. French

EDITOR
Linda Starke

CONTRIBUTING RESEARCHERS
Lester R. Brown
Derek Denniston
Christopher Flavin
Hilary F. French
Hal Kane
Nicholas Lenssen
Michael Renner
David Malin Roodman
Megan Ryan
Aaron Sachs
Peter Weber
John E. Young

W·W·NORTON & COMPANY

NEW YORK   LONDON

The text of this book is composed in Baskerville, with the display set in Caslon.
Composition and manufacturing by the Haddon Craftsmen, Inc.

First Edition

ISBN 0-393-03717-7
ISBN 0-393-31261-5 (pbk)

W. W. Norton & Company, Inc., 500 Fifth Avenue, New York, N.Y. 10110
W. W. Norton & Company Ltd., 10 Coptic Street, London WC1A 1PU

1 2 3 4 5 6 7 8 9 0

This book is printed on recycled paper.

Acknowledgments

This is the only place in all our publications where we get to thank the staff at Worldwatch as well as our friends outside the Institute—the Worldwatch Board of Directors, the foundations and individuals who fund our work, and the many people who reviewed each year's chapters. We're not sure if it is the least read part of *State of the World* or the one some people turn to first!

Some of the people we turn to from time to time are the funders who support our work. Core funding for the research and writing of *State of the World* comes from the Rockefeller Brothers Fund, Rockefeller Financial Services, and the Winslow Foundation. Chapter 1 this year draws on our research on food and population, which was funded by the Wallace Genetic and Weeden foundations and the McBride Family Fund. The research on fisheries in Chapter 2 was supported by the Curtis and Edith Munson Foundation. And the research in Chapter 4 was funded in part by the Energy and Joyce Mertz-Gilmore foundations. Others that support the Institute's work include the Geraldine R. Dodge, George Gund, W. Alton Jones, John D. and Catherine T. MacArthur, Andrew W. Mellon, Edward John Noble, Surdna, Turner, Wallace Genetic, and Weeden foundations; the Pew Memorial Trust; the Lynn R. and Karl E. Prickett Fund; and the U.N. Population Fund. Peter Buckley has provided a personal grant for general support.

This is the first *State of the World* without Sandra Postel's name on the cover. Sandi is now Director of the Global Water Policy Project in Boston. She remains a Senior Fellow of Worldwatch, however, and we thank her for overseeing the preparation of Chapter 3 this year. Marcia Lowe has also left the Institute and now lives in North Carolina, where she continues to work on transportation issues. The authors of Chapter 7 would like to thank Marcy for the research and initial drafts she did on pollution in China.

Behind the names on the various chapters this year lie the hard work of our enthusiastic research staff: Anjali Acharya (Chapter 7), Nancy Chege (Chapter 10), Anne Platt (Chapter 2), and Elena Wilken (Chapter 1). Gary Gardner and Odil Tunali joined the Institute just as this year's volume was completed, and gave a welcome hand with proofreading. Lori Baldwin assisted with research on Chapter 9 in addition to being responsible for the Worldwatch Library. Library Assistant James Porter kept information flowing to all researchers from the enormous number of magazines and journals received at the Institute.

Responsibility for letting the world know the results of our research rests with our capable communications team: Director of Communications Jim Perry, Deputy Director Denise Byers Thomma, Communications Associate Steve Kaufman, and Administrative Assistant Tara Patterson. One important avenue for disseminating the results of our work is *World Watch*. Thanks for our award-winning bimonthly magazine, which presents complex information in a compelling and highly readable fashion, go to Editor Ed Ayres, joined this year by Associate Editor Chris Bright.

One of the busiest parts of the Institute after *State of the World* comes out is our publications office, which responds to your orders. We are grateful for the careful, behind-the-scenes work of Publication Sales Coordinator Robin Hinegardner, Publications Assistants Joseph Gravely and Millicent Johnson, and Receptionist Laura Malinowski.

Rounding out the administrative side of Worldwatch are Vice President and Treasurer Blondeen Gravely, Executive Assistant to the President and Computer Systems Administrator Reah Janise Kauffman, Assistant Treasurer Barbara Fallin, and Administrative Assistant to the Vice President for Research Suzanne Clift. Without them, the Institute would not function at all.

Outside the Institute, thanks go to Hai Pei Xue for preliminary research on Chapter 7. And once again, we relied on independent editor Linda Starke to polish our prose and get the whole manuscript pulled together on time. Getting through a production schedule that leaves no room for error would be impossible without the understanding and good humor of Iva Ashner and Andrew Marasia at W.W. Norton & Company. Ritch Pope prepared our index this year.

The list of outside experts who gave freely of their time to comment on early drafts of chapters is, as usual, long. We know that mention here is scant compensation for the hours they spent reviewing our work, but we hope the following will accept our sincere thanks: Craig Anderson, Nicole Ball, Jayanta Bandyopadhyay, Paul Bartlett, Scott Bernstein, Soontorn Boonyatikarn, Barbara Bramble, Mark Broyles, Sarah Burns, Elizabeth Byers, John Caddy, Mac Chapin, Adele Crispoldi, Jessica Hamburger, Eric Howard, Nigel Howard, Frances Irwin, Jack Ives, Sarah Jackson-Han, Vlad Kaczynski, Frank Kensill, David Kirkpatrick, David Korten, Lee Eng Lock, Eduardo Loayza, Marcia Lowe, Alair MacLean, Louis Malin, Charlie Manlove, William Mansfield III, Jocelyn Mason, Chris Newton, Patti Petesch, D. Jane Pratt, Martin Price, Donald Rogich, Daniel Rosen, Amelia Salzman, S. Jacob Scherr, Peter Schmid, Polly Shaw, Katherine Sierra, Vaclav Smil, Lisa Speer, Lisa Surprenant, Kunio Uchino, Brenda Vale, Robert Vale, Mike Weber, Alex Wilson, John Wise, Carrie Wood, Jim Wood, and Herbert Wulf.

We sincerely thank all these individuals—and all the people inside and outside of Worldwatch who support us—for helping to make *State of the World* one of the most widely translated and used public policy reports. And we thank you, our diverse readers—whether international civil servants, grassroots activists, environmental entrepreneurs, educators, or concerned citizens. We count on you to ensure that words are translated into action.

Lester R. Brown, Christopher Flavin,
and Hilary French

Contents

Worldwatch Database Diskettes

The data from all graphs and tables contained in this book, as well as from those in all other Worldwatch publications of the past year, are available on diskette for use with IBM-compatible or Macintosh computers. This includes data from the Vital Signs *series of books,* Worldwatch Papers, World Watch *magazine, and the Environmental Alert series of books. The data are formatted for use with spreadsheet software compatible with Lotus 1–2–3 version 2, including all Lotus spreadsheets, Quattro Pro, Excel, SuperCalc, and many others. For IBM-compatibles, both 3½ (high-density) and 5¼ (low-density) diskettes are supplied. To order, indicate either IBM or Macintosh and send check or money order for $89.00, or credit card number and expiration date (Visa and MasterCard only), to Worldwatch Institute, 1776 Massachusetts Ave., NW, Washington, DC 20036 (tel: 202–452–1999; fax: 202–296-7365).*

List of Tables and Figures

LIST OF TABLES

List of Figures

Chapter 4. Harnessing the Sun and the Wind

Chapter 5. Creating a Sustainable Materials Economy

Chapter 6. Making Better Buildings

Chapter 7. Facing China's Limits

Chapter 8. Leaving Home

Chapter 10. Forging a New Global Partnership

Foreword

A few years after *State of the World* was launched in 1984, the Institute received a letter from an obscure publishing house in Romania called Editura Tehnică, asking for the rights to publish *State of the World* in Romanian. We were pleased at their interest, which coincided with our goal of publishing this annual volume in all the world's principal languages, and responded affirmatively.

The head of the publishing house had not risen to that position after years of hard work in publishing. He had been demoted to it after having been a rising young star in the Communist party. He had been Minister of Youth before a parting of the ways with Nicolae Ceaucescu. After a 1971 visit to the socialist countries of East Asia, Ceaucescu came back determined to build a disciplined, authoritarian society along the lines of the North Korean model. At this point, our promising young Party leader dissented. Five demotions later, he found himself the head of Editura Tehnică.

In late September 1994, the former head of this obscure publishing firm, Ion Iliescu, travelled to Washington for a state visit—as president of Romania. On his way to a White House meeting, he stopped at the Institute to meet the research team whose work he had translated and published. We were impressed with his intimate knowledge not only of the issues covered in *State of the World* over the years, but of who had worked on each topic.

At the White House, Iliescu met with another head of state who has a long-standing familiarity with *State of the World*. President Clinton had been reading the book for years, thanks to Ted Turner's regular distribution of the annual reports to the nation's 50 governors. In addition to this distribution, Turner also gives copies to members of Congress and the Fortune 500 CEOs.

We are indebted to everyone who distributes our materials to the world's key decisionmakers. In Europe, Izaak van Melle gave copies of *State of the World 1994* to the 1,100 participants at the World Economic Forum in Davos, Switzerland. This annual meeting at the end of January typically attracts leaders in the corporate and financial communities from every continent, making it the world's largest gathering of chief executive officers. In addition, van Melle distributed 1,200 copies of *Full House: Reassessing the Earth's Population Carrying Capacity* to participants at the International Conference on Population and Development in Cairo. He did all this because of his own personal commitment to building an environmentally sustainable global economy, one that is within the limits of the earth's carrying capacity.

In 1994, we added two new titles to our Environmental Alert Book series. The first, just mentioned, was *Full House*—our contribution to the Cairo conference. The second, *Power Surge: Guide to the Coming Energy Revolution*, is our effort to anticipate the enormous changes in prospect in the world energy economy.

Although we almost always deal with issues at the global level, we occasionally focus on individual geographic regions, as we did in *State of the World 1985* for Africa and in *State of the World 1991* for Eastern Europe and the Soviet Union. This year, we have devoted an entire chapter to China, in recognition that the surging demands of its 1.2 billion people could alter the global supply/demand balances for grain, petroleum, minerals, forest products, and fibers while complicating efforts to control such global pollutants as carbon dioxide. Never before have the incomes of such a large number of people risen so rapidly as in China today. The economic repercussions of this huge nation's emergence as a modern consumer economy will be felt around the world for decades to come.

Last year we reported launching a database diskette, which includes all the data from the tables and graphs published in all Worldwatch publications for the most recent year. These include the Worldwatch Papers, the Environmental Alert books, *World Watch* magazine, and our two annuals—*State of the World* and *Vital Signs*. Demand for the Worldwatch database diskette is growing rapidly, far exceeding our expectations. Much to our surprise, Norway has emerged as the second largest market, thanks to marketing efforts at Worldwatch Institute Norden.

Taking advantage of new technologies to disseminate the results of our research, Worldwatch now has an electronic on-line conference on EcoNet, a worldwide environmental network on the Internet. The on-line conference contains highlights from all our publications, including tables of contents, ordering information, and a list of publications. Inquiries and publication orders can be sent to wwpub@igc.apc.org.

As always, we welcome your suggestions to improve future editions of *State of the World*. You may send them by mail, fax (202–296–7365), or e-mail.

Lester R. Brown
Christopher Flavin
Hilary French

Worldwatch Institute
1776 Massachusetts Ave., NW
Washington, DC 20036

December 1994

STATE OF THE
WORLD
1995

1

Nature's Limits

Lester R. Brown

In September 1994, the 179 national delegations assembled in Cairo at the International Conference on Population and Development reached agreement on a plan designed to stabilize world population. The World Population Plan of Action may be the boldest initiative ever undertaken by the United Nations, dwarfing some of its earlier achievements, such as the eradication of smallpox. On the twenty-fifth anniversary of the 1969 moon landing, we can paraphrase American astronaut Neil Armstrong: Cairo was a giant step for humankind.[1]

In the preparatory meetings leading up to the conference, delegates had rejected the notion that population growth would continue on the high trajectory, reaching 11.9 billion by 2050. Instead, they opted for an extraordinarily ambitious plan to stabilize population between the medium projection of 9.8 billion by 2050 and the low projection, where population would peak at 7.9 billion by 2050. Their strategy reflects a sense of urgency—a feeling that unless population growth can be slowed quickly, it will push human demands beyond the carrying capacity of the land in many countries, leading to environmental degradation, economic decline, and social disintegration.

Among other things, the plan calls for quickly filling the family planning gap—for providing services to the estimated 120 million women in the world who want to limit the number of their children but lack access to the family planning services needed to do so. But more important, it addresses the underlying causes of high fertility, such as female illiteracy. It calls for universal primary school education for girls, recognizing that as female educational levels rise, fertility levels fall—a relationship that holds across all cultures.[2]

Twenty years earlier, the first U.N. population conference, in Bucharest, had agreed that access to family planning services was a human right. In Cairo, the focus was on gender equity. Kaval Gulhati, a veteran family planning leader from India, may have put it best: "Unless women can manage and control their own fertility, they cannot manage and control their own lives."[3]

The goals set in Cairo will be extraordinarily difficult to achieve, but if the world succeeds in stabilizing human numbers at 8 or 9 billion, it will satisfy one of the conditions of an environmentally sustainable society. The plan recognizes both the earth's natural limits and the need to respect those limits.

In the mid-nineties, evidence that the

world is on an economic path that is environmentally unsustainable can be seen in shrinking fish catches, falling water tables, declining bird populations, record heat waves, and dwindling grain stocks, to name just a few.

The world fish catch, which climbed more than fourfold during 40 years, is no longer rising, apparently because oceanic fisheries cannot sustain a greater catch. The failure to coordinate population policy with earlier carrying capacity assessments of fisheries means the world now faces a declining seafood supply per person and rising seafood prices for decades to come.[4]

Concern over water scarcity is rising in many areas. A prolonged drought in northern China, for example, and the associated water shortages have raised questions about the suitability of Beijing as the national capital and renewed discussion of a 1,400-kilometer (860-mile), canal that would bring water from the south to the water-deficit north. Although the cost of building this enormous conduit—comparable to bringing water from the Mississippi River to Washington, D.C.—was initially estimated at $5 billion, the total could ultimately be several times larger. Among other things, it will challenge engineers because it must cross 219 rivers and streams, including the Huang He (Yellow River), en route to Beijing.[5]

Although collapsing fisheries and water scarcity attract attention because of their immediate economic effects, the decline of bird populations may be a more revealing indicator of the earth's health. Recently compiled data by Bird-Life International of Cambridge, England, show populations dropping on every continent. Of 9,600 species, only 3,000 are holding their own; the other 6,600 are in decline. Of these, the populations of some 1,000 species have dropped to the point where they are threatened with extinction. The precise reasons for this vary, but they include deforestation, particularly in the tropics; drainage of wetlands for farming and residential construction; air and water pollution; acid rain; and, for some species, hunting.[6]

After two decades of steadily rising global average temperature, including the highest on record in 1990, the June 1991 eruption of Mount Pinatubo in the Philippines gave the world a brief respite from global warming. The explosion ejected vast amounts of sulfate aerosols into the upper atmosphere, which quickly spread around the globe. Once there, the aerosols reflected a minute amount of incoming sunlight back into space, enough to exert a cooling effect. By early 1994, however, almost all the aerosols had settled out, clearing the way for a resumption of the warming trend.[7]

Evidence of new temperature highs was not long in coming. A premonsoon heat wave in central India lasted several weeks with temperatures up to 46 degrees Celsius (115 degrees Fahrenheit), taking a heavy toll on humans and livestock in the region. For the western United States, hundreds of new records were set, creating hot dry conditions that led to a near record number of forest fires.[8]

Japan had the hottest summer on record. Intense heat led to excessive evaporation and water shortages so severe that many utilities and manufacturing firms in Tokyo and surrounding areas were forced to import water by tanker from as far away as Alaska. Over a thousand miles to the west, Shanghai—with little air conditioning—suffered during July through 14 days above 35 degrees Celsius (95 degrees Fahrenheit) and 16 days between 33 and 34 degrees Celsius. And in parts of Northern Europe, including Germany, Poland, and the

Baltic states, mid-summer temperatures soared well above 32 degrees Celsius, exposing both residents and ecosystems to unaccustomed levels of heat.[9]

On the food front, developments were particularly disturbing. Even though in 1994 the United States returned to production all the grainland that had been idled under commodity supply management programs, global food security declined further as the world's projected carryover grain stocks from the 1994 harvest dropped to the lowest level in 20 years. A combination of spreading water shortages, declining fertilizer use, and cropland losses, particularly in Asia, led to another harvest shortfall and the drawdown in stocks.[10]

Thus in various ways, nature's limits are beginning to impose themselves on the human agenda, initially at the local level, but also at the global level. Some of these, such as the yield of oceanic fisheries or spreading water scarcity, are near-term. Others, such as the limited capacity of the atmosphere to absorb excessive emissions of carbon without disrupting climate, will manifest themselves over the longer term.

THREE IMMINENT LIMITS

One of the key questions that emerged as the world prepared for the Cairo conference was, How many people can the earth support? Closely related was, What exactly will limit the growth in human numbers? Will it be the scarcity of water, life-threatening levels of pollution, food scarcity, or some other limiting condition? After considering all the possible constraints, it appears that it is the supply of food that will determine the earth's population carrying capacity.

Three of the earth's natural limits are already slowing the growth in world food production: the sustainable yield of oceanic fisheries, the amount of fresh water produced by the hydrological cycle, and the amount of fertilizer that existing crop varieties can effectively use.

Nature's limits are beginning to impose themselves on the human agenda, initially at the local level, but also at the global level.

More than 20 years have passed since a marine biologist at the U.N. Food and Agriculture Organization (FAO) estimated that oceanic fisheries could not sustain an annual yield of more than 100 million tons. In 1989, the world fish catch, including that from inland waters and fish farming, reached exactly that number, an amount equal to world production of beef and poultry combined. (See Chapter 2.) During the following four years, it has fluctuated between 97 million and 99 million tons, dropping the fish catch per person 8 percent in four years. Recent FAO reports indicate that all 17 oceanic fisheries are now being fished at or beyond capacity. With the total catch unlikely to rise much above 100 million tons, the decline in the seafood supply per person of the last few years will continue indefinitely—or at least until the World Population Plan of Action succeeds in stabilizing population.[11]

A combination of pollution and overharvesting is killing many inland seas and coastal estuaries. The Aral Sea, for instance, once yielded 44,000 tons of fish per year; the wholesale diversion of river water to irrigation has shrunk that body of water, raising its salt content and making the salt in effect a pollutant. All 24 species of fish that were once fished there commercially are believed to be extinct. In the Caspian Sea, the famous sturgeon harvest has been reduced to perhaps 1 percent of the level of 50 years ago through pollution and overfishing.[12]

The Black Sea, which is the dumping point for the Danube, Dniester, and Dnieper Rivers, is the repository for chemical and organic pollutants for half of Europe. Of the nearly 30 species that once supported commercial fisheries there, only 5 remain. During the last decade the total catch has dropped from nearly 700,000 tons to 100,000 tons—a result of pollution, overharvesting, and the accidental introduction of destructive alien species of fish.[13]

The U.S. Chesapeake Bay, once one of the world's most productive estuaries, is deteriorating rapidly from a lethal combination of pollution, overharvesting, and—for oysters—disease. Formerly a major source of this delicacy, the bay's annual harvest has dropped from nearly 100,000 tons of edible oysters (roughly 1 million tons in the shell) around the turn of the century to less than 1,000 tons in 1993. (See Figure 1–1.)[14]

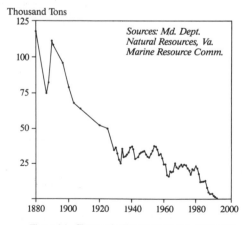

Figure 1-1. Chesapeake Bay Oyster Catch, 1880–1993

With land-based food stocks, limits on production are being imposed by the amount of fresh water supplied by the hydrological cycle. Today, two thirds of all the water extracted from rivers and underground aquifers is used for irrigation. In parts of the world where all available water is now being used, such as the southwestern United States or large areas of northern China, satisfying future growth in residential and industrial demand will come at the expense of agriculture.[15]

Although there are innumerable opportunities for increasing irrigation efficiency, only limited potential exists to expand freshwater supplies for irrigation. For example, roughly one fifth of U.S. irrigated land is watered by drawing down underground aquifers. A recent study of India found that water tables are now falling in several states, including much of the Punjab (India's breadbasket), Haryana, Uttar Pradesh, Gujarat, and Tamil Nadu—states that together contain some 250 million people. The drop ranges from less than one meter to several meters a year.[16]

In many parts of the world, the diversion of water to nonfarm uses is also reducing water for irrigation. In the western United States, for instance, the future water demands of rapidly growing Las Vegas will almost certainly be satisfied by diverting water from irrigation. Similarly in China, most cities suffer from severe water shortages, and many of them will meet their future needs by taking water away from irrigation.[17]

The physiological limit on the amount of fertilizer that current crop varieties can use is an even broader threat to world food expansion. In countries where fertilizer use is already heavy, applying more nutrients has little or no effect on yield. This helps explain why fertilizer use is no longer increasing in major food-producing regions, such as North America, Western Europe, and

East Asia. During the last several decades, scientists were remarkably successful in increasing the responsiveness of wheat, rice, and corn varieties to ever heavier applications of fertilizer, but in recent years their efforts have met with little success.[18]

Worldwide, fertilizer use increased tenfold between 1950 and 1989, when it peaked and then began to decline. During the following four years it fell some 15 percent, with the decline concentrated in the former Soviet Union following the withdrawal of subsidies. In the United States, fertilizer use peaked in the early eighties and has declined roughly one tenth since then. With China, the other leading food producer, the peak seems to be occurring roughly a decade later. Some countries, such as Argentina and Vietnam, can still substantially expand their use of fertilizer, but the major food-producing countries are close to the limit with existing grain varieties.[19]

For nearly four decades, steadily rising fertilizer use was the engine driving the record growth in world food output. The generation of farmers on the land in 1950 was the first in history to double the production of food. By 1984, they had outstripped population growth enough to raise per capita grain output an unprecedented 40 percent. But when the use of fertilizer began to slow in the late eighties, so did the growth in food output.[20]

The era of substituting fertilizer for land came to a halt in 1990. (See Figure 1–2.) If future food output gains cannot come from using large additional amounts of fertilizer, where will they come from? The graph of fertilizer use and grainland area per person may capture the human dilemma as the twenty-first century approaches more clearly than any other picture could. The world has quietly and with little fanfare entered a new era, one fraught with un-

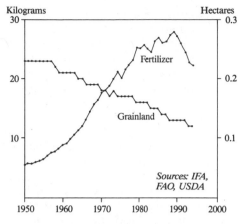

Figure 1-2. World Fertilizer Use and Grainland Area Per Person, 1950–94

certainty over how to feed the projected massive growth in world population.[21]

Unless plant breeders can develop strains of wheat, rice, and corn that are much more responsive to fertilizer, the world may not be able to restore the rapid growth in grain output needed to keep up with population. Either science will have to come up with a new method of rapidly expanding food production, or population levels and dietary patterns will be forced to adjust to much tighter food supplies. With the prospect of no growth in ocean-based food supplies and of much slower growth in land-based food supplies, the world is facing a future far different from the recent past.

THE ECONOMIC EFFECTS

The depletion of natural capital—of forests, rangelands, topsoil, underground aquifers, and fish stocks—and the pollution of air and water have reached the point in many countries where the economic effects are becoming highly visible, including a loss of output, of jobs, and of exports. Some countries have lost entire industries.

As the global demand for seafood overruns the sustainable yield of fisheries or as pollution destroys their productivity, for instance, fisheries collapse—raising seafood prices, eliminating jobs, and shrinking the economy. The economic wreckage left in the wake of these collapses can be seen around the world: Fishing villages that once lined the Aral Sea are now ghost towns. In Newfoundland, the collapse of the cod and haddock fishery has left 33,000 fishers and fish-processing workers unemployed, crippling the province's economy. And in New England, families who for generations have made their living from the sea are selling their trawlers and searching for other jobs.[22]

Seafood prices are likely to keep rising for as long as population continues to grow.

Even as fisheries are being destroyed, the world demand for seafood is rising. Seafood was once a cheap source of protein, something that people ate because they could not afford meat. In 1960, a kilogram of seafood cost only half as much as a kilogram of beef. In recent years, that margin has narrowed and disappeared as seafood prices have risen above beef. During the last decade the world price of seafood, in real terms, has risen nearly 4 percent a year. (See Figure 1–3.)[23]

In a few cases, prices have reached astronomical levels. In November 1993, for instance, a 300-kilogram bluefin tuna caught in the North Atlantic was sold for $80,000 to an agent for top-of-the-line sushi restaurants in Tokyo. While this is not, by any means, an average price for bluefin tuna, prices are climbing and will

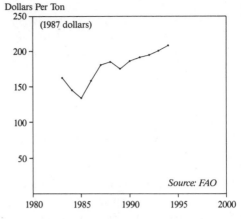

Dollars Per Ton

(1987 dollars)

Source: FAO

Figure 1-3. World Price of Seafood, 1983–94

undoubtedly go higher since the breeding population in the Atlantic has dropped from 250,000 to 22,000 as a result of overharvesting. A giant Caspian Sea beluga sturgeon, laden with prized caviar, can sell for almost as much as a bluefin tuna.[24]

When the price of fresh swordfish hit $18 a pound in Washington, D.C., a local supermarket chain started buying frozen swordfish from more distant fisheries at $10 a pound. This merely brought closer the day when swordfish scarcity would be worldwide. Not only has seafood become more costly, but prices are likely to keep rising for as long as population continues to grow, forcing ever larger numbers of people to compete for limited supplies and reducing seafood consumption among the poor.[25]

In some economies, overcutting forests has done even more economic damage than overfishing. The clear-cutting of tropical hardwood forests by lumber companies has almost completely destroyed this valuable resource in some developing countries, devastating their economies. Côte d'Ivoire, for example, enjoyed a phenomenal economic expansion in the sixties and seventies as its rich tropical hardwood forests yielded export earnings of $300 million a year. It became a development model for the rest of Africa, but as in many other countries that did not practice sustainable forestry, clear-cutting decimated its forests; exports dropped to $30 million a year in the early nineties. The loss of this major source of employment and export earnings, coupled with declining prices for other export commodities and other economic setbacks, led to a steady decline of the economy. Within just half a generation—from 1980 to 1994—income per person fell by half.[26]

Similar forest destruction in other tropical countries, such as Nigeria and the Philippines, also led to industry collapse and to job, income, and export losses. Nigeria was once a major exporter of logs; by 1988, the nation was spending $100 million to bring in forest products. In the Philippines, exports peaked at $217 million per year in the early seventies, disappearing entirely by the early nineties.[27]

As noted earlier, in many farming areas the claims on underground water supplies now exceed aquifer recharge rates. For farmers in northern India, where wheat and rice are double-cropped, the rate at which the water table is falling—more than a meter per year in some areas—may soon force a shift to less intensive cropping practices. Most likely this will mean a replacement of rice with a less water-demanding, lower-yielding staple crop, such as sorghum or millet. Although this may arrest the fall in the water table, it is not a welcome development in a country whose population is expanding by 17 million per year and is projected to reach a billion within the next six years.[28]

In the agricultural regions surrounding Beijing, farmers no longer have access to reservoir water. They must now either drill their own wells and pursue the falling water table downward or switch to less intensive rain-fed farming.

With some 300 cities in China reportedly now short of water, and 100 of them seriously short, similar adjustments will undoubtedly be made by farmers in the agricultural belts surrounding countless other Chinese cities.[29]

In the southwestern United States, the need to supply booming cities with water and the depletion of aquifers is eliminating irrigated agriculture in many locations. In arid Arizona, the diversion of irrigation water to the rapidly growing sunbelt cities of Phoenix and Tucson means that large areas of productive farmland have returned to desert. In the Texas panhandle, where the southern reach of the Ogallala aquifer has been largely depleted, farmers have reverted to dryland farming. Although agriculture continues in this region, the drop in intensity, and hence of output, reduces employment in both the agricultural input and service industries and the agricultural processing industries. As a result, some rural communities are being partially depopulated.[30]

In situations where years of overpumping is depleting aquifers, reductions in irrigation lie ahead. If the rate of groundwater pumping in an area is double the rate of recharge, for example, the aquifer will eventually be depleted. As it nears depletion, the withdrawal rate necessarily will be lowered by half, because it cannot exceed the recharge rate, so the irrigated area will be reduced accordingly.

One of the commodities most affected by aquifer depletion is rice. Its production is now being constrained by the limits of aquifer yields, the scarcity of land suitable for production, and the capacity of available rice varieties to use more fertilizer effectively. In contrast to wheat and corn, which are largely rain-fed, the production of rice depends heavily on irrigation. This makes yield trends easier to analyze simply because the effect of weather fluctuations is much less.

The precariousness of the balance between world rice consumption and production is becoming more evident each year. In the fall of 1993, world rice stocks were at their lowest level in 20 years. When the Japanese government announced that an uncommonly cool, wet summer had reduced its harvest from 9.6 million tons in 1992 to 7.0 million tons, forcing it to consider emergency imports of close to 2 million tons, the price rise was dramatic. With the market already delicately balanced, these additional Japanese claims doubled the rice futures price in the United States, the world's leading exporter, between late August and mid-November.[31]

A shortfall of 2 million tons of rice is minute compared with a world rice harvest of some 350 million tons—scarcely one half of 1 percent. Nonetheless, when stocks are as low as they are today, even a relatively small shift in the world supply/demand balance can have global repercussions. Fortunately for consumers, particularly those in low-income rice-importing countries, the price of rice began to return to more normal levels in the spring of 1994 as the early rice harvest in tropical Asia neared maturity.[32]

Growth in the irrigated area in Asia, where 90 percent of the world's rice is grown and consumed, has slowed to a snail's pace. Most remaining available sites for large-river diversion projects are either too costly to develop or would displace too many people. The potential for expanding irrigation using underground water is limited by aquifer recharge rates; as noted earlier, overpumping is already lowering water tables in key food-producing regions of Asia.[33]

The other key constraint on rice output, of course, is the capacity of existing varieties to use fertilizer. On much of Asia's riceland, applying more fertilizer has little, if any, effect on yields. In some countries, fertilizer use is declining slightly as farmers fine-tune applications, matching them more precisely with crop needs.[34]

With irrigation growing very slowly and fertilizer use levelling off, the rise in cropland productivity is also slowing. The rise in rice yield per hectare, which halted in Japan a decade ago, is now slowing nearly everywhere, edging up only 2 percent from 1990 to 1994.[35]

As the rise in rice yields has slowed during the nineties, the loss of cropland to nonfarm uses has speeded up during accelerated industrialization, particularly in China—the world's largest rice producer. Other large countries, including India and Indonesia, are also losing cropland to industrialization and residential development. With the decline in harvested rice area of 2 percent since 1990 offsetting a 2-percent rise in rice yield per hectare, the harvest has ranged narrowly between 350 million and 352 million tons. (See Figure 1–4.) A new rice variety under development at the International Rice Research Institute in the Philippines, which promises to boost rice yields by 20–25 percent after being released around the turn of the century, will help offset some of the riceland losses in prospect for the next several

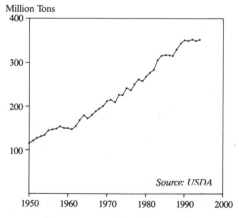

Million Tons

Figure 1-4. World Rice Production, 1950–94

decades. With production stalled since 1990, carryover rice stocks have fallen in each of the last four years, dropping to the lowest level since 1972, leaving the world vulnerable to sharp price rises. The political leaders of Asia—a region adding 57 million people annually—face no more pressing question than how to restore growth in the rice harvest.[36]

An even more telling indicator of the loss of momentum in expanding grain output is the drawdown in world stocks since 1987. Then, world carryover stocks of grain from the 1985 harvest totalled 465 million tons, an all-time high and equivalent to 104 days of consumption. During the following eight years, grain stocks were reduced to 302 million tons, a drop of 163 million tons or some 20 million tons a year. (See Figure 1–5.) This annual drawdown exceeds the yearly growth in the world grain harvest during this period, which averaged roughly 10 million tons. Stated otherwise, a substantial part of the growth in world grain consumption since 1987 has come from consuming stocks, a trend that cannot continue much longer because current stocks represent only 59 days of consumption—little more than pipeline supplies.[37]

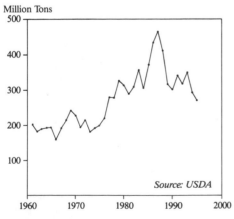

Million Tons

Figure 1-5. World Grain Carryover Stocks, 1961-95

In response to the decline in grain stocks in 1993, the United States released for production in 1994 all grainland idled under its commodity supply management programs. Even with this land returned to use, and even with fair to excellent growing conditions in the world's major food-producing regions, stocks continue to decline. If grain stocks cannot be rebuilt in years of good harvests, when will they be rebuilt?[38]

In the absence of a dramatic new technological advance in agriculture comparable to the discovery of fertilizer or the hybridization of corn, there is now a real possibility that grain production could continue to lag and that prices could begin to rise in the years ahead, following those of seafood upward. The unfortunate reality is that with carryover stocks at such a low level, the world is now only one poor harvest away from chaos in world grain markets.

The collision between continuously expanding human demands and nature's various limits affects not only the world food supply but also overall economic growth. A 1993 study published by the World Bank notes that environmental damage takes many forms, including land degradation, pollution damage, the loss of biological diversity, deforestation, and soil erosion. Using a dozen or so examples, the two authors—both economists—show that the annual costs to countries of various forms of environmental damage can range from less than 1 percent to as much as 15 percent of gross national product. (See Table 1–1.) If the data were available to calculate all the economic costs of environmental degradation in its many forms, they would undoubtedly show an enormous loss. The authors observe: "If you asked any economist at the World Bank today if the environment is important to the country they work on, they would say 'Yes.' A few years ago, they wouldn't have said that."[39]

Table 1-1. Estimates of Environmental Damage in Selected Countries

Country and Year	Form of Environmental Damage	Annual Costs as a Share of GNP
		(percent)
Burkina Faso (1988)	Crop, livestock, and fuelwood losses from land degradation	8.8
Costa Rica (1989)	Deforestation	7.7
Ethiopia (1983)	Effects of deforestation on the supply of fuelwood and crop output	6.0–9.0
Germany (1990)[1]	Pollution damage (air, water, soil pollution, loss of biodiversity)	1.7–4.2
Hungary (late eighties)	Pollution damage (mostly air pollution)	5.0
Indonesia (1984)	Soil erosion and deforestation	4.0
Madagascar (1988)	Land burning and erosion	5.0–15.0
Malawi (1988)	Lost crop production from soil erosion	1.6–10.9
	Costs of deforestation	1.2–4.4
Mali (1988)	On-site soil erosion and losses	0.4
Netherlands (1986)	Some pollution damage	0.5–0.8
Nigeria (1989)	Soil degradation, deforestation, water pollution, other erosion	17.4
Poland (1987)	Pollution damage	4.4–7.7
United States[2] (1981)	Air pollution control	0.8–2.1
(1985)	Water pollution control	0.4

[1]Federal Republic of Germany before unification.   [2]Measures the benefits of environmental policy (avoided rather than actual damages).
SOURCE: "Environmental Damage Robs Countries' Income," *World Bank News*, March 25, 1993, based on David Pearce and Jeremy Warford, *World Without End* (Washington, D.C.: World Bank, 1993).

The crossing of sustainable yield thresholds in sectors such as forestry and fishing and in aquifers, combined with the slowdown in the growth in world grain production, directly affects the performance of the world economy.

To begin with, these primary producing sectors play a unique role in the global economy. If the growth in production of food from both land- and ocean-based sources falls far behind growth in demand, the resulting rise in prices could destabilize some national economies.

Economic growth, peaking at 5.2 percent a year in the sixties, dropped to 3.4 percent in the seventies and to 2.9 percent in the eighties. Thus far, during the nineties, it has averaged 1.4 percent, which means that the per capita output of food, energy, housing, and the other goods and services that determine living standards has declined by roughly 0.3 percent a year. (See Table 1–2.)[40]

Several trends are contributing to slower economic growth, such as a near saturation of markets in some advanced industrial societies for basic consumer goods—automobiles and household appliances, for example. In some developing countries, burdensome external debt has slowed growth, and in Eastern Europe economic reforms have taken a toll. But also included among the reasons for slower world economic growth is the lack of growth in the fishing and farming sectors. Indeed, the 1994 fish catch was an estimated 3 percent smaller than in 1990, while the grain harvest was down nearly 2 percent. In addition, the economic uncertainty and, in some cases, instability associated with colliding with limits undermines confidence in the future. The bottom line is slower economic growth.[41]

Although projections by the Interna-

tional Monetary Fund show economic growth accelerating in the years immediately ahead, these could be derailed by the instability associated with food scarcity. The nineties could turn out to be the first decade since the Great Depression when income per person for the world as a whole actually declines. Incomes fell in some 53 countries containing more than 800 million people during the eighties, many of them in Africa. But that incomes might fall for the entire world during the nineties has not been anticipated in any long-range economic projection.[42]

UNSUSTAINABILITY FEEDS INSTABILITY

Once the demand for a particular product, such as seafood, exceeds the sustainable yield of the resource base, the traditionally stable relationship between demand and supply becomes unstable. With thresholds for sustainable yields now being crossed for so many resources, relationships that have been stable for centuries or millennia are becoming highly volatile in the late twentieth century.

Analysis of the relationship between the level of human demand and the sustainable yield of various systems is severely handicapped in many cases by a lack of data. For example, it is known that water tables are falling in many countries because water pumping now exceeds aquifer recharge. As noted earlier, some 21 percent of irrigated cropland in the United States depends on drawing down underground aquifers. But for most of the world, data on sustainable aquifer yields are not available. Few communities or countries know when rising water demand will exceed

Table 1-2. World Economic Growth by Decade, Total and Per Person

Decade	Annual Growth	Annual Growth Per Person
	(percent)	
1950–60	4.9	3.1
1960–70	5.2	3.2
1970–80	3.4	1.6
1980–90	2.9	1.1
1990–94 (prel.)	1.4	−0.3

SOURCE: Worldwatch Institute, based on sources documented in endnote 40.

aquifer recharge; overpumping is often discovered after the fact.[43]

We are also handicapped in analyzing the effects of excessive demand on natural systems by the interaction of biological, economic, and political systems. While academic specialists may understand the workings of individual systems and how they respond to stress, they seldom comprehend the interactions. Fortunately, a new effort to better understand this relationship—the project on Environmental Scarcities, State Capacity, and Civil Violence—was recently launched by the University of Toronto in cooperation with the American Academy of Arts and Sciences in Boston.[44]

At some point, severe ecological stresses begin to manifest themselves economically on a scale that has political consequences. Rwanda is one tragic example of this, recently much in the news. While the attention of the world in the summer of 1994 focused on the tribal conflict between the Tutsis and the Hutus, there was ample evidence that tensions had been building as the relationship between all Rwandans and the natural systems on which they depend deteriorated.

Between 1950 and 1994, Rwanda's population increased from 2.5 million to 8.8 million. The average number of children per woman in 1992 of 8 was the highest in the world. Despite impressive gains in overall grain production, output per person declined by nearly half between 1960 and the early nineties. Land scarcity intensified as increasingly small plots were subdivided from one generation to the next. As population grew, the freshwater supply per person dropped to the point where Rwanda was officially classified by hydrologists as one of the world's 27 water-scarce countries.[45]

But beyond these numbers was the quiet desperation that comes to an agrarian society when population growth overwhelms the carrying capacity of the land. Just as a lightning strike in forests in the American West is more likely to turn into an uncontrollable conflagration when it is unbearably hot and dry, so too are ethnic conflicts more likely to erupt when there are underlying tensions about food and the ability to earn a living.

Another essentially agrarian economy where the situation is in some ways even worse is Haiti. Once richly forested, it has lost all but 2 percent of its forests and much of its topsoil. In contrast to Rwanda, where the overall harvest has continued to rise, grain production in Haiti was one third less in the early nineties than it was in the mid-seventies, which means that grain production per person has plummeted. Political scientist Thomas Homer-Dixon observes that "the irreversible loss of forests and soil in rural areas deepens an economic crisis that spawns social strife, internal migration and an exodus of 'boat people.' " He concluded that even when Aristide was returned to power, "Haiti will forever bear the burden of its irreversibly ravaged environment, which may make it impossible to build a prosperous, just and peaceful society."[46]

The ecological symptoms of unsustainability include shrinking forests, thinning soils, falling aquifers, collapsing fisheries, expanding deserts, and rising global temperatures. The economic symptoms include economic decline, falling incomes, rising unemployment, price instability, and a loss of investor confidence. The political and social symptoms include hunger and malnutrition, and, in extreme cases, mass starvation; environmental and economic refugees; social conflicts along ethnic, tribal, and religious lines; and riots and insurgencies. As stresses build on political systems, governments weaken, losing their capacity to govern and to provide basic services, such as police protection. At this point, the nation-state disintegrates, replaced by a feudal social structure governed by local warlords, as in Somalia, now a nation-state in name only.

One of the difficulties in dealing with the complex relationship between humans and natural systems is that once rising demand for seafood or firewood crosses the sustainable yield threshold of a fishery or forest, future growth is often maintained only by consuming the resource base itself. This combination of continuously rising demand and a shrinking resource base can lead from stability to instability and to collapse almost overnight.

When sustainable yield thresholds are crossed, the traditional responses proposed by economists no longer work. One common reaction to scarcity, for instance, is to invest more in production. Thus the key to alleviating seafood scarcity is to invest more in fishing trawlers. But in today's world this only exacerbates the scarcity, hastening the collapse of the fishery. Similarly, as food prices rise, there is a temptation to spend more on irrigation. But where water tables are already falling, investing in more wells simply accelerates the depletion of the aquifer and the eventual decline in irrigation.

Once the demand on a particular system reaches a limit, the resulting scarcity sometimes spills over to intensify pressure on other systems. As seafood became scarce, for example, many expected that fish farming would take up the slack. But maintaining the historical growth in seafood supplies of 2 million tons per year over the last four decades by turning to aquaculture, where 2 kilograms of grain are needed to produce 1 kilogram of fish, requires 4 million tons of additional grain a year for fish raised in cages or ponds. Growth in the seafood harvest, which once relied primarily on spending more on diesel fuel to exploit ever more distant fisheries, now depends on expenditures on grain as more fish are produced in marine feedlots. With grain supplies tightening, the feed may not be available to sustain rapid growth in aquacultural output.[47]

Some effects of crossing sustainable yield thresholds are indirect. If excessive demand for forest and livestock products leads to deforestation and rangeland degradation, the amount of rainfall runoff increases and the amount retained and absorbed for aquifer recharge decreases. Thus, excessive demand for timber and livestock products can reduce aquifer yields.

The combination of continuously rising demand and a shrinking resource base can lead from stability to instability and to collapse almost overnight.

As another example of an indirect effect, when carbon emissions exceed carbon fixation, as is happening with the massive burning of fossil fuels, the level of carbon dioxide in the atmosphere rises, altering the earth's heat balance. The principal effect is to trap heat, raising temperatures. This in turn affects all the ecosystems on which humans depend, from estuaries to rangelands.[48]

Crossing sustainable yield thresholds of natural systems can alter world markets. Ever since World War II, the challenge to agricultural policymakers, except for a brief period in the early to mid-seventies, has been how to manage surpluses. Exporting countries typically insisted on using subsidies to bring farm prices above world market levels. This stimulated overproduction, leading to the use of export subsidies and competition for inadequate import markets for grain. Now that production is no longer keeping up with growth in demand at current prices, policymakers may once again be faced with managing scarcity and dealing with the politics of scarcity as the historical decline of grain prices is reversed. This new trend is already evident in the seafood market.

Managing scarcity could test the capacity of national governments and international institutions. For example, overseeing fisheries was relatively easy when the catch was far below the sustainable yield. But when the catch overruns that level, reestablishing a balance between the catch and the regenerative capacity of fisheries can be difficult. Similarly, countries that share water basins find it relatively easy to manage water supplies when there is a surplus, but if water becomes scarce and there is no longer enough to go around, the problem of management increases inordinately.

The natural systems on which the economy depends—whether it be the hydrological cycle or rangelands—are not merely sectors of the global economy. They are its foundation. If their productivity is diminished, then the prospect for the global economy will deteriorate. In an urbanized world where attention focuses on growth in telecommunications and computers and on the construction of the information superhighway, it is easy to forget that it is these natural systems that underpin the global economy.

One unfortunate and little noticed consequence of these various trends of environmental and economic decline is that international assistance programs are focusing more on aid and less on development. In effect, expenditures are shifting from crisis prevention to crisis management. Nowhere is this more evident than at the United Nations, where the budget for the U.N. High Commissioner for Refugees is nearly as high that of the U.N. Development Programme. The same trend can be seen in Somalia,

where social disintegration and conflict reached the point where military intervention was needed just to deliver the food supplies needed to end famine. When deterioration reaches this point, military intervention can easily cost 10 times as much as the food assistance being given.[49]

The bottom line of the growing instability between human societies and the natural systems on which they depend is political instability. This in itself is beginning to make economic development and agricultural progress difficult, if not impossible, in many countries. In some countries, the crossing of thresholds has international repercussions. When the growth in demand for food in a country as large as China begins to outstrip domestic productive capacity, the economic effects can spread far beyond national borders, altering the food supply/demand balance for the entire world.

THE CHINA FACTOR

The breathtaking pace of economic expansion in China promises to push demands on some of the earth's natural support systems beyond their sustainable yields. (For a more extensive discussion of China's environmental situation, see Chapter 7.) When Western Europe, North America, and Japan industrialized during the century's third quarter, establishing the foundations of the modern consumer economy, they were home to some 340 million, 190 million, and 100 million people, respectively. By contrast, China, which is entering the same stage, has a population of 1.2 billion and an economy that is expanding much faster than the others did earlier. Given recent rates of economic growth, the World Bank projects that by 2002, greater China (which includes Hong Kong and Taiwan) will overtake the United States and become the world's largest economy.[50]

We have no yardstick by which to assess the effect of this on demand for the earth's basic resources—simply because consumption levels have never risen so rapidly for so many people. Yet a sense of the potential effects on at least the world food economy is beginning to emerge. The escalating demand for food in China—where 14 million people are added each year and where the incomes of 1.2 billion people are rising at a record rate—could convert the world grain market from a buyer's to a seller's market, reversing the historical decline in grain prices.[51]

The prospect of a massive grain deficit in a country that has essentially been self-sufficient comes on the heels of four decades of agricultural progress—progress that was particularly impressive following the agricultural reforms of 1978. These transferred land from production teams to individual families, unleashing energies that boosted the country's grain production by half—from 200 million tons in 1977 to more than 300 million tons in 1984. This put China ahead of the United States as the world's leading grain producer and raised output from the subsistence level of roughly 200 kilograms per person to nearly 300 kilograms.[52]

On the demand side, China is projected to add 490 million people between 1990 and 2030, swelling its population to 1.6 billion—the equivalent of adding another Beijing every year for the next 40 years. Because its population is so large, even a slow rate of growth means huge absolute increases. Meanwhile, from 1991 to 1994, the economy expanded by a phenomenal 40 percent—an unprecedented rise in incomes for such a large number of people.[53]

As incomes rise, people diversify their diets, shifting from overwhelming dependence on a starchy staple, such as rice, to more meat, milk, and eggs. When the economic reforms were launched in 1978, only 7 percent of grain was being used for animal feed; by 1990, that share had risen to some 20 percent, most of it used to produce pork. Now, demand for beef and poultry is also climbing. More meat means more grain—2 kilograms of grain are needed for each kilogram of poultry, 4 for pork, and 7 for each kilogram of beef added in the feedlot.[54]

The escalating demand for food in China could convert the world grain market from a buyer's to a seller's market.

China has eclipsed the United States in total red meat consumption largely on the strength of pork consumption alone. At 21 kilograms per person in 1990, China's consumption of pork is approaching the 28 kilograms (62 pounds) consumed by the average American each year. Although the consumption of beef, poultry, and milk in China is still minuscule compared with that of Americans, these too are beginning to rise.[55]

Poultry was once a rare luxury in China, and the average person still eats only one tenth as much as an American, but people are quickly gaining an appetite for chicken. During the nineties, poultry consumption, starting from a small base, is expanding at double-digit rates. So, too, is the consumption of eggs. And the good life for newly affluent Chinese does not stop with meat and eggs: they are also acquiring a great enthusiasm for beer, and raising individual consumption for all adults by just one bottle takes another 370,000 tons of grain.[56]

As the conversion of cropland to nonfarm uses continues, the experience of three other countries that were densely populated before serious industrialization got under way—Japan, South Korea, and Taiwan—gives a sense of what to expect. Over the last few decades, the conversion of grainland to other uses in these countries has cost Japan 52 percent of its grainland, South Korea 42 percent, and Taiwan 35 percent.[57]

As cropland losses proceeded, they began to override the gains in land productivity, leading to steady declines in output. While production was falling, rising affluence was driving up the overall demand for grain. As a result, by 1993 Japan was importing 77 percent of its grain, South Korea 64 percent, and Taiwan 67 percent.[58]

Now the same changes are commencing in China as its transformation from an agricultural to an industrial society progresses at a breakneck pace. Building the thousands of factories, warehouses, and access roads that industrialization needs requires sacrificing cropland. The modernization of transportation is also claiming cropland as highways and railroads replace dirt roads and footpaths. Sales of cars and trucks, which totalled 1.3 million in 1992 and are expected to approach 3 million a year by the decade's end, will translate into claims on cropland for roads and parking lots.[59]

Along with the continuing disappearance of its farmland, China is also facing the extensive diversion of irrigation water to nonfarm uses—an acute concern in a country where half the cropland is irrigated. With large areas of north China now experiencing water deficits, existing demand is being satisfied partly by depleting aquifers. In late 1993, Minister of Water Resources Niu Mao Sheng stated that "in rural areas, over 82 million people find it difficult to procure water. In urban areas, the shortages are even worse. More than 300 Chinese cities are short of water and 100 of them are very short." Satisfying future urban and industrial demand for water means diverting it from irrigation.[60]

With the cultivated area declining inexorably, China's ability to feed itself now rests entirely on raising the productivity of its cropland. Rice yields in China, which have been rising toward those in Japan, are starting to level off, suggesting that the potential for lifting them further is limited to the potential gain of 20–25 percent associated with the forthcoming new variety mentioned earlier. (See Figure 1–6.)[61]

With wheat, China's other food staple, the rise in yield is also slowing. In the early eighties, China's wheat yield per hectare surged past that of the United States and has remained well above it, at roughly 3 tons per hectare. The big jump came immediately after the economic reforms of 1978, as yields climbed 83 percent from 1975–77 to 1984. During the following nine years, however, they rose only an additional 16 percent.[62]

At issue is how much cropland will be lost and how fast. Rapid industrialization is already taking a toll, as grain area has dropped from 90.8 million hectares in 1990 to an estimated 87.4 million in 1994. This annual drop of 850,000 hectares, or nearly 1 percent—remarkably

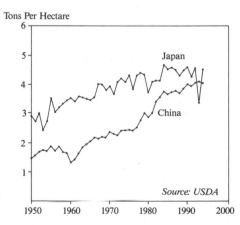

Figure 1-6. Rice Yields, China and Japan, 1950–94

similar to the loss rates of China's three smaller neighbors in their industrialization heyday—is likely to endure as long as rapid industrialization continues.[63]

Taking all these factors into account, it now appears likely that China's grain production will fall by at least one fifth between 1990 and 2030 (0.5 percent a year). This compares with a 33-percent decline in Japan since its peak year of 1960 (a fall of roughly 1 percent a year), a 31-percent decline in South Korea since its peak in 1977 (1.9 percent a year), and a 19-percent decline in Taiwan, also from a peak in 1977 (1.2 percent a year). Seen against this backdrop, the estimated decline of one fifth by 2030 in China may, if anything, be conservative. (See Figure 1–7.)[64]

The resulting grain deficit is huge—many times the 28 million tons of Japan, currently the world's largest grain importer. In 1990, China produced 329 million tons of grain and consumed 335 million tons, with the difference covered by net imports of just 6 million tons. Allowing only for the projected population increase, China's demand for grain would increase to 479 million tons in 2030. In other words, even if China's booming economy produces no gains in the consumption of meat, eggs, and

beer, a 20-percent drop in grain production to 263 million tons would leave a shortfall of 216 million tons—more than the world's entire 1993 grain exports of 200 million tons.

But even this is understating the problem, for China's newly affluent millions will of course not be content to forgo eating more livestock products. If grain consumption per person were to rise to 400 kilograms (the current level in Taiwan and one half the U.S. level), total consumption would climb to a staggering 641 million tons and the import deficit would reach 378 million tons. (See Figure 1–8.)[65]

The Chinese themselves have apparently been making similar calculations. Professor Zhou Guangzhao, head of the Chinese Academy of Sciences, observed in early 1994 that if the nation continues to squander its farmland and water resources in a breakneck effort to industrialize, "then China will have to import 400 million tons of grain from the world market. And I am afraid, in that case, that all of the grain output of the United States could not meet China's needs."[66]

Will China have enough foreign exchange to import the grain it needs? China's trade surplus with the United

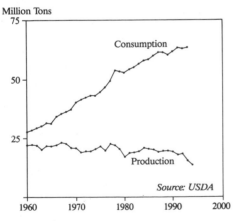

Million Tons

Figure 1-7. Combined Grain Balance, Japan, South Korea, and Taiwin, 1960–94

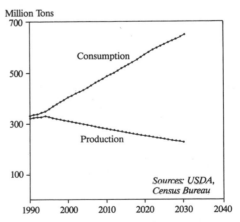

Million Tons

Figure 1-8. Projected Grain Production and Consumption in China, 1990–2030

States alone in 1993 was $23 billion, enough to buy all U.S. grain exports, with some to spare. Given the likely continuing growth in China's exports, it could import 200 or even 300 million tons of grain at current prices if its leaders were willing to use a modest share of export earnings for this purpose. Of course, this would mean cutting back on capital goods imports, which in turn could diminish the inflow of technology needed to sustain rapid economic growth.[67]

But the far more difficult question is, Who could supply grain on this scale? The answer: no one. Since 1980, annual world grain exports have averaged roughly 200 million tons, close to half of which comes from the United States. But the United States, with a projected addition of 95 million people during the next four decades, is simultaneously facing growth in grain demand and losses of cropland and irrigation water to non-farm uses. As a result, the U.S. exportable surplus may not increase much, if at all.[68]

At the same time, huge deficits are projected for other parts of the world. Africa, notably, is expected to need 250 million tons of grain by 2030—10 times what it currently imports. The Indian subcontinent is likely to rack up a deficit several times larger than its present one. Scores of countries with rapid population growth—among them Iran, Egypt, Ethiopia, Nigeria, and Mexico—will find themselves facing huge food deficits in the years ahead. In these circumstances, the vast deficit projected for China will set up a fierce competition for limited exportable supplies, driving world grain prices far above familiar levels.[69]

No one knows exactly when this competition among importing countries will develop, converting the world grain market from a buyer's to a seller's market. If China turns to the outside world for imports, as projected, rising food prices will forcibly curb demand for food worldwide—reducing consumption among rich and poor alike. For the former, this will mean fewer fat-rich livestock products and, happily, less cardiovascular disease. But for hundreds of millions of low-income rural landless and urban poor, it means tightening their belts where there are no notches left.

Acute food scarcity and the associated political instability could bring the Chinese economic miracle to a premature end. At a minimum, this prospective deficit in China will force other governments—however reluctantly—to reassess painstakingly their national population carrying capacity and the closely related questions of population and consumption policies.

The bottom line is that when China turns to world markets on an ongoing basis, its food scarcity will become everyone's scarcity. Its shortages of cropland and water will become the world's shortages. Its failure to check population growth soon enough will affect the entire world.

It will probably not be in the devastation of poverty-stricken Somalia or Haiti but in the booming economy of China that we will see the inevitable collision between expanding human demand for food and the limits of some of the earth's most basic natural systems. The shock waves from this collision will reverberate throughout the world economy with consequences we can only begin to foresee.

2

Protecting Oceanic Fisheries and Jobs

Peter Weber

Fishers around the world are worried about the future as they work harder and catch less—or, in some cases, are banned outright from pursuing their traditional livelihood. The catch has fallen in all but 2 of the world's 15 major marine fishing regions; in 4 of them, it has shrunk by more than 30 percent. (See Table 2–1.) Since 1989, the global oceanic catch of fish, crustaceans (such as lobster), and mollusks (such as clams) has fallen by 5 percent and stagnated.[1]

Until the recent stagnation in the world catch, the supply of fish per person had been rising steadily. Marine fishing boomed after World War II, increasing seafood available for consumers around the world and far surpassing the catch from freshwater lakes and rivers. (See Figure 2–1.) Today in Asia, an estimated 1 billion people rely on fish as their primary source of animal protein, as do many people in island nations and

the coastal states of Africa.[2]

Worldwide, fish and other products of the sea account for 16 percent of the animal protein consumed—more than either pork or beef—and for 5.6 percent of total protein intake. Once considered the poor person's protein, fish is becoming expensive even for consumers in industrial countries, and some species that were once common in supermarkets are no longer readily available.[3]

The fundamental problem is fishers' own expanded ability to catch fish and counterproductive government policies that have pulled more people and boats into the business even after the point of diminishing returns. After decades of buying bigger boats and more advanced hunting technologies, the oceans are nearly fished to the limits. Analysts from the U.N. Food and Agriculture Organization (FAO) found overfishing in one third of the fisheries they reviewed; they found some depleted fish populations in nearly all coastal waters around the world.[4]

Numerous studies have attempted to

An expanded version of this chapter appeared as Worldwatch Paper 120, *Net Loss: Fish, Jobs, and the Marine Environment*.

State of the World 1995

Table 2-1. Change in Catch for Major Marine Fishing Regions, Peak Year to 1992

Region	Peak Year	Peak Catch	1992 Catch	Change[1]
		(million tons)		(percent)
Atlantic Ocean				
Northwest	1973	4.4	2.6	−42
Northeast[2]	1976	13.2	11.1	−16
West Central	1984	2.6	1.7	−36
East Central	1990	4.1	3.3	−20
Southwest	1987	2.4	2.1	−11
Southeast[2]	1973	3.1	1.5	−53
Mediterranean and Black Seas[2]	1988	2.1	1.6	−25
Pacific Ocean				
Northwest	1988	26.4	23.8	−10
Northeast[2]	1987	3.4	3.1	− 9
West Central	1991	7.8	7.6	− 2
East Central	1981	1.9	1.3	−31
Southwest	1991	1.1	1.1	− 2
Southeast	1989	15.3	13.9	− 9
Indian Ocean				
Western	still rising		3.7	+ 6[3]
Eastern	still rising		3.3	+ 5[3]

[1]Percentages were calculated before rounding off catch figures. [2]Rebounding from a larger decline. [3]Average annual growth since 1988.
SOURCE: U.N. Food and Agriculture Organization, fisheries database (FISHSTAT-PC), Fisheries Statistics Division, Rome, 1994.

gauge the limits of the oceanic catch. Today, fishery scientists use 100 million tons per year—about 20 million tons more than the 1993 marine catch—as a rough estimate of the potential for all commercially viable marine species in the foreseeable future. Although such estimates are inherently uncertain, the decline of major fisheries and the recent faltering of the world catch overall suggest that fishers are running into natural limits. Further gains appear possible, but according to FAO, the marine catch is unlikely to reach and maintain the 100-million-ton mark unless fish stocks are better managed.[5]

In addition to overfishing, the marine environment suffers from pollution and habitat destruction, leading to the loss of several million tons of edible marine fish a year. These two problems disproportionately affect fish that spend at least part of their lives in rivers, bays, estuaries, coastal wetlands, coral reefs, or semienclosed seas: these are the marine ecosystems that people have degraded the most. Development has destroyed about half of all coastal wetlands around the world, for example—along with many of the creatures that live or spawn in these areas.[6]

Already, declining catches have translated into job loss among the world's 15–21 million fishers. In the last few

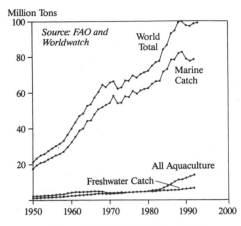

Figure 2-1. World Fish Catch, 1950–93

years, more than 100,000 fishers have lost their source of income. One hundred times that number could be out of work in the coming decades as fishery managers and policymakers try to come to grips with the great disparity between the capacity of the world's fishing fleets and the limits of the oceans.[7]

Income generated from marine fishing fuels only a small portion of the global economy, perhaps 1 percent. But in coastal and island regions, the occupation takes on greater importance. In Southeast Asia, more than 5 million people fish full-time, contributing some $6.6 billion toward the region's national incomes. In northern Chile, fishing accounted for 40 percent of income, 18,-000 jobs, and $400 million worth of exports in 1990. Iceland was founded on marine fishing, which today accounts for 17 percent of the national income and 12–13 percent of employment. Around the world, some 200 million people depend on fishing and fish-related industries for their livelihoods.[8]

Tight times in marine fishing particularly harm coastal communities and cultures. From Canadian maritime regions to South Pacific island cultures, fishing is a social mainstay. Lost opportunities can turn fishing towns into ghost towns, and cause fishing cultures to disappear. Small-scale fishers—who get the least support from governments—form the backbone of community and cultural diversity along the world's coasts.

THE ROOTS OF OVERFISHING

Despite warnings of a slowdown in the marine catch in the seventies and eighties, the fishing industry geared up. Today it has something like twice the capacity needed to make the annual catch. Between 1970 and 1990, FAO recorded a doubling in the world fishing fleet, from 585,000 to 1.2 million large boats. According to FAO fisheries analyst Chris Newton, "We could go back to the 1970 fleet size and we would be no worse off—we'd catch the same amount of fish."[9]

Almost invariably, when a country looks closely at its fisheries, it finds overcapacity. Norway, for instance, estimates its fishing industry is 60 percent over the capacity necessary to make its annual catch. And European Union nations are estimated to have 40-percent overcapacity.[10]

Individual fisheries have shown even greater overcrowding. In the late eighties, the Nova Scotia dragger (trawler) industry was estimated to have four times the capacity needed to make the yearly quota for cod and other bottom-feeding fish (groundfish). In the United States, a simulation in 1990 indicated that as few as 13 boats would be sufficient for the East Coast surf clam fishery; at the time, there were 10 times that number.[11]

How did this overcapacity develop? Many fisheries are open to all comers. In its simplest form, open access allows people to fish at will. If regulators want to limit the total catch, they must calculate the potential take of all boats and adjust the length of the open season accordingly. Fishers then race each other to get the biggest catch possible. As the number of fishers or their capacity increases, the season gets shorter. In the extreme case of the Alaska halibut fishery, the season is restricted to just two or three 24-hour periods a year.[12]

If overfishing becomes too severe, the fishery can collapse, bringing an employment crisis.

Under open access, boats continue to enter the fishery well after fish yield and profits begin to fall. As stocks decline, fishers often buy bigger, faster boats with more advanced equipment and gear. The pressure to overfish, to under-report the catch, and even to poach can undermine management programs. If the cycle of overfishing and overcapacity continues, profits decline until people start to go out of business, fewer people take up fishing, and fishers have no incentive to increase their effort. At this point, the catch in the damaged fishery may stabilize—but at a level below its sustainable potential.

As more and more fishers slide to the brink of financial ruin, pressure on politicians can trigger subsidies that keep overextended individuals in business, maintaining overcapacity. If overfishing becomes too severe, the fishery can collapse, bringing an employment crisis.

FAO estimates that countries provide on the order of $54 billion annually in subsidies to the fishing industry—encouraging its overexpansion in recent decades. European Union member-states, for instance, subsidize their fishing fleets to the tune of at least $500 million a year, not including fuel, tariff protection, and local government subsidies. And Malaysia, having launched a program to modernize its fisheries after independence in 1954, offered subsidies that the World Bank characterized as among the highest in the world. The government laid out $30 million for equipment alone between 1977 and 1981.[13]

Because of the importance of fuel in operating costs, subsidies for this input became increasingly common with the oil shocks in the seventies and eighties. Among Taiwanese fishing companies, for instance, fuel accounts for 60–70 percent of operating costs, and the government disbursed approximately $130 million in fuel subsidies in 1991. Before its collapse, the Soviet Union spent several billion dollars annually on fuel subsidies. In the United States, fishers are exempt from paying the 20–22¢ tax on diesel fuel, which works out to roughly a $250-million annual subsidy.[14]

In addition to contributing to overcapacity, government subsidies often favor larger-scale operations. For example, the Indian state of Kerala pursued a policy of "modernization" in the sixties and seventies that supported commercial fishers over traditional small-scale ones. Kerala paid for 25 percent of the hull and 50 percent of the engine for commercial fishing vessels, and provided low-interest loans for the rest; most of the monies went to more privileged people who knew the ins and outs of how the government works.[15]

Modernization projects have failed for a number of reasons. One is that development projects aimed at improving the lot of poor fishing communities more often end up serving people who have the resources to take advantage of the new technologies and trade possibilities. Modern equipment can provide the means, and commercial markets the motivation, for depleting fish stocks in ways that are not likely in traditional fisheries. Also, lack of expertise and spare parts can quickly make even outboard motors useless, as can the cost of importing fuel in debt-ridden countries.

International development agencies have helped underwrite fishery failures by contributing to the overcapacity of commercial fisheries and undermining traditional fishers. In an evaluation of its own fishery development projects, the World Bank concluded that the "results have not been satisfactory." In the past, development agencies such as the Bank focused primarily on the purchase of equipment, with the major objective being to increase production for export and generate foreign exchange. Traditionally, more than 60 percent of the total aid went toward development of large-scale fisheries, including large vessels, fishing harbors, onshore facilities, technical assistance, and marketing and processing capabilities. The World Bank, among other lenders, is now in the process of revamping its fishery program.[16]

But subsidies to small-scale fishers can also be detrimental if they lead to overcrowding and overcapacity. In Kerala, the government reversed its fishery development policy after small-scale fishers started to hold protests and threaten commercial fishers physically. It first eliminated boat subsidies to commercial fishers in 1978, and then started providing small-scale fishers with subsidies for outboard motors, small boats, and modern gear. The previous subsidies had led to overfishing by commercial fishers; the new policy caused the same problem, just from a different source.[17]

An alternative approach would have been to support more traditional forms of fishing. With its fisheries declining, in 1984 the Kerala government appointed an expert committee to study the problem. The committee cited overcapacity as the culprit and advised emphasizing small-scale, traditional fishing to maximize employment and protect the livelihood of the poorest fishers. The committee recommended reducing the number of trawlers from 2,807 to 1,145, eliminating all 54 boats that used purse seine nets, cutting back on motorized small boats from 6,934 to 2,690, and keeping all 20,000 of the non-motorized craft. If the government had followed this advice, Kerala's fisheries might be in better shape today.[18]

TOO MANY FISHERS?

With many of the world's fisheries declining under the burden of an overextended fishing industry, the phrase "too many fishers chasing too few fish" has become a cliché. Like many such catchphrases, the statement contains some truth, but it also oversimplifies the situation. It is not just the number of fishers that counts, but also the size of their nets, the number of their hooks, the girth of their boats—in short, their capacity to fish.

The structure of the fishing industry varies considerably from country to country. Japan, for instance, is the world's top marine fishing country and catches nearly twice as much as China. Yet only 200,000 fishers work in Japan, compared with China's 3.8 million.[19]

Of the world's 15–21 million fishers, more than 90 percent are small-scale operators, using either traditional equipment or small, relatively modern boats. (See Table 2–2.) The definition of small-, medium-, and large-scale fishing is somewhat arbitrary, but the basic differences are evident from country to country, whether comparing dugout canoes and a 20-meter steel trawler, or the same trawler and a 100-meter factory freezer-trawler.[20]

Table 2-2. Comparisons Among Fishers by Scale of Operation

Comparison	Large-Scale	Medium-Scale	Small-Scale
Number of fishers employed	200,000–300,000	900,000–1 million	14–20 million
Earnings per fisher (dollars per year)	15,000	8,000	500–1,500
Marine fish caught for human consumption (million tons per year)	15–20	15–20	20–30
Marine fish caught for fish meal, fish oil, and so on (million tons per year)	10–20	10–20	almost none
Bycatch (million tons per year)	5–10	5–10	almost none
Fishers employed per $1 million investment	1–5	5–15	60–3,000
Fuel consumption (million tons per year)	7.6	12.8	26.2
Fish per ton of fuel (tons of fish)	2.6–3.9	1.6–2.3	0.8–1.1[1]

[1]Several million small-scale fishers use nonmotorized boats.
SOURCE: Worldwatch Institute, based on FAO and other sources documented in endnote 20.

Although the contribution of all three sectors to the food supply is approximately the same, smaller-scale operations have a number of important advantages. To catch a given amount of fish, these outfits tend to employ more people, produce less waste, and require less capital. In addition, smaller-scale fishing supports a greater diversity of coastal communities. However, fuel consumption is high on average for small-scale operators, and has been increasing particularly among traditional fishers, who are buying outboard motors in large numbers. Nonetheless, several million fishers still use nonmotorized boats.

On average, small-scale fishers earn considerably less than their more mechanized counterparts. FAO estimates that the crew on the largest boats earn about $15,000 per person annually, while small-scale fishers may take in less than $500 per person a year. As an example of the discrepancies, in 1982 in Newfoundland the small-scale fishers formed the majority, yet they brought in only 35 percent of the total catch—worth about $8,590 per person. In Asia, traditional fishers are generally poor, despite accounting for 1–5 percent of national incomes and catching a third of the fish in the region. An estimated 98 percent of traditional fishers in India fall below the poverty line. As a result, most people who fish must also hold other jobs.[21]

From a strictly economic perspective, it appears to be irrational and inefficient for a person to continue being a small-scale fisher. But such decisions are made within the context of fishing communities and cultures. Furthermore, fishers in remote coastal areas have few lucrative employment options. Where there are alternatives, people fish because they like the freedom, the sea, the life-style, the continuity of tradition.

Today, however, even the economic efficiency argument does not always favor large-scale fishing. Whereas before only the huge boats of large-scale operators could weather the high seas, technological improvements are letting smaller boats venture further from shore. Small, powerful boats, miniaturized electronic equipment, and modern fishing gear allow fishers to do the job of the larger vessels, even travelling hundreds of kilometers out to sea. They can also respond more rapidly to market fluctuations, making them more profitable. In the Mediterranean and the Persian Gulf, smaller boats are replacing the industrial fishing ships because of these advantages.[22]

If governments are to control overfishing, a basic problem they must confront is the excess capacity of the industry. Choosing to emphasize larger-scale fishing over smaller-scale fishing will yield very different results, however. Reducing the large-scale fishing industry by half would eliminate some 100,000 jobs. Cutting the medium-sized industry in half would affect 500,000 jobs. But halving the small-scale fishing industry would destroy 7–10 million jobs. Each group has roughly the same capacity to bring in fish. The employment and other social implications of these sectors are, however, very different. In recent years many governments have emphasized industrialization and large vessels: if this continues, virtually the entire smallscale fishing sector could be wiped out— at a cost of some 14–20 million jobs.[23]

FOOD AND FAIRNESS

While fish supplies have stagnated, world population continues to grow approximately 1.6 percent a year, adding the equivalent of the population of Mexico annually. At this rate, the total supply of fish (marine, fresh, and aquaculture) would have to rise from today's 100 million tons per year to 120 million tons by 2010, and then add another 20 million tons to the annual supply by 2025, just to maintain today's per capita fish supply.[24]

Although the long-term prospects are limited, marine fisheries could continue to contribute to the growth in the world fish supply for the next 20–30 years if they were better managed. Rehabilita-

tion of stocks could potentially increase the annual marine catch by 20 million tons. Aquaculture, currently growing by approximately 800,000 tons per year, could make up the difference.[25]

One crucial question must be addressed, however: who would benefit from these increases? Current trends— rising prices, increasing exports from developing to industrial countries, and limits on access to fisheries—have severe implications for low-income people and subsistence cultures who rely on marine fish as a dietary staple. Already the distribution of fish is skewed toward consumers in industrial countries, where average consumption per person is three times the level in developing nations. Marine aquaculture has contributed to this disparity. Unless countries manage their marine fisheries for the purpose of maintaining and improving nutrition, increased fish catches will serve only the affluent.[26]

The nutritional benefits of marine fishing are closely tied to the scale of production. Small-scale maritime operations tend to sell or trade their catch locally, particularly in developing countries and traditional cultures; largerscale operations mostly supply commercial markets, which sell to the highest bidder.

This dichotomy has created two global classes of fish consumers. The one linked with local small-scale fishers consists of people with low incomes or in traditional cultures, for whom fish is an integral part of the diet. Consumers connected to commercial markets, which is most consumers in the industrial world, primarily eat fish as a luxury item or supplement to an already balanced diet. In countries such as Sierra Leone and Philippines, for example, people eat fish to raise their overall protein intake to a healthy level. In industrial countries such as the United States and France, however, where protein consumption is twice the recommended level, people on average could greatly reduce or eliminate their fish consumption without significantly affecting their nutrition.[27]

Historically, fish has been considered the poor person's protein because of its relatively low price with respect to meat. Over the last two decades, however, fish prices have risen relative to beef, pork, and chicken because of the combination of rising demand in industrial countries and tightening world supply. (See Figure 2–2.) Today they are more in line with meat prices. Except perhaps for specialty items such as lobster, if prices rise much further, people will substitute chicken or other meats for fish, so meat prices will constrain those of fish in wealthier nations.[28]

Consumers in developing countries, however, face a far more dramatic rise in fish prices as local fishers tie into lucrative markets in industrial countries. In Kerala, India's number one fishing state, prices for shrimp skyrocketed from 240 rupees ($50) per ton to 14,120 rupees ($1,300) between 1961 and 1981 with the rise in commercial fishing for export. Per capita consumption fell from 19 kilograms in 1971 to 9 kilograms in 1981. Sardine and mackerel prices increased tenfold. Local consumers were no longer competing on the local market at local prices, but on the international market at international prices.[29]

The incentive to export is, of course, cash. In the last two decades, developing countries have increased their share of the marine catch, and in 1989 they surpassed the catch of industrial countries. But they are exporting an increasing share of their haul in order to gain foreign exchange to pay off foreign debts and import fuel, food, medicine, and other supplies. Exports of ocean products from developing countries have increased twice as fast as those from industrial nations. Conversely, industrial countries import nearly seven times as much as developing ones do. And the trend is likely to continue: Vietnam, for instance, plans to more than double its fish exports by the end of this decade, to between $900 million and $1 billion per year.[30]

Increased participation in commercial markets not only raises prices in developing countries; it can reduce the domestic supply, disrupt traditional cultures, and lead to hunger. Anthropologist James McGoodwin has documented a case in Mexico where the government limited a local community's fishing rights in favor of more "efficient" commercial shrimpers in the export market. This traditional fishing community had no access to agricultural land. In late summer, when the regulators would close the fishing grounds, local people went hungry, violent crime increased, children ate dirt or sand to alleviate hunger pangs, and death rates appeared to rise for old people and infants.[31]

Another portion of the catch from the waters of developing countries never touches the nearby shore. Instead, foreign fleets pay to fish and ship the catch home. The European Union, for example, pays $200 million annually in access fees, half of it to African nations. Approximately half the catch off western

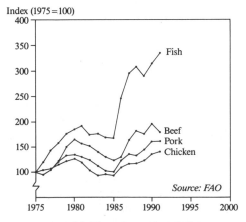

Figure 2-2. Comparison of Fish, Beef, Pork, and Chicken Export Prices, 1975–91

Africa and a third of the catch off south-western Africa is taken by foreign fleets that return home with most of the fish. In the southwest Pacific, foreign fleets take about a third of the catch, and in the eastern central Pacific, about a fifth.[32]

The economic power of industrial countries has helped create this imbalance. The United States, Canada, Europe, and Japan account for 84 percent, by value, of world fishery imports. Their wealth allows them to continue to gain access to fish by outbidding poorer domestic consumers.[33]

With 123 million well-off consumers getting half their animal protein from fish, Japan is the biggest force in the international market. Still the world's top marine fishing nation, Japan is also the number one importer of seafood. With increasing restrictions on where it can fish, the nation has reduced its own catch in recent years while increasing imports. Japanese companies are gaining greater control over processing and marketing, while leaving harvesting to others. In particular, Japan is working to develop links with developing countries that can supply it with seafood. The Japanese semipublic Overseas Fishery Cooperation Foundation (OFCF) coordinates attempts by fishing and trading companies to set up commercial links with developing countries. OFCF offers cheap loans, and the trading companies offer technical assistance.[34]

If people made an effort to establish more balance between need and supply, the current oceanic catch could fill the projected shortfall for the neediest customers. Consumption of fish in industrial countries could drop by 50 percent—which would still allow a generous supply for healthy diets and would mean the supply in developing countries could increase by almost 50 percent. If this transition occurred over the next 15 years, developing countries could maintain their current per capita supply of fish until the year 2010 without any increases in the annual catch.[35]

Distribution issues extend beyond the portion of the world catch that goes to people. Approximately a third of the marine fish catch goes to other uses—primarily animal feed for pets, livestock, and pond-raised fish. The world's top producer of animal feed is Peru, which converts nearly all 6 million tons of its anchovies, jack mackerel, and pilchard to 1.3 million tons of fish meal.[36]

Still the world's top marine fishing nation, Japan is also the number one importer of seafood.

Fishers sell their produce for fish meal when they can catch large quantities easily but the fish are too small, oily, bony, or otherwise undesirable to command a viable price on the consumer market. This portion of the marine catch now benefits primarily people in more privileged communities, who eat feed-fed livestock or fish, or buy the fish meal in the form of pet food.

But "undesirable" species do indeed feed people and could feed more, despite current trends. In Chile, for instance, despite large gains in jack mackerel production in the past decade, domestic consumption of fish has fallen by half because the fish meal market for export is more lucrative than selling to poor people. Ninety percent of jack mackerel production goes for animal feed. Yet John Kearney, a fisheries anthropologist based in New Brunswick, Canada, reports that boys from the neighborhood near a processing plant in Talcahuano, Chile, jump into moving trucks that carry jack mackerel the single block from the wharf to the processing plant. They kick as many fish as they can out before the truck reaches the plant, while others gather the fish from the pavement to take home or sell on street corners.[37]

For perspective, if the portion of the world catch that now goes for animal feed were offered for human consumption, the world food fish supply would go up by 40 percent. This would maintain today's average supply of 13 kilograms per person until the year 2017 without having to increase the supply of fish from other sources. And if this fish went solely to consumers in developing countries, it would preserve today's per capita consumption level until 2030.[38]

Expanding marine fish farming will do little to meet the needs of those poised to lose as the wild marine supply tightens.

The momentum in marine fisheries, however, is moving in the wrong direction for low-income consumers. Not only have prices risen, but in the past decade the largest increases in supply have come from either low-value species used primarily for animal feed, or from high-priced species such as tuna and squid. Neither of these extremes benefit low-income consumers.

AQUACULTURE: NO PANACEA

Although people have farmed fish for thousands of years, aquaculture's contribution to the world fish supply has been negligible on a global scale until the last four decades. During the last 10 years, it has been the fastest growing supplier of fish worldwide. Today, as a result of increased freshwater aquaculture production, two farmed species have displaced marine ones in the top 10 in the world catch (which includes marine and freshwater species): silver carp and grass carp have taken over the seventh and tenth positions, accounting for 1.6 million and 1.3 million tons per year respectively.[39]

As a result of the slowdown in the ocean catch, people have turned to fish farms for increased supplies. In general, however, aquaculture serves as a distraction from facing the limits of marine fisheries. Policymakers may be tempted to assume that we can make up for mistreating the oceans and small-scale fishers by farming fish. But despite rapid growth, aquaculture's contribution to the welfare and nutrition of coastal people who have traditionally relied on marine fisheries has been minimal.

For instance, the marine aquaculture industry has made extraordinary efforts to increase the supply of such high-value species as shrimp: although the wild catch has stagnated around the world, the shrimp supply has continued to grow because of aquaculture. The shrimp farming industry was producing about 500,000 tons a year by the end of the eighties, about a quarter of the total shrimp supply. At the same time, salmon aquaculture was producing about 250,-000 tons per year of this high-value species: again, about one quarter of total production.[40]

A rapidly growing industry, saltwater aquaculture has largely fueled exports. Therefore, expanding marine fish farming will do little to meet the needs of those poised to lose as the wild marine supply tightens. An increasingly common practice, in fact, is to catch wild fish and use them as feed for farmed fish. If people cannot outbid a fish raised in a pond for one caught in the sea, how can they hope to afford the raised fish? Some fishers who sell feed go so far as to use fine-mesh nets to make a clean sweep— biomass fishing. Everything caught is ground up and fed to farmed fish.

Theoretically, aquaculture could employ fishers who lose their jobs. But fish farming involves a quite different set of skills. Furthermore, the logical alternative for coastal fishing communities is marine aquaculture, which is predominantly tied into the commercial sector. On Java, intense competition in the coastal aquaculture sector fueled consolidation. Many small-scale fish farmers had to sell out as input prices rose, land prices escalated, and large-scale fish farms started to underbid them. As ownership became more concentrated and the number of absentee owners increased, fewer workers were needed to raise the same quantity of fish.[41]

Marine aquaculture is also a major cause of coastal habitat destruction, which undermines marine fisheries. One major reason people cut down mangrove forests—half of which have been destroyed worldwide—is to make artificial shrimp ponds. But coastal wetlands are essential nurseries for wild fisheries, and their destruction directly undermines marine fishing. In Honduras, tensions between shrimp fishers and shrimp farmers have led people on both sides to arm themselves; some claim that a conservation-minded fisher was murdered by vigilantes hired by shrimp farmers. Similar conflicts over shrimp farming have flared up around the world.[42]

In addition to destroying coastal habitats, shrimp farming and other forms of marine aquaculture have contributed to coastal water pollution, the introduction of alien species and new diseases, and the loss of genetic diversity in wild populations.[43]

To feed needy people while protecting the environment, freshwater aquaculture holds more promise than marine farming. Freshwater fish farms produce less expensive species such as carp and tilapia, which low-income people are more likely to be able to afford. Carp production, in particular, has soared in

the past two decades. Furthermore, fish farmers have developed systems that integrate fish ponds with crop production, so that waste from the ponds fertilizes crops instead of causing pollution.

In the Mampong Valley in eastern Ghana—an area characterized by depleted soils, hillside or terraced agriculture, and seasonal rainfall—small farms have benefited from building fish ponds on marginal and unused land. In Vietnam's Mekong Delta, freshwater prawn aquaculture systems have flourished in integrated systems on farms. Farmers have even integrated vegetable and rice crops with marine shrimp and freshwater fish species. These systems typically consist of agricultural land divided into a series of ditches and levees connected to the main source of water.[44]

Although fish farming has potential for maintaining supplies for inland markets and privileged consumers, people currently dependent on marine fisheries are not poised to reap many benefits. The greatest hope for continuing to meet the needs of coastal peoples lies in the small-scale fishers who currently serve them. Thus, rehabilitating marine fisheries and maintaining access for small-scale operators is not only a matter of employment and community support, it is also a question of nutrition for many of the world's poorest fish consumers. For these people in particular, the tightening in world fisheries is increasingly threatening. Without preventive action, marine fisheries will cease to play much of their current vital nutritional role.

OVERREACTING TO OVERCAPACITY

Despite the benefits of smaller-scale fishing, government after government is implementing consolidation programs that encourage bigger boats and smaller fleets to address the problems of over-capacity and overfishing. Taiwan has stopped issuing licenses to boats smaller than 1,000 tons and started a buy-back program for boats more than 15 years old. Malaysia plans on using higher capacity, more modern boats—and in the process expects to cut the number of fishers from 100,000 to 60,000. The European Union has set annual targets for individual nations to reduce the number of fishing vessels. As part of Iceland's plan to improve the economic efficiency of its fisheries, the country plans to cut its fishing capacity by 40 percent. In Canada, the Ministry of Fisheries imposed a quota system on one Nova Scotia fishery that dropped the number of active boats from 455 in 1990 to less than 170 in 1993.[45]

Management systems that promote consolidation also concentrate wealth and can be devastating for coastal communities.

Although consolidation is arguably necessary in many cases, poorly considered programs can eliminate badly needed sources of employment, concentrating the benefits of the fishery in the hands of privileged people. In the United States, a consolidation program started in 1990 for the East Coast surf clam fishery did not involve crew members or address employment issues. In the course of two years, the number of boats dropped by 53 percent, and the amount of labor by an estimated one third. Employment would have fallen more if the boat owners had not already begun rotating employees among their boats. At the beginning of the program, three firms controlled 33 percent of the

surf clam boats, as well as a number of processing plants, while only 21 percent of the boats were owner-operated. The consolidation effort led to even further integration of the industry.[46]

At the request of the surf clam boat owners, regional regulators had put in place a market-based system known as individual transferable quotas (ITQs). Under this, each boat owner received a share in the annual catch, and quota holders could buy, sell, or lease them like property. For boat owners, who did not have to pay for fishing rights that they could now sell, ITQs yielded a windfall profit, and small operators who were having hard economic times were able to sell out or lease their portion of the quota. For the unemployed crew members, the implications are obvious. The unexpected results were that a leaner and presumably more efficient fishery nevertheless did not lower the price of clams—nor did it raise income for most of the remaining crew, despite longer working hours.[47]

Although the results can be questionable, as this example shows, ITQs are one of the most widely discussed management solutions for overcrowded fisheries. They have a certain appeal because, through transferable fishing rights, market forces can direct the allocation of resources, presumably increasing economic efficiency. ITQs have the benefit of allowing marginal shareholders to get out of the fishery with some money. The down side is that such systems allow a small number of individuals or companies to buy control over the fishery.

When New Zealand was in the process of instituting an ITQ system, highly capitalized fishing companies expanded their operations beyond the level of catch they could sell profitably so that they would control a higher percentage of the fishery at the time of the initial allocation of quotas. If regulators do not act to prevent such "capital stuffing," ITQs can reward the very fishers who overcapitalized the fishery in the first place, while squeezing out smaller operations.[48]

Limitations on the transferability of an ITQ, such as restricting the portion an individual or company may own, could help limit consolidation. Under an ITQ system for Alaska's halibut fishery, which is scheduled to begin in 1995, quotas for small boat owners would be allocated in blocks. No single owner could own more than five blocks. In principle, these regulations will keep the small-boat portion of the quota in the hands of small operators.[49]

But before going this route, policymakers should recognize that management systems that promote consolidation also concentrate wealth and can be devastating for coastal communities, particularly if changes come rapidly and without support for developing new jobs. Small-scale fishers are too numerous—and too vital to coastal communities—to sacrifice in an effort to control overfishing.

FENCING THE OCEANS

As one of the great global commons, the oceans fall within the realm of international governance. A fundamental challenge to managing marine fisheries is determining who has jurisdiction where. For centuries, freedom of the seas was the reigning doctrine, and the waters beyond 3 nautical miles were open to all.

With the boom in marine fishing after World War II, fishers began to engage in sometimes fierce competition over fishing grounds. In the seventies, as conflict mounted, the world community took the first major step toward curtailing freedom on the high seas—at least in the

realm of fishing. As part of the Third United Nations Conference on the Law of the Sea, governments agreed to establish a zone no more than 200 nautical miles wide within which a coastal country has sole rights to natural resources. Known as an exclusive economic zone, or EEZ, this area includes the most productive fishing grounds in the oceans. By 1976, more than 60 countries had laid claim to the waters 200 nautical miles from their shores. Today, more than 122 nations have claimed EEZs.[50]

The EEZ system is a compromise. It removes the richest portions of the oceans from the global commons and confers sovereignty over them to individual coastal nations. These countries are arguably in the best position to manage the adjacent fisheries, but landlocked and other nations lose access to what had been open territory. Outside the EEZ, however, freedom of the seas still largely stands.

The Law of the Sea itself officially went into force in November 1994, but it is vague on the matter of high-seas fishing. Small portions of Canada's Grand Banks extend more than 200 nautical miles into the Atlantic, for example. The Canadian government accuses foreign fishers who work these waters of depleting cod stocks. In one case, Canadian enforcement officials boarded and seized a trawler, the *Kristina Logos*, despite the fact that it was 28 miles outside Canada's EEZ.[51]

The *Kristina Logos* had taken advantage of the most significant fishing loophole in the Law of the Sea: a dearth of enforceable restrictions on fishing on the high seas. Regional agreements cover various high-seas fisheries, including the one outside the Grand Banks, but these lack teeth beyond the power of diplomacy. If a country does not wish to comply with restrictions imposed by an agreement, it can refuse to participate, as Norway did with the whaling moratorium; or it can simply quit, as Iceland did with the International Whaling Commission. When the home nation of a vessel enters into a regional agreement that might restrict fishing, the vessel's owners can avoid the restrictions by adopting a flag of convenience—the flag of a nation that has not signed the agreement. Such was apparently the case with the *Kristina Logos*, whose Portuguese captain and crew were flying a Panamanian flag.[52]

The most dramatic failure of high-seas diplomacy involves bluefin tuna, the world's most valuable fish, which fetch up to $260 per kilogram in restaurants in Japan. In principle, the International Commission for the Conservation of Atlantic Tuna (ICCAT), an organization of nations whose fishers hunt tuna in the Atlantic Ocean, manages this industry. But despite ICCAT oversight, bluefin tuna populations have dropped precipitously. The population that spawns in the Gulf of Mexico has dropped by 90 percent since 1975, and the one that spawns in the Mediterranean has declined by half.[53]

Under the threat of endangered species listing under the Convention on International Trade in Endangered Species of Wild Flora and Fauna, ICCAT chose a phased cut of 50 percent by 1995. But the prospects for bluefin tuna recovery remain dim. ICCAT members complain that up to 80 percent of the catch may be taken by non-ICCAT fishing vessels flying flags of convenience— some 500 of which are thought to be hunting bluefins in the Atlantic.[54]

Conflicts over high-seas stocks precipitated international negotiations at the United Nations beginning in July 1993. To date, negotiators have been unable to reach agreement. Two camps have formed—one primarily of countries with major fishing grounds who want a binding international treaty, and one mainly of nations with long-range fishing fleets, who want only a guideline.[55]

To reduce international tensions over high-seas fishing, however, international negotiators will have to acknowledge that the doctrine of freedom of the seas is no longer viable for oceanic fishing. Just as the western frontier in the United States disappeared behind fences, the oceans will eventually have to be completely divided up by diplomacy to allow for conservation of high-sea fisheries.

PROMOTING FISHERS AND HEALTHY FISHERIES

Two decades after the nations of the world convened for the Third Conference on the Law of the Sea, coastal countries control the prime fishing grounds—but the number of fish populations that have collapsed or are at risk is higher than ever. Coastal countries have replaced overfishing by foreign fleets with overfishing by their own. For many fishers, the crisis point that nations worked 20 years ago to avert has arrived.

More effective fisheries management would not only save jobs, it would also save taxpayers tens of billions of dollars a year. Governments could save some $54 billion annually by eliminating subsidies, and earn another $25 billion per year in rents, with a net budgetary benefit greater than the current gross value of the entire marine catch. Meanwhile, if stocks are allowed to recover, FAO estimates that fishers could increase the annual catch by as much as 20 million tons—worth about $16 billion at today's prices.[56]

To make the transition to healthy fisheries, governments and fishers have to move beyond the current political deadlock. In virtually all cases, a combination of government oversight and community-based management promises the best integration of conservation while maximizing community benefits. The basic tenets of fishery management—closed seasons, restricted areas, size limits, species restrictions, quotas, and equipment regulations—are well known. However, the indispensable element all too often lacking today is local, community-based control. Fishers readily subvert management systems that do not involve them. In addition to outright illegal methods of enlarging their catch, they bend the rules by increasing their capacity with bigger boats, nets, and so on. In fisheries with restricted boat length, the boats become almost as wide as they are long. Short of draconian monitoring, centralized management often fails.[57]

Examples of successful management involve a high level of community involvement. In Maine, lobster fishers developed their own effective system of limited access without any government involvement. Each local harbor has its own territory, which is further subdivided among local fishers. The system's success is based on the tight-knit communities. The rules are taken so seriously that violence occasionally flares when fishers break them.[58]

Japan manages its coastal fisheries under a two-tiered system with roots in village customary law of the feudal era. During the Edo Period, from 1603 to 1867, the nation developed detailed fishing regulations and institutionalized a system of local sea tenure. For example, seaweed harvesting was banned during spawning season to protect the fish eggs attached to seaweed, gill nets for bottom species were outlawed, and night fishing with torches was limited during the mid-nineteenth century. As the government of Japan became increasingly centralized, local communities nevertheless continued to control coastal fisheries. Japan passed the national Fisheries Law

in 1901 to formalize the existing system of control and access through Fishing Cooperative Associations (FCAs).[59]

Essentially, the FCA owns the local fishing grounds; all members have a share, just as a stockholder owns a share of a company. The FCAs form the link between the government and local fishers. They organize all coastal fishers and enforce control over the fisheries. As a result, long-time Japanese fishers are relatively well-off, in sharp contrast with fishers in many other parts of the world. And the basic two-tier structure of fisheries management—stable for hundreds of years—forms a model promising for other countries as well. Higher levels of government set guidelines, but local people work out the details.[60]

More effective fisheries management would not only save jobs, it would also save taxpayers tens of billions of dollars a year.

Similarly, small-scale fishers in the Maluku Islands in Indonesia have modified their traditional management system, known as *sasi*, to adapt to changes brought by interaction with commercial markets. *Sasi* combines management and spiritual practices to maximize the catch. Starting in the sixties, fishers there began gathering trochus, a reef mollusk, to export the shells to Italy, Japan, and other Asian markets for buttons and pigments. Overharvesting in the eighties led to declines in the catch, which the fishers blamed on failing to please ancestral and environmental spirits. The government stepped in and banned the harvest in 1990. Over time, the local fishers modified *sasi* to take into account scientific notions of environmental dynamics—and trochus gathering began again on a sustainable basis.[61]

Enforcement is critical to the success of any management system. To the extent that a management system gives them a strong sense of ownership, fishers have more of an incentive to steward the fishery for the long term. For example, in the United States individual fishers often lease their own shellfish beds. Close oversight is therefore not necessary because it is the individual fisher who stands to lose if he or she overexploits it. Likewise, a community-based fishery can be self-policing if the community is tight-knit and they understand the ecology of the fishery.

Fisheries are part of the public trust, and governments have a responsibility to maintain them for future generations.

Theoretically, market-based systems that give individual fishers a share in production (such as ITQs) can also give fishers a long-term interest in the resource base. But if the species move around, if the fishing grounds lie far offshore, or if there are many fishers, any given individual is likely to act as if it were an open access system. ITQs can even make enforcement more difficult because fishers can fish when they want. With an open-ended season, they can get around the system by not reporting catches and by high-grading—that is, discarding lower-value fish and keeping only the more valuable ones to maximize the value of the catch. In some fisheries, a defined season can be easier to manage and lead to less abuse because enforcement officials know that fishing in a particular region is only allowed at certain times. Likewise, violation of no-fishing zones, which can serve as undisturbed habitat for reproduction and growth, is

obvious. No one management system is appropriate in all cases.

Ultimately, fisheries are part of the public trust, and governments have a responsibility to maintain them for future generations. Ideal management systems would require little government participation, but there is always a role for government, whether enforcing the right of a community to bar outsiders and manage its own fisheries, or pursuing more active regulation and patrolling.

In the Philippines, for instance, the government grants local communities 25-year contracts to manage the coastline. With this authority behind them, several communities have restored hundreds of hectares of mangroves, established no-fishing zones, and limited fishing—with resulting increases in the sustainable fish catch. Communities that did not have government backing found that commercial fishers encroached on their territory.[62]

Developing countries commonly establish a coastal zone where only traditional, small-scale fishers may work. But these zones are vulnerable to encroachment and to fishing further offshore by commercial fishers. In Sierra Leone, the catch of traditional fishers dipped significantly as commercial fishing intensified. Greater control of large-scale fishing offshore would thus directly benefit small-scale fishers.[63]

Once a country decides how to manage its fisheries, the next step is to make sure that financial incentives support the overall strategy. As noted earlier, all too often governments subsidize overcapacity and overfishing even as the catch declines. Further, governments often forgo potential royalties for the use of fishing grounds that are, after all, a public resource. As in the management of grazing, logging, or mining on public lands, fees can be an integral part of limiting exploitation and compensating the public for use of commonly held resources. At a minimum, fisheries should be self-supporting, with the fees covering management. If a community decides to take a market-based approach to its fisheries, it can require fishers to pay for tradable fishing rights, which would also eliminate windfall profits from giving away rights that can subsequently be sold.

In an innovative tradable quota system, the Australian government takes a percentage of each fisher's allotment each year, which it then sells to cover management costs and to give new fishers the opportunity to enter the fishery. In other Australian fisheries, rents have ranged from 11 to 60 percent of the gross value of the catch, with a weighted average of 30 percent.[64]

Governments can adjust royalties according to social and conservation goals. For example, small-scale fishers could be exempt from payments. Fees for commercial fishers can increase as the stocks become more depleted. Many countries already charge foreign fishing vessels for access to their fishing grounds. Domestic charging is much less common. In the United States, licensing fees fail to cover the cost of fishery management, even for foreign vessels.[65]

Countries may have rich marine resources from which they derive little benefit because of mismanagement, poaching, and corruption. After studying fisheries management in West Africa, Vlad Kaczynski at the University of Washington School of Marine Affairs concluded that foreign fishing fleets were essentially robbing poor nations. Guinea, for instance, received about 1 percent of the value of the catch by foreign vessels, compared with 25 percent royalties in many industrial countries.[66]

To put fishing on a sustainable path will mean at least a slowdown in the take from major fisheries while fish populations recover. Programs to help ease the transition are vital. A few are already being assembled, including a $30-million package for New England fishers and their communities. Of this total, $12 million is earmarked to help individuals move on to other fisheries and into other industries. If, however, such programs encourage fishers to simply pursue species that are not yet overexploited, then the vicious cycle of reaching out to new fisheries and depleting them may continue.[67]

The bottom line is that oceanic fisheries have limits, and the fishing industry is undermining these natural systems by overfishing. Fishers and fishery managers widely acknowledge that overcapacity is one of the primary forces driving the declines in marine fisheries, but given the ominous potential for job loss, few policymakers have been willing to take strong stands on fishery conservation, which only allows the situation to get worse.

To combat overfishing and overcapacity, policymakers can reorient their policies so that 1–2 million large- or medium-scale fishers are out of work. Or they may find that 5 million, 10 million, or even 20 million small-scale fishers will lose their jobs, with all that implies for coastal communities. Given the social consequences, policymakers would do well to help keep small-scale fishers in business.

If fishers, regulators, and coastal communities stay on the current path, marine fisheries will continue to decline, millions of people will lose their jobs, and coastal communities and low-income consumers will suffer disproportionately. If instead these groups work together to improve fishery management, the oceans will be able to continue to yield fish—and economic and social benefits—for the foreseeable future.

3

Sustaining Mountain Peoples and Environments

Derek Denniston

In 1937, James Hilton wrote *Lost Horizon*, his classic novel about a mystical Shangri-La ensconced in an unknown recess of Tibet. The book describes the surreal abduction of four westerners to a Buddhist paradise of content peasants and ageless monks. Perhaps more than any other, this work of fiction sculpted the western literary notion of mountains as remote and sparsely inhabited fortresses, secure in their immensity and transcendent in their beauty. Notwithstanding all this aesthetic appeal, we remain grossly ignorant of mountain peoples and environments and the increasing threats they face.[1]

Mountains span one fifth of the landscape and are home to one tenth of humanity. An additional 2 billion people live downstream from them, and depend on their ample water, hydropower, grassland, timber, and mineral resources. And 7 of the world's 14 tropical "hotspots" of endemic plants threatened by imminent destruction have at least half their area in tropical mountains. The enormous layers of complexity of mountain landscapes—their climates, vegetation, and wildlife—have spawned great cultural diversity as well. For instance, several million tribal farmers and pastoralists reside in the mountains of Afghanistan, China, Iran, Nepal, Pakistan, and the central Asian nations of the former Soviet Union.[2]

Mountain cultures and ecosystems face three primary threats from the expanding world economy: land scarcity fueled by inequitable ownership patterns and control of public resources, intensive resource extraction, and mass tourism and recreation. Around the world, mountain peoples risk increasing cultural assimilation, debilitating poverty, and political disempowerment. After millennia of intensive human transformation of the surrounding lowlands and flatlands, mountains have become vertical islands of cultural and biological diversity surrounded by seas of biological impoverishment and cultural homogeneity. This enormous diversity makes mountains one of the last major opportunities for conserving natural and human variety.

VERTICAL VALUES

Mountains and highlands span every latitude, altitude, and continent on earth. They cover at least 30 million square kilometers and in 1994 were home to about 560 million people. Although even basic data on the area and population of many ranges are hard to come by, what is available shows that mountains contain wide geographic and demographic diversity. Two fifths of the world's mountain peoples are concentrated in the Andes, the Himalaya-Hindu Kush ranges, and dispersed African mountains. (See Table 3–1.) Contrary to the sparse populations of northern mountains, portions of some tropical ranges—such as some parts of the highlands of Papua New Guinea, Mount Kenya, and the Virunga volcano region of Rwanda—have more than 400 people per square kilometer.[3]

One major reason for the ignorance of mountains has been the confusion about exactly what the term means. No universal definition exists: one person's mountain can be another's hill. The generic meaning of a mountain is "a landmass that projects conspicuously above its surroundings and is higher than a hill."[4]

A common criterion for identifying mountains is relative relief, defined as the "elevational distance between the highest and lowest points in the area." Early European geographers felt that at least 900 meters was the relief required for an area to be considered mountainous, but geographers in the eastern United States consider 300 meters sufficient.[5]

A second basis for distinguishing mountains from hills is that a mountain's rise in altitude creates climates, soils, and vegetation that are significantly different from those in surrounding lowlands. Ecologists call this "altitudinal zonation." A recent ecological map of the world shows more than 23 percent of the earth's landscape with this characteristic. Although they lack relative relief, high plateaus are usually included in definitions of mountains because their elevation induces short growing seasons, and thus the low biomass productivity that is common to many steep-sloped environments. Local perceptions of topography will continue to determine local definitions, but progress toward a more generally accepted, ecologically based definition of mountains is urgently required for effective conservation.[6]

While consensus emerges on this definition, a useful distinction regarding mountain peoples and environments is the characteristics created by their unique vertical dimension. Mountains share common physical attributes of steepness, instability, and ecological complexity that create natural hazards, microclimates, niches of biodiversity, and inaccessibility. These shared physical and environmental characteristics predispose their inhabitants to being at the margins of cultural, economic, and political power.[7]

The collision of continental plates—the major cause of mountain uplift and slope—creates numerous natural hazards, including earthquakes, volcanic eruptions, landslides, avalanches, and floods. These structural instabilities not only add major costs and efforts to build-

Table 3-1. Area and Population, Selected Mountain Ranges and High Plateaus[1]

Region	Area	Population, Circa 1990
	(thousand square kilometers)	(million)
N.E. Siberia/Russian Far East	3,813	1.7
Himalaya[2]	3,400	121
African Mountains and Highlands[3]	3,000	100
Tibetan Plateau	2,500	6.4
Andes	2,000+	65
Alaskan Ranges[4]	1,060	0.17
Western Canadian Ranges[5]	1,365	3.3
Antarctic Ranges	1,346	0
Other Former Soviet Ranges[6]	836	2.4
U.S. Rockies[7]	818	3.4
Central Asia/Kazakhstan	522	11
Sierra/California Coastal/Cascades	380	17.1
Brazilian Atlantic Range[8]	300	25
Alps	240	11.2
Caucasus	179	7.7
Appalachia/Adirondacks	176	10

[1]Figures are not strictly comparable due to varying definitions of mountains and highlands. [2]Includes Hengduan, Hindu Kush, and Karakorum. [3]Includes East African mountains and highlands, Atlas mountains, isolated West African mountain peaks, dispersed southern African mountains, and mountains and highlands of Madagascar. [4]Includes Ahklun Mountains, Alaska Range, Aleutians, Brooks Range, Pacific Coastal, Pacific Gulf, Seward Peninsula, Upper Yukon mountains, and Yukon Intermontane Plateaus. [5]Includes portions of Alberta, British Columbia, Northwest Territories, and Yukon Territory. [6]Includes Altai, Sayan, Urals, high latitude mountains, Crimea, and the Ukranian Carpathians. [7]Includes New Mexico-Arizona and Nevada-Utah mountains. [8]Includes Chapada Diamantina, Serra do Espinhaço, Serra da Mantiqueira, Serra do Mar, and Serra Geral.
SOURCE: Compiled by Worldwatch Institute from sources cited in endnote 3.

ing infrastructure such as roads, dams, and tunnels, they can make human settlement dangerous. On May 31, 1970, for example, an earthquake caused a large mass of ice to tumble from Mount Huascarán in the Peruvian Andes, creating a massive mudflow that hurtled toward the town of Yungay 12 kilometers away. Fifteen minutes later, 18,000 villagers were dead.[8]

The slope and altitude of mountains create variations in climate—including temperature, radiation, wind, and moisture availability—over very short distances. Mountains include both the wettest place on earth—Cherrapunji, India, which receives almost 12 meters of rain annually—and one of the driest—Chile's Atacama Desert, which has had no measurable precipitation in 27 years. With high daily, seasonal, and annual fluctuations, weather is a key controlling factor in the complex distribution and variety of soils and the biological and human adaptations to these environments. Even the shade of a single rock can provide an unique microhabitat for an alpine wildflower found nowhere else. Similarly, mountain farmers can have quite different seeds and sowing, cultivation, and harvesting practices for fields that differ only by 50 meters in altitude or by their orientation to the sun.[9]

Mountains function as the earth's

water towers by attracting much of its precipitation. By intercepting the global circulation of air, they force air upwards, where it condenses into clouds that provide rain and snow. Thus most of the world's rivers form in mountains, giving the upper portions of watersheds immense importance for environmental and geopolitical security. About 1 billion Chinese, Indians, and Bangladeshis, for instance, depend directly on waters that form in the Himalaya. Most of California's 31 million residents depend on rivers originating in the Sierra Nevada. At least half of humanity relies on water captured in mountains for drinking, domestic use, irrigation, hydropower, industry, and transport.[10]

One distinguishing mountain characteristic is fragility or vulnerability to disturbance, again largely a function of the vertical dimension. Unlike more productive lowland environments, mountain ecosystems are typically less able to recuperate from substantial perturbations such as widespread soil erosion or loss of vegetation. Not only are the soils usually thin and poorly anchored, but gravity-powered erosion accelerates silt and sediment movement. Because a doubling in water speed produces an eight- to sixteenfold increase in the size of the materials that water can transport, the erosive power of rapid runoff in mountains is immense.[11]

Life in the mountains is as complex and diverse as the underlying rock formations found there. The diversity of wild plants constitutes a global gene bank that is vital to future food security. In addition to natural diversity, including plants for food and medicine, mountain communities are also the custodians to vital crop species, helping ensure genetic variety as well as disease and pest resistance. On the top of a 2,880-meter mountain in the Mexican Sierra de Manatlan, for example, are the only known stands of the most primitive wild

relative of corn (or maize). Indigenous Andean crops include amaranth, quinoa, cocoa, and more than 200 species of potatoes. At the annual fair in Dali, in China's mountainous Yunnan province, thousands of Bai, Yi, Naxi, Tibetan, Lisu, and Lahu people trade as many as 550 species of native herbal medicinal plants in addition to hundreds of food plants.[12]

Such areas also function as sanctuaries and refugia for plants and animals long since lost from transformed lowlands. Freestanding mountains, such as Mount Kenya or the Tatra Mountains (shared by Poland and the Czech Republic), are islands of biodiversity in seas of humanly transformed landscapes. The extraordinary number of ecological niches in mountains is typified by Mount Kinabalu in Malaysia's Sabah, home to about 4,500 species, more than one quarter as many plant species as exist in the entire United States. More than 1,400 varieties of flowering plants and 100 species of trees grow in the Great Smoky Mountains National Park in the United States, more than found in all of Europe.[13]

Freestanding mountains, such as Mount Kenya, are islands of biodiversity in seas of humanly transformed landscapes.

Mountains are rich in another measure of biodiversity: endemism, the occurrence of species only within narrow ranges, typically after centuries or more of isolation. Centers of endemism are areas where many such species occur together, and therefore are typically found on true islands or terrestrial islandlike habitats such as isolated mountains. A BirdLife International study published in 1992 revealed that 20 percent of the known 9,600 bird species were confined to just 0.5 percent of the earth's land surface in pockets of endemism, where large numbers of other endemic animals and plants also occur. Subsequent analysis revealed that 53 percent of these 247 endemic areas are in tropical mountains. The mountains of South America alone have 40 of these, many of which are confined to rare tropical montane cloud forests.[14]

Mountains are perhaps the supreme example of a less recognized but equally critical type of biodiversity—the variety between habitats and ecosystems. On tropical mountains with high relative relief, vegetation belts may range from moist submontane forest to dry or wet montane tropical forest, subalpine forest, alpine heaths, cloud forests, grasslands, tundra, and permanent snow and ice fields. Each of these life zones—even the ice fields—has its own assemblages of plants and animals. Disintegration of this ecological variety impairs ecosystem functions, evolutionary processes, and the viability of species that rely on a range of ecosystems for their survival (such as salmon, grizzly bears, and snow leopards).[15]

Because mountains tend to be inaccessible places and challenging environments in which to earn a living, they often have provided sanctuary to refugees, indigenous peoples, and ethnic minorities. Mountain people typically live on the economic margins as nomads, part-time hunters and foragers, traders, small farmers and herders, loggers, miners, or wage workers, or in households headed by women while men pursue seasonal work elsewhere. With men largely involved in the cash economy, mountain women are the primary custodians of natural resources and biodiversity. Given the imperative to survive, these people have acquired unique knowledge and skills by adapting to the specific constraints and advantages of their fragile, inhospitable environments. They possess millennia of experience in shifting cultivation, terraced fields, medicinal use of native plants, migratory grazing, and sustainable harvesting of food, fodder, and fuel from forests.[16]

"Cultural diversity is not an historical accident. It is the direct outcome of the local people learning to live in harmony with the mountains' extraordinary biological diversity," says Anil Agarwal, founder and director of the Centre for Science and Environment in New Delhi. Estimates of the number of remaining indigenous (or tribal or native) peoples vary from 200 million to 600 million. Although no total figures exist on the numbers living in mountains, the proportion is clearly high since mountains account for a substantial portion of the landscape that has not been transformed by modern economies. For instance, more than 10 million Quechua, descendants of the Incas, reside in the central Andes. And more than 16 million indigenous people live throughout the 19 major mountains ranges of the former Soviet Union.[17]

Whether in the Swiss Alps or the Ethiopian highlands, the Appalachians or the Andes, the relative and absolute poverty of mountain people is striking. More than 60 percent of the rural Andean population lives in extreme poverty. Most of China's 98 million people considered absolutely poor are ethnic minorities who live in mountains. Similarly, residents of the Appalachians are among the poorest in the United States. Although subnational statistics for comparing mountainous regions to the lowlands are scarce, those that have been compiled document pressing needs for development. (See Table 3–2).[18]

People in these areas are further marginalized by their frequent position astride disputed political borders or as ethnic groups resisting the control of their national government. Not surprisingly, war and insurrection are common

Table 3-2. Per Capita Income and Literacy Rates, Selected Himalayan Regions and Countries

Country	Region	Average Annual Income Per Capita		Adult Literacy Rate	
		National[1]	Regional	National[1]	Regional
		(dollars)		(percent)	
Bangladesh	Chattagram Hills	210	228[2]	35	16[2]
Bhutan	entire country	190	n.a.	38	n.a.
China	Tibet Autonomous Region	370	106[2]	73	33[2]
India	Himalchal Pradesh	360	166[3]	48	43[3]
Nepal	Dhadhing district	180	150[1]	26	25[1]
Pakistan	Baluchistan (rural)	400	72[2]	35	10[3]

[1]1990. [2]Late eighties. [3]Early eighties.
SOURCE: Adapted from Jayanta Bandyopadhyay, "The Himalaya: Prospects for and Constraints on Sustainable Development," in Peter B. Stone, *State of the World's Mountains: A Global Report* (London: Zed Books Ltd., 1992); national data from United Nations Development Programme, *Human Development Report 1993* (New York: Oxford University Press, 1993); Tibet data from State Statistical Bureau, *China Statistical Yearbook* (Beijing: 1991 and earlier years).

in the mountains. In 1993, 34 major armed conflicts involving state forces were ongoing in 28 countries; 22 took place in mountains, and another 8 included such areas. Since World War II, the Caucasus, northern Iraq, the Hindu Kush, Kashmir, Tibet, the Peruvian and Colombian Andes, the Vietnamese and Laotian mountains, and the Ethiopian highlands have been damaged by major military activities.[19]

Finally, sacred places abound in the mountains. Regardless of their form, location, or size, mountains have a unifying quality that evokes deep religious meaning or has inspirational appeal. Examples of sacred mountains include Sinai and Zion in the Middle East, Olympus in Greece, Kailas in Tibet, T'ai Shan in China, Fuji in Japan, and the San Francisco Peaks in Arizona. Although increasing secularism, urbanization, and industrialization have distanced westerners from any sense of sacred attachment to the land, mountains are places of vital spiritual value for hundreds of millions of people.[20]

IMPACTS OF THE MOUNTAIN ECONOMY

In most mountain countries, economic development policies have led to the expropriation of customary land rights and their redistribution to vested commercial interests for agriculture, ranching, logging, hydropower, or mining.

Converging on most subsistence mountain farmers are two driving forces: increasing land scarcity as populations grow both naturally and from immigration, and insecure land tenure and the inequitable distribution of and access to local natural resources. Increases in agricultural productivity often have not kept pace with population growth rates.

As pressures mount to adopt commercial farming practices, traditional methods of resource management developed over centuries are lost. This dynamic often leads to increased soil erosion and degradation on open-access mountain forests, rangelands, and marginal croplands.[21]

In the East African highlands of Burundi, Kenya, Rwanda, Tanzania, and Uganda, the population has mushroomed 700 percent in the last 80 years. Although simmering ethnic rivalries certainly sparked the horrific Rwandan massacre in 1994, a powerful contributing cause was land scarcity: Rwandans had on average less than 0.03 hectare of arable land per person, equivalent to a square plot about 17 meters on each side, almost completely on steep slopes. The Indian Planning Commission found that population densities in relation to arable land in the mountainous districts of Himalchal Pradesh and Uttar Pradesh are quadruple those of adjacent plains, while productivity is much lower. Subholdings are divided into nonviable fragments, with a single family working up to 25 tiny pieces of land; as much as 60 percent of the family income comes from remittances from men working in the plains. In Nepal, almost all the 55 hill districts are now classified as food-deficit areas.[22]

Especially in the Himalaya, mountain farmers often have been blamed for causing downstream floods through their upstream deforestation. Long-term scientific research, however, has revealed a much more complicated reality: while cultivation of steep slopes can accelerate soil loss, many other factors often contribute more to sediment loads in flooding rivers, especially natural erosion in large watersheds following heavy rains.[23]

By coincidence of the right soil and climate conditions and the poverty of peasant farmers, virtually all the world's cocaine and heroin production is concentrated in three small mountain regions. Mountain farmers in southeast Asia's Golden Quadrangle (northern Thailand, Myanmar, Laos, and southwestern China) and southwest Asia's Golden Crescent (northern Pakistan and Afghanistan) provide nearly all the poppies used in opium and heroin production. Similarly, virtually all coca leaves for cocaine and crack production are grown in the White Triangle of the Andean regions of Bolivia, Colombia, and Peru. Although prices paid to farmers for these crops may prove irresistible, drug production and trade create environmental and cultural devastation—deforested hillsides, declining soil fertility, soil erosion, and water pollution, not to mention drug addiction, AIDS, and violence among competing drug lords. Between 1979 and 1987, Peruvian cocaine producers cleared some 180,000 hectares, about one tenth of the deforestation during that period.[24]

Farmers are far from the only ones having an impact on mountain regions. With the incursion of roads, bridges, and tunnels, mountains have been transformed into steep storehouses of meat, timber, hydroelectricity, and minerals for export to the plains. Large-scale interventions, extractive industries, and commercial operations often cause exceptional ecological and cultural damage in mountains because they ignore the dynamic soils, fragile ecology, and cultural diversity.[25]

Ecological burdens from intensive livestock operations include loss of native vegetation, decline of fisheries as water is diverted for irrigation and stream habitats are degraded, diseases in native herbivores, and major changes in fire frequency, soils, hydrology, and other ecosystem processes. Seventy percent of the western United States is grazed. In California, livestock now use nearly one third of all irrigation water.

Because livestock congregate in riparian ecosystems, which are among the biologically richest habitats in arid and semiarid lands, the ecological costs of grazing are magnified. Half of U.S. rangeland, most of it in the mountainous West, is now considered severely degraded, with its livestock carrying capacity reduced by at least 50 percent.[26]

In Peru, the government has made huge investments in the Amazon since the fifties to establish a cattle herd of 228,000 that today produces about 9,000 tons of meat annually, 5.7 percent of the nation's total consumption. During this process, more than 8.5 million hectares of forest have been replaced by marginally productive agriculture and grasslands, most of which has now been abandoned. By comparison, poor Indians and mestizos produce 31,000 tons of fish and 13,000 tons of wild game from the same region with little, if any, government investment.[27]

Forest destruction is moving up mountain slopes in most tropical countries. In a recent assessment of tropical forests, the U.N. Food and Agriculture Organization found that hill and mountain forests were more susceptible to ecological damage from excessive population densities than all three types of lowland forest. During the last decade, tropical mountain forests have had the fastest rates of both annual population growth and deforestation.[28]

Several practices of commercial forestry can be especially destabilizing to slopes and damaging to mountain ecosystems: road building, clear-cutting, slash and burn, dragging, skidding, hauling, the introduction of exotic plants, and the spraying of herbicides and pesticides. These practices erode hillsides, reduce the structural and species diversity of the forest, and impair ecosystem processes. In 1992, the Swiss government passed a new law to subsidize the management of forests that are critical to protecting roads, railways, and settlements from natural hazards such as avalanches, floods, and rockslides.[29]

Mountains attract most of the world's hydroelectric power projects, and many irrigation reservoirs as well.

Because their slopes permit gravity to increase the power of flowing waters, mountains attract most of the world's hydroelectric power projects, and many irrigation reservoirs as well. In the Swiss Alps, almost every possible site for a hydroelectric power facility has been developed. Many mountain river systems have been converted into stepped sequences of linked reservoirs, including the Tennessee, Colorado, and Columbia Rivers. In the continental United States, Norway, New Zealand, and Mexico, most of the commercial hydropower potential has already been developed.[30]

Most developing countries with major hydropower potential, on the other hand, are seeking out big projects to meet drastic shortfalls in electricity supplies, despite frequent local or international opposition. As "a showpiece of industrial progress," Malaysia is spending $5.8 billion to build the 2,400-megawatt Bakun dam in Sarawak. This project will require construction of a 210-meter-high dam, the relocation of more than 8,000 tribal people, inundation of 69,500 hectares (an area larger than Singapore), and the clearing of 80,000 hectares of mostly intact moist forest for 670 kilometers of power lines.[31]

In eastern Nepal, the World Bank leads a group of donors providing loans for the Arun III project, a $760-million dam in the Arun River valley south of the Nepal-Tibet border. Although the dam is a run-of-the-river 403-megawatt scheme that will flood only 43 hectares, the 122-kilometer access road will open up to land-hungry settlers the Arun Valley's 4 million hectares of pristine wilderness and homelands of 450,000 tribal peoples. The dam's construction will bring in at least 20,000 workers and their families to a region of chronic food deficits. Its projected cost exceeds the annual national budget of Nepal, one of the world's poorest countries. Project promoters claim Nepal will need up to 50 percent of the project's output when it comes on-line in the next decade; the surplus power is slated for export to India.[32]

Project critics question the assumptions used by World Bank staff regarding the project, including the rate of return from power sales, the equitable distribution of the project's benefits, and the adequacy of measures taken to ease cultural and environmental impacts. Even though several smaller hydro schemes operated by Nepalese already function efficiently, Bank staff have consistently ignored them as cost-effective alternatives. In spite of a high-profile campaign against the project led by the Kathmandu-based Alliance for Energy and Arun Concerned Group, the Bank's Board of Directors seemed likely to grant final approval to the project.[33]

Of all the economic activities in the world's mountains, nothing rivals the destructive power of mining. Environmental impacts include habitat destruction, increased erosion, air pollution, acid drainage, and metal contamination of water bodies. Each year, for instance, Peru's Ilo copper mining and smelter operation emits 600,000 tons of sulfur compounds and dumps nearly 40 million cubic meters of tailings containing copper, lead, zinc, aluminum, and traces of cyanides into the sea, harming marine life in a 20,000-hectare area. In the Khaniara area of India's Himachal Pradesh, nearly 1,000 small- to medium-sized slate mines have stripped up to 60 percent of the forest cover and triggered countless landslides.[34]

Now that the Andean countries have rewritten their mining codes to encourage foreign investment, dozens of multinational companies from Australia, Canada, South Africa, and the United States are rushing to extract the rich deposits of copper, silver, and gold there. And in Colorado, Galactic Resources of Canada declared bankruptcy in 1992 and abandoned its gold mine in Summitville while the mine leached cyanide, sulfuric acid, and toxic heavy metals into 28 kilometers of the Alamosa River. Summitville is a Superfund hazardous waste site that will cost $100 million to clean up.[35]

The Ok Tedi open-pit copper and gold mine in the Star mountains of western Papua New Guinea is the country's second largest mine, and a vital source of income. In 1991, the mine shipped 600,000 tons of copper concentrates to Japanese smelters. This remote area is also home to the Wopkaimin, for whom the mountain is sacred. By the time the mine closes, the 2,330-meter mountain will have been virtually levelled. After the failure in 1989 of a partially built tailings dam, the mining company received government permission to dump heavy-metal-laced tailings directly into the Fly River, the country's second largest. As the dumping continues, 30,000 villagers recently filed a $3-billion class action suit against the company for pollution of the river and damages to its fish stocks and the adjacent fields.[36]

EMERGING THREATS

In 1898, a founder of the U.S. conservation movement, John Muir, wrote, "Thousands of tired, nerve-shaken, overcivilized people are beginning to find that going to the mountains is going home; that wilderness is a necessity; and that mountain parks and preservations are useful not only as fountains of timber and irrigating rivers, but as fountains of life." Today, so many lowlanders are taking Muir's advice that the problems they had hoped to leave behind are following them up the slopes.[37]

In glossy magazines and slick television commercials, enticing images of pristine mountain wilderness lure legions from the plains for respite and sport. In industrial countries, mass tourism and recreation are now fast overtaking the extractive economy as the largest threat to mountain communities and environments. A recent Wilderness Society study of the Yellowstone region in the United States found that during the last 20 years, 96 percent of the new jobs and 89 percent of the growth in labor income occurred in sectors outside agriculture, logging, and mining. The study also found that oil and gas, mining, timber, and grazing in the ecosystem's seven national forests accounted for just 5 percent of the area's total employment, while recreation generated the majority of direct jobs in all but one of these forests.[38]

Since 1945, visits to the 10 most popular mountainous national parks in the United States have increased twelvefold. (See Figure 3–1.) Tourists overwhelm mountain areas in the tropics as well. Each year, for example, more than 100,000 people visit Machu Picchu, the fifteenth-century stronghold of the Incas, leaving behind garbage, vandalized stonework, and polluted streams. In the Gangotri region of the Indian Himalaya, more than 250,000 Hindu pilgrims annually visit the sacred source of the Ganges River.[39]

Mass tourism in the Alps is now a $52-billion business that results in 100 million visitor-days to the region a year and creates 250,000 jobs. Each weekend on

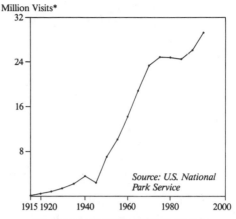

Million Visits*

Source: U.S. National Park Service

* Denali, Glacier, Grand Teton, Great Smoky Mountains, Hawaii Volcanoes, Mount Ranier, Olympic, Rocky Mountain, Yellowstone, and Yosemite

Figure 3-1. Recreation Visits to 10 Mountainous U.S. National Parks, 1915–93

the Swiss St. Gotthard pass, automotive traffic deposits 30 tons of nitrogen, 25 tons of hydrocarbons, and 75 kilograms of lead, often creating layers of black soot on the snow. At the urging of those living near the pass, Swiss citizens voted in 1994 that all heavy trucks passing through the country must move on railroad flatbeds by 2004.[40]

Infrastructure for leisure and recreation in the mountains can approach the absurd. In 1990, there were 100 Alpine golf courses; in 1992, 250; and by the end of 1996, 500 are expected. The lure of golf in the mountains is not restricted to rich countries: tropical montane forests in Malaysia's Gentian Highlands are now being cleared for golf courses, and China is building a golf course and luxury hotel near the remote Yulongxue Shan in northwestern Yunnan.[41]

Thundering helicopters bring well-heeled skiers to untracked slopes in not only the Rockies and Alps, but also the Indian Himalaya, Chilean Andes, Japanese Alps, Polish Tatra, and New Zealand's Southern Alps. To expand or just maintain their business, many ski resorts now consume massive amounts of water to make snow at the very time of the year when mountain water is least available. The populations of many small ski towns—like Vail, Colorado, and Park City, Utah—have more than doubled since 1980, causing new home construction and retail sales to increase at double or even triple the national average. In the wake of this migration have come new versions of suburban sprawl: 16 hectares per residential lot and "trophy" homes with more than 500 square meters in floor space.[42]

In both the Appalachians and the Alps, proximity to industrial-urban corridors has proved damaging, or even deadly, to mountain forests. Since 1950, European vehicle-miles have increased fifteenfold; carbon monoxide emissions, fivefold; hydrocarbon emissions, sevenfold; and nitrous oxide emissions, nineteenfold. One of the most extreme examples is along the Czech-Polish border, where most of the forests of the Jizera and Giant Mountains have been damaged or destroyed by acid rain from the industrial smokestacks and automotive tailpipes in southeast Germany, southern Poland, and the northern Czech Republic. Damage is greatest in the highest spruce forests, where the airborne acids concentrate in the clouds and on the needles of trees. Those at upper tree line are particularly affected because the airborne toxics concentrate just below the inversions that often form at this altitude.[43]

Potential climate change particularly threatens mountain ecosystems. Because mountains typically have steep temperature gradients over short distances, plants and animals there are among the most vulnerable to climate change. A warming of 3 degrees Celsius by 2050—certainly possible, given scientists' projections of 1.5–4.5 degrees of warming—would be roughly equivalent to an altitudinal shift upwards of about 500 meters. Species already confined to the tops of mountains or below impassable barriers like rock outcroppings or highways could be exterminated as they are ecologically squeezed out of their potential habitat.[44]

Surveying 26 summits, Austrian researchers recently found that as mean annual temperatures had increased 0.7 degrees Celsius in this century, nine plant species had migrated upward at an average rate of one meter per decade. Given an average decrease of 0.5 degrees Celsius for every 100 meters increase in altitude, the observed warming theoretically should have led to a shift in altitudinal vegetation belts at a rate of 8–10 meters per decade. For the first time, the Austrian study documents that the rate of plant migration is slower than would be required to adapt to recent and anticipated warming.[45]

On the vast Tibetan Plateau, an increase of even 2 degrees Celsius in annual mean temperature would cause most of the current ecosystems to disappear and, in the central and northern sections, be replaced with desert, according to one recent computer simulation. Since changes in climate would coincide with habitat degradation and other human stresses on biodiversity, the cumulative impacts on mountain biodiversity could be severe.[46]

INTEGRATING CONSERVATION AND DEVELOPMENT

More than 100 years ago in New Zealand, Maori people—fearing exploitation of sacred peaks by European sheep farmers and other colonists—found a unique solution: the Tongariro Mountains were given to Queen Victoria, and New Zealand's first national park was born. Globally, approximately 8 percent of the world's mountains are now in some form of protected area, accounting for 42 percent of the world total area of this category of land. Although these reserves span every continent, altitude, and biogeographic realm, they are far from evenly distributed. (See Table 3–3.) Underrepresented areas include the Atlas Mountains, Antarctica, the Alps, Papua New Guinea, the Hindu Kush, and the mountains of Myanmar and Laos.[47]

With years of slashed budgets, national parks are straining just to provide the services demanded by visitors; preservation of untrammelled wilderness has become increasingly secondary. Many park designs are "doughnut holes," often including only the higher zones above treeline and excluding the biologically richer lower flanks. In the case of endemic species, failure to protect the single site or the small number of localities where a species occurs can lead to extinction. Additionally, many mountain species are especially vulnerable to harm from alien (non-native) organisms, since many mountains are essentially island habitats with no evolutionary adaptations to invading species. Especially damaging alien species are feral pigs in Hawaii and Costa Rica, goats in Venezuela, and foreign grasses in Puerto Rico.[48]

With so many pressures on mountain reserves, preserving biodiversity will require much more than parks. To address effectively the problems that mountain peoples face in sustaining their livelihoods and ecosystems, innovative approaches need to build on the principle that the richness and fragility of mountain ecosystems combined with the diversity of their cultures create distinct constraints as well as offer comparative advantages. Several nongovernmental organizations (NGOs) are pioneering new community-based approaches that integrate conservation and development. (See Table 3–4.)[49]

Instead of imposing a rigid conservation plan derived from a foreign culture, these projects have taken a practical approach to conservation by combining it with the pursuit of equity, empower-

Table 3-3. Inventory of the World's Mountain Protected Areas, 1992

Geographic Region	Biogeographic Realm[1]	Number	Total Area
			(hectares)
Antarctica and New Zealand	Antarctic	11	2,086,861
Australia	Australia	3	2,649,148
Europe, North Asia, North Africa, and Middle East	Palearctic	147	30,270,611
Latin America and the Carribbean	Neotropical	90	30,969,739
North America[2]	Nearctic	96	153,804,175
Pacific	Oceania	8	3,598,032
South and Southeast Asia	Indomalayan	52	8,794,398
Sub-Saharan Africa[3]	Afrotropical	35	10,986,512
World Total		442	243,159,476

[1]Classification of world's biomes from M.D.F. Udvardy, *A Classification of the Biogeographical Provinces of the World,* IUCN Occasional Paper 18 (Gland, Switzerland: 1975).   [2]Includes Greenland National Park, which has an area of 97 million hectares.   [3]Includes Atlas mountains.
SOURCE: Adapted from James W. Thorsell and Jeremy Harrison, "National Parks and Nature Reserves in Mountain Environments of the World," *GeoJournal,* May 1992.

Table 3-4. Integrated Conservation and Development Projects in Mountain Communities, Selected Examples

Project/Program, Organization	Location	Activities and Accomplishments
Makalu-Barun Conservation Project, Woodlands: The Mountain Institute and Nepal's National Parks and Wildlife Conservation Department	Makalu-Barun region, eastern Nepal	In region of intact forests and high biodiversity, created 830-square-kilometer conservation area around Makalu-Barun National Park for the 32,000 residents of seven distinct hill tribes; created 13 skills training programs and 10 cultural conservation projects; preserved some of Nepal's last riverine tropical forest; established 33 community forest user groups that manage 2,000 hectares of forests, two nurseries that can produce 60,000 seedlings each year, and kerosene depots at the trailhead to Makalu basecamp; project model now being replicated with technical and cultural modifications in Bolivia and Peru.
Hindelang, Alp Action	Algäu, Bavarian Alps, Austria	To reverse trend of abandoned farms and deteriorating fields, 88 farmers formed organic farming cooperative; produce cheese, milk, vegetables, and meat sold at a premium in exchange for $60,000 a year from corporate sponsor; intact communities and landscapes have enhanced ecotourism.
Hill Area Development Foundation	Chiang Rai province, northern Thailand	In heavily deforested watersheds, works with 28 villages of four tribal groups to build terraces, plant and rotate indigenous crop species along contours, form community forests, teach literacy, and help secure land tenure.
Fundación Pro-Sierra Nevada de Santa Marta	Sierra Nevada, northern Colombia	In steep, biodiverse watershed threatened by logging, cocoa production, colonists, and concentration of landownership in a few hands, foundation is forging regional consensus to conserve the mountain; established community conservation centers that teach holistic farming, aquaculture, and forest use.
Ladakh Project, Centre for Ecological Development	Ladakh, India	For a traditional culture undergoing rapid development, project promotes appropriate development strategies, including passive solar construction, solar ovens and water heaters, wind turbines, low-cost ram water pumps; sponsors performances and exhibits of traditional culture.

Table 3-4. (*Continued*)

Project/Program, Organization	Location	Activities and Accomplishments
Mattole Restoration Council	Mattole River Valley, northern California	To reverse effects of soil erosion (produced by logging and overgrazing) on salmon and trout spawning, coalition of 100 community groups has planted thousands of trees to control erosion and released 250,000 salmon and 50,000 steelhead fingerlings since 1980 to help restore fisheries.
Bauda-Bahunipati Family Welfare Project, World Neighbors	Sindhupalchowk District, eastern Nepal	Project nursery producing 15,000 fodder, fuel, and timber seedlings a year; family planning adopted by 22 percent of fertile couples, and fertility rate reduced from 5.8 to 3.2 children per couple; built 55 new drinking water systems and 525 pit latrines; project now replicated in 38 villages of 153,000 people and run by local groups.
Integrated Family and Communal Gardening Project, AIDESEP[1]	Peruvian Amazon	In response to abandoned farms, low-productivity cattle pastures, dwindling territories, and assailed cultures, project provides training in organic crop production to 120 communities of 36 indigenous organizations; soil restoration has had 90 percent success rate, reducing toxicity from pesticides by 70 percent; supported 39 model gardens; now studying alternative land use model for granting communal land titles.

[1]Interethnic Association for the Development of the Peruvian Amazon.
SOURCE: Compiled by Worldwatch Institute from sources cited in endnote 49.

ment, indigenous rights, and local control of natural resources. Shanti Basnet of the Bauda-Bahunipati Family Welfare Project in Nepal says, "We cannot preach development outside the context of village needs. But once people have a stake in their own future, anything is possible." The overarching premise of these projects is the inextricable link between local cultures and local ecosystems: one cannot be saved without the other. Although they are still the exception, they are blazing a trail for mountain peoples and organizations everywhere.[50]

One exemplary project is found in the Annapurna region in central Nepal. Stretching from subtropical lowlands and lush temperate rhododendron forests in the south to dry alpine steppe in the north, this region features a wide variety of plants and animals, including 100 species of orchids and 60 percent of Nepal's medicinal plants. The natural richness is rivalled by the cultural diversity: 116,000 people belonging to 14 distinct ethnic groups inhabit the 762,900-hectare area. The scenic grandeur belies an inherent vulnerability, however. More than 50,000 trekkers ascend the trails every year, each with on average one porter. The local population is growing by 2.8 percent a year, meaning it would double in just 25 years at current growth rates. More than 90 percent of the residents are subsistence farmers who depend on the depleted forests for food, fuel, fodder, and timber. Overgrazing by livestock and cultivation of crops on marginal lands add to hillside instabilities and soil erosion, estimated at 20–50 tons per hectare a year.[51]

In response to the impending ecological and economic crisis, the King Mahendra Trust for Nature Conservation (KMTNC) founded the Annapurna Conservation Area Project. It relies on local participation in the design and implementation of development programs and natural resource management. The project began with the villagers' priorities: a clean water supply and health care. Only when these were established could resource management issues be approached with participatory methods to enable villagers to maintain control over their local resources—such as forests and pastures—through such activities as community forest management committees, tree nurseries, fodder and fuel plantations, and self-help training courses for farmers and tourist-lodge owners. To help depleted rhododendron forests recuperate, project staff and villagers have marked the entire conservation area off in various land use zones, including areas for strict conservation, low impact use, and intensive use. At the initiative of villagers, subsequent programs have included family planning and literacy training for women and children. KMTNC now uses similar approaches in other Nepalese conservation areas.[52]

Similarly, for the last decade the Peruvian Foundation for the Conservation of Nature (FPCN) in partnership with the World Wildlife Fund has worked closely with several villages around the 1.5-million-hectare Manú National Park in the southeastern Peruvian Andes, another of the biologically richest areas in the world. The park's span of elevations (250 to 4,600 meters) includes a broad array of plant communities, ranging from humid tropical rain forest to *paramo* grassland, and more than 850 bird species—about 9 percent of the world total. Threatening the park from several sides are colonization, logging, cattle grazing, gold prospecting, poaching, oil extraction, and road development.[53]

The fundamental ingredient to FPCN's success has been the extensive public planning consultation with local communities. Project staff spent years living in the area, listening closely to people's pressing needs. Only then were a diverse mix of projects launched in a multiple-use zone surrounding the protected area of the park: growth and preservation of medicinal plants for people and animals (since villagers cannot afford modern medicine or veterinary help); assistance with creating markets for crops; small-scale agricultural projects to improve the integration of crops, livestock, and fish farming; and technical education for locally hired park staff. The project's approaches have been adapted for use in several other areas of Peru.[54]

In the arid mountain canyon country of western New Mexico, the Zuni Tribe has launched a comprehensive Sustainable Resource Development Plan, one of the first community-level strategies built on the structure of the Earth Summit's plan for action, Agenda 21. One important outcome of this has been the Zuni Conservation Project, now staffed by up to 80 people working with the 10,000 residents of the tribe's 192,000 hectares of lands. With some of the elders' intricate wisdom about dryland and irrigated agriculture at risk of disappearing, the project staff recognized that it was vital for ancient practices to be preserved. The project works closely with young members of the tribe, teaching traditional methods. Farmers have established a seed bank to preserve customary varieties of maize, chile, squash, and other traditional crops, for both subsistence and commercial use.[55]

Directed by the project's hydrologist and two technicians, in 1994 a seasonal crew of 40 workers used tribal techniques to arrest soil erosion on two drainage systems covering almost 2,500 hectares by building 300 rock and brush structures, reseeding with native grasses, closing some roads, and rebuilding older structures. The watershed restoration will help decrease siltation in the check dams for irrigation and in water supplies for livestock and wildlife. In connection with this restoration, other project staff work individually with ranchers to create grazing management plans that reduce grazing in highly erodible or overgrazed areas, especially near streams. To quantify their results, field staff used stream flow stations to measure in-stream siltation precisely. Project leader James Enote now shares his experience in sustainable community development with other indigenous organizations around the world.[56]

Integrated programs at the community level are the linchpin to success in empowering local people to meet their needs while conserving mountain ecosystems.

Integrated conservation and development projects provide no guarantee of success, however. They are complex and time-consuming to implement due to the intrinsic problems of reconciling the fundamentally distinct goals of conservation and development. In a recent study by Stanford's Center for Conservation Biology, only 5 of 36 projects reviewed had positively contributed to the conservation of wildlife. The authors concluded that comprehensive ecological oversight of projects is usually lacking. They recommend two types of monitoring: first, to assess the total effects of the projects on biodiversity and overall ecosystem health by tracking indicator species across space and through time; and second, to observe human impacts by comparing target species diversity and abundance in unregulated areas, managed buffer zones, and core protected areas through time.[57]

Since mountains are so physically, biologically, and culturally diverse, integrated programs at the community level are the linchpin to success in empowering local people to meet their needs and aspirations while conserving healthy mountain ecosystems. Although the paths to this success will be just as distinct as the local customs, ecosystems, and people involved, the recent pioneering approaches have proved that such goals are not beyond reach.

MOVING MOUNTAINS UP THE AGENDA

Agendas for action in mountains need to originate from the people who live there. A major step in this direction will take place in February 1995 at the first global conference of mountain NGOs in Lima, Peru. Since the mountain chapter of Agenda 21 was negotiated without benefit of full debate and negotiation among governments or NGOs, the U.N. Commission on Sustainable Development (CSD) asked those involved in these issues to deliberate and approve an action plan for implementing the chapter's recommendations. The Mountain Agenda Consultation should help coalesce an NGO mountain constituency.[58]

On a parallel track, the CSD also has coordinated a series of intergovernmental meetings for reviewing national progress made in implementing the mountain chapter; these should help spur governments to focus on funding integrated conservation and development mountain programs. A global conference on sustainable mountain development is planned for early 1997. If innovative partnerships among mountain communities, NGOs, research institutions, and development assistance and government agencies are forged, institutional momentum is sure to build.[59]

Helping mountain peoples solve their own problems will require policies and institutions designed specifically for mountains: the complexity and fragility of the ecosystems and the poverty and diversity of those who live there urgently demand new approaches. To elevate the status of mountain peoples and conserve their ecosystems, national governments and international development agencies need to focus on policy reform in five areas: helping people secure land tenure and control over local resources; reducing the impact of producing mountain beef, timber, hydropower, and minerals in mountains; creating regional networks of conservation areas; performing integrated scientific research and environmental monitoring; and creating institutions and cooperative agreements for each major range.

Today's prices ignore the full costs of denuded forests, eroded hillsides, and dammed or polluted rivers.

Perhaps the single best hope for deflecting growing pressures on relatively intact mountain ecosystems and for improving the welfare of poor inhabitants lies in reforming the inequitable patterns of private landownership and public resource control that currently keep the best lands and resources in the hands of a small group of powerful elites. Major components of this reform include comprehensive social and ecological assessments of all major development projects (a frequently violated requirement of multilateral development banks), along with genuine consultation with local people before projects that would affect them are funded.[60]

Most important for indigenous peoples is mapping, demarcation, and recognition of ancestral homelands, and the creation of organizations to fight for land and resource rights through the courts. Evaristo Nugkuag of Peru's Aguaruna tribe is a prominent example of how to pursue land rights through indigenous organizations. Realizing that all Indians in the Peruvian Amazon basin faced the same threats from cattle ranching, mining, and logging, he helped organize the Interethnic Association for the Development of the Peruvian Amazon (known as AIDESEP), a coalition of tribal groups that work collectively to protect land rights. In 1984, Nugkuag went on to help found the Coordinating Body of the Federations of Amazonian Indians (COICA), representing more than 1.2 million people and 219 different tribes, many of whom live on the eastern slopes of the Andes. COICA has forged a strategic alliance with northern conservationists in their efforts to preserve the Amazonian rain forest.[61]

An equitable and sustainable balance between the conservation and use of mountain resources must be found. Three fundamental reforms in natural resource policies could dramatically lessen the impacts of mountain mining, ranching, logging, and hydropower. First and simplest is more efficient use of every log and ore extracted and of every kilowatt and pound of animal product produced. If the United States, the world's largest consumer of wood, adopted currently available methods of waste reduction, recycling, and manufacturing efficiency, overall wood consumption could be cut in half at least. For reasons of immediate cost savings, resource efficiency is already revolutionizing many industries. (See Chapter 5.)[62]

The second needed reform is eliminating the massive subsidies governments grant these environmentally destructive operations. Reflecting only the present economics of extraction and distribution, today's prices do not tell the ecological truth; they ignore the full costs of denuded forests, eroded hillsides, and dammed or polluted rivers— not to mention the incalculable social costs of uprooting people living atop the resource. Large dams can be built without massive social and environmental impacts. Most of the Andes, Himalaya, and mountainous Turkey, Ethiopia, and southwest China abound with unpopulated sites with little or no vegetation, enormous opportunity for hydropower, and potentially small reservoirs. Whether future projects will focus on sites with potentially minimal impacts remains to be seen.[63]

Third, to encourage progress toward full-cost pricing, shifting a portion of taxes from income to consumption of virgin materials and resources will ensure that environmental costs are considered even in private consumption decisions. Together, these reforms can lessen a source of social inequity and free up funds that could be used to improve the welfare of mountain people.[64]

Counteracting mountain peoples' marginalization does not necessarily mean integrating them fully into industrial market economies. For years, some community activists in the mountains have been advocating life-styles of simplicity instead of extravagance. Sunder Lal Bahuguna, a Gandhian leader of the Save the Himalaya movement in India, calls for using local natural resources only to achieve regional self-sufficiency; banning all future commercial logging,

mining, and building of dams; and donating 12 percent of all electricity generated by large hydropower projects to local villages.[65]

To safeguard the variety of mountain ecosystems, it is critical to create regional networks of conservation areas. Andean conservationists are developing plans for "corridors" of protected areas along the entire length of the range. In the continental United States, the two best prospects for regional conservation are, not surprisingly, both mountain ranges: the northern Rockies and the southern Appalachians. Given the recent demise of the Montana wilderness bill, however, near-term prospects for congressional designation of large areas of U.S. wilderness appear dim.[66]

In the Mount Everest region, an innovative set of partnerships has been created for regional conservation. A group called Woodlands: The Mountain Institute, based in West Virginia in the United States, has worked with the Nepalese and Chinese governments to create two multiple-use conservation areas that adjoin three existing Nepalese national parks. Together, the parks and preserves now span more than 4.1 million hectares, an area as large as Switzerland. Home to about 100,000 people, this regional protected area provides a full elevational range of habitats and migratory corridors for wildlife, vital to wide-ranging predators like the endangered snow leopard.[67]

A fundamental impediment to raising mountains on the agenda of policymakers is lack of knowledge and information, combined with pervasive scientific uncertainty about the planet's most complex landscapes. Data on mountain areas are often nonexistent or incomplete. Thus comprehensive research and long-term monitoring programs are critical to establish baseline scientific information on mountain ecosystems and the rapid natural and human-caused changes occurring there. Three successful examples are the Swiss Man and the Biosphere project, the International Potato Center's Sustainable Andean Development project in the high Andes, and the African Mountain Association's Mount Kenya Ecological Programme. A steady stream of scientific indicators on the social welfare and ecological health of mountain peoples and environments will give policymakers a much sounder basis for making decisions.[68]

Forging mechanisms for cooperation and coordination on transboundary mountain problems is essential. The Andes, for instance, are divided among seven countries. Movements of water, soil, weather, and life—especially in the mountains—defy human-imposed boundaries. Thus institutions and cooperative agreements for each major mountain range should be encouraged. The Alpine Convention negotiated in 1992 by the environment ministers of Austria, France, Germany, Italy, Liechtenstein, Slovenia, and Switzerland was ratified by most of these countries in late 1994. It provides an encouraging model for international cooperation on transboundary problems, and includes legally binding protocols on tourism, traffic, regional planning, protection of nature, and mountain farming and forestry. Although such commitments are decades off in other major international ranges, the Alpine Convention will continue to provide a vital precedent for range-wide agreements.[69]

Eleven years ago, the eight countries that share the Hindu Kush-Himalaya ranges founded the International Centre for Integrated Mountain Development (ICIMOD) to promote sustainable development. By training numerous local institutions and organizations in technical aspects of development, ICIMOD has played an important role in building human capacity in the region and raising awareness among policymakers about mountain problems. Since many of the member countries have had political tensions or even war along their borders, ICIMOD has been one of the few organizations to promote scientific cooperation within the area. Creating similar institutions for the Andes and African mountains would provide critical support for integrated research and development work in those regions.[70]

Genuine progress for mountain peoples will require development agencies to recognize mountain conservation and development as distinct funding priorities. Analysis of 1,588 World Bank projects worth $151 billion over the last six fiscal years indicates that a mere 13, with $493 million in foreign-exchange costs, dealt directly with improving the lives of mountain peoples or protecting mountain environments. Lending records of the other multilateral development banks appear comparable.[71]

Most development investment decisions are still made by economists and engineers, for whom environmental protection and cultural conservation are at best peripheral considerations. Until ecologists and anthropologists attain equal footing, sustaining mountain peoples and environments will remain secondary to maximizing internal rates of return and erecting costly infrastructure. To meet their primary mandates of alleviating poverty and promoting environmentally sustainable development, the development banks will have to shift their lending priorities to strengthening the institutional capacity of the thousands of effective, grassroots groups already working throughout the world's mountains. The same imperative also applies to the U.N. Environment Programme (UNEP), the U.N. Development Programme (UNDP), and the Consultative Group on International Agricultural Research. Not every institution, however, is blind to the distinct needs of mountain peoples. The Rome-based International Fund for Agricultural Development has focused on poverty alleviation in mountainous areas in 40 percent of its Asian projects and 70 percent of its Latin American ones.[72]

One logical source of funding for some integrated mountain initiatives is the Global Environment Facility (GEF), the fund jointly administered by UNEP, UNDP, and the World Bank that provides grants and concessional loans to developing countries for addressing global environmental problems. Three of GEF's primary funding priorities—biodiversity, climate change, and international water issues—are highly relevant to mountain environments. Integrated watershed management projects are one example of how funding mountain projects could simultaneously satisfy more than one GEF objective. Watersheds provide the link between upstream causes and downstream effects. Reforesting the degraded slopes above a hydropower reservoir would help conserve biodiversity, improve the quality of headwaters, and reduce the carbon emissions that might otherwise have resulted from deforestation.[73]

Another vital avenue for channeling funding will continue to be the swelling ranks of NGOs. Each year, about 4,000 northern NGOs disperse about $3 billion in development assistance, usually working with 10–20,000 southern NGOs who help up to 100 million of the world's poorest people. Shifting a tenth of these funds directly toward the tenth of humanity who live in mountains would leverage substantial new financial resources. Additional funds could be raised if donor governments were to accept UNDP's 20:20 Compact on Human Development, targeting 20 percent of aid funds to human development priorities in developing countries. (See Chapter 10.)[74]

One way to help increase mountain people's access to productive assets would be to create national microenterprise banks in each of the Andean, Himalayan, and African mountain countries. These could be modeled upon the highly successful Grameen Bank in Bangladesh, which focuses on improving financial opportunities for women and boasts a 98-percent loan repayment rate; small loan programs to women's cooperatives in Bolivia, Ecuador, and Uttar Pradesh, India, also have been successful. Since mountain women in developing countries seldom own property or have access to credit, the banks would make loans to small groups of village women willing to guarantee each other's repayments, in lieu of traditional collateral. In regular meetings with village-based bank staff, women could also learn basic literacy skills, infant and maternal health care, and family planning. Only if gender biases are removed will mountain women escape the trap of poverty and become full partners in conservation and development efforts.[75]

Mountain people urgently need equitable and sustainable human development. Today, the impacts of the ecological, economic, and social challenges they face extend far beyond the 2 billion people who live downstream. Their environments are integrally connected to the lowlands through the movements of water, animals, people, and products. To restore and maintain the quality of life of mountain residents and the ecological health of mountain ecosystems, global efforts toward sustainable development must be integrated with efforts to sustain mountain peoples and places. If successful, these actions will enrich all humanity and help preserve for future generations many of the most intact cultures and ecosystems left on earth.

4

Harnessing the Sun and the Wind

Christopher Flavin

When representatives of the world's seven most powerful economies met at their annual Economic Summit in July 1994, one of the most contentious issues was how to help Ukraine shut down the notorious nuclear power plants at Chernobyl. The Ukrainian government asked for compensation, including help in replacing the power generated by the reactors. Responding to pressure from their nuclear lobbies, the governments of France and Germany urged the West to assist Ukraine by financing the completion of several other nuclear plants.[1]

In response, the U.S. government put several proposals on the table, including projects to help Ukraine improve the efficiency of its industry and buildings. Although the assembled diplomats had little reaction to most of these ideas, the American officials had an additional suggestion that provoked laughter from several European colleagues: a U.S. com-

pany was ready to install thousands of wind generators on Ukraine's Crimea Peninsula, which according to data the officials presented would be cheaper than finishing some of the nuclear reactors.

This scene says at least two things about the current status of wind and solar energy technologies. First, they are becoming economically competitive in many parts of the world—often far less expensive than nuclear power plants or other so-called conventional technologies. Indeed, three countries at the summit—Germany, the United Kingdom, and the United States—already have sizable wind power installations, and all the others have projects in operation or on the drawing board. The second point is that these new energy sources are still generally underestimated by most policymakers, not to mention by many in the energy industry itself.

Although they have been pursued by scientists, entrepreneurs, and visionaries for two decades, solar and wind energy have never claimed the large share

This chapter is adapted from *Power Surge: Guide to the Coming Energy Revolution*, coauthored with Nicholas Lenssen (New York: W.W. Norton & Company, 1994).

of the mainstream energy market that proponents hoped they would. Many people, not surprisingly, gave up on the heady promises made in the seventies, and decided that these "new" energy sources were unlikely to find a place in the modern energy world.

Yet 1994 brought a series of developments that suggest the time has come for solar and wind energy to compete directly with fossil fuels. Major wind power projects were announced in India, China, Germany, and Argentina, to name but a few countries—setting off a boom in wind turbine construction. At the same time, tens of thousands of homes, found everywhere from Sri Lanka to Switzerland, were equipped with solar cells for electricity generation. A number of major corporations, including Enron, Westinghouse, and Siemens, recognized the growing size of the renewable energy markets when they announced new investments in solar and wind energy technologies.[2]

These energy sources are also taking on a glossy, twenty-first century image, as U.S. Secretary of Energy Hazel O'Leary discovered when she led an energy trade mission to India in July 1994. In contrast to the department's traditional missions focusing on coal and nuclear power, this one concentrated mainly on solar and wind energy technologies, reflecting the priorities of the Clinton administration. The renewable energy executives who accompanied Secretary O'Leary met with an enthusiastic reception from their Indian hosts, particularly in the private sector, where wind and solar markets are booming. By the end of the trip, several projects had been agreed to, and at least one U.S. company had set up an office in New Delhi.[3]

With world leaders struggling to cope with problems such as urban air pollution, acid rain, and global climate change, pressure is growing to begin the transition to the world's two most abundant energy sources: the equivalent of nearly 1,000 trillion barrels of oil that strike the earth's atmosphere in the form of sunlight each year, and the winds that flow from it.[4]

GOING WITH THE WIND

Among the golden rolling hills of California and along the pancake-flat plains of northern Europe, a fresh new energy source sprouts dramatically from the landscape. In large and small clusters, thousands of sleek, white turbines, 20–30 meters in diameter, stand up like large airplane propellers. Denmark had roughly 3,600 wind turbines in operation by 1994, supplying 3 percent of the country's electricity; California had an even greater concentration—15,000 wind turbines, generating as much power as the residents of San Francisco use each year. Altogether, the world had roughly 20,000 wind turbines in operation by the end of 1993, producing 3,000 megawatts of electricity. (See Figure 4–1.)[5]

In the early eighties, wind machines typically cost $3,000 per kilowatt and

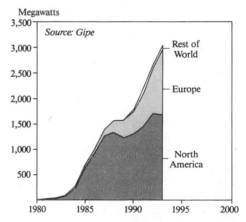

Figure 4-1. World Wind Energy Generating Capacity, 1980–93

produced electricity for more than 20¢ a kilowatt-hour (1993 dollars). By the late eighties, the machines were larger and more efficient and their capital cost, including installation, had fallen to about $1,000–1,200 per kilowatt. At an average wind speed of 6 meters per second (13 miles per hour) and a maintenance cost of a penny per kilowatt-hour, this yields a generating cost of 7–9¢ per kilowatt-hour for U.S. wind turbines installed in the early nineties, compared with 4–6¢ for new plants fueled by natural gas or coal.[6]

More than a dozen American and European companies, many with government assistance, are pursuing advanced wind technologies that are believed capable of closing the remaining cost gap with fossil fuel plants. According to one study, the average capacity factor of Californian wind turbines—the percentage of their annual power potential generated—rose from 13 in 1987 to 24 in 1990. These machines are now estimated to be "available" to operate 95 percent of the time, which is better than most fossil fuel plants.[7]

In India, a major wind boom was under way in 1994.

The machines now entering the market generate 300–750 kilowatts per turbine rather than the 100-kilowatt average of the late eighties' models. They have lighter and more aerodynamic blades made of synthetic materials, improved rotor-hub connections and drive trains, new blade controls, and more advanced power electronics, including some that operate at variable speeds, which allows the turbines to run more efficiently in a range of winds. The new designs are less expensive and can be deployed in more moderate wind

regimes. In 1994, wind developers using the new technology signed contracts to sell wind-generated electricity for as low as 4–5¢ per kilowatt-hour.[8]

As wind power has gained acceptance as a reliable, economical source of power, a number of U.S. utilities have begun to incorporate it into their plans. California, for example, is poised to move forward with some 1,500 megawatts' worth of projects that were bid successfully in a power auction finalized in 1994. Sizable wind power projects are also being built or planned in Iowa, Maine, Minnesota, Montana, New York, Oregon, Texas, Vermont, Washington, Wisconsin, and Wyoming.[9]

An even bigger wind rush is under way in Europe. Prompted by environmental concerns, several governments stepped up their efforts to promote carbon- and sulfur-free renewable energy sources in the late eighties, including increased R&D support and additional subsidies. In northern Germany, a relatively high power-purchase price allows private wind power developers to receive 13¢ per kilowatt-hour for their electricity. Germany added 98 megawatts of wind capacity in the first half of 1994, with the installed capacity expected to have reached 500 megawatts by the end of the year. In the Netherlands, an integrated wind power development program is a prominent part of the National Environmental Policy Plan. And in the United Kingdom, power companies are required to reserve a portion of new power contracts for "non-fossil" sources, a provision intended for nuclear power but now benefiting wind energy.[10]

Denmark continues to add to its wind power installations, but its total capacity could soon be surpassed by Germany and the United Kingdom, each of which hopes to develop at least 1,000 megawatts of wind-generating capacity by 2005. Greece, Spain, and the Netherlands have ambitious plans as well. Altogether, members of the European Union aim to install 4,000 megawatts of wind power capacity by 2000 and 8,000 megawatts by 2005. By mid-1994, some 1,400 megawatts were already in place in Europe, and the figure could reach 2,000 megawatts by the end of 1995.[11]

In India, a major wind boom was under way in 1994, as the government opened up the power grid to independent developers, and offered tax incentives for renewable energy development. By mid-year, 120 megawatts of wind turbine were in place—half installed in the previous 12 months—and another 970 megawatts were awaiting approval. Most of the projects involve joint ventures with European and U.S. wind turbine manufacturers who are now rushing to sign up local partners and break ground on assembly plants. One result: land values in some parts of Tamil Nadu jumped to between 8 and 20 times previous levels.[12]

Other wind projects are under way in China, Ireland, New Zealand, Switzerland, and even Quebec, Canada, where despite a long-standing commitment to large hydro projects on James Bay, provincial officials suggested in 1994 that the region's energy future lies in wind power. One of the most intriguing recent developments is in Ukraine, where despite the skepticism of diplomats and the breakdown of the local economy, in 1994 the state electric utility Krimenergo and Kenetech Corporation of San Francisco together embarked on a 500-megawatt wind power project on the Crimea Peninsula. Argentina, which has some of the strongest winds, is also developing a 500-megawatt wind power scheme. Both Argentina and Ukraine are building most of the wind turbines domestically in jointly owned local factories.[13]

Although wind power still provides less than 0.1 percent of the world's electricity, it is fast becoming a proven power option, considered reliable enough for routine use by electric utilities. In many regions of the world, wind is now fully competitive with new coal-fired power plants, and experts predict that as wind turbines enter mass production, costs should fall to less than $800 per kilowatt (below 4¢ per kilowatt-hour, including operating costs) by the end of the decade, and perhaps one day to $600 per kilowatt or 3¢ per kilowatt-hour, making wind one of the least expensive electricity sources.[14]

It is also one of the most abundant. Even excluding environmentally sensitive areas, the global wind energy potential is roughly five times current global electricity use. Since the power available from wind rises with the cube of the wind speed, most of the development will occur in particularly windy areas. In the United States, where detailed surveys have been conducted, it appears that wind turbines installed on 0.6 percent of the land area of the 48 contiguous states—mainly in the Great Plains—could meet 20 percent of current U.S. power needs. Indeed, even resource estimates that exclude large environmentally sensitive areas show that three states—North and South Dakota and Texas—could in theory supply all the country's electricity.[15]

Among the countries that have enough wind energy to supply most or all their electricity from this source are Argentina, Canada, Chile, China, Russia, and the United Kingdom. Egypt, India, Mexico, South Africa, and Tunisia should easily be able to push their reliance on wind power to 20 percent or more. Europe as a whole could obtain between 7 and 26 percent of its power from the wind, depending on how much land is excluded for environmental and aesthetic concerns. In addition, many regions with limited wind power potential may find that the constraints end at the water's edge: New England, the United

Kingdom, and Poland are among the areas that could obtain most of their power from wind farms located on off-shore platforms in shallow seas. At least 20 small subtropical island countries have nearly constant trade winds that could meet a large share of their electricity needs, replacing the expensive diesel generators they now rely on.[16]

Relying on wind power as a major energy source will inevitably generate some land use conflicts. On the plus side, while it is true that wind farms would "occupy" large areas (1 percent of the land of the United States to supply one third of the country's electricity), most of it would be land where few people or wildlife reside. Moreover, wind machines occupy land mainly in a visual sense. The area surrounding the turbines can be used as before—usually for grazing animals or raising crops—and provide farmers with supplementary income. In Wyoming, for instance, a hectare of rangeland that sells for $100 could yield more than $25,000 worth of electricity annually. In many windy regions, harnessing the wind might enhance land values by acting as a windbreak and reducing soil erosion.[17]

Still, the accelerating pace of wind power development in the nineties has led to a few environmental controversies. From Rattlesnake Ridge in the state of Washington to the green hills of Wales, local groups have protested wind power as a visual blight on the landscape. Some developers have sought to dismiss or bully the opposition—a practice they have later come to regret. Many opponents have raised valid concerns, and unless these are addressed carefully, wind power is unlikely to become a major energy source. On the other hand, experience suggests that in many regions the aesthetic appeal of wind farms has grown over time.[18]

Another problem gained prominence in 1994: the potential of wind turbines to kill birds. This issue was first identified in northern California's Altamont Pass, where a number of golden eagles have been killed; dead birds have also been found on the Spanish wind farm near the Strait of Gibraltar. According to ornithologists, some bird species are attracted to the windy areas that are good for producing power, though the issue needs much more research in order to understand the nature and scale of the problem. Officials at the National Audubon Society and the U.S. Fish and Wildlife Service have expressed alarm about bird kills, but are working closely with the industry to study it and propose solutions. Experts hope that means can be found to scare birds away from the wind farms, and believe that as wind power development moves from mountain passes to the open plains, there will be less conflict with birds.[19]

One constraint to reliance on wind power is the distances that separate some of the world's large wind resources from major population and industrial centers. This problem is seen clearly in the United States, where nearly 90 percent of the country's wind resource is in the Great Plains, more than 1,000 kilometers from Chicago and 2,000 kilometers from New York or Los Angeles. In some cases, new transmission lines will be needed to carry wind energy to where it is needed, or existing lines will have to be beefed up, perhaps using new electronic controls or superconducting ceramic wires, each of which is under development.[20]

Building the new lines is feasible, but will take time and money. Moreover, developers face a chicken-and-egg problem: until large power projects are started, there is no incentive to build a long transmission line, but no one wants to invest in a wind farm unless they are sure they can get the power to market. In addition, new lines face siting problems that are far more severe than those faced by wind farms, as a result of growing controversy over the potential health effects of electromagnetic radiation from high-voltage lines. Among the possible solutions: direct current lines that do not produce such radiation, or placing lines underground.[21]

The economics of remote wind power also appear favorable. A 2,000-kilometer, 2,000-megawatt transmission line would cost roughly $1.5 billion, which would add only about a penny per kilowatt-hour to the cost of wind energy. This would still allow wind to be fully competitive even with the cheapest coal-fired power. To ensure that the new power lines operate at close to capacity, wind farms may need to be packaged with gas turbine or hydropower projects that can be operated when the wind is not blowing.[22]

SOLAR POWER HEATS UP

Ever since the Arab oil embargo of 1973, government and private researchers have struggled with a variety of means for turning the most abundant energy source of all—sunlight—into electricity. Much funding has been devoted to this effort, including the construction of several giant central receivers. None of these efforts has proved itself commercially, but a more practical approach is now taking hold, relying on technologies originally invented more than a century ago.

In the 1870s and 1880s, at the height of the Industrial Revolution, French and U.S. scientists developed an array of solar cookers, steam engines, and electricity generators, all based on a simple concept: a parabolic-shaped solar collector that is coated with a mirrored surface to reflect light coming from different angles onto a single point or line. These include parabolic "dishes," which resemble satellite television receivers, and trough-shaped parabolic collectors that concentrate sunlight onto a tube rather than a single point. By the turn of the century, clever inventors had built a wide array of solar engines that did everything from running a printing press in Paris to pumping irrigation water in Arizona. Within a few years, however, the era of cheap oil had begun, and the efforts were abandoned.[23]

Seven decades later, in the aftermath of the 1973 oil embargo, parabolic solar dishes and troughs made a comeback as scores of scientists and engineers developed new designs. Though their efforts were not as well funded as the larger "power towers," the results have been more promising. Late-twentieth-century inventions such as inexpensive reflective materials, improved heat transfer fluids, more-efficient solar receivers, and electronic tracking devices have greatly improved the effectiveness of a nineteenth-century technology, allowing engineers to reduce the cost of these systems.

The most successful effort to commercialize solar trough technology was launched in Israel in 1979. Arnold Goldman designed a system of mirrored troughs 9 feet high and 40 feet long to concentrate the sun's rays onto oil-filled tubes that run parallel to the mirrors along their focus. The troughs were mounted on a device that allowed them to follow the arc of the sun, keeping it focused on the collection tube. Goldman's original concept was to mount these collectors on the flat roofs of industrial buildings, providing heat for textile production, food processing, and other industries.[24]

Although this approach failed to catch on, Goldman was attracted to another market in the early eighties: the generous power purchase contracts and solar tax credits being offered in California. Soon his firm, Luz International, had lined up several large contracts to deliver electricity to the Southern California Edison Company, and was at work on a series of solar generators. In Luz's design, the solar trough heats a working fluid that circulates to a power station where water is superheated into steam, which then powers an electricity-producing turbine. By burning natural gas as a backup fuel, Luz is able to keep its turbines running even when the sun is not shining.

The Luz plants now convert 23 percent of sunlight into electricity during peak sunny periods and 14.5 percent on an annual basis. The power plant built at Harper Lake, California, in the Mojave Desert in 1989 is a good example. Spread over 750 hectares, hundreds of rows of gleaming solar collectors produce enough power for about 170,000 homes for as little as 9¢ per kilowatt-hour, which is competitive with generating costs in some regions, and far below the 29¢ from Luz's first plant in 1984. Without using natural gas for backup, the latest Luz plant can generate electricity for 13¢ per kilowatt-hour, with the potential to cut that figure to less than 10¢ by scaling up production. Between 1984 and 1990, Luz installed nine plants with a capacity of 354 megawatts of generating capacity, making it one of the top 10 Israeli exporters.[25]

The Luz plants now convert 23 percent of sunlight into electricity during peak sunny periods.

Luz's fortunes took a bad turn in 1989, when falling natural gas prices drove the company's power purchase price down at the same time the vagaries of a tax-incentive-driven market caught up with it. By 1990, Luz had declared bankruptcy. Still, even after its demise, the company's nine plants continued to churn out power in the Southern California desert. Belgian investors purchased the rights to the technology from Luz's creditors, calling the reorganized company (which is still based in Israel) Solel. In 1994, Solel was working to raise the efficiency and improve the storage of its systems, while rumors were rampant of negotiations under way to build one or more 200-megawatt solar power plants, possibly in Brazil, India, Israel, or Morocco.[26]

Other research teams also were developing solar troughs in the early nineties, including an innovative design by David Mills of the University of Sydney. Tests reveal that improved collector surfaces, polar axis tracking, and a better trough design can increase sunlight collection by nearly one fourth. By also adding vacuum insulation to the heat-carrying pipes, Mills estimates that the annual efficiency of the system may reach 20 percent, with peak efficiency between 25 and 30 percent. The new design has the ability to run for eight hours without sunlight by storing heat in an inexpensive bed of rocks, and to provide power for around 6¢ a kilowatt-hour.[27]

The parabolic dish collector is also mounting a strong comeback. Each dish follows the sun individually, with double-axis tracking that allows sunlight to be focused onto a single point where heat can be either converted directly to electricity or transferred by pipe to a central turbine. Parabolic dishes are generally more thermally efficient than troughs. Moreover, since dishes (like troughs) are built in moderately sized, standardized units, they allow generating capacity to be added incrementally as needed. And they can attain temperatures three to four times that of trough systems, thus producing higher quality steam and more electricity.[28]

The U.S. Department of Energy expects parabolic dishes to produce power for 5.4¢ a kilowatt-hour early in the next century, and some experts believe that such systems will outperform troughs economically. One system has been designed at the Australian National University, and an initial 2-megawatt plant was being built in 1994 in Australia's remote Northern Territory. The project is being funded by a consortium of electric utilities under pressure to reduce their heavy reliance on coal. Twenty-five dishes will feed steam to a turbine to produce power for the isolated community of Tennant Creek.[29]

Meanwhile, advances in Stirling engines (also known as heat engines) are opening up another use of dish-shaped solar collectors. Mounted at the focal point above the dish, the Stirling engine directly converts heat to electricity, reaching conversion efficiencies as high as 29 percent. These systems can heat homes and factories, but may be particularly practical as a way of providing small amounts of power in remote areas.[30]

Another approach to collecting the sun's heat is to rely on abundant and cheap salt water. The difference in temperature between warm surface water and deeper water layers can be used to drive a heat engine to generate electricity. When cold water passes warm water in a heat exchanger, the warm water vaporizes and drives a low-pressure steam turbine to produce power.

Two variants of this technology have been developed: solar ponds and ocean thermal energy conversion (OTEC). The first, which involves an artificial lake of salty water, was developed by Israeli scientists in the seventies to generate 5 megawatts of electricity on the shores of the Dead Sea. Smaller systems were also built in Australia and California. The low conversion efficiencies of these systems are countered by their modest cost per square meter. Still, solar ponds have yet to attract serious commercial interest,

and may not have the long-run economic potential of other solar thermal technologies.[31]

The ocean thermal variation of the solar pond concept may have greater promise. Solar energy that strikes the oceans can be captured in a similar manner in regions where surface and deeper waters differ in temperature by at least 20 degrees Celsius. OTEC uses the difference between sun-warmed surface waters in tropical areas and deep, cold water to power a heat engine, and could supply electricity around the clock. A pipe as long as 1,000 meters is used to pump huge volumes of water to the surface, where it is run through a heat exchanger. One variant on the design couples a deep-water collection system with an on-shore solar pond, raising the temperature differential and lowering the amount of water that must be moved.

Although large OTEC systems face many hurdles, and some analysts have questioned their economics, the value of these systems is enhanced by the fact that they can produce two other valuable commodities: fresh water, and fish that can be raised in enclosed pens supported by the deep-water nutrients brought to the surface by an ocean thermal system. A prototype system in Hawaii is used to desalinate water, cool buildings, and supply nutrient-rich water for vegetables and aquaculture, all while generating 210 kilowatts of power. In tropical, coastal areas of the developing world, ocean thermal energy appears to be an especially promising technology.[32]

Given the rocky development path that solar thermal energy has followed so far, it is difficult to anticipate the course of future developments. Low fossil fuel prices have cooled the interest of utilities, but the attractions of a new pollution-free power source, coupled with the niche markets opening up in many countries, may be sufficient to spur a takeoff. A 1994 World Bank study concluded that solar thermal power plants would be economical in many developing countries; in response, the Bank launched a solar initiative aimed at financing such projects.[33]

One possibility that is being explored in the U.S. Southwest is to convert existing coal-fired power plants into solar thermal power stations that use natural gas for backup—already close to being economical for plants that face legal requirements to cut the amount of sulfur and nitrogen oxides they emit, according to one set of calculations. Another possibility is to link a field of solar troughs or dishes to a gas turbine power station, allowing the solar collectors to substitute for the boiler in a combined-cycle plant, which would increase the overall efficiency.[34]

The sheer abundance of solar energy suggests that it will be the foundation of a sustainable world energy system a century from now. Indeed, if we could harness just one quarter of the solar energy that falls on the world's paved areas, we could meet all current world energy needs comfortably. Moreover, according to several studies, solar thermal technologies should be able to provide power at 5–7¢ per kilowatt-hour by 2000, which could be broadly competitive with electricity derived from fossil fuels.[35]

PHOTONS INTO ELECTRONS

During the past few years, the basic energy needs of some of the world's poorest people have been met by what is arguably the most elegant and sophisticated energy technology yet developed. People around the world are now getting electricity from solar photovoltaic (PV) cells, which can be used in everything from handheld calculators to suburban rooftops and large desert power stations. Solar cells turn sunlight directly into electricity—without aid of mechanical generators—and many experts expect the devices to be ubiquitous in the early part of the next century. But the greatest short-term impact of solar photovoltaics will be in the rural Third World, providing power to many of the more than 2 billion people who do not yet have it.[36]

Solar photovoltaic cells are semiconductor devices made of silicon—similar to but far less expensive than the chips used in computers—that convert the energy from sunlight into moving electrons, avoiding the mechanical turbines and generators that provide virtually all the world's electricity today. French scientist Edmund Becquerel discovered in 1839 that light falling on certain materials could cause a spark of electricity, but it was not until Bell Labs in the United States built the first silicon solar cell in 1954 that practical applications for the effect were identified. By the late sixties, solar cells were widely used on U.S. space satellites.[37]

Starting in the late seventies, industrial-country governments and companies invested billions of dollars in advancing the state of photovoltaic technology. By the eighties, solar cells were deployed at telephone relay stations, microwave transmitters, remote lighthouses, and roadside callboxes—applications where conventional power sources are either too expensive or not reliable enough. The technology continued to advance during the next decade, and by 1993 the wholesale price of photovoltaics had dropped to between $3.50 and $4.75 a watt, which translates to 25–40¢ a kilowatt-hour, thanks to both higher efficiencies and more automated manufacturing processes. As costs fell, sales rose—from 6.5 megawatts in 1980 to 29 megawatts in 1987 and then to 60 megawatts in 1993. (See Figure 4-2.) The worldwide industry, including activities such as retail sales and installation, did about $1 billion worth of business in 1993.[38]

Although still too expensive to compete head-to-head with conventional generating technologies, photovoltaic cells have found ever-larger niches in the global energy market. The technology's versatility was best demonstrated in the mid-eighties, when Japanese electronics companies came up with an ingenious new application, attaching tiny solar cells to handheld pocket calculators and wristwatches. These require only a trickle of electricity, well within the capability of a small solar cell—even when operating in a dimly lit room. Since the late eighties, the Japanese have sold an average of about 100 million such devices each year, an application that absorbs 4 megawatts of solar cells annually, 7 percent of the global market.[39]

By the early nineties, thousands of villagers in the developing world were using photovoltaic cells to power lights, televisions, and water pumps, needs that are otherwise met with kerosene lamps, lead-acid batteries, or diesel engines. More than 200,000 homes in Mexico, Indonesia, South Africa, Sri Lanka, and other developing countries have obtained electricity from rooftop-mounted solar systems over the past decade. Most of these efforts have been pioneered by nongovernmental organizations and private businesses, with only limited support by government and aid agencies.[40]

Perhaps the best example of the new approach to solar electrification is in the Dominican Republic, where more than 2,000 homes have been "solarized" in the past nine years, largely through the efforts of Enersol Associates, a U.S. nonprofit group, and the Asociación para el Desarrollo de Energía Solar. Starting with $2,000 in seed money, they provided loans to several families for the purchase of rooftop solar systems, and as the money was repaid, additional families were able to finance similar systems.[41]

Since 1990, similar organizations have been established in China, Honduras, Indonesia, Sri Lanka, Zimbabwe, and elsewhere. In Sri Lanka, $10 million is enough to electrify 60,000 homes, estimates Neville Williams, founder of the Solar Electric Light Fund, a U.S.-based nonprofit that facilitates PV electrification in Asia and Africa. Still, at early-nineties prices (roughly $500 for a 50-watt system that includes not just a PV panel but also light bulbs, wiring, a battery for storage, and a charge regulator that monitors the battery), only a few people can afford PVs. Further price cuts will increase the number, as will smaller systems. A recently developed solar lantern, for example, uses a 2.6-watt panel to charge a battery that can light one or two fluorescent lamps—providing light that even poor families can afford.[42]

Still, solar electrification projects start with a large disadvantage, since most developing-country governments heavily subsidize the extension of grid electricity to rural areas, as well as the installation of diesel water pumps. Simply levelling the playing field—reducing the subsidies

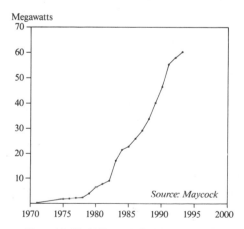

Megawatts

Source: Maycock

Figure 4-2. World Photovoltaic Shipments, 1970-93

to conventional power or providing equivalent funding for solar energy—could lead to a boom in solar electrification. Slowly, a growing number of Third World governments and international aid agencies have begun to respond to this need, mainly by setting up new ways of funding solar power projects. One of the biggest success stories is in Kenya, where during the past few years 20,000 homes have been electrified using solar cells, compared with only 17,000 homes that were hooked up to the central power grid during the same period.[43]

Some of the recent impetus has come from the Global Environment Facility (GEF), a fund set up in 1990 under the joint management of the World Bank, the United Nations Development Programme, and the United Nations Environment Programme to finance projects that are not quite economical today but that could benefit the global environment by keeping carbon dioxide and other pollutants out of the atmosphere. In Zimbabwe, a $7-million GEF grant approved in 1992 will finance a revolving fund to electrify 20,000 households in five years; another $55-million World Bank loan and GEF grant will support a program to install 100,000 solar lanterns and other projects in India.[44]

Among the leaders in PV home installations are Spain, Switzerland, and the United States.

The World Bank is also making or considering solar loans to China, Indonesia, the Philippines, and Sri Lanka. Some of the new grants and loans are to strengthen nascent PV industries in developing countries, which can create economic opportunities and jobs in rural areas. The Zimbabwe grant, for example, supports six small PV installation companies and a larger enterprise that imports cells and assembles them into commercial panels.[45]

The use of solar electric systems in rural homes is growing in industrial countries as well, spurred by the popularity of vacation cabins and the cost of reaching them with power lines, which in the United States runs between $13,500 and $33,000 per kilometer for even small local distribution lines. In contrast, a 500-watt PV system—enough to power an efficient home's lights, radio, television, and computer—would cost less than $15,000, including batteries for storage. Norway already has 50,000 PV-powered country homes, and an additional 8,000 are being "solarized" each year. Among the other leaders in PV home installations are Spain, Switzerland, and the United States. All four nations have extensive forests or mountains, and a middle class with the money and leisure time to enjoy them.[46]

Electric utilities are beginning to serve the remote home market as well, in effect redefining their structure to include potential users who are not actually connected to the utility's web of power lines. In the rugged mountains and remote basins of the northwestern United States, the Idaho Power Company is purchasing, installing, and maintaining PVs for homeowners located off the grid. Instead of a bill based on electricity use, customers pay a set monthly fee based on the cost of installing and maintaining the system. Several of Brazil's state-owned utilities have similar programs.[47]

Although the remote power market will expand, and will have an enormous impact on people, it is dwarfed by the $800-billion annual global market for grid-connected power. Even if 4 million homes (1 percent of those now lacking electricity) installed a PV system each year, a total of only 200 megawatts—less than four times world production in 1993—would be produced. Meanwhile, the world's electric utilities install 70,-000 megawatts of generating capacity each year. If the PV industry were able to garner even 1 percent of this market, annual production of solar cells would rise tenfold. Capturing 10 percent of this market would allow a hundredfold increase in production.[48]

Over the past decade, several dozen grid-connected solar buildings have been built. The Sacramento Municipal Utility District plans to purchase an average of more than 1 megawatt of distributed photovoltaic systems each year until the end of the decade. It launched its effort with a 1993 procurement of 640 kilowatts, installed on 100 residential rooftops and at an electrical substation. By the end of 1994, it had brought rooftop power to another 100 homes, and reduced their installed cost to $7 per watt.[49]

Prospects for using solar photovoltaics in ever-wider applications hinge on how rapidly the technology evolves. Prices will need to be cut by a factor of three to five before large-scale grid-connected applications become economical. Most PV experts believe that such reductions can be achieved by continuing the advances in cell efficiency and manufacturing processes of the past two decades and by capturing the cost-savings of mass production. The only question is which of many promising PV technologies will win out.

As of the mid-nineties, single-crystal silicon still has nearly half of the global market; polycrystalline silicon—a related material—also has a large share. Several other promising solar electric devices are starting to go into commercial production. The new technology that has captured the most scientific attention is the thin-film solar cell. Some cells are reaching the 10-percent efficiency threshold, and are projected to generate power at about $1 per watt or 10–12¢ per kilowatt-hour—less than a third of the average cost of PV electricity in 1993. Automation could bring the cost of solar electricity down to 10¢ a kilowatt-hour by 2000, and even to 4¢ by 2020.[50]

If so, photovoltaics could become one of the world's largest industries, as well as one of its most ubiquitous energy sources. Developments in 1994 indicate that this day may be approaching faster than most experts expected. Dramatic price cuts now appear to be around the corner as a result of new technologies and scaled-up production. One indication of this came in July when Enron Corp, a major natural gas company, shocked the PV world by bidding to develop 100 megawatts of solar PV plants in the Nevada desert and to sell the power at 5.5¢ per kilowatt-hour—one fifth the current world price.[51]

What Happens After Sunset?

Solar and wind energy technologies are now economical for many applications. (See Table 4–1.) The remaining challenge with these intermittent generators is integrating them into the electricity grid. In the past, engineers have argued that fluctuating energy sources would create havoc in their systems, and require costly investment in backup generators or storage. But experience to date with wind generators in California and elsewhere suggests otherwise. Wind power has been easily integrated into the existing mix of generators—reaching as

**Table 4-1. Cost of Electric Power
Generation in the United States, 1985,
1993, and 2000**

Power Source	1985	1993	2000
	(1993 cents per kilowatt-hour)		
Natural Gas	10–13	4–5	3–4
Coal	8–10	5–6	4–5
Wind	10–13	5–7	4–5
Solar Thermal[1]	13–26	8–10	5–6
Nuclear	10–21	10–21	—[2]

[1]With natural gas as backup fuel. [2]No new
plants being planned for 2000.
SOURCE: Christopher Flavin and Nicholas Lenssen,
Power Surge: Guide to the Coming Energy Revolution
(New York: W.W. Norton & Company, 1994).

high as 20 percent of the total in some regions—and has actually increased the reliability of a few systems.

Still, utility engineers must deal with the fact that intermittent renewable power sources do not fit easily within the traditional hierarchy of generators. The challenge of integrating intermittent renewables into a grid is in many ways similar to one that utilities mastered long ago: meeting the rapidly fluctuating demands of customers. California's Pacific Gas and Electric Company has shown that a diverse array of intermittent power sources can meet one third of a utility's load at no additional cost, and up to one half at an additional cost of only 10 percent. The ease of integrating these sources depends in part on how well their availability matches patterns of consumer demand; experience shows that while in some regions peak winds coincide nicely with peak power demand, in others they do not.[52]

If intermittent power sources are to supply 20 percent or more of a region's electricity, adjustments may be needed, however. In regions with extensive hydropower, such as the northwestern United States, little if any additional backup is required since hydro provides a reserve supply. In addition, new gas turbines are sufficiently inexpensive that they make economic sense even if operated partly on standby, raising the possibility that in the future, independent power producers might build combination gas-turbine and wind-turbine plants, providing an attractive combination of high reliability and low installation and operating costs.[53]

As reliance on renewable energy sources grows, backup storage will be needed in some areas. The most commercially ready alternative is pumped hydro storage, in which electricity produced during low demand is used to pump water up to a reservoir from which it is released to generate power when demand is high. Another alternative that is economically feasible in many areas is compressed air storage, in which underground rock fractures are filled with high pressure air. A third option is to store heat produced during the day in hot rocks, water, or another medium, which can then be used to keep the system's turbines running long after the sun has set. Studies show that heat storage can extend the operating period of such a plant by several hours at only minor additional cost. Even more revolutionary storage technologies are on the horizon: small mechanical flywheels and superconducting magnets that can be used to store electricity economically within individual buildings.[54]

Although intermittent renewables will continue to present challenges for utility engineers, most are amenable to economical solutions. In the end, with the help of new electronic controls, renewables are likely to improve both the reliability and cost-effectiveness of many utility systems.

A REPLACEMENT FOR FOSSIL FUELS?

The potential for wind and solar energy to one day be leading sources of electricity is clear. Although electricity is an economically essential (and relatively expensive) form of energy, it accounts for only 15–20 percent of the energy actually used in most countries; the rest is used mainly in the form of oil or gas (and some coal or wood). Many of these applications involve relatively low-temperature heat, for which electricity is an expensive and inefficient energy carrier. Means are needed, then, to convert solar and wind energy into a form that can be easily stored and used by consumers. Such needs can be met in part by household conversion systems—solar water heaters, for example—but a new energy carrier is also needed.[55]

The fuel most likely to fill this niche is hydrogen, the simplest of the chemical fuels—in essence a hydrocarbon without the carbon. Hydrogen is the lightest element as well as the most abundant. When combined with oxygen to produce heat or electricity, the main emission product is water. (Another product of combustion is nitrogen oxides, though it can be controlled using a variety of techniques.) The logic of a transition to hydrogen has been argued by scientists and writers for more than a century. In the 1870s, Jules Verne wrote that hydrogen would be a good substitute for coal. Although hydrogen has a reputation as a particularly dangerous fuel, this is largely a myth. It can be explosive in the right conditions, but this is true of gasoline and natural gas as well. If properly handled, hydrogen could be safer than the major fuels in use today.[56]

Electricity can be used to split water molecules into hydrogen and oxygen through electrolysis, a century-old technology already used commercially. Although it is relatively expensive today, costs would come down as the technology is scaled up. As far as water is concerned, the requirements are relatively modest. In fact, all current U.S. energy needs could be met with just 1 percent of today's U.S. water supply. Even in most arid regions, water requirements will not be a major constraint. The water needed by a photovoltaic power plant producing hydrogen is equivalent to just 2.7 centimeters of rain falling annually over an area the size of the plant. And in the long run, hydrogen may be derived from seawater.[57]

The real challenge comes in finding inexpensive sources of electricity to split water. Most of the early hydrogen advocates came from the aerospace and nuclear industries, and they developed a centralized vision of a hydrogen-powered economy. Some predicted massive offshore nuclear islands that would produce enough hydrogen to serve whole countries; others suggested that orbiting satellites could beam concentrated solar energy to gargantuan hydrogen production centers on earth. None of these schemes is remotely practical or economical, and all ignore one of the key advantages of hydrogen: the equipment to produce it is almost as economical on a small scale as on a large one. Both in production and use, hydrogen lends itself to a decentralized system in which waste is minimized.[58]

The obvious candidates for hydrogen production are thus wind and solar energy, supplemented by biomass gasification. As large wind farms and solar ranches appear in windy and sunny reaches of the world, they can generate electricity that is fed into the grid when power demand is high, and produce hydrogen when it is not. Additional hydrogen could be produced in individual homes and commercial buildings using rooftop solar cells. Hydrogen can either be stored in a basement tank for later use or be piped into a local hydrogen distribution system. In either case, it would gradually fill the niches occupied by oil and natural gas today—including home and water heating, cooking, industrial heat, and transportation. Hydrogen-powered cars have already been developed by several companies, with the main future challenges being an improved storage tank and an inexpensive fuel cell engine.[59]

The key to the practical use of hydrogen is efficiency. According to research carried out at Princeton University and the German Aerospace Research Establishment, even if the marginal cost of the electricity used to produce hydrogen were only 1–2¢ per kilowatt-hour, which may be possible in well-sited facilities built to produce power as well as hydrogen, the delivered cost of the fuel would still be more than three times as much as U.S. consumers now pay for natural gas, though roughly equal to what Europeans pay for gasoline (including taxes). But hydrogen lends itself to highly efficient applications, and as a result, the actual delivered costs of energy services to customers could well be lower than they are today.[60]

One means of using hydrogen efficiently is the fuel cell, which can produce electricity directly from the fuel at an efficiency as high as 65 percent. Indeed, the fuel cell may one day be thought of as the silicon chip of the hydrogen economy. Many homes could have reversible fuel cells—capable of producing hydrogen from electricity and vice versa.[61]

Eventually, much of the world's hydrogen is likely to be carried to where it is needed through pipelines similar to those now used to carry natural gas. This is more efficient than the oil or electricity distribution systems in place today. Power lines, for example, are expensive to build, and over a distance of 1,000 kilometers lose 3–5 percent of the electricity sent. Moving energy in the form of compressed gas is substantially less expensive, though hydrogen will cost 30 percent more than natural gas to move, as it is a lighter element that is more difficult to compress. In the early stages of the transition to hydrogen, the new energy gas can be added to natural gas pipelines in concentrations up to 15 percent—a clean-burning mixture known as hythane. In the long run, engineers believe that it will not be too difficult to modify today's natural gas pipelines so that they will be able to transport hydrogen. The fuel could also be produced from natural gas, either in central facilities or right at the gas station.[62]

Over time, solar- and wind-derived hydrogen could become the foundation of a new global energy economy. All major population centers are within reach of sunny and wind-rich areas. Although renewable energy sources are more abundant in some areas than others, they are far less concentrated than oil, with two thirds of proven petroleum reserves being in the Persian Gulf.[63]

Many people assume that producing sufficient hydrogen and other fuels from renewable energy sources requires such huge swaths of land that extensive dependence on them is impractical. In fact, solar and wind energy are far less land-intensive than many of the energy sources now in use. (See Table 4–2.) Today's giant hydro dams and strip mines claim extensive land areas—often rendering them unusable for anything else for centuries.

The amount of land required for renewable energy development is surprisingly modest. To provide as much solar energy as the world currently gets from hydro and nuclear power combined, the world would need an area about half the size of Costa Rica or Bhutan, or less than a twelfth the size of Arizona. And supplying the same amount from wind energy would require an area the size of Vietnam, or less than the area of Montana.

Table 4-2. Land Requirements for Electric Generation Technologies

Technology	Land Requirement
	(square kilometer-years per exajoule)[1]
Dedicated Biomass Plantation	125,000–250,000
Large Hydro	8,300–250,000
Small Hydro	170–17,000
Wind[2]	300–17,000
Photovoltaic Central Station	1,700–3,300
Solar Thermal Trough	700–3,000
Bituminous Coal	670–3,300
Lignite Coal	6,700
Natural-Gas-Fired Turbine	200–670

[1]End-use energy figure averaged over assumed 30-year life cycles for power plants, mines, and so on.   [2]The lower range for wind includes only land occupied by turbines and service roads, while the higher number includes total area for a project.
SOURCE: Keith Lee Kozloff and Roger C. Dower, *A New Power Base: Renewable Energy Policies for the Nineties and Beyond* (Washington, D.C.: World Resources Institute, 1993); Paul Gipe, Gipe and Associates, Tehachapi, Calif., private communication and printout, March 29, 1994; David Mills, University of Sydney, Australia, private communication and printout, March 25, 1994.

The land needed for solar and wind development is in each case small enough that environmentally sensitive areas can be withheld from development without significantly diminishing the available energy.[64]

THE POLICY CHALLENGE

When the leaders of 106 nations met at the Earth Summit in Rio de Janeiro in June 1992, few doubted the historic nature of the gathering. But after all the inspiring speeches and media hoopla, it was the two global treaties signed in Rio that were the summit's signal accomplishments. One of these, the Framework Convention on Climate Change, commits the world community to an ambitious but crucial goal: bringing stability to the global atmosphere.[65]

During the two years following Rio, as the treaty reached and then surpassed the 50 ratifications needed to bring it into force—Portugal was the fiftieth—the significance of this goal began to sink in. The world has now pledged to transform fundamentally an energy system that has served us well for many decades but that puts our future at risk.[66]

Sadly, most of the leaders gathered at the Earth Summit went home to domestic energy policies that are a far cry from the lofty rhetoric of Rio. The list of countries that ratified the treaty in the first year hints at the challenge ahead— ranging from the desperately poor country of Mauritius, which still relies heavily on wood fuel, to the United States, the world's largest fossil fuel user (and one of the most reluctant treaty signers), to the tiny Maldives, an island nation whose very existence may be threatened by climate change. Heavy subsidies for coal, research budgets dominated by unpromising nuclear technologies, and uncompetitive market structures are among the many barriers to reforming the world energy system.

What few of the leaders gathered in Rio realized is that some of the solar and wind energy technologies needed to help reduce carbon emissions are ready to go. But the pace of change will be heavily influenced by the ability of societies to overcome the remaining policy barriers. Carl Weinberg, the former director of R&D at the Pacific Gas and Electric Company, and Princeton University scientist Robert Williams note: "The rules of the present energy economy were established to favor systems now in place. Not surprisingly, the rules tend to be biased against solar energy."[67]

The needed policy changes number in the hundreds, but most fall into one of five categories: reducing subsidies for fossil fuels and raising taxes on them to reflect environmental costs, redirecting R&D spending to focus on critical new energy technologies, accelerating investment in the new devices, rechanneling energy assistance to developing countries, and opening previously closed energy markets to more participants and greater competition.

In most areas, greater reliance on the market and less direct government involvement are called for.

One priority is to spur the expansion of commercial markets for new technologies. Creating larger markets will encourage companies to scale up production and reduce the costs of these manufactured devices. Economists who track such price reductions use a "learning curve" to measure the gains. As a general rule, each time cumulative production doubles, the average unit price falls 20–30 percent. For example, between 1909 and 1923, Henry Ford reduced the price of the Model T by two thirds, as annual production rose from 34,000 to 2.7 million.[68]

Solar and wind technologies are still in the early stages of what is likely to be an extended period of cost reduction. Total production of wind turbines, for instance—from all companies combined—was less than 2,000 units a year in the early nineties. Some of the most rapid cost gains are likely to come in photovoltaics, which since 1975 have dropped 33 percent in price for each doubling of cumulative production. The faster these markets grow in the future, the more economical the technologies will become.[69]

One role for governments is to catalyze market-driven, multiyear purchases, so that production can increase through reliance on either direct purchasing programs or partnerships with industry. Solar generators, for example, could be purchased in bulk for use on military bases or government buildings. Following this model, the U.S. Department of Energy has established a Solar Enterprise Zone at its nuclear test site in southern Nevada, and plans to purchase 900 megawatts of solar electricity from the lowest bidders.[70]

Similarly, a group of U.S. utilities recently arranged a bulk purchase of solar cells, albeit on a scale that may have to be expanded in order to achieve major cost reductions. And the World Bank hopes to catalyze similar advances in developing countries through a Solar Initiative it launched in 1994. By providing financing that will expand production of solar technologies, the Bank hopes to spur substantial cost reductions.[71]

Many of these measures will require recasting the role of government, which in the past has been more centrally involved in the energy sector than in almost any other part of the civilian economy. But in most areas, greater reliance on the market and less direct government involvement are called for. The concept that the government alone can invent a new energy technology and unilaterally push it to market—which was tried so unsuccessfully with nuclear power—is even less appropriate to renewable energy development. Government's main role in the future is to facilitate commercial entry of new technologies, and to remove the many impediments to change.

In sum, it is hard not to be optimistic about the prospect for renewable energy sources in the late nineties and beyond. Indeed, during 1994, a number of countries announced major new efforts to encourage the adoption of solar and wind energy, including Brazil, China, India, Japan, the Netherlands, and the United States. With efforts like these, and a renewed commitment by the private sector, the next decade is bound to be sunny.

5

Creating a Sustainable Materials Economy

John E. Young and Aaron Sachs

The town of Arcata, California, was founded on virgin materials. Almost all the original settlers, back in the mid-nineteenth century, either prospected in the gold fields of nearby mountains or worked the lumber camps in surrounding forests. Subsequent generations have worked mostly for the town's numerous sawmills and timber processing plants. Like so many other small towns in resource-rich areas, Arcata long managed to thrive in geographic isolation by selling its local bounty to the outside world.

Unlike many similar communities, though, Arcata continues to flourish today—because it has broken its cycle of dependence on virgin resources. Other logging towns in the Pacific Northwest are beginning to disintegrate as forests disappear and as large companies replace workers with machines and export

An expanded version of this chapter appeared as Worldwatch Paper 121, *The Next Efficiency Revolution: Creating a Sustainable Materials Economy*.

raw materials instead of processing them locally. But Arcata is not only processing materials—it is also reprocessing used and discarded materials, and remanufacturing goods from within the community that have reached the end of their useful life.

Local entrepreneurs have made sizable profits and created hundreds of jobs by starting businesses that mine the town's industries and its highly successful municipal recycling program for reusable materials. Cascade Forest Products, for instance, is able to make marketable composts and mulches at a very low cost by obtaining 100,000 cubic yards of discarded wood materials each year from local sawmills and wood products plants. It employs 35 people, and last year reported sales of more than $3.3 million. A new firm, Fire & Light Originals, has cultivated a direct link with the city's recycling infrastructure and is marketing decorative glass tiles made with 100 percent post-consumer glass. Arcata's 7-Up bottles will soon become shower doors in the town's bathrooms.[1]

The extractive industries that created communities like Arcata will never disappear, since new quantities of materials will always be needed to replace those that are dissipated or rendered unusable as they move through the global economy. But virgin production could be cut back to much less destructive levels. A necessary first step would be to develop secondary industries like those of Arcata throughout the global economy. Yet the list of potential reforms extends far beyond the increased use of secondary materials, because the traditional materials economy is vastly inefficient on all fronts. Poor product design, sloppy extractive and processing techniques, and the ethos of casual consumption all contribute to industrial societies' use of far more materials than necessary to meet their needs. (See Table 5–1.)

A few observers now believe that dramatic reductions in materials use are not only possible but essential for the long-term health of the planet. Friedrich Schmidt-Bleek, of Germany's Wuppertal Institute, argues that creating a sustainable materials economy would now require a 50-percent reduction in worldwide materials consumption—which translates into a 90-percent reduction in industrial countries. The task is a daunting one, necessitating significant changes not only in the ways businesses and industries operate but also in how people decide what to eat, how to work and enjoy themselves, and what to discard. Since our happiness in the end seems to depend more on clean and healthy communities than on the number of goods we can use and then discard, we may never feel that our needs are being satisfied unless we cease defining ourselves primarily as consumers.[2]

SOCIETY'S CONSUMING PASSION

The culture of consumption that has spread since mid-century from North America to Western Europe, Japan, and a wealthy few in developing countries has brought with it an unprecedented appetite for physical goods—and the materials from which they are made. People in industrial countries account for only about 20 percent of global population, yet they consume 86 percent of the world's aluminum, 81 percent of its paper, 80 percent of its iron and steel, and 76 percent of its timber.[3]

Sophisticated technologies have let extractive industries produce these vast quantities of raw materials, and have helped keep most materials prices in decline. But the growing scale of those industries has also exacted an ever-increasing cost: raw materials production has brought about unparalleled ecological destruction during the last half-century.

The traditional materials economy is vastly inefficient on all fronts.

The environmental costs of waste disposal, ranging from toxic incinerator emissions to the poisoning of groundwater by landfills, have been documented with increasing frequency. But even greater damage is caused by the initial extraction and processing of raw materials by an immense but rarely noticed complex of mines, smelters, petroleum refineries, chemical plants, logging operations, and pulp mills. Just four primary production industries—paper, plastics, chemicals, and metals—account for 71 percent of the toxic emissions

Table 5-1. Inefficiency of the Materials Economy and Opportunities for Improvement

Activity	Example	Opportunity
Extraction	Mining high-grade ore and then moving on to a new site because land is artificially cheap, while ignoring lower-grade ore on the already-disrupted site.	Higher land prices (through elimination of subsidies and addition of full costs of environmental disruption) would increase incentives to use more-efficient extraction technologies, reducing the area of land disrupted.
Manufacture	Making paper from 90- to 100-percent virgin wood fiber.	Most paperboard, paper packaging, and office paper can be made with less than 50-percent virgin input, with no loss of quality, potentially saving millions of trees each year—as long as community recycling programs are in place to provide a steady supply of secondary paper.
Product Design	Designing "discount" products—from umbrellas to televisions to houses—that compete for low retail price but do not last.	Design emphasizing durability and repairability would reduce the number of times the consumer has to replace the product and thus reduce materials consumption.
Community Development	Planning communities in which residences are far from workplaces and services.	Planning that puts people closer to what they need and that makes efficient use of already-developed land would reduce the use of cars and thus the need for materials-intensive construction projects such as roads and bridges.
Direct Consumption	Stressing immediate convenience of consumption and disposal as the ultimate good, without considering the prospects for sustainable consumption.	Making changes in our consumption patterns to promote a culture of conservation—copying on both sides of the page, reading books from the library instead of buying new copies, taking public transportation—could ultimately save both money and materials.

from all manufacturing in the United States, for example. And the search for virgin resources has increasingly collided with the few indigenous peoples who had remained relatively undisturbed by the outside world.[4]

Though few of the world's mostly city-dwelling consumer class comprehend the impacts and scale of the extractive economy that supports their life-styles, the production of virgin materials alters the global landscape at rates that rival the forces of nature. Today, mining moves more soil and rock—an estimated 28 billion tons per year—than is carried to the seas by the world's rivers. Mining operations often result in increased erosion and siltation of nearby lakes and streams, as well as acid drainage and metal contamination by ores containing sulfur compounds. Whole mountains, valleys, and rivers have been ruined by mining in Papua New Guinea, Peru, the United States, and many other countries. In the United States, 59 former mineral operations are now slated for remediation under the federal Superfund hazardous-waste cleanup program, at a cost of billions of dollars. Many of them rank among the most expensive sites to clean up.[5]

Cutting wood for materials plays a major role in global deforestation, which has accelerated dramatically in recent decades. Since 1950, nearly a fifth of the earth's forested area has been cleared. Industrial logging has more than doubled since 1950, and is now particularly important in the destruction of primary rain forests in Central Africa and Southeast Asia. Production of agricultural materials also has dramatic environmental impacts. In the former Soviet republics of Kazakhstan and Uzbekistan, for instance, decades of irrigated cotton production have contaminated large areas of farmland with toxic chemicals and salt.[6]

The chemical industry has since mid-century become a major source of materials, including plastics, which have increasingly been substituted for heavier materials, and synthetic fibers, which have become crucial to the textile industry. The impacts of chemical production—from hazardous-waste dump sites like Love Canal to industrial accidents such as the release of dioxin from a Seveso, Italy, plant in 1977—are generally more familiar than those from mining, logging, and agriculture, since chemical facilities are usually located closer to urban areas.

Raw materials industries are also among the world's biggest consumers of energy. Mining and smelting alone take an estimated 5–10 percent of world energy use each year. Just five primary materials industries—paper, steel, aluminum, plastics, and container glass—account for 31 percent of U.S. manufacturing energy use. This thirst for energy contributes significantly to such problems as global warming, acid rain, and the flooding of valleys and destruction of rivers for hydroelectric dams.[7]

Despite the environmental impacts of the materials economy, the principal subject of debate over materials policy in the last several decades has been how soon we are likely to run out of non-renewable resources. Yet the ecosystems that provide us with renewable resources could well collapse long before we reach that point.

Extractive activities caused severe local environmental problems even in Roman times, but rates of raw materials production remained relatively low until after the Industrial Revolution. Of course, large population increases have contributed to environmental degradation, simply because the number of people consuming at high levels has increased. But growth in the materials economy has far outstripped that of population.

In the United States, for example, the

Bureau of Mines estimates that total consumption of virgin raw materials was 14 times greater in 1991 than in 1900, a span during which the country's population grew just a little over threefold. (See Figure 5–1.) Most of the growth occurred during the fifties and sixties, when millions of homes were built, new roads connected them with stores and offices, and thousands of factories were created to produce consumer goods. Between 1945 and 1973, U.S. paper and industrial minerals consumption more than tripled, while that of metals more than doubled. Consumption of plastics grew by 35 times. Other industrial nations experienced similar increases in materials consumption.[8]

Since the seventies, growth in industrial nations' raw materials consumption has slowed. Some observers believe that these countries have reached a consumption plateau, for much of their materials-intensive infrastructure—roads and buildings—is already in place, and markets for cars, appliances, and other bulky goods are largely saturated. But the plateau they sit on is a lofty one, and the consumer culture is still going strong.[9]

Even with demand for raw materials appearing to level off in industrial countries, world use is still rising. Between 1970 and 1991, total world materials consumption rose 38 percent. (See Figure 5–2.) Consumption of agricultural materials grew 40 percent, forestry materials 44 percent, metals 26 percent, nonmetallic minerals 39 percent, and nonrenewable organic chemicals—the feedstocks for plastics and synthetic materials production—69 percent. The continuing increase in demand stems in part from population growth and in part from increasing per-person use of materials in newly industrialized countries.[10]

Materials use has reached such extraordinary levels in industrial countries because of an outdated global economic framework that depresses virgin materials' prices and, most important, fails to account for the environmental costs of their extraction and processing. Prices have continued to fall even as the environmental costs of the global materials economy have risen sharply. During the past decade, almost every major commodity has gotten significantly cheaper throughout the world—a trend that in turn allowed consumption rates to continue their steady growth.[11]

There is a distinctly nineteenth-century character to the national policies

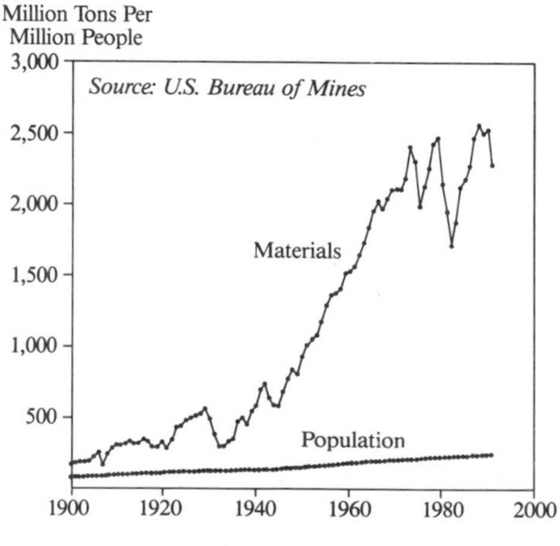

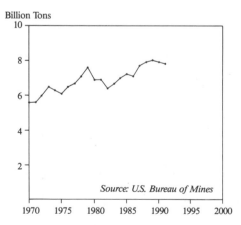

Million Tons Per
Million People

Figure 5-1. U.S. Materials Consumption and
Population, 1900–91

Billion Tons

Figure 5-2. World Materials Consumption, 1970–91

and international rules that affect materials production and trade. U.S. policies, for instance, are still determined by laws originally designed to foster development and settlement of the frontier, such as the 1872 General Mining Act. This archaic law gives miners the right to purchase mineral-bearing government lands for $5 an acre or less, and does not require them to pay royalties on production or to ensure that the land is reclaimed afterward. As of October 1994, large mining companies that are the law's principal beneficiaries had managed to stall current congressional efforts to change this law. Mining and timber companies also benefit from special tax exemptions not offered to other industries.[12]

International trade rules and the policies of industrial nations also tend to reinforce materials consumption patterns that date back to the colonial era, when empires were assembled to secure access to raw materials for manufacturing industries in home countries. The development assistance policies of former colonial powers tend to favor the production and export of primary commodities, which they often still receive in large quantities from the countries they once ruled. World Bank and International Monetary Fund planners generally advise commodity-exporting developing countries—many of which are deeply in debt—to invest heavily in those sectors to gain foreign exchange. Such policies, combined with tariffs that are lower for primary commodities than for processed intermediates or manufactured goods, have tended to depress prices of primary material commodities as compared with recovered materials.[13]

At the other end of the materials cycle, industrial countries commonly subsidize waste disposal as well. In the United States, where national policy officially favors waste reduction, reuse, and recy-

cling over landfilling and incineration, actual practice has been the reverse. Local communities have spent billions of dollars to finance construction of disposal facilities, while cheaper, more environmentally sound waste management options have received little funding. A large share of these waste disposal costs are hidden in property taxes or utility assessments rather than being paid for directly per unit of waste. Thus there is little incentive not to throw things away. Between 1960 and 1990, the annual tonnage of U.S. municipal solid waste more than doubled. Recycling has picked up considerably over the last decade, but until the late eighties, the rate at which U.S. municipalities recovered their solid waste did not pass 10 percent.[14]

Industrial wastes often cause even worse problems than municipal wastes, and the quantities involved can be greater. For example, in 1985, Japan's manufacturers produced 132 million tons of waste—2.6 times the country's municipal waste output. U.S. industries produce an estimated 180 million tons per year of hazardous wastes, and another 11 billion tons of industrial wastes not subject to hazardous-waste regulations.[15]

Favoring disposal over waste reduction, reuse, and recycling squanders not only materials but also the large amounts of energy embodied in products that are buried or burned. A 1992 study of the relative energy benefits of recycling and incineration found that while significant amounts of energy can be recovered through burning, three to five times more can be saved by recycling municipal solid waste. The potential savings are substantial: increasing the recovery of materials in U.S. solid waste so that at least 60 percent of all the materials are recycled could save an estimated 1.8 exajoules of energy per year—the equivalent of 315 million barrels of oil.[16]

BUILDING A SECONDARY MATERIALS ECONOMY

Preserving the natural resource base will require the creation of an economy that produces much less waste and can function with relatively small inputs of virgin materials. Eventually, of course, the overall efficiency of the system will have to improve on a massive scale: all the goods and services our economy produces will have to be designed to need far fewer materials. On a more immediate level, though, we must learn to look at "wastes" and secondary materials in an entirely different light. Our throwaway culture of "convenience" and planned obsolescence must be discarded in favor of an approach that seeks value in products even after people think they have finished using them.

The practical consequences of this attitude will be complex and varied. Perhaps most important, entrepreneurial and employment opportunities would grow rapidly in the recovery and reprocessing of used materials, as secondary businesses like those in Arcata forge closer ties with rapidly expanding municipal recycling systems. A wide variety of items—from bottles to shipping containers—could be reused dozens of times and then collected for remanufacturing. Car owners might bring their tires to a local auto parts dealer to get retreaded and, later perhaps, to be melted down into completely different products. Composted kitchen, yard, and sewage wastes would be plowed back into gardens and farms. Recycled-paper mills would outnumber those equipped only for virgin fiber, and smelters fed by recycled metals would replace a major share of mining operations. In general, cities—where used resources, factories, and labor are concentrated—would become a more important source of materials than rural mines or forests.

Bringing about change on this scale is going to require more than today's incremental increases in governments' environmental budgets, curbside pickup of newspapers, and the occasional trip to the community bottle bank. The job demands an infusion of capital, design skill, imagination, and public commitment comparable to the U.S. economic mobilization during World War II. Like that process, this one will have to proceed from public policies, but its principal players will be industrialists, financiers, engineers, designers, and thousands of small businesses. In the long run, efficient use of materials should mean not only less environmental damage but also a more stable economy, better long-term investment opportunities, and more skilled jobs, especially in design industries.

The most obvious place to start is with the current subsidization of virgin materials extraction. Raw material production should be taxed rather than subsidized: a reformed tax system could force industries to cover the full environmental costs of their activities, instead of leaving the bill for the public to pay. By raising prices to more realistic levels, such a system would provide strong incentives not to degrade the natural resource base in the first place. Market forces need to be aligned for, rather than against, materials efficiency.[17]

A related policy could force households and businesses to pay the full cost of disposing of their waste—with the clear understanding that a more efficient economy would make it well worth their while. Some countries are already taking their first, faltering steps in this direction. In Germany, policymakers are addressing the waste issue by making manufacturers responsible for the ultimate fate of their products. The most famous of Germany's waste laws deals with packaging materials, and has resulted in the establishment of a separate, industry-run collection and recycling system. It has also led to the virtual elimination of certain types of redundant packaging, such as boxes containing tubes of toothpaste or cans of shaving lotion. Similar programs are now being developed for automobiles and electronics. The idea that consumers might lease, rather than own, many goods, so that ownership—and responsibility—for those items would eventually revert to their makers, is also being considered.[18]

Truly taking responsibility for our garbage, though, will involve far more than just paying a little extra for its disposal. The ultimate goal is to develop comprehensive systems for collecting waste and transforming it into new products—which will be possible only if many consumer goods are redesigned to be easily reused and recycled. For some recycling and reuse activities, a functional infrastructure does already exist in many places, even if it is sometimes hard to find. In most of Europe and the developing world, beverages usually come in refillable bottles, and there is an extensive network of bottle collection and washing facilities. Even some complex products such as automobiles commonly get recycled in places that have developed markets for used parts. Much more work needs to be done, however, to facilitate reuse and to connect consumers with supplies of secondary products that are already being salvaged.[19]

Other products, such as many of those made from plastics, have almost never been recycled, so countries have to develop recovery systems for them from scratch—or switch to materials that are easier to recycle. They also need to revive a few long-standing reuse and recycling practices that have fallen into decline. In the United States, for instance, the recycling of wool and cotton textiles was once common, but the used-textiles market declined after the passage of the Wool Products Labeling Act of 1939, which required recycled-content labelling on goods containing reprocessed wool and cotton. The labels rapidly acquired a negative image, which was fostered by makers of virgin textiles. But carefully designed incentives both to save old clothes and to produce recycled textiles could result in a new boom for wool and cotton remanufacturers and for consumers as well. If we could develop a sustainable supply of inexpensive used textiles, reprocessed clothes might even become fashionable.[20]

The ultimate goal is to develop comprehensive systems for collecting waste and transforming it into new products.

Right now, the key to moving beyond traditional disposal systems may be simply getting governments to make serious investments in the secondary materials economy—to encourage less wasteful consumption patterns and product designs, to develop markets for recycled goods, and especially to gather more information about wastes and secondary materials. Details on how much waste communities or countries are generating and where it is going are still exceedingly rare. Without such data, it is difficult to make accurate assessments of opportunities for reuse, recycling, and waste reduction—or to establish meaningful goals and incentives.

DESIGNING FOR EFFICIENCY

Recovering secondary materials and reintegrating them into the economy will be crucial in the struggle to reduce our need for virgin resources. Over the long term, though, we will have to go beyond the establishment of sophisticated recycling systems. It will be necessary to make basic design changes in the materials economy that reduce its overall throughput by eliminating materials needs and wastes right at the source.

Two decades ago, when the world faced an energy crisis, skeptics scoffed at the idea that efficiency was the key to a sustainable energy policy. Since then, new lighting, heating, cooling, insulation, and manufacturing technologies have made it possible to cut energy use by three fourths or more in many applications. The improved technologies are now often cheap enough to make energy efficiency a better investment than energy production.[21]

The more durable a product is, the less frequently the cycle of processing or reprocessing has to start over again.

Efficient design can follow directly from a more careful consideration of exactly what ends consumers are trying to achieve. People do not necessarily want houses that use lots of materials and energy, for instance; they just want a sturdy, livable, shelter-providing structure with a comfortable temperature and hot showers. Houses can be designed to save materials without sacrificing comfort—and even the boards the house is made of could be produced more efficiently. In recent years, managers of industrial sawmills, frustrated at how much wood was being lost as sawdust, realized that they could achieve considerable savings simply by using thinner blades to saw logs: the thinner blades cut just as well as the originals but left more of the wood intact. By combining similar

technologies already available—ranging from two-sided copying in offices to the adoption of efficient architectural techniques—the United States, for example, could cut its wood consumption in half.[22]

Efficiency policies will have to cover a wide range of issues, but on the most basic level they all need to spark smarter design. Of course, smarter design is not a simple task, but three principles may help designers, architects, engineers, planners, and builders work together to make it happen.

The first is to promote sharing. For years, consumers have obtained reading materials from free public libraries instead of buying increasingly expensive books that they would probably read only once. Many people would likely welcome the opportunity to apply the same concept of sharing and reuse to thousands of other everyday items—power tools, bottles and jars, cars, or computer data, for example.

A second principle is to maintain the value added to materials. Extraction, processing, refining, and manufacturing all add value to a raw material. These processes also have major environmental costs. The materials efficiency of a product can be judged in part by how well it holds the value added to it. If a computer becomes worthless a few months after its purchase because a much better, cheaper model has hit the market, the economy has wasted all the effort and environmental damage that went into the computer's manufacture. But the item would lose value much more slowly if it were designed specifically to be easily repaired or upgraded. The more durable a product is, the less frequently the cycle of processing or reprocessing has to start over again.

The third is to design goods and services in context. A product design is most likely to be materials- and energy-efficient if it is considered as part of the whole system in which it functions. It is often more efficient to substitute a broad systemic change for an individual product. An instructive model for this kind of interdisciplinary approach can be found in the design of energy-efficient buildings. (See Chapter 6.)

Synergistic gains between components of design are not realized simply by plugging in efficient technologies or materials. They emerge only when design professionals work together from beginning to end—as they did, for example, when the National Audubon Society built its new headquarters recently in New York City. Audubon achieved massive improvements in lighting, heating, cooling, ventilation, and overall indoor air quality. The architects drew up floor plans to take full advantage of natural light; the contractor installed windows that let just the right amount of light and heat pass through them; the lighting technician knew, accordingly, that the building would need fewer lamp fixtures; and the interior designer arranged surfaces and finishes to get the most out of the lamps.[23]

Such integrated design costs perhaps three times as much as conventional design. But according to Amory Lovins, whose Rocky Mountain Institute has done pioneering studies on the subject, the resulting efficiency improvements can yield as much as 25 percent more floor space in a building of the same size. The extra expense, then, may be recovered immediately in materials savings—fewer ducts will be necessary, for instance, if climate-control systems are smaller—and a good design would yield substantial energy-saving dividends over the life of the structure.[24]

This truly thoughtful design would no doubt be more common if society rewarded it more directly. Currently, an engineer's commission is usually based on a percentage of the overall project budget—a practice that in many cases rewards oversizing. Taking the opposite approach, the Canadian utility Ontario Hydro recently announced that it would reward design that met certain energy-efficiency standards with a rebate equivalent to three years' energy savings, to be shared by the developer, architect, and consulting engineers. By basing the rebate on the finished product—the building's actual energy performance—the utility was also adding an incentive for the design professionals to stay involved and ensure that their ideas were executed properly during the building's construction, operation, and maintenance. Although materials efficiency is harder to measure than energy efficiency, similar methods of compensating designers for work that reduces materials intensiveness could be just as effective.[25]

Even with such incentives, however, smarter design will remain difficult until information systems are in place that give fuller descriptions of products and materials. The "green labels" now seen in several countries are intended to encourage purchases of environmentally preferable products, but they provide little detailed information and are directed primarily at consumers. More promising would be in-depth green labelling for designers and builders. Information on a material's origin, its capacity for reuse and recycling, the environmental costs of its production, and so forth will have to become an essential part of its design specifications.[26]

The use of concrete in the United States, for example, is governed by 17 sets of specifications, according to the Construction Specifications Institute—but none include any environmental information. Developed by government agencies and professional societies, such stipulations are what guide designers in choosing materials. But they usually address only such qualities as weight, strength, durability, safety, appearance, and shelf life. Sometimes specifications even work against sustainable design, as when virgin materials are called for where used materials would suffice.[27]

Systematically reworking materials specifications to include environmental information would be a step in the right direction—and some countries, such as the United Kingdom, have already begun "greening" their building sector. (See Chapter 6.) Accomplishing this reform on a broad scale, though, will require a much clearer understanding of how materials production and use actually affect the environment. Currently, detailed information on that topic is just as scarce as information about waste. Yet materials-efficient design will ultimately be impossible without it. Data need to be developed at every level of society, from corporate materials audits—which should help firms identify opportunities for efficiency improvements—up to national and international accounting of materials flows. These statistics also need to be linked with data on the amount of energy, pollution, and economic activity associated with materials production and use.[28]

Systematically reworking materials specifications to include environmental information would be a step in the right direction.

There have been at least a few promising initiatives in this area. In the United States, the Bureau of Mines has started compiling limited but extremely useful data on materials production, consumption, and recycling. The eventual goal is to track comprehensively the quantities of materials flowing into and out of the U.S. economy, allowing progress in materials efficiency to be measured. Similarly, the U.S. Department of Energy has begun to collect more detailed energy-

use statistics. Combining the two data sets will undoubtedly uncover valuable opportunities for saving energy through more efficient materials use.[29]

Data on pollution and hazardous waste generation from production processes, exemplified by the information collected annually in the U.S. Toxics Release Inventory (TRI), are also useful. Unique in the world, the U.S. Environmental Protection Agency's TRI lists the reported output of several hundred toxic substances by U.S. manufacturers. Data are available by the specific facility or company, by geographical area or industrial sector, or by chemical. The TRI has its flaws—including limited coverage of industries and chemicals, and poor quality control on its data—but it is a good starting point for the kind of comprehensive system that is needed. It would also be very useful if such a system included data on raw materials that flow into industrial facilities—a reform Massachusetts has already implemented on a limited basis through its toxics-use reduction law.[30]

In the long run, materials-data collection efforts—like energy-use tracking—make sound economic sense, since they could inspire efficiency improvements that would far outweigh the cost of amassing the information. They could also help us make materials choices, by facilitating quick assessments of the energy use, pollution, jobs, and waste associated with production of a given material or product—a virtually impossible task today.

NEW MARKETS, NEW INVESTMENTS

Once we gather sufficient data about materials flows, we will be much closer to having the tools needed to make a materials revolution pay for itself. Initially, though, every element of the transition to a sustainable materials economy is going to cost something. Materials policies, then, will have to support the process, contributing directly to the establishment of everything from municipal recycling programs to materials information systems to an infrastructure for interdisciplinary, materials-efficient design. Perhaps most important, though, these policies will have to spur the development of markets for used materials.

Articles on recycling's marketing difficulties have become a staple in U.S. and European newspapers. Market problems for secondary materials are real, but their importance is often exaggerated. They are largely a symptom of the promotion of recycling only as a waste management option rather than part of a broader materials policy. Many market crises happen for a simple reason: it can take years to develop the facilities that use secondary materials, while collection programs start yielding substantial quantities of materials as soon as the trucks roll. Most communities turn to recycling because they see it as a cheaper disposal option with less potential long-term liability than landfilling or incineration. They are usually right—even if they are forced virtually to give away the materials they collect—but often suffer when revenues from materials sales fail to meet projections. When thousands of communities or facilities begin collecting recyclables at the same time, prices of these used materials can plummet, as has happened in both the United States and Europe.

In the United States, the number of curbside pickup programs for recyclables grew from 1,042 in 1988 to 6,678 in 1993, according to *BioCycle* magazine's annual waste management survey. As a result, the share of municipal waste being recycled or composted rose from around 9 percent to 19 percent, and the total quantity being recovered grew by at least 30 million tons. Thirty-nine percent of Americans are now served by

municipal curbside recycling programs. In Germany, the Duales System Deutschland (DSD)—a private, non-profit consortium of more than 600 companies formed in response to the 1991 packaging ordinance—collected 3.9 million tons of packaging for recycling from its member companies' products in 1993. The DSD has collected more used material than Germany's existing recycling infrastructure can handle, and some of Germany's materials—particularly plastics—have overflowed into other countries' markets, lowering prices.[31]

There is nothing inherently wrong with collection programs; they are a crucial element of an efficient materials economy. Unfortunately, though, recycling planners and local governments have often failed to set aside sufficient reserve funds to tide them over during periods of market difficulties. This problem could be addressed by taking recycling programs at least partly off of general-revenue-funded budgets (where they compete with other municipal programs such as schools, police, and firefighters) and "capitalizing" them: funding them through bond issues and other long-term sources of capital, the way incinerators and landfills are funded.

Since recycling programs require far less capital to put in place than incinerators—usually viewed as the main alternative waste management method—such funding should save money. In Massachusetts alone, more than $1 billion has been spent on nine solid waste incinerators, while recycling was left to languish for years. Two Massachusetts Institute of Technology researchers have calculated that the state could have saved more than $200 per ton of waste if it had chosen recycling over incineration as its principal strategy.[32]

Collection programs would also be much more effective if they were planned in conjunction with sufficiently aggressive measures to develop markets for what they collect. Perhaps the quickest, most effective market stimulation measure available to governments is to require that their own procurement offices purchase goods made from secondary materials whenever possible. The United States recently took a long-awaited step in this direction by enacting an executive order requiring the federal government—the world's largest consumer of paper, at 300,000 tons per year—to purchase only paper containing 20 percent or more post-consumer waste. By 2000, the content requirement will rise to 30 percent.[33]

The most effective market stimulation measure available to governments is to require that their procurement offices purchase goods made from secondary materials.

Directly encouraging or requiring commercial use of secondary materials can also help. Again in the United States, 13 states have set minimum recycled-content standards for newsprint, and 15 more have negotiated voluntary agreements with newspapers; these standards have stabilized the demand for non-virgin newsprint, spurring a sharp growth in recycling. In 1988, there were only 9 newsprint recycling plants in North America; now there are 29. Governments can also encourage secondary materials market development—and the economic development that goes with it—through tax exemptions or credits for recycling enterprises, creation of recycling market development zones, and technical assistance programs. Twenty-seven states have recycling tax incentive programs in place, and 23 have established grant or loan programs for the same purpose.[34]

Another important way to make recycling more secure for both businesses and communities that collect materials is to develop official, organized markets for secondary materials. Conventional commodities markets boast complex systems, such as futures contracts based on standard specifications, which insulate buyers and sellers against sharp fluctuations in price or supply. If a firm wants to be sure it can buy pork bellies or sheet steel in six months' time at a predictable price, it can purchase a contract guaranteeing that it will be able to do so. Few secondary materials are traded through such sophisticated markets.

This situation is changing, however. Trading of secondary aluminum began on the London Metals Exchange in 1992, and another, broader initiative in the United States shows great promise. The Recycling Advisory Council, a program of the National Recycling Coalition, has been working with the Chicago Board of Trade, one of the world's premier commodities markets, to develop a formal trading system for recycled materials. The system initially will be a cash market, but the feasibility of futures markets will be investigated. Secondary newsprint, cardboard, plastic, glass, steel cans, and aluminum containers all have the potential to be included. The system will begin a demonstration phase in early 1995.[35]

To ensure that secondary materials are eventually plowed back into the economy—substituted for virgin materials—support is needed not only for municipal programs but also for the many private firms, for-profit and nonprofit, that are trying to collect and process secondary materials into forms usable by manufacturing industries. For the most part, the collection and distribution centers and the numerous other facilities of the new materials infrastructure will likely be in private, not government, hands. And government appropriations—though important for leveraging private investment—will provide only a fraction of the funding for such facilities.

Firms established to collect and process used materials may face greater obstacles than other new businesses. Like many industrial operations, they tend to have trouble finding appropriate sites and sorting through elaborate permitting processes. But financing may be even more difficult to come by. The more innovative they are, the harder it is to get credit. Reprocessors of recovered goods, for instance, often require specialized equipment that banks will not accept as loan collateral since they are uncertain of its market value. Or it may be difficult to reassure financiers that a facility's raw materials or cash flow will be consistent enough to allow for regular loan payments, given the current instability of secondary materials markets.

Such problems are not insurmountable, though. A model for getting the capital for a sustainable materials infrastructure can be found in the area of low-income housing finance. A few decades ago, there was no effective bridge between large holders of capital—banks, pension funds, and so on—and borrowers in many U.S. low-income and minority communities. One important factor that helped bring much-needed mortgage loans to low-income communities was the advent of intermediary institutions, such as community development banks, that understood both the communities involved and the complexities of capital markets.[36]

Now springing up are similar intermediaries that attempt to facilitate financing of a sustainable materials infrastructure. The Recycling Advisory Council, for instance, has launched a project that seeks to hook up interested investors with start-up recycling operations through an on-line matchmaker service. One institution more directly involved in financing is the Materials for the Future Foundation (MFF), established in California in 1992 to provide grants, loans, business advice, and policy advocacy for community-based recycling and reuse enterprises. In conjunction with the Californians Against Waste Foundation, MFF has convened a working group on strategies for financing small recovered-materials enterprises in California. The group issued a detailed report on the subject in 1993.[37]

THE ECONOMIC OPPORTUNITY

Paying for the redesign of an entire economy will be difficult at first, but it will not launch an era of global penance. On the contrary, a materials revolution would bring with it significant economic opportunities. Its benefits would quickly outweigh its costs. The biggest payoff may eventually be an increase in one of society's most precious assets: jobs.

Industries founded on secondary materials will allow pioneering companies to open up entirely new economic sectors. Even when such industries are portrayed simply as branches of waste management, their job intensity is striking. Every million tons of solid waste tends to generate 1,600 recycling jobs; if the same million tons were put in a landfill, only 600 workers would be involved, and incinerating that amount of waste would require only 80 workers.[38]

Secondary materials industries constitute much more than simply recycling, however. As we make the transition to a new materials economy, thousands more people will be needed to collect, recollect, sort, repair, clean, process, and reprocess materials and products that used to be simply discarded. And others will operate behind the scenes, creating new design standards, implementing new manufacturing techniques, and developing new markets. Moreover, though more jobs may mean higher labor costs, capital costs should fall, and the financial return from working with secondary materials could easily make secondary industries a good investment even by conventional measures. In short, the global imperative to use materials more efficiently is likely to create as many new professions, companies, and industries as the communications revolution did during the past century.

Of course, communities and regions dependent on primary materials production may initially feel an economic crunch with the shift to a lower level of extraction. Workers there will need help from employers and government to switch over to sustainable livelihoods. Over the long term, though, metals recovery and paper recycling should supply far more jobs than do mines and logging operations. Processing is much more job-intensive than extraction: logging 1 million board-feet of U.S. timber generates only 3 jobs, for example, while milling it into lumber creates 20 and turning it into furniture generates 80. And reprocessing jobs can be sustained indefinitely, because they do not rely on finite supplies of minerals or harvestable timber.[39]

Logging and mining towns have tended not to make very stable communities. In fact, they are often not communities at all but merely frontier outposts, built to be abandoned: many former "boom towns"—places like Deadwood, South Dakota, and Potosí, Bolivia—have been so devastated by extraction that these days they are more like ghost towns.

Primary industries have long ranked near the bottom in jobs per unit of economic output, but in recent decades, especially in industrial countries, they have declined in absolute numbers of jobs as well. Between 1980 and 1992, for example, U.S. employment in metal mining dropped 45 percent and that in primary metal manufacturing, 38 percent. Almost every country with a large mining industry has experienced a similar decline.[40]

For industrial countries, part of this decline has been caused by a shifting of extractive industries to the developing world. Even there, though, primary industries have created few jobs: they have had to confront limits imposed not only by environmental liabilities but also by their need to become increasingly mechanized in order to stay competitive. All over the world companies are "downsizing" and increasing automation—using technologies that increase output per worker, which in its final effect means cutting jobs. Widespread technological advances in the logging industry, for instance, are allowing companies to cut more timber with fewer employees. Teams of highly skilled lumberjacks have been replaced by lone operators of bulldozers or huge "feller-bunchers." Subsequently, the pace of logging has quickened so dramatically that the forests around many communities can no longer grow back fast enough to provide local loggers with a continuous yield, so they need to look elsewhere for employment.

Timber workers and miners who claim that the environmental lobby is the principal threat to their livelihoods fail to acknowledge that the internal practices of their own industries are a much more significant source of job loss. Even regions where entire economies were founded on extractive industries are shifting to other sources of income. In the American West, for example, only a tenth of 1 percent of all workers are still employed in metal mining. Montana, Wyoming, Oregon, Nevada, and Colorado have all largely switched over to service economies focused mostly on tourism—an industry that depends on a healthy landscape unmarred by toxic tailings ponds and clear-cut wastelands.[41]

For the past couple of decades, recycling, reprocessing, and repair services have in fact been among the world's most reliable "growth industries." In the United States, between 1970 and 1992 the total recovery rate for paper nearly doubled, rising from 22 to 39 percent—reflecting the booming business being done by post-consumer paper collectors, sorters, recyclers, manufacturers, and distributors. And employment in the American auto repair business increased 50 percent between 1980 and 1990—while jobs in the manufacture of new motor vehicles increased a mere 3 percent. In reprocessing industries overall, employment is actually underreported, because workers in this sector often are not classified separately. These industries use scrap inputs instead of virgin, but from that point on the processing requires similar skills and equipment.[42]

In other words, the infrastructure already exists in many primary industries to take on more reprocessing and remanufacturing. A recent multiyear study found that iron foundries can safely use scrap steel cans as a feedstock without any embrittlement or loss of strength in their cast-iron products. Now many foundries have begun mining local recycling programs for a convenient, inexpensive supply of steel cans.[43]

Not only existing industrial processes and plants but also existing marketing and distribution systems are coming into play. In Chicago, a tire-retreading company called Lakin General has formed a partnership with Sears' extensive automotive network to guarantee a steady supply of about a million tires a year, which keeps 365 employees busy. Lakin General either repairs the tires as they are, gives them entirely new treads, or reprocesses them as products ranging from snowblower blades to conveyor rollers.[44]

Similar entrepreneurial efforts in the developing world are doing well too. In the Philippines, in and around Manila,

the Women Balikatan (Shoulder to Shoulder) Movement has joined with scavengers and junk dealers both to improve the recovery of solid waste and to promote community development. Scavengers in certain districts collect discarded items for the dealers, who then resell them to local artisans and industrialists. In the 11 years since Balikatan's initiative was launched, Metropolitan Manila has become much cleaner, the recovery rate for solid waste has risen considerably, and hundreds of scavengers and junk-shop owners have been able to establish permanent microbusinesses. Regular junk-shop customers, who like to reuse or recycle the salvaged goods, can now count on steady supplies.[45]

Reprocessing jobs can be sustained indefinitely, because they do not rely on finite supplies of minerals or harvestable timber.

Today's fledgling secondary industries are at least nudging us down the right path. Of course, they do carry certain imperfections, both economic and environmental. They are sometimes highly mechanized, requiring significant capital but not creating many jobs; and they sometimes generate their own toxic emissions. On the whole, though, they tend to offer brand-new employment opportunities, and they are clearly able to sustain themselves, even in wildly fluctuating markets and damaged environments. Sometimes they can even help ease other social stresses: Gulf Coast Recycling, for instance, a nonprofit organization operating in a high-unemployment region along Mississippi's shoreline, focuses specifically on using recycling to create jobs, and employs mostly minority women and single mothers.[46]

In addition, as demonstrated in Manila, secondary industries tend to clean up communities more than they pollute them. Maureen Smith, a researcher at the University of California at Los Angeles, recently compared the virgin and recycled paper industries by studying TRI data. She found that switching from virgin to recycled newsprint tends to result in a 99-percent decrease in the amount of ammonia and chlorine released into the environment. Of course, the sludges that result from deinking processes at recycled newsprint facilities have so far been fairly toxic—but only because so many printers are still using toxic inks, which could be replaced with other inks that are ecologically safe, widely available, and competitively priced.[47]

Implemented carefully, reforms that allow secondary industries and their affiliates a toehold could eventually lead to the revitalization of entire communities. Most of today's urban areas, after all, already have a huge, underused labor pool and are overwhelmed with materials now going to waste. These are the resources of the future. Since reprocessing businesses have the potential to close materials loops within communities' own borders, they can increase self-reliance quite dramatically.

It is essential that industrial nations—the world's materials gluttons—sharply improve their materials efficiency.

Instead of paying—in both financial and ecological terms—for commodities to be extracted, refined, fabricated, and transported from afar, cities could reclaim and reprocess products locally, salvaging some of the value that has already been added to them. In the process, they would both save money and create jobs for local people, in fields ranging from aluminum reprocessing to market research for secondary fabrics. And perhaps the largest job growth would come in all kinds of well-paid planning and design professions—contrary to myths about recycling being little more than the drudgery of sorting through wastes—since so many facets of the local economy would have to be completely overhauled.

A REVOLUTIONARY PARTNERSHIP

The current materials economy presents a classic political problem: those who benefit from the status quo (mining and timber companies, waste disposal firms, bulk commodity producers) are well organized and politically powerful. The rest of society, which is paying the price for inefficient use of materials, is dispersed and for the most part does not perceive that there is a common solution—an efficiency strategy—to the wide range of problems that stem from materials use. But the ecological benefits of reduced virgin materials production and waste disposal, and the economic benefits of building an efficient economy based on used materials, are great enough—and offer enough benefits to a wide range of constituencies—to build a powerful and broad political coalition for reform. The first step is for everyone to recognize the common roots of our problems; the next is to organize well enough to generate the political will for change.

A model for how a coalition could be built around an efficient materials policy can be found in the successful struggle for a more sustainable and broadly beneficial transportation policy in the United States. Traditionally, transportation legislation was not generally known as such; instead, it was the annual "highway bills." Not surprisingly, these emphasized road-building at the expense of other priorities. But this situation was altered in 1991, when a coalition of community development, civil rights, and environmental organizations came together with local governments to support the passage of the Intermodal Surface Transportation Efficiency Act (ISTEA). The law forced transportation agencies to shift their focus from building highways toward an integrated approach to transportation, development, and air-quality planning. Only by building this new, broader coalition could the grip of the entrenched constituency that supported the old status quo—the highway builders—be loosened.[48]

The same kind of political development could spark the transition to a sustainable materials economy. It could provide a common rubric for groups concerned with environmental problems caused by extractive activities in wilderness areas, for recycling and waste reduction activists, and for advocates of urban economic development. And the potential benefits are even greater than those made available to the constituencies that supported ISTEA: materials use is crucial not only to transportation, but also to construction, communication, and almost every other important human activity.

Since the current materials economy threatens global ecosystems, this coalition-building also needs to be pursued globally. Though the economic development spurred by a materials revolution might have the most potential impact on a local level, the scope of such a revolution would nevertheless have to be worldwide. It is essential that industrial nations—the world's materials gluttons—sharply improve their materials

efficiency. But poorer countries also need to adopt efficiency policies, even as they develop. A world of 10 billion or more people consuming as much material per person as Americans, Europeans, or Japanese currently do would have unthinkable ecological consequences. Indeed, such consumption levels might well be physically impossible to achieve for any extended period of time, given the current fragile state of many forest and agricultural systems. The global consequences of unchecked growth in materials use range from lost biodiversity in countries whose ecosystems are shattered by logging and mining to increased emissions of greenhouse gases from energy-intensive virgin materials industries.[49]

Developing nations will not be denied their right to economic improvement. If they are to avoid the mistakes of their predecessors in industrialization, though, they will need new technologies and technical assistance from the wealthier nations. Industrial nations must improve their own materials performance and lead the drive toward efficient design and production, or developing countries may see no reason to step away from the beaten path of inefficient growth. And development and foreign aid agencies should rethink the economic development strategies they promote, moving away from an emphasis on materials-intensive infrastructure—highways, bridges, dams—toward a focus on meeting human needs with a minimum of materials and energy use.

Development planners need to recognize that though we will never completely eliminate virgin materials production, extractive industries need to shrink substantially as the world moves toward greater materials efficiency and more use of secondary materials. The transition will not be painless, and it will have the greatest impacts on countries whose economies rely heavily on virgin resource exports. Money needs to be devoted to retraining and education for workers in industries that are forced to reduce employment, with an eye to shifting these people to sectors that will grow as a result of the changes under way. Much of the money that now goes toward funding virgin materials projects—mines, logging projects, and the like—could be redirected to such efforts.

An all-out effort is also needed to find creative solutions to the debt crisis, and tariff and trade agreements need to be modified in such a way that countries can become more self-sufficient and maximize the value they add locally to the materials they do export. Such new policies should also generate more economic spinoffs—related economic development—than do current policies, which largely prop up "enclave" industries that are more closely connected to processing firms in other countries than to local economies.

Developing an ecologically sound economy presents tremendous opportunities. As economist Herman Daly put it, "the end of growthmania is no cause for despair; it is a hopeful new beginning." In the materials economy, as with energy and water, the key to the shift will be a change in values, a new emphasis on quality over quantity. Instead of defining success as getting the most materials, we need to move to a new standard: getting the most *from* materials.[50]

6

Making Better Buildings

Nicholas Lenssen and David Malin Roodman

As durable cultural artifacts, buildings leave for posterity much information about the societies that made them. The Acropolis of the ancient Greeks, Angkor Wat in the forest of Cambodia, and the Incan Machu Picchu perched on a ridge in modern Peru—each speaks volumes about the values and structure of a dead civilization.

Today's buildings will also reveal a great deal about us. Luxurious suburban homes from Stockholm to San Francisco and gleaming skyscrapers from Brasilia to Bangkok are, on their own terms, spectacular triumphs of the modern industrial age. They are equipped to deliver myriad services once undreamed of: indoor plumbing (including hot water on demand), precise climate control, lighting at the flip of a switch, refrigeration, communication, and even entertainment. Though such buildings are concentrated in industrial countries, steel and glass office buildings and concrete block houses can now be found in every major city in the world.

Less obvious, though, is the destructive legacy of today's built environment. When asked to list major sources of pollution, most people in industrial countries would likely point first to their cars and factories. The buildings they spend more than 90 percent of their lives in would escape blame. Even at their most alienating, modern buildings present an inert facade to the world, seemingly incapable of massive environmental damage.[1]

Yet as much as a tenth of the global economy is dedicated to constructing and operating homes and offices. And dollar for dollar, this activity uses several times as much wood, minerals, water, and energy as the rest of the economy: buildings consume one sixth to one half of the world's physical resources. Responsibility for much of the environmental damage occurring today—destruction of forests and rivers, air and water pollution, climate destabilization—belongs squarely at the doorsteps of modern buildings. At the same time, many buildings do harm on the inside. They may subject their occupants to stale and unhealthy air or alienating physical environments, making workers less productive or residents ill.[2]

These symptoms, along with broader problems such as sprawling development patterns that consume land and clog highways, point to a fundamental conclusion: modern building design takes place out of context. Designers are almost completely detached from the people and the ecosystems that their work affects. Recognizing this, some architects, engineers, and builders have begun to search for alternative approaches. Often they blend traditional design solutions with advanced technologies to create buildings that supply modern amenities yet are healthier, more affordable, more durable, and more efficient.

The Internationale Nederlanden (ING) Bank's new headquarters in Amsterdam provides a striking example of how much better buildings can be. The bank's directors chose to build an "organic" building that was highly efficient in its use of energy and other natural resources, and that integrated natural shapes, green plants, and art into something that celebrated the human spirit. When completed in 1987, the new headquarters used one fifth of the energy of a new office building next door, and less than a tenth as much as the bank's previous headquarters. Lower energy expenditures covered the additional costs of construction in just four months of operation.[3]

A few months of building construction can consume more resources and generate more pollution than a decade of building operation.

Small numbers of similar buildings are now appearing around the world. Yet many obstacles remain to a wholesale transformation of the building business, among them the resistance to change in a dispersed and competitive industry, and a spreading global culture that is often more attuned to the transient whims of consumers than long-term economic or environmental considerations. Only a concerted effort on the part of governments, builders, and occupants will ensure that people can provide shelter for themselves without jeopardizing the livability of their greater home—the planet.

CONSTRUCTION DESTRUCTION

The problems of modern buildings have their roots in the early stages of the Industrial Revolution. The motive forces of industrialization—mechanization and specialization—have produced an economy that straddles the globe and produces a vast array of goods and services. Paradoxically, it is an economy in which individuals fill ever narrower roles, giving them little appreciation of their relationship to the larger world. The simultaneous expansion and differentiation of economic society has had many effects on buildings.

Mechanization enabled miners and loggers to do their work on destructive scales and to transport their raw products to builders far away. Builders gained access to a dramatic variety of new materials, although distance insulated them from the environmental consequences of their choices. Over time, inventors formulated high-strength and often energy- and pollution-intensive new materials, such as steel and plastics, that could be made and used anywhere. Coal, which provided coke for steel, and petroleum, which was a feedstock for plastic, were also burned in large amounts to generate the high temperatures needed to produce these and other new substances.

Today, much of the environmental impact of a building occurs before people ever set foot in it. A few months of building construction—particularly production and transportation of building materials—can consume more resources and generate more pollution than a decade of building operation.[4]

Buildings account for roughly 40 percent of the materials entering the global economy each year: some 3 billion tons of raw materials are turned into foundations and walls, pipes and panels. The lion's share of this is essentially dirt and rocks—stone, clay for bricks, and gravel and sand for concrete. (Where buildings are put also affects their environmental impact: much of the rest of the materials flow becomes roads, bridges, and vehicles to connect structures.) Getting these materials out does not normally have many off-site impacts, but quarrying can obliterate the foliage and landscape in local areas, scarring the earth with giant pockmarks. (See Chapter 5.)[5]

Heavily processed and manufactured materials used in the building sector—such as copper, iron, bauxite, and plastics—have far more environmental impact than quarried materials because they must be purified from low-grade ores or undergo heavy processing. For example, nearly half the copper used in the United States—some 530,000 tons a year—ends up in buildings, primarily for pipes and electrical wires. A fifth of this is recycled material, but the rest is extracted from low-grade virgin ores, using a purification process that produces huge tailing piles. The final smelting stage releases large amounts of poisonous heavy metals, including arsenic and cadmium, as well as sulfur dioxide, which contributes to acid rain.[6]

Polyvinyl chloride, better known as vinyl or PVC—a chlorinated plastic that is widely used in piping, siding, and windows—is little better. It is difficult to recycle, and its production and incineration (if that is how it is disposed of) generate numerous water and air pollutants, including carcinogenic dioxins and vinyl chloride monomers. Various bodies, including Germany's Health Ministry and the American Public Health Association, have called for PVC use to be phased out where viable substitutes exist.[7]

In many regions where it is available, wood remains the material of choice for house-sized structures: it is strong, light, and easy to transport and build with. Globally, building construction accounts for more than one quarter of the world's voracious appetite for wood, as trees are converted to lumber, plywood, particle board, veneer, and other products. In North America and Scandinavia, almost all new houses are made from wood, and in Japan, wood's popularity has risen in tandem with incomes since World War II. (Additionally, half of the world's wood use, some 1.9 billion cubic meters in 1992, is burned by people primarily in developing countries to cook food and heat homes.)[8]

In the last century, global forest cover has shrunk by a fifth; more than half of what remains is isolated forest fragments or commercial stands. Most timber production in primary forests is really timber mining: it is far above sustainable levels, and must eventually fall. Symptomatic of the spreading forestry crisis, many nations have surpassed the capacity of their own lands to supply wood, and have taken to importing large amounts. Japan, by far the world's largest importer, put up 750 million square meters of wood buildings during the eighties, mostly with timber from dwindling Pacific Rim forests.[9]

People in buildings rely heavily on two additional natural resources: energy and clean water. Of these, the impacts of energy use are more diverse and far-flung. Between 1971 and 1992, primary energy use in buildings worldwide grew on average 2 percent annually. In 1992, structures accounted for about a third of total world energy consumption, including 26 percent of fossil fuels, 45 percent of hydropower, and 50 percent of nuclear power.[10]

These figures, though, only count the energy buildings use once they are up and running, ignoring everything that went into making them. Steel, glass, and brick require large amounts of fossil fuels for high-temperature manufacture. (See Table 6–1.) Transporting materials to the building site takes still more energy. For the United States, adding in the "embodied energy" in structures pushes the building sector's share of energy consumption from 36 percent to roughly 45 percent—more than any other use.[11]

Systematic study would probably reveal that buildings dominate the global energy economy as well. They would thus account for nearly half the emissions of heat-trapping carbon dioxide from fossil fuel burning and of sulfur dioxide and nitrogen oxides. By extension, buildings deserve much of the blame for other environmental side effects of energy use—oil spills, nuclear waste generation, river ecosystem destruction from dams, toxic run-off from coal mines, and mercury emissions from coal burning.[12]

A survey of water use in buildings tells a similar story. From Beijing to Los Angeles, rapid growth in urban water use is depleting groundwater and leading to remote projects that siphon supplies away from agriculture. Nuclear and fossil fuel power plants use still more water as a coolant, much of which drains into rivers, carrying thermal and chemical pollution and damaging downstream ecosystems. These two uses—direct domestic consumption and power production—contribute about equally to the one-sixth share of global water use accounted for by buildings.[13]

Putting structures up also produces large amounts of waste, as does tearing them down. Erecting a typical 150-ton home in the United States sends some 7 tons of refuse to the local dump. At the same time, for every six houses or apartment buildings constructed in the coun-

Table 6-1. Energy Used in Production and Recycling of Selected Building Materials, United Kingdom[1]

Material	Virgin Production	Recycling
	(gigajoules per ton)	
Concrete	0.5–1.5	0.5–1.5[2]
Brick[3]	2.5–6.1	
Wood (Domestically Harvested)[3]	4–5	
Glass	13–25	10–20
Plastics	80–220	50–160
Steel	25–45	9–15
Copper	70–170	10–80
Aluminum	150–220	10–15

[1]The wide ranges in these data reflect variations in manufacturing processes from plant to plant, and in distances materials are transported. [2]Using old, crushed concrete for aggregate and all new Portland cement. [3]Generally not recycled, though can be reused or made into other products.
SOURCE: Nigel Howard, Davis Langdon Consultancy, London, printout, September 20, 1994, and private communication, September 27, 1994; recycling energy use for glass and plastics are Worldwatch estimates, based on ibid. and on data from Jeffrey Morris and Diana Canzoneri, *Recycling Versus Incineration: An Energy Conservation Analysis* (Seattle, Wash.: Sound Resource Management Group, 1992).

try, one falls to the wrecking ball—about 150,000 each year. In the European Union, construction and demolition activities produce 50 percent more waste than municipal garbage generation does, although it garners far less public attention.[14]

In addition to despoiling the forests, the land, the air, and the water around them, many modern buildings create dangerous indoor environments for their inhabitants. "Sick building syndrome" occurs in as many as 30 percent of new or renovated buildings. Ventilation systems installed to avoid such problems often actually create them, subjecting occupants to stale air for hours on end, or harboring and spreading unhealthy molds. Sealed, climate-controlled buildings also trap volatile organic compounds (VOCs), particularly formaldehyde, that can seep out from adhesives and drying agents in furniture, carpets, and paint and can lead to air concentrations hundreds of times higher than just outside.[15]

The medical and productivity costs of unwell and uncomfortable workers in sick buildings are thought to run into the tens of billions of dollars each year. In addition, some researchers believe that forced air circulation in modern buildings could facilitate the spread of airborne diseases like the common cold and influenza. If their suspicions are correct, the economic impact could run to hundreds of billions of dollars annually. Meanwhile, in developing countries, poorly vented and inefficient biomass- or coal-burning stoves and furnaces are common for cooking and heating, leading to homes with high indoor concentrations of particulates in urban areas.[16]

Though modern buildings have made living easier for millions, they have also resulted in more subjective problems. Traditionally, local materials and the demands of climate tended to give each indigenous architecture a distinctive character. What shapes modern buildings are the abstract theories of academic architects, the careful calculations of corporations and developers, and the short-run economics of the highly competitive building business.

The result everywhere has been monotonous business and commercial neighborhoods mixed with garish commercial strips. These buildings rarely offer visitors a sense of connection to the fabric of a place, or, by extension, to a community. Modern offices cut workers off from the outside world, making them uncomfortable with their work environments and less productive. If the aesthetic freedom granted by industrial materials and fuels carries with it a certain responsibility, then designers and builders have often been derelict in their duties—not just to the natural ecosystems from which life is drawn, but to the people who live and work in their creations.[17]

MATERIAL CONCERNS

One reason that construction today consumes so many more natural resources than before is that people expect more from buildings in terms of floor space and features. As people move more frequently, as industries rise and fall, and as cities undergo convulsive development, people become less interested in investing in these massive capital assets for the long term. As a result, even as buildings become more opulent, they often wear out in a matter of decades or are torn down to make way for newer ones even sooner, compounding the waste. To make the process of turning trees and rocks into modern homes and offices less destructive, builders will have to put up structures that are durable and adaptable, make them out of carefully chosen materials, use these efficiently, and reuse and recycle materials as much as possible.

Since World War II, the average size of houses in industrial countries has grown while family size has shrunk. Even the oil shocks of the seventies failed to slow this trend. (See Figure 6–1.) In the United States, for example, floor space per person more than doubled in new homes between 1949 and 1993. As Gopal Ahluwalia of the National Association of Homebuilders explains, "everybody wants a media room, a home office, an exercise room, three bathrooms, a family room, a living room, and a huge, beautiful, eat-in kitchen that nobody cooks in." Similarly, Japan added some 2.25 billion square meters of residential floor space between 1982 and 1991 even though its population was nearly stable.[18]

Though buildings are getting wider and taller, they are not lasting as long. Sixty percent of West Germany's buildings survived the onslaught of World War II, but only 15 percent weathered the rapid economic development of the ensuing 30 years, according to European planner Leon Krier. Skyrocketing land values in postwar Tokyo translated into a churning building market in which, by the eighties, buildings lasted only 17 years on average before being demolished and replaced with taller ones.[19]

According to writer Stewart Brand, buildings can become more adaptable in several ways, so that they can endure in today's rapidly changing world. They should be built solidly, yet in a way that makes them easy to add on to later. Rather than being specialized for today's narrow uses, they should be general-purpose, to adapt to the unforeseeable demands of future occupants. Piping and wiring should not be embedded in a building's structural components, so that upgrading for future needs can be done more easily.[20]

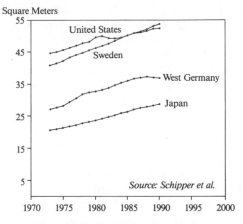

Figure 6-1. Residential Floor Space Per Person, Selected Countries, 1973–90

Several recent projects demonstrate the environmental and economic advantages of rehabilitation over construction from scratch. KBI, a large nonprofit housing association in Denmark, upgraded old three-story apartment buildings by adding another floor at the top. This gave them 33 percent more floor space but used much less material than new construction would, and at two thirds the cost. Along the way they added energy- and water-saving features, so that total resource use in the buildings stayed the same. Similarly, when the National Audubon Society moved its New York headquarters, it decided to refurbish an eight-story brownstone in lower Manhattan rather than erecting a new structure in the suburbs. It also used the latest in technology and design—such as an efficient cooling system and insulating windows—to cut energy use in the building by 60 percent and reduce water use. All the improvements will pay for themselves within five years, and will continue generating savings thereafter.[21]

Modern buildings are not only growing bigger, they are multiplying. Perhaps a billion people live and work in western-style buildings today. If rapid economic and population growth continues, many billions more eventually will, intensifying the environmental impact of the global building stock. It is thus essential that those putting up new buildings—most of which will be in developing countries—avoid the mistakes of the past, and instead seek to minimize the amount of material taken from the natural environment.[22]

As designers think about how to make buildings go farther, they should think about how to make the materials in them do the same. The art of using wood efficiently is perhaps the most advanced because primary forests are already disappearing in many places. For instance, the Center for Resourceful Building Technology in Missoula, Montana, recently built a home to demonstrate how to build more efficiently with wood. Walls had insulation sandwiched between panels of glued-together wood scraps, instead of normal timber framing, which requires long beams from mature trees. The floor incorporated I beams also made from wood scraps, shaped like their steel counterparts to leave wood only where it provides the most strength, cutting material needs by 75 percent. With similar techniques, the Davis Energy Group and the Pacific Gas and Electric Company put up a framed house in Davis, California, that uses roughly half the wood of its neighbors.[23]

Key components of large, modern buildings—steel and glass—are much more energy-intensive than wood. As a result, it takes two to four times as much energy per square meter to make an office building as it does a house, according to U.K. data. But like wood, industrial materials can be used much more efficiently. Steel use in new office buildings has already fallen by two thirds in the United States since the sixties, in favor of less energy-intensive steel-reinforced concrete. In 1993, a concrete that contains thousands of hair-sized steel wires instead of standard reinforcing

bars was developed in France. It is strong enough to do the work of conventional concrete that is three to four times as thick. Such technological improvements are particularly useful for developing countries.[24]

Several recent projects demonstrate the environmental and economic advantages of rehabilitation over construction from scratch.

Builders can also make materials go even further by reusing and recycling them. In this respect, inorganic materials actually tend to work better than wood. Bricks and manageably sized concrete blocks are easy to rescue intact from a building destined for demolition, and can last for millennia. St. Albans Abbey, still standing in southern England, was built 900 years ago partly out of bricks from nearby Roman ruins now twice as old. Monolithic concrete—cast into large molds on-site to make entire walls—can also be crushed and mixed with additional cement to make new concrete, an increasingly common practice as landfilling becomes more costly. A demolition crew in Sydney, Australia, recently knocked down an entire skyscraper, sorted the glass, steel, and concrete, and sent it all off to the recyclers.[25]

Finding new customers for short, nail-filled wood timbers can be more difficult, but some companies have begun to turn wood and other tree products into new beams and panels by grinding them down and reusing the fiber—in a process similar to paper recycling. One start-up company in California makes a material from old newspapers, cardboard boxes, and timbers that is carefully molded to maximize strength while minimizing weight. It is likely that entire homes could soon be built from beams, studs, and panels made from gridcore, as the product is known. The company has already picked up some high-profile customers, including the electronics giant Sony and some Hollywood studios.[26]

Wood, though, can only be recycled a limited number of times because—as with paper—the organic fibers degrade each time they are processed. Some parts of the world—particularly where the building stock is growing rapidly—may have to move away from wood altogether. People in climates where organic materials are sparse have long made their dwellings out of the earth itself, a material with many environmental advantages. Ancient Chinese builders rammed mud into rigid molds to make the Great Wall. Archaeologists have found millennia-old adobes (sun-dried mud bricks) in the Indus Valley and the Middle East. And much of Europe, from the British Isles to the Balkans, turned to adobe and rammed earth after razing their own forests. Today, roughly two fifths of humanity lives in earthen dwellings.[27]

Unlike concrete and brick, rammed earth or adobe bricks do not require energy-intensive high-temperature firing. Earth suitable for construction lies close at hand in many parts of the world, which keeps transportation impacts low, and traditional earthen building techniques involve little machinery and much hand labor—a balance that still works well in developing countries, where jobs and capital are scarce. Builders in Niger and Mali, for example, have worked with a French nongovernmental organization called Development Workshop since 1980 to perfect a new technique for capping hundreds of their buildings with earthen domed roofs, using no wood, but remaining strong, safe, and water-resistant.[28]

In industrial countries, where labor is much more expensive, some companies have mechanized earth building in order to compete with standard materials. Small diesel- or electricity-powered machines that make as many as 900 compressed earth blocks per hour have been commercialized in Australia, Germany, Switzerland, and the United States. The ecological price of using these machines—in terms of energy use and pollution generated—is one fortieth that for concrete.[29]

DESIGNING WITH CLIMATE

Le Corbusier, creator of the residential high rise, proclaimed prophetically in 1937, "I propose one single building for all nations and climates." His gray concrete monoliths, which once would have been livable nowhere, are now lived in everywhere—with air conditioners, elevators, and showers kept running on massive energy and water flows.[30]

The use of remote fossil fuel and water supplies has made obsolete an essential part of traditional architecture: using craft to make the most of local, often scarce resources. Whereas architects once carefully sited buildings close to water supplies or to capture prevailing breezes or the winter sun, they now shape, size, and position their structures according to other expedients—confident that hidden, energy-guzzling mechanical systems will compensate for what would otherwise be ludicrous design.

The most resource-efficient approach to architecture is to shun the use of machinery in favor of careful manipulation of the basic elements of design, often employing ancient techniques. The result is structures tailored to harness natural forces—for example, wind and sun—at times while buffering against them at others, in order to create comfortable indoor climates through all seasons at minimal environmental cost.

Since about two thirds of the energy used in buildings goes into producing an artificial indoor climate—heating, cooling, ventilation, and lighting—the potential savings from designs that co-opt natural forces to do the same thing can be quite large. The methods, though, vary from structure to structure. Small buildings in cold climates have a lot of heat-leaking exterior surface for the amount of indoor space, which makes insulation a priority. In contrast, large buildings lose less heat when it is cold outside, and gain less when it is warm—but special design techniques are needed to make the most of what little sunlight they capture for illumination. Climate-sensitive design must also, by definition, adapt to regional variations in the availability of resources like sunlight, wind, and rain. For both of these reasons, resource-efficient buildings tend to vary in design more than resource-wasting ones do.[31]

Like warm-blooded animals, all buildings—but particularly small ones—need effective skins to control internal temperatures throughout the day and the year. The oil shocks of the seventies catapulted this simple idea into the public consciousness in many countries, leading millions to add insulation to their walls and roofs and to weatherstrip their windows. Partly as a result, the amount of external heating required for each square meter in an average home in the United States was cut by more than 40 percent between 1973 and 1990; in Denmark, the reduction was more than 46 percent.[32]

Meanwhile, some builders discovered that designing from the ground up for airtightness and thermal integrity can reduce energy use even more dramatically. During the past decade, more than 100,-000 "superinsulated" homes with extra-thick insulation and careful construction

to block air leaks have been built in Scandinavia and North America. So hermetic are these homes that the warmth wafting up from people, lights, and appliances goes a long way toward heating the entire space.[33]

Climate-sensitive design must, by definition, adapt to regional variations in the availability of resources like sunlight, wind, and rain.

New technologies have particularly revolutionized windows, which are often the leakiest parts of buildings. Advanced windows—those with two or three panes of glass separated by thin, insulating layers of argon gas, and even with thin metallic coatings that allow visible light to pass but block invisible infrared radiation (which transmits only heat)—are increasingly popular in industrial countries. The residential market share in the United States for these types of windows rose from 1 percent in 1985 to 38 percent in 1991. (See Figure 6-2.)[34]

This shift now saves homeowners

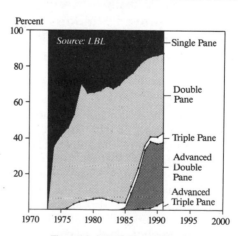

Figure 6-2. U.S. Residential Market for Various Glazing Technologies, 1974–91

some $5 billion in heating and cooling bills each year—an impressive figure, but one that falls far short of the $22 billion additional savings that is technologically feasible. Not only can advanced windows insulate as much as six times as well as traditional single-pane glazings, but by admitting sunlight, they can actually capture more energy than they lose. Winning entries built for the Canadian government's Advanced Houses competition demonstrated that even at high latitudes, homes that combine improved windows with superinsulation can get half of their heat from the winter sun.[35]

The basic principles of solar architecture date back at least to the ancient Greeks, who, confronted with a fuelwood supply crisis, turned to the sun for their heat. Though they lacked glass for windows, the Greeks oriented many of their buildings with large south-facing openings. These captured rays from the sun in winter, when it rode low in the sky—exactly when it was most needed and most scarce. But during the summer, when the sun climbed high overhead, much less sunlight would enter.[36]

Even at high latitudes, homes that combine improved windows with superinsulation can get half of their heat from the winter sun.

In hotter climates more common to developing countries, the design challenge is not making the most of solar heat, but getting rid of it. Along with proper solar orientation, deep eaves and recessed windows can shield buildings from the sun. Studies also suggest that planting trees around some buildings can provide enough shade to cut cooling needs by 30 percent. And light-colored roofing and cladding materials that reflect sunlight can cut peak cooling needs by as much as 40 percent.[37]

Some architects also exploit a technique known as daylighting, which supplants artificial light with sunlight by using skylights, atria, and other approaches. For schools and offices that are occupied primarily during the day, daylighting is particularly cost-effective in cutting peak electricity demand. At the same time, it improves lighting quality, aesthetics, and worker satisfaction—benefits that may outrank the energy gains. Top executives in one Chicago skyscraper vie not for window offices but for rooms fronting onto one of three daylit atria. Technologies such as window-mounted mirrors, or "light shelves," can deflect the sun's rays deep into a building, spreading the benefits of daylighting in a more egalitarian fashion.[38]

Another important technique that architects in temperate climates are rediscovering is thermal storage. Like reservoirs that set aside water from heavy rains to tide cities over during dry times, thermal storage allows buildings to make more flexible, efficient use of heat from the sun. Many traditional cultures in dry climates, from the Ladakhi in the Himalaya to the Pueblo in what is now New Mexico, built their homes with massive adobe walls that absorbed the sun's heat during the day and returned it to the air at night, moderating temperatures around the clock. Many builders today use water tanks, clay tiles, or adobe bricks to perform the same service.[39]

Taken together, climate-sensitive design could cut heating and cooling energy use by 70 percent in residential buildings, and total energy use by 60 percent in commercial buildings in the United States, according to scientists at the National Renewable Energy Laboratory (NREL) in Golden, Colorado. Many examples already suggest that these estimates are quite conservative. In fact, two NREL researchers used solar design and superinsulation to cut their home's heating bills to one fortieth those of its neighbors. Not far away, the Rocky Mountain Institute's headquarters in Snowmass, Colorado, gains 99 percent of its heat from the sun (and from the people and appliances inside) despite a frigid mountain climate.[40]

Perhaps no one has gone as far in integrating climate-sensitive design techniques into modern building forms as Malaysian architect Ken Yeang. In designing his skyscrapers, Yeang first orients his buildings to minimize solar gain and to capture prevailing breezes to assist natural ventilation. He then incorporates sun shading—often with vegetation-filled balconies or courtyards high above the ground—to further reduce solar gain. In addition, wind ducts draw fresh air into the inner areas of the building. Yeang hopes to provide a model for other architects, particularly those in developing countries, to pursue designs adapted to their specific climate instead of simply producing a cookie cutter rendition of the standard Chicago or New York high rise.[41]

MACHINES FOR LIVING

Although environmentally concerned designers always seek first to minimize the need for electrical and mechanical systems, it is nearly impossible to provide all modern amenities without them. And since it is difficult to incorporate climate-sensitive design into a structure after it is built, most improvements can be made by enhancing add-ons such as heaters, lights, and plumbing fixtures. The challenge in every modern building is to use machinery to provide the

amenities people expect but with a minimum of environmental damage. The result will often be buildings that are more pleasing and productive for their inhabitants.

Unfortunately, the very complexity of machinery can lead to waste. Because mechanical systems are hard to understand and harder to see, even efficient ones often malfunction and are not repaired. In U.S. homes with forced-air climate control, up to 30 percent of heating and cooling energy escapes unnoticed from leaky or uninsulated duct work. Anecdotes of long-unobserved malfunctions are common in commercial buildings as well. Thus the first challenge in making modern building systems efficient is designing them to be easier to monitor, maintain, and fix.[42]

Nevertheless, well-designed technologies can generate dramatic improvements in the efficiency and livability of buildings. The history of lighting has demonstrated this repeatedly. Incandescent lamps are more than 10 times as efficient as oil lamps, provide better light, and are more convenient. Modern fluorescent lights are four times as efficient again, last even longer, and produce light of comparable quality. The compact fluorescent lamp (CFL) that can replace the incandescent bulb has caught on in recent years, capturing 15 percent of the market. In Japan, where electricity is expensive, savings can reach $40 per bulb; not surprisingly, CFLs now fill 80 percent of the country's home fixtures.[43]

Likewise, though the remaining potential is large, household appliances and fixtures such as furnaces, toilets, and air conditioners have all become more efficient in recent years, more than covering the sometimes higher up-front costs. (See Table 6–2.) Electricity use in new U.S. refrigerators, for instance, fell roughly by half between 1972 and 1992, thanks to better insulation, more-effi-

Table 6-2. Resource Consumption of New U.S. Appliances and Prototypes in Early Nineties, Compared with Average Appliance Sold in 1985

Technology	Average For Sale, Early Nineties	Best For Sale, Early Nineties	Prototypes
	(percent reduction[1])		
Electricity			
Refrigerator	18	35	55–82
Central Air Conditioner	5	45	52–59
Water Heater	6	66	71–77
Gas			
Furnace	8	23	23
Water Heater	8	20	36
Cooking Range	20	40	60
Water			
Toilet	54	100[2]	100[2]
Showerhead	38	50	63

[1]Indicates reduction in resource use compared with average of appliances that were for sale in 1985.
[2]Composting and incinerating toilets use no water.
SOURCE: Howard S. Geller, "Energy-Efficient Appliances: Performance Issues and Policy Options," *IEEE Technology and Society Magazine,* March 1986; Mark D. Levine et al., "Electricity End-Use Efficiency: Experience with Technologies, Markets, and Policies Throughout the World," American Council for an Energy-Efficient Economy (ACEEE), Washington, D.C., 1992; John Morrill, ACEEE, Washington, D.C., private communication, May 21, 1993; Steven Nadel et al., "Emerging Technologies in the Residential & Commercial Sectors," ACEEE, Washington, D.C., 1993; Amy Vickers, "Water-Use Efficiency Standards for Plumbing Fixtures: Benefits of National Legislation," *Journal of the American Water Works Association,* May 1990; Amy Vickers, Amy Vickers & Associates, Boston, Mass., private communication, September 6, 1994.

cient electric motors, and other modest improvements; a new model introduced in 1994 uses even 30 percent less electricity. Other technologies likely to enter the market during the next decade could cut total appliance energy and water use by more than 25 percent.[44]

In buildings where cooling is a big energy user, every efficiency improvement carries an extra financial bonus, since the less power a machine consumes, the less heat it generates. Engineers can specify a smaller air conditioning system, which reduces the capital and operating costs of the new structure. Also, energy-efficient buildings often have more usable space. Since they need less cooling, smaller air-handling ducts and blowers can be used, allowing designers to reduce the hidden area between floors. So much space can be saved that

for each four stories, a fifth one can be added in a highly efficient structure, giving the developer more square meters to rent or sell, and making the project more profitable.[45]

To reduce consumption of scarce or polluting resources even further, renewable, on-site supplies can be tapped. For example, most buildings could easily be made to channel rain into toilet tanks instead of sloughing it off into storm drains. Solar water heaters, once popular in California and Florida before the advent of cheap fossil fuels, experienced a revival after World War II and again after the Arab oil embargo of 1973, particularly in countries concerned about availability of fuel supplies. More than 900,000 solar units in Israel heat 83 percent of the country's domestic hot water, and in Japan, some 4.5 million units were installed by 1992. Thousands more are used in developing countries, including Botswana, Colombia, and Kenya.[46]

As solar cell prices continue to fall (see Chapter 4), integrating them right into a building's facade or roof, rather than attaching separate solar panels, may soon become common. The large German glass manufacturer Flachglas has integrated solar cells into a semitransparent window glazing that provides filtered light while generating electricity. The company has installed several grid-connected prototypes in commercial buildings in seven German cities. Meanwhile, companies in Japan, Switzerland, and the United States are testing new types of solar cells that also function as roofing shingles. In western Germany, rooftop photovoltaics on existing buildings could generate up to 50 gigawatts, or one quarter of the region's total current power output. Even in the cloudy United Kingdom, the potential in recladding building facades with solar cells is estimated to equal half the country's power supply.[47]

As designers push the technological limits of efficiency, pieces of building machinery that were once separate become connected. For instance, water consumption can be dramatically reduced by simply rerouting "gray water" from sinks and baths to toilets. Similarly, buildings that need plenty of artificial heat can capture the waste heat during on-site electricity generation from combusting natural gas in small engines or from battery-like devices called fuel cells. A single system could then provide heating, cooling, hot water, and power for ventilation, lights, and appliances.[48]

One of the best-known interactions between separate building functions is the tension between the need for fresh air and the energy benefits of supertight construction. Most superinsulated homes resolve this conflict with mechanical ventilators with built-in heat exchangers. These transfer heat from the exhaust to the cool incoming air (and vice versa in summer), assuring a fresh air supply while minimizing heat loss. Using this arrangement, the 10 winners in Canada's Advanced Houses competition require so little artificial warmth that the heater has become a small add-on to the ventilation system.[49]

Companies in Japan, Switzerland, and the United States are testing new types of solar cells that also function as roofing shingles.

Most researchers believe that energy efficiency measures need not preclude healthy indoor air. Rather, the problem usually lies in the sources of indoor pollutants, such as cigarette smoke, VOCs, and radon (which seeps into buildings from the earth). In designing healthy buildings, it is best to attack both sides of the problem at once, making sure that ventilation systems are adequate while selecting paints and furniture that do not contain VOCs, and sealing basement walls and floors.[50]

Recent projects have demonstrated that integrating a variety of environmental design features makes buildings more attractive, healthy, and productive places to be. One of the best examples is the government-initiated Ecolonia housing project in the Netherlands. Each of 101 homes had to satisfy stringent requirements on materials choices, energy efficiency, and indoor air quality, while undertaking additional measures in one of these areas. Some save rainwater for the toilet tanks; some are roofed with sod; and most use solar water heaters and recycled concrete. All the units pay particular attention to the choice of paint and materials to avoid indoor pollution.[51]

Because they were pioneering, experimental buildings, Ecolonia's homes cost roughly 10 percent more than the typical Dutch house, but buyers quickly snatched them up anyway, and are apparently quite pleased. One mother says, "We want to stay here forever," because her five-year-old daughter no longer gets serious asthma attacks.[52]

Pleasant and healthy buildings translate into more productive employees who are more likely to show up for work.

Commercial building occupants are more interested in what the quality of a work space might do for employee productivity. For a typical company, employees' salaries are so high that a productivity boost of just 2 percent is worth more than eliminating utility bills entirely. At the ING Bank, one surprising result of the energy-efficient design was a 15-percent drop in employee absenteeism. Thus, pleasant and healthy buildings translate into more productive employees who are more likely to show up for work.[53]

Indeed, a recent review of eight buildings by Joseph Romm of the U.S. Department of Energy and William Browning of the Rocky Mountain Institute identified a gain of 6–16 percent in the productivity of people who work in such buildings. A new facility for Lockheed Corporation in Sunnyvale, California, that uses daylighting, automatic light dimmers, and other features cut lighting bills by 75 percent, with the measures paying for themselves through reduced energy costs in four years. And the higher quality lighting along with other measures reportedly led to a 15-percent increase in worker productivity, a bonus that dwarfed the energy savings by a factor of four.[54]

BLUEPRINT FOR BETTER BUILDINGS

When projects like Ecolonia and the Lockheed building demonstrate how much better the bulk of today's buildings could be, and at comparable cost, it is hard to understand why this is not happening everywhere. Experience over the past two decades has shown that changing how buildings are made and run does not come easily. The obstacles are various and knotty, ranging from a lack of information and the complexity of the industry to economic policies that favor virgin materials extraction over recycling. Making the global building industry sustainable will require that everyone from architects to government policymakers takes action on many fronts.

Unlike the automotive industry, the building business is fragmented in most market economies, and its patrons are generally far from being educated consumers. As many as 25 independent actors—from developers and mechanical engineers to bankers and maintenance staff—can be involved in the design, construction, and operation of a single office building in the United States. Each participant behaves according to the imperative he or she faces, whether that be minimizing up-front costs, maximizing a commission, or meeting a deadline. The industry produces what is best for it: generic, quick-to-build structures that tend to neglect long-term costs and health concerns. Meanwhile, future occupants often lack the knowledge or tools to gauge a structure for some of the key characteristics they care about: low running costs and healthy interiors.[55]

Centrally planned economies have traditionally produced even worse buildings, as meeting production quotas overrode concerns for quality. Lacking thermostats, Russians often resort to opening windows to cool down over-heated apartments. Chinese buildings use three times as much energy for heating as comparable U.S. buildings, even though inside temperatures remain colder.[56]

Buildings like the ING Bank and the National Audubon Society headquarters illustrate that the team-oriented management style that helps Japanese car companies focus on customer concerns works for buildings too. Both projects brought engineers, architects, contractors, interior designers, scientists, building managers, and occupants together in a working group so that each could learn how the decisions he or she made affected others and the project as a whole—an experience that can be surprisingly rewarding.[57]

This integrative process seems so critical to sustainable buildings that "before you design a building, you have to redesign the building process," says John Picard, a Los Angeles-based consultant. In fact, major Japanese construction firms already combine design, engineering, construction, maintenance, and building operation services under one roof, though in their case the environment is no more of a concern than it is elsewhere.[58]

Reinventing the industry will require changing the values it holds as a culture, and the process by which they are transmitted: education. This is being done in some places. A U.K. government-industry collaboration resulted in the 1994 publication of an environmental code of practice for buildings by the Building Services Research and Information Association. It sold 700 copies—more than any of their other publications—in its first three months alone. The American Institute of Architects publishes an Environmental Resource Guide that covers energy, land use, and detailed assessments of the impacts of various materials. For the broadest impact, such educa-tional material needs to enter the curricula of schools of architecture, engineering, and related disciplines. Professional schools also need to focus on integrative, interdisciplinary design processes.[59]

Flagship projects, such as Ecolonia, Canada's Advanced Houses, and the ING Bank headquarters, are an effective way to educate professionals and the public. The ING Bank, for example, is now the best known building in the Netherlands, according to national surveys.[60]

Other countries are beginning to launch high-profile demonstration projects. On Earth Day 1993, President Bill Clinton announced the "Greening of the White House." By late 1994, some 50 steps had been initiated, including a retrofit of lighting and water fixtures to improve efficiency, with additional measures planned for the next 20 years. The demonstration value of a project like this—capable of reaching 1.5 million visitors a year—is far greater than the immediate savings. And in mid-1994, the Thai government announced it would put up a 25-story office building in Bangkok that aims to use only a fifth of the energy of a standard building. It hopes to stimulate the use of passive design and advanced cooling technologies suited to tropical climates.[61]

Governments can work in a variety of ways to influence the building process directly. Building codes and appliance standards have long helped make buildings more energy- and water-efficient, and industrial countries are extending these to protect indoor air quality in commercial buildings. Such codes are particularly critical for developing countries, where building booms are driving up energy and water use. Rapid development of offices, stores, and homes presents these countries with a fleeting and valuable opportunity to curtail resource waste in buildings for decades to come.

Mexico adopted strict national limits on water use in new plumbing fixtures in 1989 as part of a program to reduce per capita water use by a sixth in its water-poor capital. And in 1994, Thailand, facing rapid growth in electricity consumption, adopted a building code much like those in the United States.[62]

Enforcing codes, though, may be difficult, especially in developing countries where governance is often weak. China, for instance, has required new apartments to be 30 percent more efficient since 1986, a level raised to 50 percent in 1993, but the code has been ignored by builders and local governments alike. Even in affluent countries, code violations often escape the notice of inspectors.[63]

Governments are experimenting with a variety of market-stimulating techniques to overcome the myriad obstacles to good design.

Codes and standards, though important, do little to educate consumers or encourage builders to innovate beyond the norm—both of which are essential to the development of a vibrant, environmentally conscious building market in the long run. As New York architect Randolph Croxton attests, any developer who proudly claims that a structure "meets every code" may actually be making a confession: "If I built this building any worse, it would be against the law." As a result, governments are experimenting with a variety of market-stimulating techniques to overcome the myriad obstacles to good design. One approach would replace codes with a "feebate" system that charged less-efficient structures a fee for connections to energy and water utilities; this revenue would then be used to reward builders of more-efficient buildings.[64]

Some independent home builders have already proved that environmental design can attract buyers. A major selling point for Bigelow Homes in Chicago, for example, is that it guarantees homeowners a rebate if their winter heating bills ever exceed $200 per heating season during the first three years. It has only had to make good on its promise four times since 1985. Nick Martin, a developer in Nottingham, England, had not even broken ground on a pioneering "environmentally correct" housing project before there were six times more interested buyers than homes planned by mid-1993.[65] *People want good if they know*

Governments in several countries are using voluntary rating systems to spread environmental marketing to a much larger portion of the building industry, and to spur the adoption of environmentally responsible design. The U.K. government started grading buildings in 1991, awarding points for features that go beyond code requirements to save energy and water, increase recycled materials use, lower toxic materials use, or reduce local environmental impacts. By mid-1994, more than 25 percent of new commercial building construction was being rated, with schemes under way for new homes and existing buildings. Some British real estate agents now use high environmental marks to promote their properties.[66]

Interest in this approach is growing in the rest of Europe, with governments in France, Norway, and Spain closest to adopting their own systems. In British Columbia, the building industry has launched a rating system for commercial facilities, and in the United States, the nonprofit Green Building Council is exploring a related plan. In countries with great climatic and geographical variety, such as the United States, rating systems should vary regionally, leaving ample room for local organizations to contribute. Austin, Texas, for example, already has a 10-year-old Green Builder program that includes a simple rating system.[67]

A variant on rating systems is labelling programs. In 1980, the Canadian government began a voluntary certification system for energy-efficient houses. Although only 8,000 homes have undergone certification to earn the "R-2000" imprimatur, the program helped commercialize and popularize a number of efficient technologies. The government revised the standard in 1994 to add requirements on materials selection and indoor toxics sources.[68]

Support from financial institutions is also crucial to transforming the building market. Since most structures are put up or purchased with borrowed money, banks, insurance companies, and other lenders have enormous influence over what gets built. Traditionally, lenders have treated innovation with skepticism—and higher interest rates—since it increases the perceived risk of a project. But recently a number of banks, often prompted by governments, have realized that by lowering utility bills, resource-efficient building designs leave owners more money to repay loans, reducing the risk of default. The Bank of Montreal, for example, cuts the interest rate on loans for R-2000 homes by a quarter point.[69]

Sweden subsidizes loans for energy-efficient homes, a program that has helped push the Swedish building industry to high standards of efficiency, affordability, and quality. In the United States, "energy-efficient mortgages," which lower the income requirements on energy-efficient homes, have been available through federal and state lending agencies as well as private banks for more than a decade. Still, most U.S. financial institutions resist making more significant changes.[70]

Multilateral financial institutions, led by the World Bank, could help developing countries improve their fast-growing building stock. The Bank loans hundreds of millions of dollars each year to East European and developing countries for housing-related projects; it has recently emphasized improving the institutional framework of housing ministries, mainly to remove barriers to housing construction, and providing adequate water and sanitation services in burgeoning cities. But in its effort to ensure basic housing services, the Bank has so far failed to include specific measures to improve energy and water efficiency or, more generally, to adopt the broad goals of sustainable development in the building sector.[71]

Electric, natural gas, and water utilities can also play a big role in ensuring efficient use of natural resources. To avoid expensive new power plants, some electric utilities provide incentives to building owners to upgrade lights and appliances. A few North American energy utilities have started helping home buyers with the down payments on new houses that are energy-efficient. Ontario Hydro offers rebates to design teams to cut energy use in new buildings, and provides additional money once savings are demonstrated. New Brunswick Power also tenders rebates for R-2000 homes, which is one reason these now account for a fifth of the new homes built in that province—the highest rate in Canada. Water and energy utilities could also perform home inspections on a regular basis, checking for inefficient heaters and fixtures, and for leaky duct work and pipes.[72]

In addition, governments can develop constructive partnerships with industry. One consequence of the competitive, fragmented nature of the industry in many countries is that architectural, engineering, and construction firms are too financially insecure to invest in R&D. Production of some components, such as windows and ceiling tiles, tends to be more concentrated, and here innovation continues at a steady pace. What can result, for example, is a home with state-of-the-art windows but leaky walls. Research into design as an integrated discipline is thus crucial to better buildings. The Swedish government spends far more on building research than most countries per capita, another reason that Swedish homes have earned a reputation for comfort and efficiency.[73]

The U.S. Environmental Protection Agency has developed an innovative set of voluntary programs to spur businesses to upgrade their facilities. The Green Lights program, which has more than 1,500 participants so far, will eventually reduce lighting energy use by about half in at least 5 percent of U.S. commercial floor space. The Energy Star Buildings program, inaugurated in 1994, carries the approach further, guiding building managers through a series of steps to improve air quality and cut energy use in existing structures an impressive 50 percent—all while saving money.[74]

Perhaps no country has moved as aggressively as the Netherlands in formulating a broad program. The Dutch campaign is part of the country's 1989 National Environment Policy Plan (NEPP), updated in 1993, which addresses a wide spectrum of environmental issues. Among the goals of NEPP's sustainable housing initiative are improving energy efficiency by 25 percent in new and renovated buildings by the year 2000, increasing the reuse and recycling of construction and demolition waste from 60 percent in 1990 to 90 percent by 2000, cutting in half the use of toxic materials such as oil-based paints, and eliminating the use of unsustainably produced tropical timber.[75]

Since 1990, the Dutch government has worked with developers, contractors, building associations, and residents' associations to assemble an action plan to meet NEPP goals. Meanwhile, a nongovernmental organization, the Association for Integral Biological Architecture (VIBA), runs an information center that recently received government funding; some 100 companies sell "green" products there certified by VIBA and provide information for builders and architects. The government has also backed high-profile demonstration projects, such as Ecolonia, to point up the advantages of the new approach to design.[76]

In addition, NEPP calls for taxes on virgin materials and on waste disposal to ensure that prices for fossil fuels, metals, and wood reflect their full environmental cost. These would encourage recycling of building materials and more efficient use of fuels and water. The Dutch and others hope that assessing environmental taxes will help consumers incorporate these costs into their day-to-day economic decisions.[77]

If governments balance such increases with cuts in other taxes—on labor, for example—the net impact can actually be positive, encouraging efficiency and increasing employment. Governments can also channel a small percentage of the money into research and development, helping to accelerate the decline in the costs of resource-efficient construction.[78]

The building industry, like any other, is a creature of its environment. If governments shift the economic calculus of the marketplace toward sustainability, and buyers match this with demands for better buildings, the industry could evolve quite rapidly.

What must ultimately change are people's values, both as citizens and consumers. The most lasting legacy our generation can leave for the next is not simply a better building stock but a new building ethic: one that recognizes the relationship between the built environment and the natural one.

7

Facing China's Limits

Megan Ryan and Christopher Flavin

For millennia, Chinese literature and philosophy have included two themes that resonate powerfully in today's world: harmony with nature and commitment to family—not only the current generation, but past and future ones as well. More than most major civilizations, China's traditions and philosophies are attuned to the modern concept of a sustainable society—one that meets the needs of current generations without sacrificing the health of the natural environment or the options available to their descendants.[1]

As the twentieth century draws to a close, however, China is putting the concept of sustainable development to a severe test, and on an unprecedented scale. With 1.2 billion people—one fifth of the world—now taking eagerly to Deng Xiaopeng's belief that "to get rich is glorious," China's use of natural resources is growing at staggering rates. If recent growth patterns continue, China's use of coal will double in the next 16 years, and its consumption of grain will rise by 40 percent. Emissions of some air and water pollutants are growing even more rapidly.[2]

China's dilemma is that it has a huge population but a far smaller slice of the world's resources. (See Table 7–1.) It is roughly the same size as the United States but has four and a half times as many people. With 22 percent of the world's population, China has only 7 percent of its fresh water and cropland, 3 percent of its forests, and 2 percent of its oil.

Despite these limits, China has managed reasonably well as a rural, agricultural, and relatively poor country. It has made substantial progress in reducing poverty, improving nutrition, and providing basic amenities such as health care and education to its people in recent decades. But with its economy now doubling in size roughly every eight years, China's shortage of resources threatens to become a serious impediment to its development plans.[3]

Its Asian neighbors, such as Japan and South Korea, have sidestepped similar dilemmas by importing much of their resources, including food, oil, and wood products, while exporting manufactured goods and pollution to countries where the extractive and dirtier industries are located. But China's size precludes this option. Recent projections cast doubt on the ability of the rest of the world to supply all the oil or food that this country may require in the decades ahead. Trying to do so could drive up world prices for basic resources, and might push parts of China out of some

Table 7-1. China's Share of World Population, Economic Output, Natural Resources, and Selected Pollutants, Circa 1990

Category	Share of World Total
	(percent)
Population	22
Economic Output[1]	7
Cropland	7
Irrigated Land	19
Forests and Woodlands	3
Protected Land	4
Roundwood Production	8
Fresh Water	7
Carbon Emissions	11
Sulfur Emissions	16
Oil Reserves	2
Coal Reserves	11

[1]Based on purchasing power parity.
SOURCE: Worldwatch estimates based on World Resources Institute, *World Resources 1994–95* (New York: Oxford University Press, 1994), on British Petroleum, *BP Statistical Review of World Energy* (London: 1993), and on Lester R. Brown, Hal Kane, and David Malin Roodman, *Vital Signs 1994* (New York: W.W. Norton & Company, 1994) for sulfur emissions.

key import markets.

Ongoing trends are also placing severe stress on the domestic environment, dirtying the air and water, and further undermining the health of China's cropland, forests, and fisheries. Already, its cities have air that is dangerous to breathe, and many regions are running short of water. Although a traditional development strategy might allow millions of Chinese to enter the middle class, the quality of life of the majority would be at risk.

The challenge for China, therefore, is to meet the expanding needs of its citizens while gradually moving onto a sus-

tainable development path, one that protects the quality of its own environment and does not make excessive demands on the world's resources. To do so, it can learn from sustainable development efforts in other parts of the world—from Costa Rica to Kerala, India. But no other society of remotely similar size has made a serious effort to pursue sustainable development. Among the major challenges are building an energy system that does not rely so heavily on coal, providing a nutritious and satisfying diet that does not stretch food production limits too far, and using water and forestry products much more efficiently.[4]

China's challenge is the world's, for the success of this huge country in forging a new development strategy will affect all others.

China's efforts will be complicated by the fact that the country is undergoing a series of historic economic, political, and social transformations that will test it in many ways. Attempts to establish a market economy, democratize the political system, protect human rights, and extend the country's social advances are all intricately linked to the goal of sustainable development. Progress in each of these areas is critical, and failure to move forward could lead to social strife and political breakdown.

Ultimately, China's challenge is the world's, for the success of this huge country in forging a new development strategy will affect all others. Like most developing countries, China has until recently had minimal effect on global environmental trends. But as its economy grows, it will begin challenging the far less populous United States as the leading contributor to many global problems. As China faces its limits, many of its development plans will have to be reconsidered; as other countries encounter the global limits raised by China's growth, they will have to reevaluate their own unsustainable economic plans as well.

CHINA RISING

Though its civilization is 4,000 years old, few countries have ever changed as rapidly as China is today. With so many economic, social, and political transformations going on simultaneously, it is hardly surprising that the China of the mid-nineties is a land of extraordinary contradictions. Despite the continuing reign of a government run by old-line Communists in their eighties, China is in a state of economic flux.

These days, the streets of Shanghai are filled with Japanese auto executives, U.S. investment bankers, and Russian entrepreneurs gathering up running shoes and radios for Vladivostok. Those same streets are traversed by young Chinese in miniskirts next to peasant farmers pulling rice-laden rickshaws. Yet amid the excitement surrounding this economic "miracle," many observers seem to have lost sight of the unique scale—and stakes—of the Chinese boom.

Virtually any discussion of China begins with the staggering size of its population. In 1994, more people lived in this one country than in all of Europe, Russia, North America, Japan, and Australia combined. China added some 13 million people to its numbers that year— the equivalent of adding another Sweden and Norway to its population.[5]

China has long had the world's largest population—430 million in the middle of the nineteenth century—but its numbers have ballooned since the revolution, more than doubling between 1950 and 1994. In the early years of the Communist reign, these trends were applauded. For example, Chairman Mao Zedong wrote in 1949: "It is a very good thing that China has a big population. Even if China's population multiplies many times, she is fully capable of finding a solution; the solution is production."[6]

This attitude did not last. As infant mortality was reduced in the sixties, it became clear that surging population growth would strain even the most ambitious production goals. In the early seventies, the government established a series of progressively more stringent population goals and family planning programs. In 1979, the one-child policy was introduced, which soon made it illegal in most provinces to have two children. Fertility fell sharply from 5.8 births per woman in 1970 to 2 in the early nineties, and the population growth rate declined from 2.7 percent a year to 1.1 percent. Today, the fertility rate in China is actually lower than in the United States, but the growth rate is roughly 60 percent higher. Because of this, demographic momentum is projected to take the population from the current 1.2 billion to 1.4 billion by 2010.[7]

China's population is often viewed as homogenous by outsiders, and for such a large country the regional and ethnic differences are indeed relatively modest. Some 92 percent of China's people are Han Chinese, and most of them speak the Mandarin Chinese of northern China. But the country does have a number of ethnic minorities, mainly in the rugged West.[8]

Even after the industrialization drives of the Communist era, China remained (and still is) a largely rural and agricultural country in which less than 30 percent of the people live in cities. Yet ever since Mao's death in 1976 and Deng

Xiaopeng's subsequent endorsement of market reforms, China has pursued an aggressive, market-oriented economic strategy in which "socialism" is more a slogan than a daily reality.[9]

The Chinese have taken to capitalism with a vengeance, particularly in the South. Where business owners were once jailed as "enemies of the people," they now drive Mercedes and vacation in Hawaii. Private companies and township and village enterprises now produce about half of China's industrial output. An estimated two thirds of the gross national product (GNP) is currently generated outside the state sector, remarkably similar to the economic makeup of France or Italy.[10]

The economy grew on average 8.4 percent annually between 1978 and 1992—faster than in any other major country—rising to a rate of more than 10 percent in the early nineties. (See Figure 7-1). Forecasters expect the size of the economy to double again by shortly after 2000. According to standard figures, China's per capita income in 1991 was only $370 per year. Adjusting that figure to account for the domestic purchasing power of China's currency, however, brings per capita income closer to

Table 7-2. Consumption Trends in China, 1978 and 1992

Goods Consumed	1978	1992
Consumption per capita of:	(kilograms)	
Grain	196.0	234.6
Edible oil	1.6	6.2
Pork	7.7	18.1
Sugar	3.4	5.3
Ownership of consumer durables:	(per 100 people)	
Sewing machines	3.5	12.8
Bicycles	7.7	38.5
Televisions	0.3	19.5
Housing space per person:	(square meters)	
Cities	3.6	6.9
Village	8.1	18.9

SOURCES: 1992 data from State Statistical Bureau, *China Statistical Yearbook* (Beijing: 1993); 1978 data from *Economic and Political Weekly*, June 26, 1993.

$3,000—more than two-and-a-half times the comparable figure for India.[11]

As incomes grow, so does the use of automobiles, appliances, and power plants. (See Table 7-2.) According to expatriate Xiao-huang Yin, "color TV sets, refrigerators, and VCRs, considered luxuries when I lived in China, can be found in almost every working-class urban household." By 1992, 83 percent of urban households had washing machines, 75 percent had color televisions, and 52 percent had refrigerators.[12]

The economic boom is surprisingly diversified, from tiny, primitive steel mills to an array of high-tech firms using advanced western and Japanese equipment to produce textiles, toys, and electronic appliances intended for export. Even services are booming, having surpassed agriculture in 1991 to become the second largest sector. The most rapid growth has occurred in the hun-

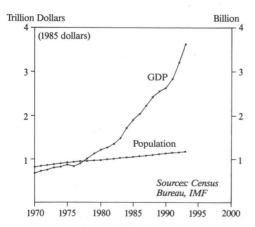

Figure 7-1. Population and Gross Domestic Product in China, 1970–93

dreds of special economic zones set up in various parts of China, although mainly in the south. These areas are free of the various restrictions that limit economic development in other regions.[13]

China's economy, largely isolated for three decades, is now a magnet for global investors. The country exported nearly $100 billion in goods in 1993, up nearly 50 percent from 1989, and imported $96 billion worth. The World Bank projects that China's trade will more than double in the next five years. Textiles and garments are the largest export earner, and the United States is the largest customer. Major imports include chemicals and electric power equipment. Much of the economic boom is financed by ethnic Chinese living abroad, who often combine business acumen with wealth and a familiarity with the language and culture. Hong Kong and Taiwan are rapidly being integrated into the Chinese economy—financial and managerial bases for enterprises located on the mainland.[14]

As many Chinese "get rich quick" and others are left behind, new social fractures common in other developing countries are opening up. Although migration was severely restricted in the past, millions of peasants are now leaving the countryside to improve their economic prospects. The government estimates that this "floating population" numbers more than 105 million. Although some find jobs, many are left destitute and without social services, since they are considered illegal migrants, ineligible for social services in urban areas. Urban poverty—which had been extremely low due to constraints on migration—is now growing, along with related ills such as crime, drug abuse, and prostitution. Rural crime increased 23 percent in 1993.[15]

China will soon become another Asian Tiger. The World Bank estimates that greater China (which includes Hong Kong and Taiwan) will have a slightly larger gross domestic product in 2002 than the United States (roughly $10 trillion). Lee Kuan Yew, former Prime Minister of Singapore, says, "The size of China's displacement of the world balance is such that the world must find a new balance in thirty to forty years." This is as true for the world's ecological equilibrium as it is for its economic or political stability. An unsustainable path could be disastrous for China—and for the rest of the world.[16]

DOWN TO THE LAST DROP

China's struggle to manage its waters goes back millennia. The Huang He (Yellow River) alone has broken through its dikes more than 1,500 times during the last 2,500 years, giving it the name "China's Sorrow." Although the country still fights to control its raging waters, recent decades have brought an additional struggle: harnessing a highly variable water supply to meet soaring water demands caused by growth in irrigation and industrial development. In northern China, supplies are so short that the government is considering a multibillion-dollar scheme to move water from south to north.[17]

The country has only 7 percent of the world's fresh water, and most of that is in the south. In recent decades, its water use has become a torrent: by the late eighties, when the current economic boom was just getting under way, usage was already nearly six times as high as in 1949. Agriculture claims the lion's share—87 percent—of the roughly 500 billion cubic meters of water that China uses each year. Fully 80 percent of China's grain—several times the figure in the United States—is grown on irrigated land, which has increased threefold since the fifties. China now has the world's most extensive irrigated area, a key to raising crop yields in recent decades.[18]

Water statistics for China are sometimes out of date or unreliable, but according to a 1987 estimate, industrial uses claimed only 7 percent, while residential uses claimed 6 percent. But this is changing rapidly as cities and industries expand. In late 1993, the Minister of Water Resources reported that more than 300 Chinese cities were short of water, with 100 in acute distress—at an estimated cost of $14 billion in lost economic output each year. If urban population grows to more than 600 million by 2010, as projected by China's Academy of Social Sciences, residential demand will soar, driven by rising use of flush toilets, showers, and washing machines.[19]

Water shortages are exacerbated by the fact that a growing share of "fresh" water is polluted. According to China's National Environmental Protection Agency, 60–70 percent of the recent shortfall results from pollution. This has led to shortages of clean water even in the humid south. Only 20 percent of industrial and residential wastewater receives even preliminary treatment, and pollution is spreading in rural areas as township and village enterprises spring up.[20]

Since the eighties, China has invested in several major water diversion works, including a 230-kilometer canal from the Luanhe River to Tianjin. In 1994, planners were debating an even more dramatic water rescue of the North China Plain, where the water table is dropping more than a meter annually. The plan is to carry water nearly 1,200 kilometers from the Yangtze Basin, at a cost of more than $5 billion. A canal would transport four times as much water as is used by New York City, or double the capacity of the largest diversion system in California. A lengthy fight over whether to approve the canal has begun.[21]

Recently, water conservation has received more attention as an alternative to costly supply projects, and leaders in southern China are calling on Beijing to fix its leaky toilets and poor pipes before asking the rest of the country to send water. President Jiang Zemin echoed these sentiments in 1994, saying, "If a country can send satellites and missiles into space, it should be able to dry up its toilets."[22]

Like many other countries, China wastes billions of tons of water through poor plumbing and inefficient production techniques. It takes two to three times as much water, for example, to make a ton of steel in China as it does in industrial countries, and producing a ton of newsprint consumes two to six times as much. But these rates are beginning to improve: In Dalian city, on the southern coast, an ambitious conservation program increased the rate of recycled-water use in industry to 80 percent, compared with the national average of 20 percent.[23]

Irrigation can also be made more efficient. On the North China Plain, 50–60 percent of irrigation water is lost to evaporation and seepage on its way to the fields. Although this is not as high as in some poor countries, it could be improved. Each kilogram of wheat in China takes 1,000 kilograms of water, compared with 600 kilograms in countries with more efficient systems. Farmers could benefit from more widespread use of microirrigation (in which water is delivered directly to crops' roots through pipes on or below the surface), which is used on less than 1 percent of the crops today. In the area surrounding water-short Beijing and Tianjin, farmers and local governments are reducing water losses by lining canals, introducing irrigation pipes, and using other water-saving techniques.[24]

In order to meet people's needs, the country has no choice but to break new ground in urban water conservation, agricultural water conservation, and a range of other strategies. As in other countries, one reason for China's inefficient water use is the artificially low water prices that are used to foster agricultural and industrial growth. Price reform is essential and could lead to large savings. Several cities are now boosting water prices dramatically in order to reduce demand.[25]

Million Tons

Source: USDA

Figure 7-2. Grain Consumption in the United States and China, 1960–94

LAND AND FOOD

Although China was the world's agricultural leader until the early nineteenth century, the struggle to provide adequate food has been a recurring theme in the country's history. A large population, shortages of arable land, frequent floods and droughts, and periodic political disruptions have combined to create some of the world's worst famines. As recently as the late fifties, at least 30 million Chinese died in a famine that followed the crash industrialization attempted during the Great Leap Forward.[26]

The country has been largely free of famine for more than three decades. Grain consumption has risen threefold since 1960, surpassing the United States in 1973. (See Figure 7–2.) Per capita food consumption has gone from 2,000 calories a day in 1965 to 2,640 in 1990—well above India's level of 2,230 and only 10 percent behind Japan. Today, malnutrition is largely confined to regions of rural poverty, mainly in the west. This has been accomplished, however, by emphasizing a grain-based diet. Four fifths of people's average caloric intake is directly from grain, though meat and egg consumption are now rising rapidly.[27]

So far, rising demand for food has been met without major imports, mainly as a result of rising yields stimulated by agricultural reforms and higher prices. The introduction of high-yielding strains, increased irrigation, and heavy fertilizer use have each had an impact, and China's grain production passed that of the United States in 1983. Recently, however, grain yields have begun to level off. Water shortages and diminishing returns from additional fertilizer use have taken a toll. Further yield increases are likely, but will not be as dramatic as those of the last two decades. (See Chapter 1.)[28]

These trends are forcing China to focus on its limited availability of arable land. With 22 percent of the world's population and just 7 percent of the farmland, China's total cropland area actually peaked in the mid-fifties, when the government attempted to reclaim marginal land for farming. Indeed, the loss of cropland has accelerated in recent years. Although the statistics are not entirely reliable, official figures show that during the past three decades, roughly 15 million hectares of arable land were converted to other uses—equivalent to the total cropland of France and Italy combined. In 1992 alone, 667,000 hectares of valuable farmland—more than 10 times the total land area of Singapore—were taken out of cultivation.[29]

Industrial and urban development, fish ponds, and orchards also are rapidly encroaching on cropland. According to the World Bank, land on the outskirts of cities that is rezoned as industrial immediately soars to 15–20 times its agricultural value. Local governments can make millions of dollars renting land at prices equivalent to those of suburban parcels in the United States. As land values rise, rents are increasing to the point where it is too expensive to farm in some areas. A farmer in Guangdong Province facing a 20-percent increase in rent for his land said "I do not know how anybody can afford to stay."[30]

As consumers become richer, they are eager to switch away from a heavily grain-based diet to one richer in meat and dairy products.

Because of centuries of intense pressure, China now has more low-quality land under cultivation than most countries: one third of the total. In some areas, such as the northeast plain, soil erosion already affects yields. In the extraordinarily deep topsoil of the Loess Plateau in northern China, soil erosion's most immediate threat is that it dumps millions of tons of sediment into the Huang He each year. Waterlogging from inappropriate irrigation practices is thought to diminish the productivity on approximately 10 percent of China's cropland, and salinization also reduces yields.[31]

At the same time that China's farmland is disappearing, its demand for grain is soaring. As consumers become richer, they are eager to switch away from a heavily grain-based diet to one richer in meat and dairy products, making China the world leader in the consumption of pork. Since its grasslands are already stretched beyond their sustainable capacity, livestock must be fed grain, which is pushing grain demand up dramatically.[32]

As diets continue to change, China is going to have more difficulty meeting its food needs. (See Chapter 1.) If per capita grain consumption rises from just under 300 kilograms in the mid-nineties to 400 kilograms in the year 2030—about the current level in Taiwan—total demand will climb more than 70 percent. Yet even with yield increases, production is likely to fall by at least one fifth, due to loss of cropland, leaving a deficit to be made up by imports of nearly 400 million tons. It is not at all clear who would supply this. Since 1980, annual world grain exports have averaged just 200 million tons.[33]

Although China's food trends are daunting, a change in policies could lessen the burden. First, it will need to increase investments in its cropland. Strategies include using high-yielding regenerative farming techniques, ensuring that plastics laid over farmland to speed the growing season are properly removed, reducing waterlogging, and so on. As part of its response to Agenda 21, the blueprint for action adopted at the 1992 Earth Summit, China has selected 10 sites for experiments that combine traditional farming techniques such as crossplanting, interplanting, and manure-based fertilizers with modern technology to try to make farming more sustainable.[34]

Planning to minimize the amount of land required for industrial and urban development is also key to China's agricultural future. If growth is planned and zoned so as to reduce the loss of prime agricultural land, it would not cut so extensively into the country's food-growing potential. Efforts to centralize and contain industrial and urban development also increase the land efficiency of waste and water treatment facilities. In addition, restrictions on the conversion of high-quality agricultural land conversion are needed. Although such laws have been passed, they have been inadequately enforced so far.[35]

The Chinese may also want to reconsider how far to move in the direction of a meat-based diet. Not only is this an inefficient way of providing nutrition, but it contributes to heart disease, a leading cause of death in countries where people consume fat-rich livestock products. Soybeans and fish are a healthier way to provide protein. China's fish harvest increased from 4 million tons in 1980 to more than 15 million tons by 1992. With the marine catch growing slowly despite an expanded fishing fleet, most of the gains have come from fish farming, which provided half the country's fish in 1993. Production leaped 50 percent between 1988 and 1993, and China is now the world's leading fish farmer. Although it is expected to continue growing, fish farming will ultimately be constrained by China's limited availability of fresh water and arable land. (See Chapter 2.) This sector already claims more than 4 million hectares, equal to all the cropland in Japan.[36]

SHRINKING FORESTS

China's forest and wood-products situation is well summarized by the saying "one hoe making forests, but several axes cutting them down." Although timber shortages have plagued China's ship and palace builders for centuries, demands have soared in recent decades.

Today, China has only 3 percent of the world's remaining forests; with a nationwide construction boom, wood shortages have appeared in many regions.[37]

Statistics on China's forests are among the least reliable figures issued by the government, and may overstate the health and size of the resource. Government data appear to show that logging increased 25 percent between 1978 and 1986; by the late eighties, forests were so depleted that, at current cutting rates, nearly 70 percent of the forest bureaus (districts) will have no mature trees in 2000. Timber imports rose 70 percent between 1981 and 1988. Although they fell in the next few years as a result of shortage of foreign exchange, they are likely to jump again to meet wood demand spurred by construction, coal mining, and other activities. Paper use is also increasing rapidly, with paper made from wood products growing from 7.4 million tons in 1982 to 20 million tons in 1992. Since wood is in such short supply, China has turned to other sources of paper: well over half of its paper pulp comes from plant fibers, including straw, hemp, bagasse, and bamboo.[38]

To address the timber shortfall, the government launched major reforestation efforts in the early fifties, and by the eighties claimed to have reforested more than 130 million hectares—an area the size of Peru. Although once heralded as ecological miracles, less than 30 percent of the new plantings survived. More recent reforestation efforts—aimed at preventing erosion and flooding as well as providing timber—appear to be more successful, in part by rewarding people for maintaining the trees. In 1990, according to the government, some 5 million hectares were planted, more than in Brazil, India, Japan, the United States, and the Soviet Union combined.[39]

China has also established an extensive system of shelter belts to protect arable lands from encroaching deserts, including a Green Great Wall of at least 7,000 kilometers in the north. Officials report that total forest coverage rose from 13 percent in 1989 to 14 percent in 1994. But felling still exceeds new growth, and because timber is scarce, the temptation to cut it illegally can be overwhelming. According to the Ministry of Forestry, reported violations rose 16 percent in 1993, with some local governments ignoring the Forest Law and other regulations in order to reap the rewards of illegal timber sales. The ministry estimates that these are causing the loss of 450,000 hectares of woodland—an area the size of two Luxembourgs—each year.[40]

As forest demands have grown, wood imports increased from 8 million cubic meters in 1980 to 14 million in 1988. Although it still imports less than one sixth as much wood as the world leader, Japan, does, the total is likely to grow simply to meet current demand as mature forest stocks are depleted before new ones replace them. Also, because China now uses just one fortieth as much industrial timber per person as the United States does, consumption is almost certain to rise in the years ahead, putting more pressure on its own forests as well as on exporters such as Canada and Russia.[41]

Timber scarcity is also threatening what remains of the country's biological resources. China is one of just 12 "megadiversity" countries, with more than 32,200 species of higher plants, 1,100 species of birds, and 394 species of mammals. This represents 12 percent of the world's higher plants, which are both a unique biological resource and a vital storehouse of traditional herbal medicines on which Chinese doctors still rely.[42]

The habitat on which this biological diversity depends has been shrinking rapidly in recent decades. For example, the forests of Xishuangbanna, along

China's border with Myanmar and Laos, are home to 4,000–5,000 species of higher plants and more than 500 species of vertebrates. This area, which used to be China's richest tropical rain forest, has lost half of its forest cover since 1950. Many of China's plants and animals are in trouble: 15–20 percent of them are classified as threatened or endangered.[43]

In the late seventies, when hundreds of China's pandas died of starvation after the bamboo in the Min Mountains of Sichuan died, the government expanded its small system of protected areas. By the end of 1991, 708 nature reserves, covering 568,000 square kilometers—more than 5 percent of the land area—had been established. Six government agencies are responsible for maintaining these reserves, but many lack sufficient resources to police them adequately, particularly given the price that species such as rhinos and tigers bring on black markets. Also, despite efforts to set aside nature reserves, habitat fragmentation continues to threaten much of China's wildlife. Panda ranges, for example, have been halved over the past 20 years, with the remaining habitat consisting of six unconnected areas of alpine bamboo forests. Only 1,100 pandas were counted in the 1985–87 census. Although China has been a party to the Convention on International Trade in Endangered Species of Wild Flora and Fauna since 1980, poaching is still common.[44]

Because of the timber constraints China is facing, it will have to become much more efficient in its use of wood, and reduce its burning of firewood in homes and industry. Also, its booming construction and coal mining industries may have to move toward less wood-intensive techniques. (See Chapter 5.) Already, most Chinese homes are made of earthen bricks rather than wood—and most paper is derived from crops. In the future, China has good reason to continue its leadership in developing new materials that can substitute for wood—and in using wood products more efficiently.[45]

AIR AND ENERGY

One of the first things that visitors to Beijing notice these days is the quality of the air, which frequently has an acrid, sulfurous odor, and carries a heavy burden of particulates that quickly blacken everything from building facades to curtains. The "Beijing cough" is heard everywhere, and gives a sense of the respiratory damage being inflicted on the city's residents. From urban air quality to acid rain and greenhouse gas emissions, China has some of the world's worst air pollution. The reasons for this deadly brew of contaminants are clear: energy demands are burgeoning, and they are mainly being met by a nineteenth-century-style system based on the direct burning of coal, much of it of low quality and some of it high in sulfur.

Coal provides 76 percent of the primary energy in China today, compared with 22 percent in the United States and 17 percent in Japan. The country is already the world's leading coal burner, and is on course to double its use during the next two decades. Despite extensive investments, hydropower provides only 4 percent of China's energy, and nuclear power, almost none. Air quality problems are exacerbated by a scarcity of even the most rudimentary pollution control devices, which China has been unable to afford. Unlike in most industrial countries, for example, only about a fifth of China's coal is washed. Moreover, pollution is aggravated by the fact that most Chinese coal is burned in small industrial boilers or in household stoves

or room heaters, where pollution control is more difficult.[46]

In some areas where metals and chemicals plants have opened in recent years, visitors report an industrial wasteland, with massive pollution streaming into nearby houses and little apparent regard for the emission standards issued by Beijing. The electrostatic precipitators and flue gas desulfurization units that are ubiquitous in Japan are largely absent in China. Natural gas, oil, and electricity are the main fuels for industrial, commercial, and residential boilers in industrial nations, but not in China. More than 60 percent of China's coal is used for these purposes, compared with 8 percent in the United States, where most coal is used to generate electricity.[47]

Energy demands are mainly being met by a nineteenth-century-style system based on the direct burning of coal.

China's cities have some of the world's highest sulfur and particulate readings—particularly in northern cities where coal is used for winter heating. Throughout the country, their concentrations frequently exceed World Health Organization standards. Particulates are known to provoke respiratory diseases such as asthma, chronic bronchitis, emphysema, and lung cancer. They can also transport toxic metals deep into the lungs, and inhibit the development of the brain and immunity system. Lung diseases are rising steeply in all major urban areas, and have recently become the leading cause of death in China, accounting for 26 percent of mortality.[48]

Sulfur is the main precursor to acid rain, and China would have a more severe acid rain problem were it not for an accident of geochemistry: in northern China, where much of the coal is burned, alkaline dust sweeps through the area, neutralizing the acidifying effects of sulfur deposition. In southern China, however, where the local coal has lots of sulfur and there is no alkaline dust, serious damage has been reported in some areas. Acid rain from Chinese coal has been measured as far away as Japan and South Korea. Acid rain's toll on crops, forests, and buildings is estimated at $2.8 billion a year.[49]

During the past decade, China has worked hard to control its air emissions, but efforts have been frustrated by poor enforcement and the rising use of coal. The National Environmental Protection Agency estimates that urban industries in the second half of the eighties reduced the coarse dust, fine dust, and sulfur dioxide emitted per unit of output by 45 percent, 35 percent, and 12 percent, respectively. But some observers believe that the government is underreporting emissions, and that air quality may be worse than official figures suggest.[50]

China's air is about to be assaulted by another major source of pollutants: motor vehicles. In a country well known for its dependence on 400 million nonpolluting bicycles, the automobile has so far had a negligible role: the entire country has only 700,000 private cars (which were illegal until a few years ago) and only as many kilometers of paved road as the United States did at the turn of the century. Yet the number of motor vehicles ballooned from 613,000 in 1970 to 5.8 million in 1990. Now the government is eager to create a world-class automobile industry, and envisions increasing the number of cars produced annually from 1.3 million in 1993 to 3 million in 2000.[51]

These cars will, of course, exacerbate China's air pollution. Ozone readings in Beijing, Guangzhou, and several other cities average about 20 micrograms per cubic meter, more than three times the average in Los Angeles. The use of leaded gasoline and the prevalence of inefficient and infrequently maintained trucks and buses make the emissions problem far worse. Unless China adopts emissions standards similar to those already in place in Japan, the ongoing auto boom will have devastating effects on China's air.[52]

Growing reliance on automobiles will create other problems as well. Many Chinese cities are already congested with bicycles, trucks, and buses, and it would not take many more cars to create gridlock. Oil presents another problem. Oil use nearly doubled since 1982 (see Figure 7–3), causing China to switch in 1993 from being an exporter to an importer; imports are projected to reach 1.3 million barrels per day in 2000. Domestic oil "has been unable to provide sufficiently for the nation's economic growth," according to Li Boxi of the state development research center. In fact, if China were to use as much oil per person as Japan does now, it would need 61 million barrels daily—nearly equal to current world production.[53]

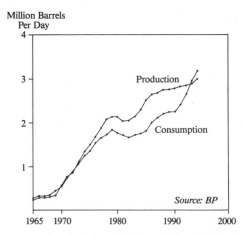

Figure 7-3. Oil Production and Consumption in China, 1965–94

Even as China struggles to cope with "traditional" pollutants and with growing oil imports, concern is spreading about its contribution to one of the most serious global threats: human-induced greenhouse warming. With its heavy reliance on coal—the fossil fuel with the highest carbon content—China is already the second largest contributor to rising atmospheric levels of carbon dioxide, the leading greenhouse gas. Its 725 million tons of carbon emissions in 1993 (see Figure 7-4) trailed only the United States, though in per capita terms it was behind 50 other nations. At current growth rates, China will become the number one emitter of carbon dioxide by 2020.[54]

If the world's climate does change, China will be among the most vulnerable countries. It has always been plagued by weather-related disasters, ranging from floods and typhoons to droughts—the kind of climatic events that are likely to become more common in a warmer world. In the spring of 1994, for example, a flood killed 1,600 people and caused $6 billion in damages. In August, a typhoon killed 700 and led to economic losses of $1.6 billion.[55]

Along with more than 100 other governments, China signed the Framework Convention on Climate Change at the Earth Summit in 1992, but so far it has taken few steps to limit its carbon output. Unlike other air pollution problems, carbon dioxide cannot be economically controlled with pollution devices. The only way to reduce the output is to use less coal, but that is the fuel that China's energy planners and their supporters at the World Bank are counting on to meet the lion's share of the country's energy needs.[56]

For the planners, coal is quite simply the energy path of least resistance. The infrastructure is in place—though it must be added to continually—and has strong supporters in the government-owned energy industry. Even so, coal development is now falling behind surging energy demand. Nor is coal inexpensive to develop. China invested 42 billion yuan (roughly $10 billion) in coal-related projects in 1990. This represents half the country's energy investments and 17 percent of its total investments. Altogether, China now spends 10 percent of its GNP on coal production, transport, and use. The question that needs to be asked is whether some of these huge sums would be better spent on more advanced energy systems.[57]

China has three energy paths open to it: copy the worst of the West (the nineteenth-century coal path), copy the best of the West (an oil-based system similar to the U.S. or German ones), or leap past the West, directly to an efficient, decentralized, twenty-first century system. The third path would involve a portfolio of new energy sources and technologies, including natural gas, solar energy, wind power, and improved energy efficiency. Together these options could allow China to reduce its air pollution drastically, while relying mainly on domestic resources.[58]

Energy efficiency is the first priority. China has already reduced its energy in-

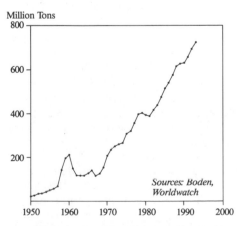

Million Tons

Sources: Boden, Worldwatch

Figure 7-4. Carbon Emissions in China, 1950–93

tensity by one third between 1978 and 1990, but it is still inefficient by industrial-country standards. One study estimates that by investing $3 billion in efficiency each year, the country could cut future growth in energy demand by nearly half, eliminating the need for $16 billion of new power plants, oil refineries, and other energy installations. Among the priorities are improved building practices (see Chapter 6) and better enforcement of existing industrial and residential appliance efficiency standards.[59]

Although official figures show little natural gas in China, foreign geologists believe the country has major resources, mostly in areas that have not yet been explored with modern technology. The government neglected gas investments in the past, but has recently opened several areas to exploration and is building long pipelines and a distribution system in Beijing. Such advances will allow the country to use gas for efficient applications such as homes, factories, and even trucks and buses. The International Energy Agency believes that China is on the verge of a gas boom. If China were able to use natural gas at the same rate that the United States does, it could meet all its current energy needs—or half the projected needs of 2010.[60]

China's largest energy resources are solar and wind energy. (See Chapter 4.) Solar power can be tapped locally throughout the country; some homes in remote areas, such as Gansu Province, are already being electrified with photovoltaic cells. In the future, wind and solar energy can replace coal: electricity and hydrogen produced in western deserts can be transported to the coast via long-distance transmission lines and pipelines. In fact, a World Bank study shows that such schemes will soon be economical. As in the United States, a tiny fraction of the area of the less populated western provinces could meet all the country's foreseeable energy needs. This will require sizable investments, but in the long run it would be less expensive than a coal-based energy path.[61]

Though solar and wind energy were neglected in the past, this is changing. The State Science and Technology Commission drew up a 1994 plan to accelerate development of these new energy technologies. One encouraging sign is that China is beginning to open up its power system to private ownership and even to joint ventures with foreign companies. This will help break the political stalemate favoring coal.[62]

MEETING BASIC NEEDS

Sustainable development is as much about people as it is about natural resources. Compared with most poor countries, China has made great strides toward meeting the basic health, educational, and nutritional needs of its citizens during the past four decades. (See Table 7–3). By putting most of its emphasis on the collective good, however, the government has often neglected the rights of individual citizens and prevented them from speaking out on policies they oppose, as symbolized by the events in Tiananmen Square in 1989. The challenge now is to continue meeting the needs of China's citizens while abandoning the authoritarian, repressive policies of the past.[63]

Since the late seventies, at least 170 million people—more than the population of Brazil or Russia—have been lifted out of poverty. According to the World Bank, the share of China's people in absolute poverty fell from one third to less than one tenth between 1978 and 1985. Most of the improvement can be traced to agricultural reforms, which raised rural incomes by more than 130

Table 7-3. China and India: Selected Social Indicators, Circa 1990

Category	China	India
Income Equality (ratio of top to bottom fifth)	6.5	4.7
Daily Calorie Intake (calories per person)	2,640	2,230
Adult Literacy (percent)	80	50
Higher Education (percent)	1.7	6.4[1]
Total Fertility Rate (births per woman)	2.3	4.0
Infant Mortality (deaths per thousand live births)	27	89
Life Expectancy (years)	71	60

[1]1985.

SOURCE: U.N. Development Programme, *Human Development Report 1994* (New York: Oxford University Press, 1994); higher education in India from UNESCO, *UNESCO Statistical Yearbook 1991* (Paris: 1991).

percent. The gains stagnated, however, and from 1985 to 1990 the number of poor held at about 98 million; some of the poorest people actually lost ground.[64]

For a developing country, China's wealth is distributed relatively equitably. Overall, the richest 20 percent have six times the income of the poorest 20 percent. This compares favorably with the ratio of 32 to one found in Brazil and almost nine to one in the United States. And income inequality is now growing. In 1993, for example, when GNP grew by about 13 percent, rural incomes grew by just 2 percent.[65]

These differences show up in the poverty rates of different provinces, since coastal areas have benefited much more from reforms. Western Gansu, an inland province, had the highest rate of poverty in a 1989 survey (although the Tibetan Autonomous Region was excluded from the survey). More than 34 percent of rural households there fell below the poverty line. Other provinces with high rates of poverty include Inner Mongolia and Xingjiang. China's ethnic minorities, which account for 8 percent of the total population, are more than twice as likely to be poor as the average Chinese.[66]

A baby born in Shanghai now has a better chance of seeing his or her first birthday than one born in New York City.

Analysts fear that as millions of peasants move to cities to improve their lot, the rate of urban poverty—now estimated at less than 1 percent—will skyrocket, and with it a range of social problems. The government is trying to stem this problem by limiting migration: Beijing is even planning to charge individuals $5,800 to move there, and employers $11,600 for residence permits for future employees. But it is rapidly losing control. To prevent an explosion of urban poverty, China will need to make social safety net programs accessible to more of its urban dwellers.[67]

China has also improved the health of its citizens in recent decades. As a result of these efforts, infant mortality fell from 150 per thousand in 1960 to 69 per thousand in 1970, 41 in 1980, and just 27 in 1992—close to Thailand's level of 26. A baby born in Shanghai now has a better chance of seeing his or her first birthday than one born in New York City. These figures vary widely by region, however. In Shanghai, infant mortality rates are 9.9 per thousand, while in Tibet, they are estimated at roughly 200 per thousand.[68]

Much of this progress was achieved by bringing primary and preventive health care to the average citizen. This is well illustrated by the extensive inoculation programs begun in the fifties, and the extension programs set up to train 2 million barefoot doctors and establish village-based cooperatives in the sixties and seventies. The Chinese government distributed penicillin to cut down on bacterial infections, and launched river cleanups to kill the snails that carry schistosomiasis. Although people in need of specialized care may not get the world's best treatment under this system, it has—at least as measured by official statistics—been successful.[69]

One disturbing side effect of China's transition to a market economy is that women are losing ground on a number of fronts.

When its agricultural communes were dismantled in the eighties, China lost the organizational and funding structure that supported much of its health care delivery system. Health brigades remain in operation, at least in some areas, but China is moving toward private, fee-based systems, and neglecting preventive health care where it is not as profitable for health care providers. It remains to be seen whether China will continue to improve the health of its poorest citizens while the economy booms.[70]

In education, as in health care, China has focused on access for the masses. Enrollment in primary education increased from 50 percent in 1952 to 97 percent in 1989, but secondary school enrollment is far lower, at 44 percent—higher than India but lower than Mexico. And only 1.7 percent of China's students attend college, compared with more

than 6 percent in India. Overall, China spends a lower share of its GNP on education than India does.[71]

Government funding of education increased during the eighties, but in poor areas, primary education is actually worsening as a result of economic reforms. As private schools spring up in China's cities and even public schools ask parents to pay school fees, the poor are often left behind. According to the World Bank, children in many poor villages are less likely to be literate today than they were a decade ago. This is having a particular impact on girls. Four fifths of the 4.8 million children who dropped out of school in 1990 were girls, mostly from remote areas and minority groups.[72]

If health care services do not improve for the majority and if girls continue to slip through the cracks of the education system, China is likely to undermine its long-term efforts to reduce its population growth rate. At the International Conference on Population and Development in Cairo in 1994, the international community agreed that raising the status of women through education and the provision of reproductive health care is essential if fertility levels are to be reduced.[73]

One disturbing side effect of China's transition to a market economy is that women are losing ground on a number of fronts. The Communist system did much to raise women's status, including banning prostitution, female infanticide, child marriages, and the sale of brides. Female participation in the labor force increased dramatically and was substantially higher than in most western countries by 1977. But according to one study, 70 percent of the 20 million workers laid off in recent years have been women; as unprofitable state enterprises reduce their work forces, factory managers are looking to cut costs for maternity leave and child care.[74]

China's family planning program is one area in which neglect of human rights is most apparent. In response to stringent national and village targets, many local family planning efforts became coercive, forcing abortions and sometimes inducing premature deliveries in an effort to meet quotas for births in a specific period. Local authorities, who are often rewarded for meeting their goals, have moved beyond giving tax breaks to families with one child to destroying the homes of people with two or more children.[75]

Family planning is not the only area of human rights abuses in China. It is illegal to form or join political parties, and in the aftermath of Tiananmen Square, thousands of political dissidents were jailed. There are believed to be thousands of political prisoners in China, many of them forced to work in labor camps. Minorities who push for local autonomy often land in prison as well.[76]

Despite continuing denial of civil liberties, some kinds of freedom appear to be emerging with a market economy, including personal freedoms, such as giving people choices of where to work, when to marry and have a child, and where to live. As people gain access to foreign broadcasts and a higher standard of living, they are beginning to want more say in their system of governance. Most outside experts expect more liberalization in the future, but this may take time. Unless the government provides people with a more direct say in their future, the road to sustainable development will be obstructed by a lack of public participation and the risk of political explosions.

SUSTAINING CHINA

During the next few years, China faces a historic crossroads that will help deter-

mine the welfare of hundreds of millions of Chinese—and perhaps billions of non-Chinese as well. Most commentators describe this juncture in political or economic terms: socialism versus capitalism, authoritarianism versus democracy. But they ignore China's vast potential to affect the health of the global environment and the sustainability of human society for many decades to come.

In one sense, the prospect of one fifth of humanity suddenly entering the consumer age will force industrial countries, which currently consume the bulk of the world's resources, to face up to the unsustainability of their current practices. Although it is clear that the world cannot afford to have another billion people driving around in big cars or eating fast-food hamburgers, it is also clear that the burden of creating a sustainable society should fall on the countries that pioneered the unsustainable life-styles, not on those that are just beginning to adopt them.

Nevertheless, even if China is not responsible for the problem, it is an essential part of the solution—and it can benefit by joining the transition early and avoiding investments in obsolete energy and industrial systems. In some instances, its participation is essential: just as industrial countries are phasing out production of chlorofluorocarbons in order to protect the ozone layer, for instance, China's production more than doubled between 1986 and 1992. Thus the pace at which China abandons these industrial chemicals will help determine global rates of skin cancer for decades to come.[77]

Fortunately, China's global responsibilities and its domestic needs coincide far more consistently than many observers seem to think. Efficient use of water and wood will strengthen China's economy, as well as protecting globally important estuaries and forest reserves.

Shifting to more sustainable agricultural techniques will provide more food for China's people, while easing pressures on world markets. Providing better educational opportunities for women will benefit society as a whole, while helping to slow birth rates and limit human numbers. And shifting to new energy sources will reduce the economic damage from local air pollution in China, while also lowering global carbon emissions.

On paper, China's government seems well aware of the resource limitations it faces, and has publicly embraced the goal of sustainable development. The constitution requires protection and improvement of the natural environment. And as a follow-up to the 1994 Earth Summit, the government has issued a several-hundred-page action plan with 62 pilot projects. But as with many countries, there has been a gap between Beijing's rhetoric and the reality of what is going on in China's vast countryside and its now bustling cities.[78]

While government planners talk of sustainable development and building a green China, local industrialists are rushing to put up steel mills and chemical plants that would have been illegal in Japan even two decades ago. Enforcement of environmental laws remains weak, the old command-and-control systems are breaking down, market incentives are often inadequate or absent, too large a share of government investment is going into megaprojects, and citizens have not been given the freedom to participate fully in environmental reform. Clearly, China faces a big challenge in converting its green words into sustainable action.

Although China is now using the market to promote economic growth, it is not yet taking full advantage of it to assign value to limited environmental resources. Water, energy, and timber continue to be sold for a fraction of their market value—which discourages efforts to use them more efficiently. Strategically limiting subsidies on these resources would go a long way toward conserving them. Beijing may also wish to adopt the kind of emission fees that are increasingly used to fight air pollution in many industrial countries.

Yet as most advanced industrial countries have already learned, the market is an imperfect solution. As China plunges headlong into capitalism, it will need to work quickly to install an adequate regulatory structure. As economist Michael Porter has noted, countries that implement strong environmental standards are generally more successful economically, since they encourage development of state-of-the-art industries that do not require remedial cleanup. China also faces the challenge of not being the dumping ground for inefficient and polluting factories that are being abandoned by industrial countries. And it will be hard to monitor and regulate the myriad village and township enterprises that are now springing up, many in violation of environmental and other laws.[79]

In addition to correcting prices and revamping regulations, the government needs to back its commitment to a healthy environment with money. China spent just 0.7 percent of its GNP on environmental protection in 1993, compared with 3.0 percent in Japan and 3.4 percent in the United States. Yet according to recent government estimates, pollution costs the country roughly $11 billion a year, nearly 7 percent of the GNP. The World Bank has urged China to spend at least 1.5 percent of its GNP on pollution control.[80]

These funds could support environmental enforcement, the dissemination of environmental technologies, the development of new energy sources, and the deployment of economic incentives to encourage sustainable practices. In recent years, China has cut research funding dramatically and laid off thousands of scientists, threatening research on soil erosion, ecology, and other areas that are vital to sustainable development.[81]

In terms of public-sector investment, government planners have yet to fully embrace the idea of smaller-scale, less-centralized projects. They continue to look for grand projects that reflect Soviet-style thinking, such as the Three Gorges Dam project on the Yangtze River, which would flood an area half the size of Luxembourg and could tie up more than $34 billion of capital—equivalent to nearly one sixth of China's current GNP. Instead of trying to improve bicycle-based transportation, the government speaks of a "world-class" auto industry and a system of roads that is likely to become gridlocked as soon as it is completed. China would get a lot more for its yuan if it focused on smaller-scale and more flexible options.[82]

An additional tool for change is found in international capital markets. Although it forged a path of financial independence from the fifties through the seventies, China is now borrowing heavily on international capital markets and is also the World Bank's single largest borrower, receiving $3.2 billion in 1993. By making environmental sustainability a focused borrowing priority and working with the World Bank and the Asian Development Bank in a more proactive way to identify projects that focus on using resources efficiently, China will be able to develop faster.[83]

The World Bank is starting to retarget its program for China, claiming that 13 percent of its lending for the 1992–95 period is for environmental projects. But it could take a more active role in pushing for cleaner energy technologies, redirecting transportation policy, and putting more emphasis on resource efficiency. International investment through joint ventures also has the potential to play a positive role. When multinationals set up plants that adhere to the world's highest standards, they are able to lead by example.[84]

The final challenge for China's government is to listen more closely to the voices of its citizens and to harness their energy. Around the world, citizens' groups—ranging from neighborhood watchdogs to international organizations—have helped lead the way toward sustainable development. (See Chapter 10.) India alone has more than 12,000 grassroots organizations. Although China has community organizations such as women's groups and associations that focus on health care, there are no environmental groups in the western sense of the word. Citizens must petition for the right to organize in China, and so far no application for an environmental group has been accepted.[85]

One thing is clear: China simply will not be able to follow for long any of the development paths blazed to date. Its abundance of people, shortage of resources, and collision with the technologies and political philosophies of the twenty-first century will force the country to chart a new and different course.

Although this is a daunting challenge, China is well equipped to face it. Throughout most of history, China has led the world in scientific and industrial development, and has charted its own course. The country that invented paper and gunpowder may now have the opportunity to leapfrog the West and show it the way to a sustainable economy. If it succeeds, China could become a shining example for the rest of the world to admire and emulate. If it fails, we will all pay the price.

8

Leaving Home

Hal Kane

Refugees and migrants move in response to the pressures of world politics, the ebbs and flows of livelihoods lost and gained, the adequacy or poverty of resources at hand, and the wars and conflicts that result. Their travels tell the story of a changing world.

For many centuries, the story they told was of a world of inequality, a world where a few people controlled many others. Migrations from 1500 until the early nineteenth century, for example, were mostly of slaves. Some 14 million people were transported against their will, mainly to South America, the Caribbean, and the Arabian peninsula (and a much smaller number to North America). Voluntary movements of people were smaller, possibly only 2–3 million people during this entire time, until voluntary migration began to rise quickly in the beginning of the last century. Thus for centuries the causes of migration centered on domination and economic ownership.[1]

During the Middle Ages, migration was rare. That lack of movement represents a history of economic isolation and political feudalism: peasant laborers worked near where they were born, and feudal systems from Europe through the Middle East, Asia, and parts of Africa kept people inside their lord's domain.

Even earlier, as tribes swept down into Central Asia and Europe from the north and east, migration told an altogether different story. It was one of conquest by people who carried their civilizations along with them, and often battled or mixed with people they met on the way. At that time, migration was less of individuals than of whole communities.[2]

Those migrations formed history, creating an ethnic mix in Asia, Central Europe, and Africa; populating the Americas with foreigners; reducing overcrowding in Europe; and subjecting people to the tragedy of slavery. But nothing on that historical map prepares us for the sheer mass of people captured in the current picture of migration, when as many people can move in one year as moved in most centuries previously. And nothing in that history hints at the remarkable increase in the diversity of reasons why people now leave their homes and countries.

This is no aberration or temporary trend. Migration has become an ordinary activity: it occurs every day and in almost every part of the world. It has come to reflect the events of our time—the breakup of the Soviet Union, the desperation in Africa, widening income disparities around the world, and many other developments. More people became refugees in 1994 than left Spain—at their leisure—to colonize the Americas in the nineteenth century, one of the times of heaviest emigration. (See Table 8–1.) More people fled Afghanistan following the Soviet invasion of 1979 than left Germany during the last century, yet the Germans became one of the largest ethnic groups in the United States.[3]

Today's massive movements tell of countries where crime by organized clans or gangs or by individuals is replacing aggression by militaries. Where internal conflict is replacing war with neighboring nations. Where young people have to look for employment abroad. And where population growth and environmental degradation are making other stresses more acute. Many of these trends are accelerating. They will add to the pressures that make people leave.

Public debate has yet to address the broad question of why so many people are leaving home. Instead, policymakers continue to focus on the refugee crisis of the moment, on immigration quotas, and on which individuals to allow into their countries. A fundamental resolution of the issues of refugees and migrants would require us to look deeper and understand why the politics, economics, and security situation in today's world is causing so many people to move. That is the first step toward making people more secure in their homes.

THE DISPLACED

The world's refugee population has risen to 23 million people living outside their countries of origin. (See Figure 8–1.) In 1989, the figure was 15 million. And as recently as the mid-seventies, only about 2.5 million people could claim refugee status—about the same number as in the fifties and sixties.[4]

But these numbers reflect the strict standard established by the 1951 United Nations Convention on Refugees, which remains in force today. This defines refugees solely in terms of persecution: any person who "owing to well-founded fear of being persecuted for reasons of race, religion, nationality, membership of a particular social group, or political opinion, is outside the country of his nationality and is unable to . . . return to it." That narrow definition is a remnant of the cold war. Its purpose was largely to weaken the former Soviet Union and other states within its domain by granting asylum to people who fled from them.[5]

Table 8-1. Major West European Migrations, 1815–1914

Source Country	Number	Main Destinations
	(million)	
England and Scotland	12.3	United States, Canada, Australia, New Zealand, South Africa
Italy	approx. 10	United States, Canada, Argentina, Brazil, Austria
Germany	5.3	United States, Canada, Argentina, Brazil
Ireland	4.1	United States, Canada, Australia, New Zealand, South Africa
Spain	approx. 2	Argentina, Brazil, Cuba, Uruguay, North Africa
France	1.5	Algeria, Morocco, Tunisia, United States
Portugal	1.4	Brazil

SOURCE: Aaron Segal, *An Atlas of International Migration* (London: Hans Zell Publishers, 1993).

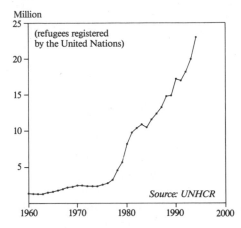

Figure 8-1. Official Refugees Worldwide, 1960–94

The official definition hardly begins to explain why people decide to leave home today. Many fall outside it because they did not flee persecution. Those who escape famine fail to qualify, even though they had no choice but to leave or perish. Those who fear that they are losing the means of feeding their children do not qualify, even though that prospect may be as terrifying as the threat of violence. Those who are pushed out by natural disasters, such as the frequent floods in Bangladesh, are also excluded. Yet all these people can find themselves in the same conditions as official refugees.

Because these people fail to qualify as official refugees, they are not eligible for asylum in other countries. (In fact, many of them do not wish to enter other countries.) So they generally join the "internally displaced"—people forced from their homes but still in their home countries. Not counting people who leave their homes for economic reasons, the internally displaced number at least 27 million worldwide.[6]

Other people who fail to qualify as refugees do manage to cross a border into another country, but they do so illegally. The total number of illegal immigrants, both those who flee out of fear and those who seek better opportunities, is un-

known but is probably at least 10 million.[7]

Some of the same pressures that force refugees out also lead other people to choose to leave; the difference is one of degree—the pressures are less urgent or severe for migrants than for refugees. Indeed, some migrants are people who had the foresight not to become refugees: they got out before it was too late in countries headed down a path toward war or economic chaos. Understanding these pressures provides insights into the situations of refugees and migrants alike.

Likewise, the reasons that some people move within their countries are often related to the reasons that others actually leave entirely. And internal migration is sometimes a first step to emigration. All these movements have at their bases the failure of societies to meet the basic needs and aspirations of their citizens.

The individuals who had moved in an attempt to improve their standard of living—migrants, not refugees—numbered about 100 million at the time of the 1985 censuses. That figure is quite rough, suffering from unreliable data from many countries, and it is also the most recent count available. Many of these individuals are simply pursuing better opportunities and could easily have remained at home. A similar group of people—those who move from rural areas to cities within their own countries—is far larger still. In China alone they number more than 100 million, and worldwide they outnumber all other kinds of migrants.[8]

All these people are a barometer of change. Their travels are symptomatic of underlying problems, from poverty to human rights abuses. Indeed, travel is one solution to the problems that migrants leave behind. From abroad they can send some of their wages home to their families or communities. They have access to education and entrepreneurial opportunities they would otherwise never have had. Migration itself is neither positive nor negative. It is simply a response to the workings of modern economies, transportation systems, and communications, to political pressures, and to individual drives.

Sometimes it is clearly bad: the fact that refugees flee in the night from the terror of persecution has no positive aspect. But others leave under bright circumstances—they move to somewhere they want to live and where they will contribute impressively to economies and cultures. Israel's innovative economy, for example, was built by Jewish immigrants and refugees who have a history of migration going back more than three millennia.

Of course, moving is not always the most desirable solution. Most people prefer to be able to improve their lives without the stress and disruption of leaving their homes or breaking up their families. They would like to have the personal security, economic well-being, and access to education, health care, and a healthy environment that would let them stay home. And many countries would like to avoid the "brain drain" of mass departure.

This human drama is still being written. Few countries have 100 million people. So imagine the novelty of a "floating" country, made up of more than 100 million souls, moving from countryside to city and from one town to another, as they are now in China. With that kind of motion, and with the economic change and population growth that have caused it, it is said that in southern China roads are being built so fast and in so many new directions that no maps are accurate. The same may be true of the way we think of demographics: so many people are on the move today, in so many different directions and for so many different reasons, that our old assumptions about demographic trends may be as out of date as the Chinese guidebooks that show rice fields where today there are small cities.[9]

Much of our thinking about migration comes from a handful of historical movements that have left a political mark on our thinking. The Exodus of the Old Testament followed a path of tribal conflict and persecution. The pilgrims of colonial America left religious persecution and oppressive government. In the twentieth century, Stalin shifted his subjects around the Soviet territories at will, Mao redistributed millions of Chinese, and the partition of India sent Hindus one way and Muslims the other.[10]

Some of the countries least able financially to cope with newcomers have been the most accepting of them.

The overwhelming majority of migrants and refugees today come from developing countries, and many of them end up in other parts of the Third World. Some of the countries least able financially to cope with newcomers have been the most accepting of them. Pakistan and Iran, for example, have been temporary homes for millions of Afghan refugees for more than a decade. (Although, at roughly the same time that the United States decided to turn away Haitian boat people, Pakistan recently limited the entry of Afghan refugees, who are now congregating near the Pakistani border.) Many African countries have allowed in people fleeing famine and war. These countries are straining under growing numbers of their own people; they are hardly in a position to be playing hosts to such influxes.[11]

The United States has been a long-time passionate defender of the principle of "first asylum," which says that people may not be returned against their will to a country where they may be endangered. Surprised by the magnitude of today's still-growing flows of refugees, however, the United States and some other governments are now backing away from this principle. In large part, this change stems from the difference between the people who fled the persecution envisioned in the 1951 U.N. definition and today's refugees, who more often flee war, social breakdown, and other problems. Western governments believed they had a vested interest in fighting the persecution they saw as a part of Communism in the former Soviet Union and China and of dictatorships in Southeast Asia and other places. (Some 96 percent of the refugees admitted to the United States during the Reagan administration were from Communist countries.) Western policymakers feel less threatened by the social, economic, and political problems of today, no matter how severe those become.[12]

This leaves refugees in a difficult position. Their numbers have not dwindled after the cold war, as many people had hoped. What has dwindled is the interest of foreign countries in absorbing them at the same time as more and more people have sought refuge from a diverse range of problems.

Once inside some of the wealthier western countries, newcomers have recently come up against growing levels of intolerance. In the United States in 1994, immigrants faced a war of intolerance waged by people who seem to forget that, in an earlier generation, their relatives were newcomers too. Citizens' groups in California, Texas, and Washington, D.C., spend time and money lobbying to reduce quotas of newcomers, for example, as well as to lower government spending on those already here. In Germany, xenophobia has exploded repeatedly into anti-immigrant violence. Throughout Europe, anti-immigrant sentiment has become a plank in political platforms.[13]

But discrimination of this sort is generally based on ill-informed fears. Most studies in the United States indicate that immigrants have not taken jobs away from natives, and that their willingness to work for lower pay has had only a slight effect on wages overall. And immigrants rarely get credit for the positive economic effects that their incomes create. According to one comprehensive study, from 1970 onwards in the United States immigrants paid a total of $70 billion in local, state, and federal taxes, generating $25–30 billion more in public revenue than they used in public services. In the words of Jeffrey Passel and Michael Fix of the Urban Institute, "that finding is sharply at odds with a number of seriously flawed studies done by groups advocating cuts in legal immigration or by governments seeking 'reimbursement' for their expenditures."[14]

It is true that the picture varies from place to place. In strong local economies, immigrants are most often found to increase economic opportunities; in weak ones, they have a small negative effect on economic opportunities for low-skilled workers. In such cases, local governments often lose revenue. Sometimes state governments do also, but studies consistently find a net gain for the federal government and a net gain overall.[15]

THE HOUR OF DEPARTURE

When the nuclear reactor at Chernobyl exploded on April 26, 1986, an estimated 180 tons of radioactive dust were spread around the surrounding landscape. Because of the fallout, some

116,000 residents eventually left the "Zone of Estrangement," as the Ukrainians call it. Their reason for moving was unusually straightforward: one day a power plant blew up, and they had to leave. Chernobyl is a vivid symbol of the kinds of pressures that arise without warning.[16]

Natural disasters are another example of these pressures. Many Bangladeshis have left their country, one of the most densely populated on earth and a nation that suffers from frequent floods and natural disasters, in search of safety in India. Their migrations, which have touched off tensions between the two countries, are the result of people living on vulnerable floodplains and in squalid squatter settlements for lack of any place better. Acute land hunger has led people to move to lands they know are risky. As the region's population grows, larger numbers of people will live on the lands most susceptible to floods, hurricanes, and other disasters. That means that in the future each natural disaster will send a larger group of people looking for sustenance in other places.[17]

Other migrants are also driven by a fairly simple rationale. Governments, for instance, may lure people away from their homes, or even force them out. China has practiced a form of "population transfer" as part of its strategy for quashing Tibetan nationalism. Chinese officials describe Tibet as a barren, inhospitable land. Nevertheless, areas that were populated entirely by Tibetans before 1950 are now majority Chinese. To accomplish that, the government doubles the pay and many rations of soldiers and settlers willing to go there. At 7.6 million, the Chinese now outnumber the 6.1 million Tibetans in their own homeland.[18]

The Chinese may have read Machiavelli. "Sending immigrants is the most effective way to colonize countries because it is less offensive than to send military expeditions and much less expensive," wrote the sixteenth-century Italian philosopher. The Dalai Lama catalogs similar moves in other parts of China: "Today, only two to three million Manchurians are left in Manchuria, where 75 million Chinese have settled. In Eastern Turkestan, which the Chinese now call Xinjiang, the Chinese population has grown from 200,000 in 1949 to seven million, more than half of the total population of 13 million. In the wake of the Chinese colonization of Inner Mongolia, Chinese now outnumber the Mongols by 8.5 million to 2.5 million."[19]

Immigrants rarely get credit for the positive economic effects that their incomes create.

Eviction is another strategy that has been used against minorities. Fearing Kurdish dissent, Saddam Hussein chased a million and a half Kurds out of Iraq and into neighboring Turkey in 1991 during a three-week period. For the same reasons, he also forced Shiite Muslims from southern Iraq into Iran.[20]

Military invasion is a clear-cut cause for flight. In Afghanistan, for instance, the Soviet invasion coupled with internal fighting between rival Afghan forces provoked an outflow of people that peaked at 6 million. Before they began to return home in 1993, Afghan refugees far outnumbered those of any other nationality.[21]

Disease can also be a major factor in migration. In the former Czechoslovakia, for instance, pollution and industrial hazards have dramatically raised rates of heart disease, cancer, respiratory failures, and birth defects. The region is one of the few where these illness rates are so high that they have noticeably reduced life expectancy. Life spans in dif-

ferent parts of the former Czechoslovakia vary by as much as five years, with the
shortest being in districts with the most
disturbed environments. The highest illness rates are in the North Moravian,
North Bohemian, West Bohemian, and
Central Slovak regions. In these areas,
divorce rates are also the highest, as are
crime rates and drug addictions—and
they have frequent "inner emigration,"
as the government has called relocations
of people from polluted regions to
cleaner parts of the country.[22]

Overcrowding has caused people to
move as well. From time to time during
history, the size of a local community
would surpass the carrying capacity of
the land, outgrowing its farmland or
water supply. Famous examples include
the Mesopotamians and the Mayans. But
today, this has become widespread. It
plays a major role in the world's rural to
urban migration. As they are divided
among more and more heirs over the
generations, for example, farms reach
the point where they are no longer viable
and some of the potential heirs must
look elsewhere for livelihoods. In Vietnam, overcrowding has caused whole
communities to move. Few places are
poorer than neighboring Cambodia, yet
that country's open spaces and fish-filled
rivers have proved irresistible for the inhabitants of overcrowded villages in
Vietnam. Hundreds of thousands of
them have moved to Cambodia over the
years (though now many are fleeing an
"ethnic cleansing" campaign by the
Khmer Rouge guerrillas).[23]

Other people leave prejudice and
head toward opportunity. One million
Jews, for instance, left the former Soviet
Union after the collapse of its Communist government. About half of them
have gone to Israel; the other half reside
in the United States and other western
countries. More people left the former
Soviet Union during the early nineties
than during the entire cold war. If, as

expected, future economic decline leads
to even greater unemployment there,
then still more people will leave. The
loss of those emigrants, many of whom
will be highly educated, could trigger additional decline. And in receiving countries, immigrants change political structures and demographic patterns.[24]

In other countries, some of the efforts
to remedy poverty have caused people to
migrate. Public works projects, for example, have a long history of prying people from their homes. Large dams flood
residential areas; roads pass over land
that once held buildings; shantytowns
are cleared to make way for power stations. A World Bank study notes that
public works projects now uproot more
than 10 million "oustees" in the developing world every year. During the past
decade, an estimated 80–90 million people have been resettled as a result of infrastructure programs specifically for
dam construction and urban and transportation development. Other sectors
have relocated millions more. As growing populations pursue economic
growth in the future, they are likely to
feel the need to build at an even faster
rate than in the past, a trend well under
way in parts of East Asia.[25]

The Indonesian government even has
a development project with the sole des-
ignated purpose of population transfer.
The goal is to reduce overcrowding. Between 1950 and 1974, the government
resettled 664,000 people through its
"transmigration" project, moving them
off of Indonesia's main island of Java.
With the World Bank adding its support
and finances beginning in 1975, almost
3.5 million more people moved. The
relocations took place despite warnings,
which later proved accurate, that the
soils on the islands of destination were
poor and could not easily support so
many people, and that the social costs of
moving the people would be high.[26]

Environmental degradation is a common cause of flight. Millions of people have left lands where soils have become too eroded to support even subsistence agriculture. Their plights anticipate what could become the largest catalyst of migration ever: climate change. Ecologist Norman Myers has estimated that if global warming becomes a reality, sea level rise and changes in weather patterns could turn 150 million people into refugees by the middle of next century, assuming a sea level rise of 30 centimeters by 2050. Disruption of agriculture and the flooding of settled areas would be the main causes of flight. Of course, uncertainty is an element in each part of that situation, from questions about climate change to unknowns of social and economic results.[27]

Some of these pressures will escalate in the future. Overcrowding will increase as nearly 90 million people are added to world population every year. Pollution will become even more widespread as economic growth and industrialization arrive in parts of Southeast Asia that have lacked them. Water tables will continue to be drawn down far faster then they can replenish themselves in many countries; soils will continue to erode. And new people will react to these pressures in the future by leaving their homes.[28]

THE MOLOTOV COCKTAIL OF INSECURITY

Most displaced people are not on the move for any single, simple reason. They are forced out by a complex of pressures often exacerbated by underlying rapid population growth, ancient ethnic animosities, and resource scarcities. Unfortunately, accounts in the popular press have often reported singular

causes for people suddenly leaving countries such as Rwanda or Georgia, creating an impression that the problems are more short-term or specific in nature.

Countries with stable populations and high levels of education and public health demonstrate a resilience against war and overt persecution, so refugee flows are rare. Many countries ravaged by high infant mortality, low literacy, eroding farmland, and hunger, on the other hand, have recently seen people leaving at record rates. Often these basic deficiencies are not the immediate cause for migration; instead, they set the stage for the despots, the politically motivated bigotry, and the extremist politics that eventually force people out.

From fewer than 10 wars at any one time during the fifties, the number of major ongoing conflicts stood at 34 in 1993.

The situation is analogous to the spread of a disease, since the causes of infection are often complex and obscure. Malnourished people, for instance, lose the resilience of their immune systems to fight disease. They rarely die of starvation, but starvation nevertheless underlies the illnesses that kill. Lack of proper sanitation increases the likelihood of a cholera epidemic, and serious mental stress sometimes predisposes people to colds and the flu. In such cases, the disease is only the final element in a series of deeper difficulties.

A frequent ingredient in the cocktail of insecurity is war, and since mid-century, warfare has spread. From fewer than 10 wars at any one time during the fifties, the number of major ongoing conflicts stood at 34 in 1993. According to one count, the average number of annual war deaths in the second half of this century is more than double that of the nineteenth century, and seven times greater than in the 100 years before that. More than 92 percent of all conflicts since World War II have occurred in developing countries.[29]

Lebanon offers a good example of how certain tensions underlie war. When the French established the state of Lebanon, they did so according to a demographic balance. At the time, half the population was Christian, mostly Maronite, and the other half was Muslim, with Sunni Muslims outnumbering Shiites. According to journalist Thomas Friedman, an unwritten but widely accepted "national pact" required that the Lebanese President be a Maronite, the Prime Minister be a Sunni Muslim, and the Speaker of Parliament, a Shiite. Parliament was to have a six-to-five ratio of Christians to Muslims.[30]

By the seventies, Christians were only a little more than a third of the population, while Muslims and Druse (a smaller Islamic sect) accounted for the remaining two thirds. Shiites were the largest single community. When the new majority demanded a greater share of the power, the Maronites resisted, and formed private armies to ensure the status quo. The Muslims and Druse established their own militias in response, and war eventually erupted. Although it was the militias that people fled from, behind the violence lay a changing demographic balance and the refusal to share power. More than a third of all Lebanese now live outside of Lebanon. The country is a place where differential population growth rates and a rigid political system converged to force people out.[31]

The most spectacular examples of the complex mix of reasons why people leave their homes are in Africa. The continent has the highest crude birth rate of any region and the highest infant mortality rate. Because of its population growth, its grain production per person is lower today than it was in 1950, despite the fact that grain yields have more than doubled. At 118 kilograms per person, annual grain production is only around half as much as would be needed, without imports, to keep people healthy. In some places, hunger alone has created refugee flows. But for most of Africa's refugees, hunger and overpopulation are not the sole causes of flight—they are two contributing factors.[32]

In Ethiopia, for instance, there is some famine even in years of good rain. The country made the news regularly in the seventies and eighties for its large flows of refugees seeking relief from a vicious circle of famine and civil war. At the end of 1993, nearly 230,000 Ethiopians lived outside the country, mostly in Sudan, and at least a half-million were internally displaced. At 57 million, Ethiopia's population has grown by 30 million within the last four decades. And the nation faces a colossal increase of 106 million during the next 40 years, based on current growth rates. It is almost impossible to imagine how Ethiopia could possibly feed so many more people. It has some of the world's most severely eroded soils; much of its cropland is on steep slopes, and its tree cover stands at a mere 3 percent. Many in Ethiopia's next generation will probably have to choose between emigration and starvation.[33]

Just as desperate but perhaps more complex is the plight of Somalia. Clan warfare had forced some half-million Somalis out at the end of 1993, with another 700,000 internally displaced, and the conflict appears to be heating up again. A history of rapid population growth has hit that country hard, as its soils are heavily eroded and overgrazed and its forests are mostly gone, with deforestation so severe that even fuelwood is scarce in many areas. One result was migration to cities, where tensions have flared. Demographic change and environmental degradation in Somalia have altered the traditional community and family structures and left people more vulnerable to the tyranny of warlords.[34]

In Kenya, which has the least cropland per person of any country in Africa and second least of any country in the world, a dispute rages that nevertheless may not involve land scarcity. Masai tribespeople have attacked Kikuyu farmers, chasing them off the land and converting it to a nomadic, pastoral economy. Yet many people believe that in Kenya's case, as in many countries, the source of conflict is political pressure from a leader who needs to manipulate ethnic tensions in order to retain power. In the future, though, with Kenya's population projected to double in 21 years, land scarcity will become progressively more acute and could easily join with political manipulation to exacerbate tensions.[35]

The recent implosion of Rwanda brought these issues to a new level of world attention. In the wake of the power struggle between Hutus and Tutsis, some 1.7 million Rwandans remained refugees at the beginning of September 1994. But despite the speed with which the crisis broke, it has its roots in long-term trends. The refugees fled hatred between two groups of people, as the mass media reported. But that hatred was based on Rwanda's colonial history, the inequities of its educational system, the ownership of its land, the control of its government, and other deep, long-standing tensions. Popular analysis of the disaster neglected to take most of those contributing stresses into account.[36]

War orphans and AIDS orphans, for example, played a role in the Rwandan tragedy. Like its neighbor Uganda, Rwanda was one of the countries hit first and hardest by AIDS. And years of internal warfare had already taken many casualties before the current tragedy. The generation of people 20 to 40 years old—today's parents—bore a disproportionate number of the deaths from both causes. This resulted in a disruption of Rwandan family structure: large numbers of boys and young men lost their parents and had dim prospects for fulfilling lives. They were more readily recruited as soldiers as a result. Tina Malone, who organizes the relief effort for Catholic Relief Services, calls these children "cannon fodder—the stuff from which you can make a militia."[37]

In the wake of the power struggle between Hutus and Tutsis, some 1.7 million Rwandans remained refugees at the beginning of September 1994.

Other demographic change is also behind some of the hatred. Rwanda is the most densely populated land in Africa. To feed itself, the country steadily expanded the amount of land in crop production until the mid-eighties, when virtually all arable land was in use. Today, the average farm size is less than half a hectare, and as land is subdivided among male heirs, plot size is dwindling. The practice of fallowing has virtually disappeared, manure is in short supply since many farms are too small to provide fodder for cattle, and yields have been declining. These are threatening trends to people with too little land to feed their children—the kind of situation that causes fear, jealousy, and hatred.[38]

These tensions were compounded by class friction between Hutus and Tutsis, who have been the enfranchised group. From colonial times, Tutsis have been better educated and richer. Of course, class resentment is sometimes a motive for slaughter. Indeed, a significant part of the fighting and killing that took place was poorer members of either group attacking richer members of the same group—social, political, and class struggle. Tutsi is not exactly the name of an ethnic group: historically it meant "people who own cattle." And Hutu meant "people who farm." Intermarriage between the groups is widespread, as it has been for years. When fighting stemmed from hatred between Hutus and Tutsis, that was largely a result of propaganda spread by disenfranchised factions who had more to gain from war than they had to lose.[39]

Malone explicitly connects some of these issues in her analysis of the Rwandan disaster. She suggests that the warfare was motivated in part by fears that family plots were too small and by poverty and past war. "People can easily turn around and blame misfortune on the fact that there's not enough land to go around," she says. "And then someone puts the idea into their heads about Hutus and Tutsis, and it starts." Had it not been for the land scarcity and demographic disruption and pressures, Rwandan society would have been more resilient. Yet those tensions will be even more powerful there in the future, with population size expected to double in 30 years.[40]

Similar forces are at work elsewhere in the world. In the new central Asian states, political leaders are trying to create national identities within borders that were arbitrarily carved out by Stalin. The republics of Tajikistan, Turkmenistan, Kazakhstan, Kyrgyzstan, and Uzbekistan have so little national cohesion that none of them demanded independence when the Soviet Union collapsed; they became independent by default. The lack of effective political structures has created a power vacuum. Widespread poverty and an abundance of weapons have exacerbated the insecurity that many people feel. In Tajikistan, the result has been fighting between rival clan, regional, and religious groups over political power. Civil war there produced a half-million refugees in 1992 and 1993, though most subsequently returned home.[41]

Farther west, the war between Armenia and Azerbaijan continues despite crippling shortages on both sides of electricity, wood, water, transportation, and food. Almost 1 million Azerbaijanis were displaced in 1993 alone. The main point of contention is the ethnic makeup of the country, which has an ethnic Armenian-majority enclave, Nagorno-Karabakh, within its borders. In Georgia, battles for succession by one region displaced a quarter-million people internally in 1993, and an additional 35,000 people left their homes following ethnic, religious, and territorial battles elsewhere in the country. With so many ethnic divisions in these countries, and with weak national identities and political structures, the involuntary movement of people in the region is likely to continue for some time.[42]

The nature of war itself is changing. Warfare in Burundi, Cambodia, Georgia, Rwanda, Somalia, Tajikistan, and many other places is taking place within states rather than between them. According to the United Nations, of the 82 armed conflicts in the world between 1989 and 1992, only 3 were between countries. The rest were the result of internal tensions, often occurring against a background of poverty, inequalities, and weak or rigid political systems. If this trend of internal war continues, it will send refugees fleeing from problems that were held in check in the past, many of them prevented by the dominating geopolitics of the cold war.[43]

Journalist Robert Kaplan has taken notions of a new kind of war one step farther. He foresees a future in which crime becomes so prevalent that it replaces "traditional" war as the principal threat to stability, and becomes a major factor in migration. Kaplan describes hordes of young men who roam the squatter settlements of Third World cities as "loose molecules in a very unstable social fluid, a fluid that [is] clearly on the verge of igniting." Some of those young men become migrants themselves; others turn to crime, which includes the smuggling of people across borders. As the process develops, it can undermine national sovereignty, as by many accounts it is already doing in West Africa. No one trend accounts for the rising crime rates there; they are caused by many developments—by an infrastructure that allows the spread of diseases that leave children orphans, by unemployment, by the disenfranchisement of particular classes or ethnic groups.[44]

In many parts of the world, people are on the move because borders are fragmenting, provinces are receiving national autonomy, and states are collapsing. Eritrea has split off from Ethiopia; Yugoslavia has disintegrated; Czechoslovakia broke apart peacefully. Many people have left their homes to move into newly created states that they prefer, or to flee new states that they find unsafe. In the crowded countries of West Africa, national governments are said to control the borders only during the day. People flow freely across them at night. In the countries of the former Soviet Union, the process can be seen in an extreme form. In the past, the Soviet regime had relocated many peoples to regions far from their homelands. For instance, almost 25 million Russians live outside Russia, dispersed throughout the old Soviet republics. In Estonia, 30 percent of the population is Russian; in Latvia, the figure is 38 percent. Today, some of these expatriates will choose to return to the country of their ethnic origin; others will remain where they are.[45]

THE PUSH OF POVERTY, THE PULL OF WEALTH

The large gap in income between the rich and the poor of the world is at the root of some of the largest movements of all. Tens of millions of workers have moved from poorer countries to richer ones to take advantage of higher wages paid in stronger currencies. Some 900,-000 Turks have relocated to Germany, Scandinavia, and other parts of Europe, for example. About 2.5 million Mexicans live in the United States. Some 400,000 South Asians and Middle Easterners were living in Kuwait before they fled war in 1991, and some 1.2 million foreign workers were in Saudi Arabia at the same time. Each of those migrations is a response to economic disparities between countries.[46]

By the end of the eighties, remittances amounted to more than $65 billion a year, larger than all official development assistance.

Globally, the remittances of migrant workers—the money they earn abroad and then send home to their families and communities—are a vital economic resource. By the end of the eighties, remittances amounted to more than $65 billion a year according to a World Bank study, second only to crude oil in their value to the world's economy, and larger than all official development assistance. Almost half these funds went to developing countries. Although that is vitally important, living abroad also poses problems: it often splits up families and communities, it can be difficult for migrant workers to adjust to their new surroundings, and it denies emigrant countries the labor and skills of those individuals. Yet without remittances, many families and communities would be in desperate circumstances.[47]

The flow of workers from poor countries to wealthier ones is likely to increase in the future. The world's labor force is projected to grow by about a billion people during the next two decades. Nine out of 10 of these new workers will reside in the Third World, and few of these countries will be able to create sufficient jobs for them. Even the countries that reach their goals for economic growth are unlikely to have enough jobs for their young workers. From 1975 to 1990, world economic production grew 56 percent, but world employment rose only 28 percent. By 2000, world production is projected to have more than doubled since 1975, but employment is expected to be up by less than half. In Mexico, 1 million new jobs will have to be created every year to match the rate at which young people are entering the work force; in Egypt, a half-million jobs a year will be needed.[48]

As young people reach working age, many will have little choice but to look for jobs abroad when there are too few at home. The countries of North Africa and the Middle East are already a major source of migrant labor, and the youthfulness of their populations virtually ensures that they will be in the future as well. More than 70 percent of Arabs have been born since 1970, for example. An even more dramatic scenario exists in Africa: there, almost half the population has been born since 1980. The same is true of Cambodia, Guatemala, Laos, and Nicaragua, among many other countries. These areas are likely to be major sources of migrant workers in the future unless they receive considerable investment in job-creating industries.[49]

The disparity between rich and poor also makes people move for reasons other than the search for jobs. Poverty and the scarcities that go with it make people wish for better places to live. Ex-hausted supplies of firewood and timber for heating and cooking and building, depleted wells, overcrowded houses and schools, and a lack of electricity all plague the regions where the poorest people live. These scarcities often band together to form a cycle of inadequacy. Felled trees, for example, no longer anchor soil, which washes away and clogs rivers, and the disrupted flows of water cause further soil erosion. People are virtually pushed out of their homelands. Often they move to the nearest city, where they are attracted by the glitter and the hope of new lives.

In 1970, a quarter of the developing world's population lived in cities; by 2025, 57 percent will, if U.N. projections prove correct. (See Table 8–2.) In industrial countries, the urban population will have risen from 67 percent to 84 percent in that same time. One daring projection even found that about 15 years from now the rural population of the Third World will begin to decrease—despite rapid overall population growth—while urban populations keep growing. Much of the urban growth will come from children born in cities, but the size of the growth is also a testament to the combined pull of urban areas and the push of poverty on rural inhabitants.[50]

Once in a city, many of these migrants

Table 8-2. Share of Population Living in Urban Areas, by Region, 1970 and 1990, With Projection for 2025

Region	1970	1990	2025
	(percent)		
Africa	23	32	54
Asia (excluding Japan)	20	29	54
Latin America	57	72	84
Europe	67	73	85
North America	74	75	85
World	37	43	61

SOURCE: United Nations, *World Urbanization Prospects, 1992 Revision* (New York: 1993).

face squatter settlements with open sewers that run through the middle of the streets where children play; they live in cardboard or sheet metal shacks, where families are crowded into one room; disease runs rampant. These cities then become international jumping off points for migration by people trying to escape difficult living conditions. It is here that shady "travel agencies" take people's last savings in exchange for clandestine passages across national borders. For Chinese migrants, a highly specialized black market exists to move them to Eastern Europe, North America, Australia, and elsewhere.[51]

The world's already large disparities of income are rising, and that is showing up in the growth of cities. Despite the recent restoration of economic growth in Latin America, U.N. economists say that no progress is expected in reducing poverty, which is even likely to increase slightly by their calculations. And this takes place in a region whose countries already have some of the world's widest income disparities. Indeed, it is not entirely a coincidence that Latin America is by far the most urbanized region of the developing world. From 1950 to today, city dwellers have risen from 42 percent of the population there to 73 percent.[52]

For some years, China has been an example of some of the most equal distribution of income in the world. But now that is changing as incomes in its southern provinces and special economic zones soar while those in rural areas rise much more slowly. (See Chapter 7.) Moreover, the new income has led to inflation, as the rich and foreign importers buy more and more goods, bidding up the prices. The poor have suffered from these price increases without benefiting from the additional income in the country. And the Chinese government counts more than 100 million "surplus farm laborers," and says that every year another 15 million are added. The Chinese Academy of Social Sciences says that by 2010, half the population will live in cities, compared with 28 percent today and only 10 percent in the early eighties. So even in formerly equitable China, widening disparities of wealth play a role in moving tens of millions of people from rural lands to cities and from one region to another.[53]

Meanwhile, in some regions almost no one is getting richer. The per capita income of most sub-Saharan African nations actually fell during the eighties. After the latest negotiations of the General Agreement on Tariffs and Trade (GATT) were completed, the *Wall Street Journal* reported that "even GATT's most energetic backers say that in one part of the world, the trade accord may do more harm than good: sub-Saharan Africa," the poorest geographic region. There, an estimated one third of all college graduates have left the continent. That loss of talented people, due in large part to poverty and a lack of opportunities in Africa, will make it even more difficult for the continent to grow richer in the future and generate opportunities for its peoples.[54]

Increased international trade affects migration. It can take jobs to workers by letting them work in their home countries and then selling their goods to large foreign markets through export. It does, however, require investment in export industries before that can happen. Trade also can take workers to faraway jobs, such as the people who move to foreign countries that are doing better at trade, or those who work in the field offices of multinational corporations. Countries that follow an export-oriented path often experience unequal growth, in which small segments of their society who own capital and industries earn considerable income but the remainder benefit much less. The resulting inequitable distribution of income can itself contribute to migration.

As with many economic subjects, wide debate rages about whether trade is more often a cause of migration or a mitigator of it. Expressing a preference for taking jobs to workers rather than the other way around, an Irish politician allegedly once said, "All my life I've seen the lads leaving Ireland for the big smoke in London, Pittsburgh, Birmingham, and Chicago. It'd be better for Ireland if they stayed here and we imported the smoke."[55]

Economic events on one side of the world can pull people from their homes thousands of miles away. For example, changes on European or North American markets in the price of soybeans or coffee have led people to leave their homes in South America and Africa. In the late seventies, coffee prices fell on markets around the world. In Brazil, a major coffee producer, farmers switched to different crops, especially soybeans. But coffee production is particularly labor-intensive, and soybean production, much less so. Unemployment rose, which led to a stream of migrants who moved into the frontier areas of uncut forests in the interior. (The massive migration was aided, to be sure, by one of the most unequal land distributions in the world, without which the numbers moving into the rain forest would have been far smaller.)[56]

Similarly with gold. In the late seventies, gold prices rose sharply, and gold mining in Brazil took off. Tens of thousands of landless workers left low-paying jobs in the coastal areas to move inland and prospect for the metal. They cleared virgin lands, opened large pits, and often forced out indigenous peoples, some of whom then had no choice but to migrate themselves.[57]

One attempt to lessen the push of poverty over the long term is the structural adjustment programs of the International Monetary Fund and World Bank. Yet when Poland had its first experience with this economic shock therapy in 1990, inflation hit 240 percent and 1.3 million people lost their jobs. Tens of thousands abandoned the country. Other East European countries have faced similar shocks. More often, though, it is cuts in social expenditures for government subsidies on food, education, health care, and home heating fuel, as well as changes in trade policies, exchange rates, and family incomes, that lead people to move.[58]

Research by the World Resources Institute on the effects of a structural adjustment program in the Philippines found that the program worsened short-term poverty in urban areas by cutting social expenditures. That led to an urban-to-rural migration to upland regions and coastal areas as people sought livelihoods from the fields, fisheries, and forests outside Manila and other cities, where they could no longer survive.[59]

An economic liberalization program in Sri Lanka beginning in the late seventies cut social programs and increased emphasis on export industries, resulting in declining real wages, food insecurity for the lowest income group, deterioration of the social welfare system, and widening income disparities. The authors of one report argue that much of the movement of Sri Lankans to the Persian Gulf was a case of "survival migration" by those in the poorest strata of society, mostly women who went to work as domestic servants.[60]

This poses a dilemma, because the very adjustment programs that underlie unwanted emigration are needed to combat the high inflation and financial chaos that also can cause people to leave. Without adjustment, in some cases, emigration will still occur, but for different reasons—because economies are completely out of control. The beginnings of a solution might come if the economists who plan adjustment programs took migration into account during their work by forecasting what movements of people could be expected.

They could then at least consider the possibility of altering programs when emigration appears too severe.

DEFUSING THE PRESSURES

The problems that drive people to leave their homelands—war, persecution, famine, environmental and social disintegration—are often treated as inevitable "givens." Many people and governments feel powerless to do anything about them. But if we identify the failures and scarcities that underlie so many of these problems, perhaps we can find ways to build more stable societies. If we see in persecution, for example, the tensions wrought by inadequate livelihoods, farmland, or water, by lack of education and health care, by the fear that our children face a bleak future, then we can reduce the mistreatment by addressing those issues. Yet today's refugee policy consists of responding to crises as they happen rather than trying to prevent them.

Once refugees have fled their homes, no amount of money or assistance can fully restore their past lives. The fundamental solutions are those that will enable people to avoid flight in the first place. Indeed, even from a purely financial perspective, it is more efficient to head off refugee crises by spending money to make societies secure economically, socially, and militarily than to try to put them back together after a disruption. Preventing the emergencies that may come 10–20 years down the road costs less, and must begin now.

In crises, of course, the international community will have to take expensive and drastic action. But even in such cases, the money and time invested yields a huge return. The troops dis-patched to Somalia in 1992 and to Rwanda in 1994, for instance, were able to save hundreds of thousands of lives by getting food, protection, and medical help to vulnerable people. Rarely have government programs helped so many people in so short a time. Faced with growing numbers of refugees worldwide every year, it may be time to create a permanent emergency response unit out of the world's militaries, one that would get temporary shelter, medicine, food, and safety to refugee camps. The alternatives are to assign that task to the militaries of individual countries, as happened with the French and U.S. militaries on the border of Rwanda in 1994, or to leave the task to underfunded and understaffed voluntary organizations.

Today's refugee policy consists of responding to crises as they happen rather than trying to prevent them.

Yet governments are not jumping at the chance to turn their militaries to such tasks. According to one account in the *Washington Post*, for example, "Defense Department officials cringe at the notion of becoming a kind of super, musclebound Red Cross or Salvation Army." These operations sap time and attention of senior officials, cut into combat training exercises, tie up equipment and personnel, and take increasingly scarce defense dollars away from other operations. Used for humanitarian goals, however, militaries clearly can make a huge difference. In addition to saving many lives in Somalia and Rwanda, troops have recently protected tens of thousands of Kurds after the Gulf War, have gotten food to desperate Bosnians, and have given relief to victims of natural disasters in the United States and Bangladesh. These successes clearly contribute to security and to the protection of people—the basic reasons why we have militaries in the first place.[61]

Of course, military action can never be a substitute for more fundamental and long-term solutions. Efforts to help people remain in their homes and countries must reach across the entire spectrum from prevention of emergencies to protection and relief during crises and rebuilding afterward. It is only through such a complete approach that the phenomenon of refugees—no longer an aberration, but an ordinary expression of the world of the nineties—can be addressed. First: prevent crises. Second: protect victims. Third: try to restore as much as possible of their past lives. The first is preferable; the second and third cost heavily in human and financial terms.

It is ironic that emergency assistance is siphoning away the funds needed to prevent future emergencies.

But while crisis-driven expenditures are rising out of necessity, efforts to attack the underlying causes of flight are decreasing. Official development assistance from the world's 25 wealthiest countries fell by 8 percent in 1993. In 1994, the United Nations expected to spend at least $1 billion more on refugees and peacekeeping than on economic development. The budget of the U.N. Development Programme is now not much larger than that of the U.N. High Commissioner for Refugees. It is ironic that emergency assistance is siphoning away the funds needed to prevent future emergencies.[62]

We do not have to and cannot achieve perfect stability. Many countries are able to absorb refugees and immigrants, and many countries need them to provide labor and to inject new vibrancy into societies. The goal should be to improve stability so that people who want to remain home can do so.

Some countries that are not sources of refugees today are likely to become so during the next few years. The United Nations recently voiced particularly strong concern about Angola, Iraq, Myanmar (formerly Burma), and Sudan. The collapse of Haiti did not come as a surprise to many observers. Zaire suffers from severe political and economic collapse, and is a likely source of insecurity in the future. Nigeria's elected government has been refused control by the military, and violent clashes have resulted, raising the possibility of a flight from that country.[63]

Efforts to head off crises and flows of refugees or emigrants from these countries will be more fruitful if they begin today rather than waiting for chaos, as happened in Haiti, Rwanda, Somalia, and elsewhere. In the words of J. Brian Atwood, head of the U.S. Agency for International Development, upon returning from a trip to Africa: "Just the other day we made a decision to contribute $35 million additional to handle this disaster [in Rwanda]. One wonders if we had had that $35 million in the previous two years whether we could have done something to avoid the killing."[64]

In this light, initiatives not normally considered relevant to refugees become central. Spending on sanitation, public health, and preventive medicine would reduce parental mortality, and intact families would give children a more secure future. Maintaining stable soils and waters for farming would defuse tensions over land and livelihoods. Investing in literacy can also have a profoundly stabilizing effect by helping people read about the actions of their governments and get more involved in solving the problems of their regions. Without such actions, the problems that people flee from will continue to return.

Many examples of attacking the underlying pressures exist. The International Conference on Population and Development in Cairo in September 1994 was one such effort. Its plan to keep world population below 9.8 billion people by 2050, and to do so by focusing on women and by spreading literacy, health care, and family planning technologies, directly attacks the underpinnings of some of the insecurities and wars that chase out refugees. Likewise, UNICEF's great successes recently at immunizing infants around the world is a significant contribution to stability. Tiny loans of a few dollars to poor villagers by the Grameen Bank in Bangladesh have brought success to people in the poorest class in one of the most densely populated countries on earth. These efforts should receive credit for their ability to enhance security.[65]

If topics like improved literacy seem far removed from the pressures that make people refugees, consider the fact that no democracy that has a relatively free press has ever suffered a major famine. If access by literate people to public debate seems too detached from warfare to be relevant, consider the fact that no two democracies have ever gone to war.[66]

Without actions that improve the stability of countries and the security of individuals, we face a future of migration and flight. Since 1976, the number of U.N.-registered refugees in the world has risen consistently on average more than 12 percent a year. If growth continues at that pace, by 2000 the world's refugee population will have doubled to 46 million. It would be better to act now to eliminate the pressures that make people leave home.

9

Budgeting for Disarmament

Michael Renner

When the cold war ended, expectations for a better world ran high. Key among these were the hope for a more peaceful and more cooperative world and the anticipation of a very sizable peace dividend—the opportunity for governments to recast their priorities from war and war preparation toward disarmament and neglected civilian needs. With this reorientation, substantial savings would occur from not spending as much money on the military as in the past.

The cover of the *Human Development Report 1994*, prepared by the U.N. Development Programme, illustrates this expectation: using what looks like a stylized staircase, it shows the evolution of recent global military expenditures and projections for future years, with a steady and ultimately significant decline.[1]

Between 1987 and 1994, the cumulative reduction in military spending amounted to some $935 billion—equivalent to skipping a year's worth of expenditures. Still, reality has not matched the optimistic expectations. The cutbacks have been quite small compared with the momentous political transformations of the late eighties.[2]

Today, military budgets are still as high as they were in the late seventies, when U.S.-Soviet détente came to an end. And they may not decline substantially more. Herbert Wulf, director of the Bonn International Center for Conversion, has pointedly noted that "to do a little less of the same is the overriding principle of governments' policy." In large parts of the Third World, meanwhile, peace remains elusive or governments eagerly build their military muscle. In the Middle East, even the unfolding Arab-Israeli peace is unlikely to lead to lower arms spending.[3]

Instead of reallocating freed-up budgetary resources from the military to the civilian realm, western governments have chosen to prune overall spending, with the goal of reducing deficits or offering tax cuts. Meanwhile, although the

An expanded version of this chapter appeared as Worldwatch Paper 122, *Budgeting for Disarmament*.

former Warsaw Pact states have curtailed their military budgets, the profound and crisis-laden transformations of their economies have yielded investment deficits rather than surpluses. Hence the peace dividend has, by and large, failed to materialize—disappearing instead into a gigantic fiscal Bermuda Triangle. (Deficit reductions and tax cuts provide only an indirect benefit.)

The initial euphoria at the end of the cold war and the hope for peace around the globe quickly evaporated in the face of large-scale conflict in the Persian Gulf. Although a number of protracted conflicts have come to an end, they have been quickly replaced by a seemingly endless stream of new battles—some of them being long-standing conflicts erupting again after a break. According to the Stockholm International Peace Research Institute, the number of major wars—those that kill at least 1,000 persons—rose to 34 in 1993, after having dropped from 36 in 1987 to 30 in 1991. And an analysis including "lesser" wars actually shows a steady upward trend since the end of World War II.[4]

The post–cold war era presents a mix of peril and promise—and hence both a need and an opportunity for a new peace policy. But in the face of this challenge, there is a palpable lack of strategic vision or leadership toward a truly new world order, an inertia that leaves policymakers stuck in traditional modes of thinking and relying on outdated policy tools.

The demilitarization imperative is threefold. First, it concerns the legacy of war and war preparation. The challenge is to assist countries emerging from the devastation of warfare in their efforts to rebuild and fashion viable civil societies and economies less susceptible to breakdown and renewed strife. The second task is to slash the enormous arsenals of destruction accumulated over decades; to adopt meaningful restrictions on arms production, possession, and trade; and to convert war-making capacities to civilian use. Finally, and this is likely to be the greatest challenge, institutions need to be created that are capable of robust peacekeeping, nonviolent dispute resolution, and war prevention.

The peace dividend has, by and large, failed to materialize—disappearing instead into a gigantic fiscal Bermuda Triangle.

How much progress is the world making toward building the foundations of a just and lasting peace? A crucial indicator is the resources that governments and international organizations are making available to accomplish the tasks just mentioned. Throughout the cold war, when a nation's coercive and deterrent power was considered central to maintaining its security, military spending was a key indicator. But there is growing recognition that security in an interdependent world requires cooperation, not confrontation, and that economic vitality and environmental stability are more important to a country's fortunes than martial qualities.

COSTS OF WAR, COSTS OF PEACE

In this era of cost-cutting and public belt-tightening, the focus seems to have shifted from the peace dividend to concern about the "costs of peace"—as if peace were perhaps unaffordable. At the same time that a considerable number of military programs continue to be pursued, peace and disarmament-related expenditures are subjected to nickle-and-dime scrutiny.

Peace obviously has its costs. But in judging expenditures associated with demilitarization and peacebuilding efforts, the distinction between costs of war and those of peace is crucial. (See Table 9–1.) Many of the bills now coming due are in effect the financial aftershocks of decades of war and war prepa-

Table 9-1. The Scope of the Demilitarization and Peacebuilding Challenge

Restitution
(Coping with Legacy of the War System)

Reconstruction
Land mine clearance
Environmental cleanup
Refugee repatriation
Demobilization and reintegration of
    ex-combatants

Transformation
(Moving from War to Peace)

Decommissioning and dismantling of
    arms
Bans or restrictions on arms production
    and trade
Treaty verification
    (monitoring/inspections)
Base closures
Conversion of military production
    facilities, bases, and land

Peacebuilding
(Building Peacekeeping and Peacemaking
    Institutions)

Peacekeeping
Conflict early-warning system
Conflict resolution/mediatren
Strengthened international legal system
    (World Court, International Criminal
    Court, War Tribunals)
Sanctions support fund
Peace research and education

ration. They will be incurred whether or not humanity succeeds in fashioning an alternative system to handle conflicts within and among countries. But if an alternative does not materialize, these aftershocks will keep reoccurring.

In environmental affairs, health care, and other issues, there is growing recognition that an ounce of prevention is worth a pound of cure. The same generally holds true for war and peace. Full-cost accounting, long overdue, would make it abundantly clear that "national security" through ever increasing military prowess carries a prohibitive price tag.

The costs imposed by the war system are manifold. They begin with the resources to maintain it. Global military spending since World War II has added up to a cumulative $30–35 trillion. The military sector absorbs substantial resources that could help reduce the potential for violent conflict if instead they were invested in human security—health, housing, education, poverty eradication, and environmental sustainability. For example, the price paid for two warships ordered by Malaysia in 1992 would have been sufficient to provide safe drinking water for the next quarter-century to the 5 million Malaysians now lacking it.[5]

Getting rid of accumulated arsenals, whether as a routine scrapping of obsolete stocks or as measures to comply with international arms treaties, is another cost of the war system. So are the outlays required to decontaminate and rehabilitate land and facilities used to produce, test, and maintain weapons and to preserve combat readiness. And the costs that arise from having to cope with the devastation and dislocation inflicted by warfare—the physical and ecological damage, the loss of harvests and industrial production, the uprooting of populations and resulting need for humanitarian assistance and refugee resettlement, and, eventually, the reconstruction efforts. (See Table 9–2.) Indications are that in each of these categories, the costs will run at least in the tens, and possibly hundreds, of billions of dollars globally.[6]

In contrast, the costs of building a robust peace system are likely to be much more modest. Creating an effective multilateral peacekeeping system, curbing or banning much of the production and trade of armaments (and coming up with effective means to verify compliance), developing mechanisms to recognize conflicts before they erupt into violence, providing means for peaceful settlements, strengthening the rule of international law—these are endeavors that can legitimately be regarded as costs of peace. If governments pursued the building of a peace system with the same seriousness as they built military muscle, in all likelihood many violent conflicts could be avoided.

A comparatively small investment—perhaps $20–30 billion per year—could make a tremendous difference in the global war and peace balance. Although there are obvious upfront costs in building a peace system and making the transition to it, these ought to be regarded not as an unwelcome expense but as an overdue investment. In the long run, the benefits—in financial savings and in human lives—would clearly be dominant. Not making these investments will condemn humanity to bear the costs of the war system ad infinitum.

Table 9-2. Economic Cost and Scope of War, Selected Examples

Region/Years	Observation
Iran-Iraq 1980–88	The war cost an estimated $416 billion just up to 1985—including money to conduct the war, the damage sustained, the oil revenues forgone, and the GNP lost. This surpasses the two countries' combined earnings of $364 billion from oil sales since they first started exporting petroleum.
Persian Gulf 1990–91	According to the Arab Monetary Fund, the Iraqi occupation of Kuwait and the war to reverse it cost the region some $676 billion. This includes the direct costs of the war and the damage it inflicted, and economic impacts such as the loss of earnings, but not the vast environmental damage.
Central America 1980–89	Estimates of direct and indirect war losses total $1.1 billion in El Salvador and $2.5 billion in Nicaragua (including the cost of the U.S. embargo). The costs for rehabilitation of land and equipment are not included.
Southern Africa 1980–88	Economic costs of South African acts of destabilization and aggression are estimated at $27–30 billion for Angola and about $15 billion for Mozambique.

SOURCE: Michael Renner, "Iran-Iraq War Produces Only Losers," *World Watch*, November/December 1988; Youssef M. Ibrahim, "War Is Said to Cost the Persian Gulf $676 Billion in 1990 and '91," *New York Times*, April 25, 1993; Benjamin L. Crosby, "Central America," and Mark C. Chona and Jeffrey I. Herbst, "Southern Africa," both in Anthony Lake et al., *After the Wars: Reconstruction in Afghanistan, Indochina, Central America, Southern Africa, and the Horn of Africa* (New Brunswick, N.J.: Transaction Books, for Overseas Development Council, 1990).

Distinguishing between war and peace costs does not imply a choice between one or the other. A lasting peace cannot be built without dealing with the remnants of the war system. Given the huge stocks of military equipment around the globe, it is difficult to imagine that antagonists will choose to rely on nonviolent means of dispute settlement. Hence, far-reaching disarmament is a prerequisite for peacebuilding. And converting military facilities to civilian use and developing other jobs for those who worked in them is essential to diminish the economic imperative for continued large-scale military spending.

Conversely, addressing only the immediate symptoms of the war system without tackling its roots will likely condemn us to repeating history. Governments may now balk at the costs of conflict prevention and peacebuilding, but failure to set in motion the transition from a war system to a peace system will impose far greater costs. It is far cheaper, and far preferable, to try to avoid violent conflict than to cope with the repercussions—massive outpourings of refugees and humanitarian emergencies.

It is far cheaper, and far preferable, to try to avoid violent conflict than to cope with the repercussions.

The annual expenditures of the U.N. High Commissioner for Refugees (UNHCR), for example, have soared from about $12 million in the early seventies to almost $1.1 billion in 1993. In the first nine months of 1993, the U.N. Department of Humanitarian Affairs, responsible for coordinating humanitarian programs of different U.N. agencies, launched 17 "consolidated appeals" for more than $4 billion of relief and rehabilitation assistance to more than 20 million people in some 20 countries—a rise

of 29 percent from mid-1992. The European Union's humanitarian aid tripled in just two years to about $700 million in 1993.[7]

Events in Rwanda provide the most recent and a particularly depressing example of the international community's shortsightedness. When the genocidal killings in that country began in April 1994, the U.N. Security Council responded by reducing the peacekeeping force already deployed there to a symbolic presence. In late April, Secretary-General Boutros-Ghali proposed boosting the force to 5,500, at a six-month cost of $115 million. Opposition by the Clinton administration delayed formal approval, and the lack of adequate offers of troops and equipment from other governments postponed the deployment for months.[8]

By July, estimates of the number of people killed had risen to a half-million. Hundreds of thousands more fled into neighboring Zaire following the victory of the Rwandan rebel army; cholera and dysentery epidemics ravaged the refugee camps. It was only then that the outside world began to act, by organizing a massive humanitarian relief effort. On July 22, 1994, Boutros-Ghali estimated that more than $434 million would be needed over six months. One week later, President Clinton announced that U.S. aid alone was surging toward $500 million.[9]

This points to a bitter irony. Presumably, concern about financial costs was one of the motivating factors, along with the perceived political costs, for blocking early deployment of a peacekeeping force that could have averted some of the bloodshed and prevented the exodus of civilians. But by not acting decisively, not only were hundreds of thousands of lives lost, but the costs to the rest of the world ended up being incomparably higher. Furthermore, by not moving decisively to help reconstitute the political and legal institutions of this shattered country, its future stability remains in question.[10]

COPING WITH THE LEGACY OF WAR

A series of long-standing conflicts have been settled in recent years or are in the process of being settled—in Nicaragua, El Salvador, Ethiopia/Eritrea, Mozambique, Namibia, South Africa, Israel/Palestine, Lebanon, and Cambodia. As elating as this must be to the people in those countries, the transition from war to peace presents a host of new challenges, many of which are interrelated and must be tackled as a whole.

Demobilizing and reintegrating ex-combatants into civil society is critical to a successful transition to peace. It not only reduces the long-term drain on scarce public budgets, it holds the promise of making the ex-fighters productive members of civil society. Delays in this process or the lack of civilian career opportunities can easily cause discontent to bubble up, presenting a severe danger to peace and stability if disgruntled ex-combatants decide to take up their weapons again.[11]

The experience in different countries has been varied. In Afghanistan, Angola, and Cambodia, demobilization was attempted but never fully implemented, and fighting has resumed. In Nicaragua and El Salvador, demobilization did take place, but reintegration has proved difficult; peace has been fragile. Efforts in Zimbabwe and Namibia were successful, in the sense that a return to conflict was avoided, but there, too, productive reintegration has been problematic. (In Zimbabwe, the transfer of many ex-soldiers bloated the country's civil service.) The process remains to be completed in Uganda and Chad. In Liberia, demobilization has come to a virtual halt, and

repeated cease-fire violations may unravel the peace agreement. In Mozambique, demobilization of government and rebel soldiers was completed more or less on schedule, but the formation of a smaller, unified army has been agonizingly slow.[12]

Ideally, following the signing of a peace agreement, the combatants are brought to locations where they are registered, disarmed, and prepared to re-enter civil society. During this so-called cantonment period (or, if possible, even earlier), assessments are made of the ex-combatants' skills, needs, and preferences, and of where they want to live. This information is crucial for designing well-tailored, effective reintegration programs. To smooth this, such programs involve assistance targetted toward both short- and long-term needs, including cash compensation, provision of agricultural land and tools, housing, extension of credits, training and apprenticeship courses, and income-generating programs. Some former soldiers have skills useful in the civilian realm, but most lack adequate education and civilian job experience, and need substantial assistance.[13]

Very often, reality is far from the ideal just described. Political will and adequate funding are among the key factors determining the outcome of demobilization programs, but frequently they are in short supply. As a 1993 World Bank report of seven countries points out, insufficient resources can cause delays in implementation and hence lengthy encampment periods, and, at a later stage, may undermine effective support programs, such as promises of land and credit for ex-combatants and their families. These difficulties can lead to a loss of confidence in the whole process, produce an uneasy and tenuous peace, and might in extreme cases even make it unravel.[14]

Given the exhausted state of the economies of countries emerging from warfare, the cost of demobilization and reintegration (see Table 9–3) are often beyond their capacity. Hence, a significant share of financing falls on foreign donors. Yet donors have been reluctant to make commitments in early stages. They often prefer to wait until they detect signs of a successful program, yet that delay reduces the likelihood of success. Without knowing how much aid they can expect during what period of time, the governments of countries returning to peace cannot adequately plan or launch a demobilization program.[15]

Efforts to remove land mines are another key ingredient to the success of post-conflict reconstruction. Scattered indiscriminately, land mines have become a ubiquitous threat and a powerful impediment to the normal functioning of a society, even long after a war has ended. Mines are mostly found in rural areas, and many of the countries suffering most from this problem depend predominantly on agriculture for income and employment. Without effective demining programs, large areas remain inaccessible, refugees are impeded or discouraged from returning home, peasants cannot work their fields, and reconstruction is hindered. And coping with the needs of mine blast survivors can easily overwhelm a poor country's health and social system.

The statistics are chilling. Of approximately 1 million persons who have been killed or maimed by land mines since 1975, the majority—some 80 percent—were civilians. Estimates of the number of mines scattered in some 62 countries range from 65 million to more than 100 million, or one mine for every 50–85 people on earth. In the 12 countries with an extremely severe problem (as judged by the U.S. State Department), there is one mine for every 3–5 people. And the mines continue to be laid far faster than they are being removed: each year, even

Table 9-3. Cost and Scope of Demobilization Programs, Selected Countries[1]

Country	Cost	Duration	Number Demobilized
	(million dollars)		
Angola[2]	125.0	1992–93	[19,833]
Chad	18.9	1992–93	9,173
Mozambique	54.4–62.6	1993–94	77,000–83,000
Namibia	46.4	1989	32,000
Nicaragua[3]	84.4	1990–92	96,000
Uganda	19.4	1992–94	30,000 proj.
Zimbabwe[4]	230.0	1981–85	75,000

[1]It is difficult to compare costs directly in different countries because some include items not reflected in others.   [2]Demobilization was aborted; 19,883 combatants had been demobilized before full-scale fighting resumed.   [3]$43.6 million for Contra demobilization; $40.8 million for Sandinista Army demobilization. It is unclear how much was actually spent on Sandinista demobilization; assistance and benefits were promised, but the government received only $5.8 million in aid from Spain and was unable to follow through on its promise.   [4]Includes cost of combatants' salaries while they were encamped for one year or more ($42 million); such costs are not included in other cases here.
SOURCE: World Bank, *Demobilization and Reintegration of Military Personnel in Africa: The Evidence from Seven Country Case Studies,* Discussion Paper, Africa Regional Series (Washington, D.C.: 1993); Humberto Ortega Saavedra, "The Role of International Financial Institutions in the Democratization and Demilitarization Processes," in Francisco José Aguilar Urbina, ed., *Demobilization, Demilitarization, and Democratization in Central America* (San José, Costa Rica: Arias Foundation for Peace and Human Progress, Centre for Peace and Reconciliation, 1994).

as governments struggle to remove roughly 80,000 mines, about 2 million new ones are put in place. More than 250 million land mines have been produced during the past 25 years, and 10–30 million are still made annually; another 100 million are thought to have been stockpiled.[16]

Mine clearance is not only extremely dangerous—as some commentators have put it, undertaken "one leg, one life at a time"—but also very time-intensive and expensive. Experience suggests that it takes 100 times as long to detect, remove, and disarm a mine as to plant it. Mines are extremely cheap to manufacture, but according to Patrick Blagden, the U.N.'s top demining expert, it could cost an astronomical $200–300 billion to clear all mines worldwide. Just removing mines newly laid in an average year could cost at least $600 million.[17]

Nothing like this large amount of money is available. Kuwait, where the government signed contracts worth about $700 million for demining after the Iraqi occupation, is spending far more than the rest of the world combined. Elsewhere, demining efforts—when undertaken at all—tend to be badly underfunded. In a number of countries with ongoing U.N. peacekeeping operations, voluntary trust funds have been set up to finance mine-clearing, but Secretary-General Boutros-Ghali has said that "this system is usually slow and inadequate to meet the need for urgent mine clearance programs." Some $25 million a year has been spent on demining efforts in the context of peacekeeping operations in Mozambique, Somalia, Cambodia, and Afghanistan in recent years, a figure expected to reach $28 million in 1995. Altogether, all U.N. agencies spent some $67 million on mine clearance and mine awareness during 1993.[18]

The International Red Cross has estimated it could take thousands of years to clear all mines in Afghanistan. Demining there is now concentrated on just 60 square kilometers of priority areas, but shortfalls in funding have impeded even that limited effort. Likewise, removing all mines in Cambodia clearly surpasses that impoverished country's capacity; it would require every Cambodian to contribute every dollar of income for several years. Human Rights Watch and the Physicians for Human Rights have called on the countries that stoked the fires of the Cambodian conflict to provide funding and other assistance for mine clearance.[19]

Of approximately 1 million persons who have been killed or maimed by land mines since 1975, the majority were civilians.

Effective mine clearance is a prerequisite for refugees to be able to return to their homes. (See Chapter 8.) Wherever conditions allow, refugees do eventually return home, many with the assistance of UNHCR and other agencies. In 1992, a record 2.4 million refugees were repatriated, equivalent to 13 percent of the refugee population that year, and UNHCR planned to help 3 million people go home during 1994. But with new conflicts breaking out across the globe, the returnees' numbers are dwarfed by legions of newly displaced people. Returnees notwithstanding, during the last two decades the total number of refugees grew in every single year except two.[20]

Although most UNHCR funds go to accommodate refugees in their host countries, a rapidly growing amount is devoted to voluntary repatriation: from $43 million in 1988 to $207 million in 1993 and a projected $382 million in 1994. Repatriating refugees can be more than twice as expensive as keeping them in camps. UNHCR provides returnees with the basics for a new start in their homeland: tools, seeds, building materials, and sufficient food before the first harvest. The agency also tries to provide or repair infrastructure such as water wells, roads and bridges, and schools and health clinics. But as Soren Jessen-Petersen, a top official, explains, "we are not able to rebuild entire countries, and there really aren't any international agencies which are. There is a real gap in the international system here."[21]

The financial requirements during the transition from war to peace in countries such as El Salvador, Nicaragua, Cambodia, or Mozambique are quite small compared with global aid flows, and certainly in contrast to the resources that for many years were devoted to sustaining wars. Still, for the countries involved, weakened by protracted conflict, the needs are substantial. (See Table 9-4.) Timely and adequate support from the international community is crucial to firm up what otherwise might be a shaky or temporary peace. Yet, as Oscar Arias, former Costa Rican President and 1987 Nobel Prize laureate, pointed out in the Central American context, "each day the hope that our countries will receive as much aid for human development as they once received for militarization grows increasingly remote."[22]

Bilateral donors and international organizations are just beginning to come to grips with the requirements and im-

Table 9-4. Financing Post-Conflict Reconstruction[1]

Country	Observation
Guatemala	The government and the URNG guerrilla force were expected to sign a formal peace agreement by late 1994 to end 30 years of conflict. The government created a "National Fund for Peace" (FONAPAZ) in 1991 to finance refugee resettlement and social and economic rehabilitation in the poorest regions affected by the conflict. With international support, FONAPAZ investments rose from $6.3 million in 1992 to $13 million in 1993 and a projected $34 million in 1994.
El Salvador	International donors pledged $800 million for peace accord's implementation and reconstruction (including demobilization and reintegration of 42,000 ex-combatants, elections, democratization and safeguarding human rights, and redistribution of land), but far less money has been forthcoming. Some $515 million of national and international funds is available for 1993–96, but at least another $376 million is needed.
Haiti	Emergency Economic Recovery Program, to be implemented in the 6–12 months following a return to democracy, will cost about $210 million; foreign donors have pledged more than $1 billion for rehabilitation purposes over five years.
Mozambique	Implementation of peace agreement—including electoral aspects—is estimated to cost close to $100 million just in 1994. Refugee repatriation, demobilization and reintegration of ex-combatants, and mine clearance will cost at least another $150 million. Rebuilding destroyed schools and humanitarian needs require many hundreds of millions of dollars.

plications of war-to-peace transitions. For them, demobilization and reintegration are still emerging issues; with ad hoc arrangements predominating, many donors are institutionally not geared up for timely and effective support.[23]

The role of the World Bank, the International Monetary Fund (IMF), and the regional lending institutions in particular needs to be rethought. The Bank is receiving an increasing number of requests for technical and financial aid for ex-combatant reintegration. It has helped Angola, Ethiopia, and Uganda, but its involvement is reluctant and so far minor.[24]

The overall lending policies of the World Bank (and the IMF) are likely to have a more significant, and possibly detrimental, impact. The conditions that both institutions routinely insist on as a prerequisite for approving loans may actually be at odds with the goals of postconflict reconstruction. First, by putting strict limits on recipient governments' public spending, structural adjustment provisions by implication also restrict outlays to help foster peace and reconciliation. Second, by imposing cutbacks in social programs that alleviate poverty and by prescribing export-oriented economic policies, these arrangements tend to accentuate domestic inequalities and may generate new discontent that could bear the seeds of future conflict. The austerity measures imposed today on

Table 9-4. (*Continued*)

Country	Observation
Palestine	In 1993, donors pledged $2.4 billion over five years to lay an economic foundation for Palestinian self-rule in Gaza and Jericho. However, relatively little money has been forthcoming ($80 million by September 1994), threatening the viability of self-rule. The U.N. Relief Works Agency, meanwhile, launched a Peace Implementation Programme with $173 million worth of projects.
Kuwait	Kuwait spent at least $8–10 billion on reconstruction contracts with foreign companies during 1991–93 following the Gulf War (including $1 billion to fight hundreds of oil well fires set by the departing Iraqi army). Cost estimates made immediately following the war were in the $20–25 billion range over five years. The government has not released any official figures.
Cambodia	Of $880 million pledged by foreign donors for reconstruction and peacebuilding in June 1992, only about $200 million had actually been disbursed by September 1993 when the newly elected government was formed.
Bosnia	The cost of restoring essential public services in war-devastated Sarajevo is estimated at $540 million, with $254 million needed urgently and $286 million for a transitional phase.

¹The term "reconstruction" is broadly used here to encompass a variety of postconflict activities, including repair of physical damage, demobilization and reintegration of ex-combatants, resettlement of refugees and displaced persons, and creation of the social, economic, and political conditions under which peace can take root. The presence and importance of each one of these varies from case to case.
SOURCE: Compiled by Worldwatch Institute from sources cited in endnote 22.

many countries emerging from conflict contrasts sharply with the generous aid that European and some Asian countries received after World War II.[25]

El Salvador and other countries emerging from war are likely to find themselves walking a tightrope between the contradictory demands of fulfilling loan conditions on the one hand and peace accords on the other. In 1990, Anthony Lake, now President Clinton's National Security Advisor, warned that "economic policies that exacerbate . . . instability may destroy the peace completely. . . . Concern for the survival of fragile democratic institutions and achievement of the political stability needed to preserve a newly won peace suggests that the World Bank and IMF should be particularly careful about the policies upon which they insist as a condition of their participation in the reconstruction of . . . war-torn regions."[26]

LAYING DOWN ARMS, RETURNING TO CIVILIAN LIFE

The late eighties and early nineties witnessed a series of unprecedented arms control and disarmament treaties on conventional, chemical, and nuclear arsenals. Of these, only one—the Chemical Weapons Convention—is global. The two Strategic Arms Reductions Treaties (START I and II) concern the United States and the former Soviet Union, but not any of the other nuclear weapons powers; the Conventional Forces in Europe (CFE) Treaty regulates, as its name suggests, armaments only on that one continent. The Third World is largely outside the framework of these new agreements.

The chemical arms treaty is also the only one that mandates the destruction of stockpiles and production facilities. The others represent no more than a thinning out of huge existing arsenals. Still, together with cuts in military spending and reductions in the number of armed forces and military bases, these agreements represent a significant break with past trends and policies. The companies, work forces, and communities that used to depend on military largesse face both a challenge—adjusting to this new reality—and an opportunity—reorienting themselves toward civilian endeavors.

In signing START I and II, the United States and the former Soviet Union committed themselves to end the relentless buildup of nuclear weapons. (Both signatories began to take measures consistent with the treaties even prior to them coming into force.) Fulfilling these commitments during the next decade will require decommissioning or destroying large numbers of ballistic missiles and missile silos, strategic bombers, and submarines; this further implies dismantlement of thousands of warheads, and storage or disposal of huge quantities of fissile materials and rocket fuels. The costs of these measures will be substantial, but will likely be more than offset by future savings. In any event, they pale in comparison with the roughly $5 trillion (in 1993 dollars) that these countries have spent since 1946 to acquire and maintain their arsenals.[27]

To satisfy START requirements, the U.S. Navy has so far spent more than $700 million to dismantle ballistic missile submarines, and the Air Force projects spending $130 million to reduce strategic bombers and land-based missiles and to destroy missile silos. The Pentagon is planning to decommission more than 1,000 of its nuclear ballistic missiles during the nineties. The U.S. Department of Energy has been dismantling 1,000–1,600 nuclear warheads a year recently. The Office of Technology Assessment has estimated annual dismantlement costs to be in the range of $500 million to $1 billion over the next decade. Following warhead disassembly, the surplus plutonium will be placed in storage, at an estimated cost of $2–3 billion for a decade, before its ultimate disposal is decided.[28]

Unclassified assessments by the Russian military are that implementing START could cost the country 90–95 billion rubles in 1992 prices (about $6 billion). The other former Soviet republics with nuclear arms on their territories have agreed to ship them to Russia for dismantlement. Strapped for funds, Ukraine has asked for international assistance of up to $2.8 billion to accomplish this, and Kazakh President Nazarbeyev has asked for $1 billion in compensation to rid his country of nuclear weapons.[29]

The convention outlawing the possession of chemical weapons and mandating the destruction of existing stocks is expected to enter into force during 1995. A new body, the Organization for the Prohibition of Chemical Weapons (OPCW), is being set up to monitor global treaty compliance. But western nations, obsessed with cost-cutting, insisted on a staff only about one third the size originally planned. The budget approved for 1994—$29.7 million—is roughly half the amount requested. Limited resources may compel the OPCW to dispatch smaller inspector teams for shorter lengths of time than originally planned, possibly threatening its ability to detect, and hence deter, treaty violations.[30]

Complying with this treaty will be very costly for the United States and Russia, the only countries that have acknowledged possession of such weapons: destroying chemical weapons is expected to cost up to 10 times as much as producing them. The program to incinerate the U.S. stockpile has experienced large cost overruns; estimates now run to some $8.6 billion (plus another $17.7 billion for old, buried chemical ammunition). Annual funding for the U.S. Army's Chemical Materiel Destruction Agency has risen from less than $200 million in the late eighties to more than $500 million. While the United States has begun to destroy small amounts of chemical weapons, Russia's program has been delayed by technical difficulties, lack of money, and popular opposition; destruction is to begin by 1997. Cost estimates have varied widely; in mid-1994, a Russian diplomat put the cost at $1.3–2.8 billion. Officials hope that 30–40 percent of this will be covered by foreign assistance and the sale of chemical by-products salvaged from the weapons stocks.[31]

The Pentagon is planning to decommission more than 1,000 of its nuclear ballistic missiles during the nineties.

The Conventional Forces in Europe Treaty sets national limits for major pieces of military equipment (such as tanks and combat aircraft) deployed between the Atlantic and the Urals. It came into force in 1992 and is to be fully implemented by November 1995. Signatories have a number of options for getting rid of excess equipment, including export to other countries, so that only a portion of the surplus items is actually to be dismantled.

Among members of the North Atlantic Treaty Organization (NATO), Germany and the United States have by far the largest expenses in carrying out the CFE

Treaty's provisions. Germany must dispose of the equipment of the former East Germany, and spent 1.5 billion deutsche marks (DM)—about $900 million—in 1991–94 on CFE and other arms control activities. The United States spent $134 million, but other signatories' annual costs are typically in the low single-digit millions.[32]

The former Warsaw Pact states have to undertake much larger reductions in their arsenals than NATO members, but they also have very limited resources for the task. Though their expenditures may not seem large by western standards, they are substantial for these economically depressed countries. They are attempting to recoup at least some of their costs by selling scrap materials from dismantled weapons. Russia has repeatedly complained about its CFE costs, and would prefer to, in effect, let weapons rust away rather than undertake the expensive process of cutting them apart.[33]

Conversion is imperative for any serious demilitarization policy to succeed.

The CFE Treaty does not regulate ammunition stocks, but many countries are reducing their holdings anyway. The global costs to dispose of explosives and restore contaminated sites could grow from more than $1 billion in 1993 to $7 billion by 2000. The United States, Russia, Belarus, Ukraine, and Germany are among those with the largest surplus. The U.S. Army demilitarized about 100,000 tons of ammunition during the second half of the eighties, and more than 300,000 tons in 1990–95; expenditures since 1990 have added up to about $300 million. That is only about as much as the Army requested for 1994 and 1995 to preserve the capacity to manu-

facture ammunition in the future. And 1990–94 congressional appropriations for new ammunition procurement amounted to a staggering $6.6 billion.[34]

Of approximately 32 million soldiers worldwide in 1990, some 2.2 million were demobilized in 1990–92; a roughly equal number is expected to be cut in later years—the largest reduction since World War II. As large numbers of military facilities are closed in the former Soviet Union, North America, and Europe, millions of civilians employed by the armed forces will lose their jobs as well. The base closure process differs markedly between East and West. Particularly in the United States, it is a highly structured and planned process that includes environmental assessments and economic adjustment programs. In Russia, the process matches the country's turbulent, even chaotic, economic situation; lacking adequate resources, bases are apparently being closed in anything but an orderly fashion.[35]

The United States is in the middle of a wave of base closures and reductions initiated in the late eighties. Closures decided on to date will cut the domestic base infrastructure by about 15 percent; the last round of closures, in 1995, could involve as many facilities as affected to date. The total costs are estimated at nearly $15 billion during 1990–99, of which $4 billion is for environmental cleanup. But the projected savings in operating funds over the same period of time would more than offset the costs. Additional costs and savings are being incurred as the Pentagon closes some 895 overseas military installations and brings some 174,000 troops home.[36]

Conversion—the process of transferring skills, equipment, and other resources from the military to the civilian realm—is imperative for any serious demilitarization policy to succeed. Internationally, it is an important confidence-building measure, to the extent that it helps make disarmament less reversible. Domestically, it can help reduce the pressure for continued high arms production and export by smoothing the impact of lower military spending on companies, employees, and communities—an impact increasingly felt during the nineties. In addition to base-closure-related job losses, at least 3–4 million of 15 million arms industry jobs worldwide are expected to be lost by 1998.[37]

Although the term conversion has entered the lexicon of decision makers, actual conversion policies remain rare. Governments are forced to prune their military industries, but they are intent on protecting, not dismantling, their "defense industrial base." The adjustment to lower military spending is largely left to the market, resulting in mergers, plant closures, and job loss. In an overview of strategies pursued around the world, Herbert Wulf of the Bonn International Center for Conversion rated conversion efforts virtually everywhere as "small or unimportant."[38]

In the United States, very limited federal funding was available for economic adjustment to lower military spending until the Clinton administration proposed providing nearly $20 billion for 1994–97. But these figures are less impressive than they appear to be. First, more than a third of this amount is funding for a variety of high-tech initiatives not specifically targeted toward conversion. Second, another 30 percent is devoted to so-called dual-use projects. Ostensibly to develop technologies with either civilian or military application, the military mission remains key to these programs; only about one third of the dual-use funds are civilian-oriented. Adjusting the Clinton budget for these components yields a less spectacular $8.5 billion.[39]

In Europe, conversion funding by central governments is marginal or nonexistent. The little money available seems mostly bound up in efforts to restructure defense industries and safeguard their survival, not their reorientation. Regional and local governments are struggling to fill the void, but frequently lack adequate resources. Among the continent's largest military powers and arms producers, Germany, Spain, and the United Kingdom have not created any national conversion budgets at all. The Italian government's 1994 budget contains a conversion appropriation of about 500 billion lire (some $320 million), but it is part of a $2.4-billion package to recapitalize the state-owned military industry firms. A Fund for Defense Restructuring created in 1991 by the French Ministry of Defense had limited impact due to insignificant resources, but a larger fund, with a capital endowment of about 700 million francs ($125 million), was created in 1993.[40]

For regions and communities struggling to move away from economic dependence on military spending, the European Union's PERIFRA and KONVER programs are an alternative to national programs. They were created to assist with job retraining, regional diversification through new enterprises, support for business innovation, and cleanup and reuse of military bases. To be eligible for grants, national, state, or local governments applying for assistance have to provide matching funds. Funding came to a relatively modest 90 million European Currency Units (ECUs, a little over $100 million) in 1991–92, but for 1994–98, a budget of 500 million ECUs ($600 million) has been proposed.[41]

China has pursued its own brand of conversion, switching a large part of its arms industries to producing civilian goods, but using at least part of the proceeds to finance investments in modern arms production. From the late seventies to 1990, the government allocated more than 3 billion yuan (about $560 million at 1991 exchange rates) to conversion and modernization of industrial production capacities. During 1991–95, a total of 6 billion yuan is to be invested. China also began demobilizing large numbers of troops in the late seventies. The costs (particularly officers' pensions) have apparently been substantial, ranging anywhere from $2 billion to $5 billion annually in recent years.[42]

When Eastern Europe moved out of the Soviet orbit, the new leadership regarded conversion as an attractive political and economic proposition. Production collapsed after 1989, and defense industries in the region went into "hibernation," as Judit Kiss, a Hungarian-born analyst, put it. Heavy debts constrained new civilian investment by arms-producing companies. Limited funds went to stabilize the arms industry and to help develop civilian production. Conversion became a dirty word when the West not only failed to provide assistance to weather the difficult transition, but went after the markets once catered to by East European arms producers. Mindful of resurgent nationalism in the region and suspicious of Russian intentions, governments tried to protect the core of their industries, with an eye to reconstructing a smaller, more modern arms industry.[43]

From the late eighties, the Soviet and then Russian government kept drawing up ambitious conversion plans that were never implemented. With drastically lower domestic weapons procurement and collapsing arms exports, the Russian military industry is in a state of disintegration. Much of the work force is idled. It did increase the volume of its civilian output, but successful conversion was prevented by political upheaval and the chaotic transition from a centrally directed to a more market-oriented economy. Estimates in 1992 put the total costs of conversion at $150 billion, far surpassing Russia's financial capacities.[44]

Russian government budgets do include an allocation for conversion (in 1993, some 1 trillion rubles—about $980 million in prices of July 1993), but there are several problems with any data: Since rapid inflation renders them almost meaningless, annual allocations are revised from time to time during the budget year. Published figures are highly unreliable, and in recent years, allocated budgets were disbursed only partially and after long delays. In addition, the funds being disbursed go not so much for a reorientation toward civilian production, but principally to stem the erosion of workers' salaries in order to prevent social unrest from breaking out. Indications are that the government is becoming more interested in boosting the industry's exports than in switching to civilian production.[45]

Given the dramatic political and economic dislocations in the former Soviet Union, the successor states are confronted with an enormous challenge in meeting their disarmament obligations—one they may not master without foreign help. A number of western countries have agreed to provide various forms of assistance to dismantle nuclear warheads, to safely transport and store the fissile materials contained in them, to convert arms factories, and to construct housing for soldiers previously stationed abroad.

Between 1990 and 1994, the Soviet Union, and then Russia, withdrew more than 700,000 soldiers and 500,000 civilian dependents from Central and Eastern Europe and from other countries—the largest peacetime military pullout in history. But the returnees are confronted with problems such as a severe housing shortage and the lack of civilian skills. Russian Defense Minister Pavel Grachev claimed in 1993 that the number of officers without proper housing

[handwritten margin notes: "talk about stupid because nuclear plants could use solar energy they maintains possibility of produce bombs"]

would rise from 120,000 in early 1993 to 400,000 in 1994. Grants and credits made available by Germany to facilitate the pullout of ex-Soviet troops from the former East Germany add up to DM12.6 billion ($7.6 billion) in 1991–95, including DM7.8 billion for housing construction and DM200 million for civilian training of officers. Other countries' assistance in this regard is almost insignificant by comparison.[46]

France, Germany, Italy, Japan, and the United Kingdom combined have so far offered some $200 million worth of nuclear-disarmament related assistance stretched over several years, with additional, larger aid pledges from the United States. Russian aid requests of $1 billion for its struggling chemical weapons destruction efforts contrast sharply with roughly $60 million worth of aid pledged by the United States and Germany.[47]

Under what is known as the Nunn-Lugar program, the U.S. Congress has given $400 million in each fiscal year since 1992 to the Pentagon to assist Russia, Belarus, Ukraine, and Kazakhstan with nuclear and chemical disarmament. But actually putting these funds to use—negotiating umbrella and implementing agreements—has proved to be an agonizingly slow progress, in part because of bureaucratic and political impediments in the Soviet successor states. Of $1.2 billion appropriated in 1992–94, budget authority for $212 million expired before proper agreements were signed. By July 1994, the Pentagon had committed some $941 million in signed agreements, but actual spending ran only to about $420 million.[48]

In addition to the Nunn-Lugar funds, the United States will purchase 500 tons of highly enriched uranium derived from Russian nuclear warheads over the next 20 years—to be diluted and used as fuel at civilian nuclear power plants. Initially, the sale may bring Russia some $240 million annually, rising later to $725 million per year. The entire deal is worth about $11.9 billion.[49]

Another area of western assistance concerns defense conversion, but these funds are meager. The Organisation for Economic Co-operation and Development maintains a comprehensive register of actual and planned conversion projects. For 1991–94, assistance added up to a paltry $200 million (though for some projects no cost estimate is given, and preliminary 1994 data understate the level of funding).[50]

The United States will purchase 500 tons of highly enriched uranium derived from Russian nuclear warheads over the next 20 years.

In a report to the U.S. Congress, Secretary of Defense Perry admitted that U.S. conversion assistance—some $40 million—"is a very small fraction of what is actually needed." Out of 1.87 billion ECUs (about $2.2 billion) made available in 1991–94 under the European Union's Technical Assistance Program to the Commonwealth of Independent States, only a tiny portion—34.5 million ECUs ($40 million)—has been devoted to conversion. The European Bank for Reconstruction and Development has a mandate that explicitly involves conversion, but its lending criteria have been unrealistic, and actual funding to date has been low by its own admission. U.S. and European programs share an unfortunate characteristic: much of the money has not paid for actual programs but for feasibility studies and fees for western consultants—75 percent in the U.S. case.[51]

A Global Demilitarization Fund

In 1994, the world's governments spent roughly $16 billion on demilitarization and peacebuilding, or about 2 percent of global military expenditures. (See Table 9–5.) Since the database that provides this estimate inevitably suffers from certain gaps, real spending is somewhat higher—at least by several hundred million dollars and possibly by a few billion dollars a year. In particular, Table 9–5 underreports expenditures associated with base closures, and some of those relating to disarmament (especially concerning the former Soviet Union). And it does not include post-conflict reconstruction due to inconsistent and partial data, a problem that can be remedied only by undertaking detailed country case studies.

As suggested throughout this chapter, the world does not spend nearly enough on peace and demilitarization: Demining efforts are badly underfunded. Postwar reconstruction suffers from the lack of donor generosity and foresight. Peacekeeping is in a chronic state of financial crisis. Expenditures to implement arms control treaties appear roughly sufficient in western nations, but not in former Warsaw Pact countries strapped for resources. Most countries are determined to spend as little as possible on treaty

Table 9-5. Global Peace and Demilitarization Expenditures, 1989–94

Category	1989	1990	1991	1992	1993	1994
			(million dollars)			
Demining	10	10	197	200	238	241
Demobilization	46	28	38	54	56	52
Refugee Repatriation	77	101	160	172	252	463
Disarmament						
Nuclear	1,174	1,214	1,706	1,775	2,007	1,998
Conventional	25	26	144	351	321	529
Chemical	180	270	317	421	591	586
Aid to Former Soviet Union	0	0	1,275	1,708	2,370	1,984
Other	126	124	199	218	206	246
Base Closures	n.a.	538	998	1,148	2,120	2,864
Conversion	93	114	511	1,302	1,609	2,707
Peacekeeping/building	749	677	760	2,149	3,450	4,080
World Court/War Crimes Tribunal	6	9	9	9	9	20
Total	2,486	3,111	6,314	9,507	13,229	15,770

Note: This table represents the first systematic attempt to compile global peace and demilitarization expenditures. The data come from a wide variety of sources, with differing degrees of reliability. Thus they are a composite of precise expenditure figures, annual averages of multiyear figures, and estimates. In some cases, data were inconsistent; in other cases, none were available. Occasionally the distinctions among the expenditure categories are blurred: peacekeeping operations, for example, now frequently encompass such activities as demining, demobilization, and refugee repatriation, but it is difficult or impossible to determine what part of an operation's budget covers these. Similarly, some conversion spending might be attributed to the base closures category.

SOURCE: Worldwatch database.

compliance and verification. And arms conversion needs are neglected by almost all governments.

Much of the spending is aimed at coping with the military legacy and at cutting the fat out of military arsenals. But little or nothing is spent on preparing for a future less characterized by reliance on military prowess. And most expenditures are either voluntary or discretionary (those incurred in implementing international treaties that imply some level of spending but do not prescribe a particular amount); few are mandatory. Although many governments have been less than exemplary with regard to payment of dues obligated by international law, nonmandatory contributions carry even more uncertainty about funds being available both in sufficient amounts and in timely fashion. Such funding is vulnerable not only to governments' whims and changing priorities but also to the political pressures of the day. Hence, substantial year-to-year fluctuations are to be expected.

The shaky nature of funding for peace is mirrored in the ad hoc quality of many demilitarization endeavors. It is impossible to construct the foundations for a more peaceful world on this basis. There is, in short, a need for reliable, permanent institutions and funding mechanisms.

Considering the rising demilitarization and peacebuilding challenge, the time is right for establishing an international fund to facilitate such endeavors. This is what Nobel Peace Prize laureate Oscar Arias proposed recently. The proposal developed here follows his arguments, but is somewhat broader in scope.[52]

The Demilitarization Fund would serve three fundamental purposes and therefore would have three distinct components. The first is to assist countries that lack adequate resources for coping with the legacy of war. This "restitution account" would provide financial support for such endeavors as demining, armed forces demobilization and reintegration, refugee repatriation, and post-conflict reconstruction.

The second component would provide the financial underpinning for weapons dismantlement and economic conversion efforts that reach far beyond contemporary measures. This "transformation account" is predicated on the adoption of international accords that mandate deep reductions or even the elimination of deployed weapons systems, and that establish meaningful barriers against future production, possession, trading, and use of arms.

The third component provides resources for building an effective, alternative global peace system. This "peace-building account" would help transform what are now ad hoc activities into more reliable and permanent ones. It would establish new international institutions and mechanisms for disarmament verification, peacekeeping, conflict mediation and settlement, election monitoring, and other purposes.

Where would the resources come from for this? The most obvious source is military budgets. Transferring money from these accounts to a Demilitarization Fund would help capture at least a portion of the elusive peace dividend. A conceptually elegant way suggested by Arias would be to earmark each year a predetermined share of the money saved from reductions in the military budget of each nation. The savings would be measured against the military expenditures in a given base year—perhaps the year prior to the establishment of the fund. As long as cuts continue to be made in military spending, the savings relative to the base year would accumulate, and the fund contributions would grow each year.

But the annual contributions would stay unchanged if military budget cuts ceased, and would decline if military expenditures increased. The magnitude of fund resources would be chronically unpredictable. Countries not reducing or increasing their spending would in effect be rewarded, while those undertaking cuts would be punished. The endeavor might come to be regarded as a "tax" on disarming, when the activity that should be "taxed" is arming.

A dual formula could counter these weaknesses—with the base tier being a percentage of the military budget, and the second tier being a share of the reductions in military spending. The fund would be less vulnerable to short-term fluctuations, because if the revenue base of one tier declined, that of the other would increase. This would also ensure that each country contributes to global demilitarization—assuming participation in the fund eventually becomes mandatory—even those not reducing their own military spending.

Initially, acceptance of "the principle of committing a portion of the peace dividend to promote global demilitarization," as Arias puts it, is most important. Contributions could at first be voluntary. But eventually, the fund needs to play more than a symbolic role; contributions could then be made a normal requirement of a country's U.N. membership, just like payments to the organization's regular and peacekeeping budgets.[53]

How much funding could be expected under the proposed formula? Arias proposes that industrial countries set aside one fifth of their peace dividend for the Demilitarization Fund, and developing countries, one tenth. The *Human Development Report 1994*'s figures for global military spending and its assumption that military expenditures will drop by 3 percent annually for the rest of this decade provide the basis for a rough calculation. Using 1994 as the base year, Arias's formula would yield about $85 billion during 1995–2000, an average of $14 billion a year. And if base-tier contributions were pegged to a value of 1 percent of global military expenditures, that would yield an additional $41 billion during 1995–2000, close to $7 billion a year. Total revenues would thus reach $126 billion. (See Table 9–6.)

Criteria on who is eligible to receive assistance under the restitution and transformation accounts would have to be developed. Two kinds of judgments would be needed: whether a country is unable to marshal sufficient domestic resources (and therefore needs assistance), and whether that country is committed to demilitarization (and therefore deserves assistance). Any country receiving fund assistance would be required to provide some matching funds. Any country applying for assistance would be expected to submit, if it had not already done so, relevant data to the U.N.'s Standardized Reporting System on Military Expenditures and its Register of Conventional Arms Transfers.[54]

Establishing greater transparency concerning national military expenditures (and criteria for what items are to be considered part of military spending) would in any event be crucial for calculating fund contributions. Resolving the transparency issue poses substantial political problems, however, since doing so confronts deeply ingrained notions of secrecy in the name of national security.

Western governments (who would shoulder the bulk of fund contributions) can be expected to balk at the expense of building a peace system—whether through the fund proposed here or in any other form. Although their leaders like to talk about moral and humanitarian values, they are unlikely to support a disarmament fund unless they perceive that their narrow self-interests would be served by it. In this context, at least three arguments can be made.

Table 9-6. Possible Contributions to a Global Demilitarization Fund, 1995–2000[1]

Fund Contributions	1995	1996	1997	1998	1999	2000	1995–2000
	(billion dollars)						
First-tier[2]	7.4	7.2	7.0	6.8	6.6	6.4	41.4
Second-tier[3]							
Industrial Countries	3.8	7.6	11.2	14.8	18.2	21.6	77.2
Developing Countries	0.4	0.7	1.1	1.4	1.7	2.0	7.3
Total	11.6	15.5	19.3	23.0	26.5	30.0	125.9

[1]Assuming military budgets will decline 3 percent a year. [2]1 percent of global military expenditures. [3]Set at 20 percent of savings in military expenditures for industrial countries and 10 percent for developing countries, relative to 1994 base year (military expenditures of industrial countries at $649 billion, of developing countries at $118 billion, with world total at $767 billion).
SOURCE: Worldwatch calculation based on projected military expenditures and cumulative military budget savings in U.N. Development Programme, *Human Development Report 1994* (New York: Oxford University Press, 1994).

First, conflict prevention is infinitely cheaper than continuation of the status quo—not an insignificant fact in the cost-conscious nineties. Simply by avoiding the duplications and inefficiencies inherent in today's ad hoc demobilization, peacekeeping, and humanitarian relief activities, a more permanent structure would save money. Second, in an era of global trade and investment, countries at war or suffering instability from unresolved disputes are in effect "lost markets" to traders and investors. And third, the societal breakdown that is typically associated with domestic conflicts today unleashes growing waves of refugees. (See Chapter 8.) It is as obvious as it is regrettable that western countries are already reaching the limits of tolerance toward admitting more people seeking political asylum. Establishing and funding effective peacekeeping and peacemaking institutions would provide benefits in all three regards.

Establishing a Demilitarization Fund would require the same sense of mission and destiny that motivated the founders of the United Nations and the Bretton Woods institutions 50 years ago. Given today's political constraints, such a fund is, realistically, a long-term prospect. But transitional measures are conceivable. U.N. peacekeeping operations, for example, already encompass an enormous variety of tasks, including demining, demobilization, and many related endeavors. Most of the nonmilitary, peacebuilding components of these operations, however, are being financed through voluntary contributions. Funding them through regular, assessed contributions levied on all U.N. members would be one modest step that could easily be taken now.[55]

To reap the benefits of peace, governments need to shed their penny-wise, pound-foolish stance. If peace is considered unaffordable, it will remain elusive. At a time when politicians' strategic thinking rarely extends beyond the next election campaign, it will take courageous leadership to launch visionary initiatives now that will yield peace dividends for generations to come.

10

Forging a New Global Partnership

Hilary F. French

In June 1992, more than 100 heads of state or government and 20,000 non-governmental representatives from around the world gathered in Rio de Janeiro for the U.N. Conference on Environment and Development (UNCED). The event was widely heralded as historic. It resulted in the adoption of Agenda 21, an ambitious 500-page blueprint for sustainable development. If implemented, this would require far-reaching changes by international agencies, national governments, and individuals everywhere. In addition, Rio produced treaties on climate change and biological diversity, both of which over time could lead to domestic policy changes in all nations.[1]

The Earth Summit marked the coming of age of "sustainable development"—the point at which this concept moved from the environmental literature to the front page, and from there into the lexicon of governments and international agencies. Significantly, the Rio conference pointed to the need for a global partnership if sustainable development was to be achieved.[2]

Since Rio, a steady stream of international meetings has been held on the many issues that were on its agenda. Governments, for instance, have been preparing for the first Conferences of the Parties of the biological diversity and the climate conventions, where the real work of getting these agreements actually implemented will begin. Similarly, the U.N. Commission on Sustainable Development (CSD), created to oversee follow-through on Agenda 21, had met twice by mid-1994 and is starting to get its feet on the ground. And the September 1994 International Conference on Population and Development (ICPD) in Cairo put the spotlight of world attention on the inexorable pace of population growth—and on the need to respond to it through broad-based efforts to expand access to family planning, improve women's health and literacy, and ensure child survival.[3]

Unfortunately, though, the pace of

real change has not kept up with the increasingly loaded schedule of international gatherings. The reality is that the initial burst of international momentum generated by UNCED is flagging, and the global partnership it called for is foundering due to a failure of political will. Though a small, committed group of individuals in international organizations, national and local governments, and citizens' groups continues trying to keep the flame of Rio alive, business as usual is largely the order of the day in the factories, farms, villages, and cities that form the backbone of the world economy.

The result is that the relentless pace of global ecological decline shows no signs of letting up. Carbon dioxide concentrations are mounting in the atmosphere, species loss continues to accelerate, fisheries are collapsing, land degradation frustrates efforts to feed hungry people, and the earth's forest cover keeps shrinking. Many of the development and economic issues that underpin environmental destruction also continue to worsen. Though some social indicators, such as global life expectancy and literacy rates, have improved in recent years, other key trends are headed in the wrong direction: income inequality is rising, Third World debt is mounting, human numbers keep increasing at daunting rates, and the absolute number of poor people in the world is increasing.[4]

Fortunately, 1995 will bring a number of golden opportunities to strengthen the global partnership called for at Rio. In March, world leaders will gather in Copenhagen for the World Summit on Social Development—an effort to generate for social ills the same high level of attention the Rio conference garnered for environmental ones. And in September, the World Conference on Women will be held in Beijing, providing an opportunity for the international community to take concrete steps toward removing gender bias as a roadblock to alleviating poverty and arresting ecological decline.[5]

Throughout the year the world will celebrate the fiftieth anniversary of the founding of the United Nations. This will be a time to reflect on how the world has changed in 50 years—and on how the U.N. must evolve if it is to remain relevant. In addition, members of the Group of Seven (G7)—the major industrial powers—are devoting their July 1995 Economic Summit in Nova Scotia to the framework of institutions required to ensure "sustainable development with good prosperity and well-being of the peoples of our nations and the world" in the twenty-first century. The summit will consider both adaptations to existing institutions and the possible need to build new ones.[6]

The global partnership called for in Rio is foundering due to a failure of political will.

The global partnership that is needed will have several distinct features. As suggested in Rio, it will involve a new form of relationship between the industrialized North and the developing South. Another feature will be a new division of responsibility between different levels of governance worldwide: Problems are best solved at the most decentralized level of governance that is consistent with efficient performance of the task; as they transcend boundaries, decision making can be passed upward as necessary—from the community to the state, national, regional, and in some rare instances the global level. A third requirement is the active participation of citizens in village, municipal, and national political life, as well as at the United Nations.

Above all, the new partnership calls for an unprecedented degree of international cooperation and coordination: the complex web of ecological, economic, communication, and other connections now binding the world together means that no government can build a secure future for its citizens by acting alone. As U.S. inventor and statesman Ben Franklin said as the 13 colonies in America declared their independence from the British crown: "We must indeed all hang together, or most assuredly we will all hang separately."[7]

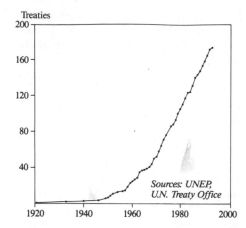

Figure 10-1. International Environmental Treaties, 1921–94

PROTECTING THE GLOBAL ENVIRONMENT

One of the primary ways the world community has responded to the environmental challenge is through the negotiation of treaties and other types of international agreements. Nations have now agreed on more than 170 environmental treaties—more than two thirds of them since the U.N. Conference on the Human Environment in Stockholm in 1972 first put the environment on the international agenda. (See Figure 10–1.) If other, less-binding types of accords are included in the total, the number of international environmental instruments on the books tops 800. Some important additions to these lists appeared in 1994: the climate and biological diversity conventions as well as the long-languishing Law of the Sea treaty all received enough ratifications to enter into force. In addition, governments signed a new accord on desertification and land degradation.[8]

Some of these agreements have led to measurable gains. Air pollution in

Europe, for instance, has been reduced dramatically as a result of the 1979 treaty on transboundary air pollution. Global chlorofluorocarbon (CFC) emissions have dropped 60 percent from their peak in 1988 following the 1987 treaty on ozone depletion and its subsequent amendments. The killing of elephants has plummeted in Africa because of the 1990 ban on commercial trade in ivory under the Convention on International Trade in Endangered Species of Wild Flora and Fauna. And mining exploration and development have been forbidden in Antarctica for 50 years under a 1991 accord.[9]

Though some treaties have been successes, many more have failed to ignite the needed changes in domestic policies. All too often, environmental accords are written in such vague terms that they commit signatories to little. Monitoring of compliance with agreements is generally cursory at best, and sanctions are rarely imposed even when violators have been identified. Developing countries are often impeded in their efforts to comply with international accords by industrial countries' failure to deliver on promises of financial and technological assistance.[10]

The broad framework of international agreements needed to protect the global environment is now in place. The challenge for the future is thus to see that existing agreements are translated into action around the world.

The hallmark of international environment governance to date is the Montreal Protocol on the Depletion of the Ozone Layer. First agreed to in September 1987 and strengthened significantly two times since then, the protocol now stipulates that the production of CFCs in industrial countries must be phased out altogether by 1996. It also restricts the use of several other ozone-depleting chemicals, including halons, carbon tetrachlorides, methyl chloroform, and hydrochlorofluorocarbons. Developing countries have a 10-year grace period in which to meet the terms of the original protocol and its amendments.[11]

In a remarkably short period of time, the Montreal Protocol has become the international law of the land. More than 100 countries have ratified the original protocol, and both amendments have received enough approvals to enter into force. Because of the quick and dramatic reduction in global CFC emissions as a result of the pact, computer models suggest that if all countries comply with their commitments, chlorine concentrations will begin to level off soon. (See Figure 10–2.) Though this will be a momentous international achievement, the world will nevertheless have paid a heavy price for earlier inaction: dangerous levels of ultraviolet radiation will be reaching the earth for decades to come, which scientists estimate will stunt agricultural productivity and damage ecological and human health.[12]

The lessons learned in the ozone treaty are now being put to a severe test, as the international community begins to confront a more daunting atmospheric challenge—the need to head off

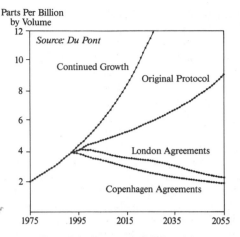

Figure 10-2. Atmospheric Chlorine, 1975–93, With Four Projections to 2055

climate change. Less than two years after it was signed in Rio, the Framework Convention on Climate Change entered into force in March 1994 after the fiftieth country (Portugal) ratified it. Unfortunately, the speed with which the treaty was ratified was in part a reflection of the fact that it contains few real commitments.[13]

The climate treaty's deliberately ambiguous language urges but does not require industrial nations to stabilize emissions of carbon—the primary contributor to global warming—at 1990 levels by the year 2000. Developing nations face no numerical goals whatsoever, though all signatories must conduct inventories of their emissions; submit detailed reports of national actions taken to implement the convention; and endeavor to take climate change into account in all their social, economic, and environmental policies. But no specific policy measures are required.

As of late 1994, most industrial countries had established national greenhouse gas targets and climate plans, but they vary widely in effectiveness. Among the most ambitious and comprehensive plans are those of Denmark, the Netherlands, and Switzerland, none of which have powerful oil or coal industries to contend with. Through the use of efficiency standards, renewable energy programs, and limited carbon taxes, these plans are likely to limit national emissions significantly.[14]

According to independent evaluations by nongovernmental organizations (NGOs), most of the climate plans issued so far will fall short of stabilizing national emissions and the other goals they have set for themselves. Germany and the United States, for example, two of the largest emitters, have each issued climate plans that take important steps but fail to tackle politically difficult policies—the reduction of coal subsidies in Germany and the increase of gasoline taxes in the United States. Neither country is likely to meet its stated goals. Reports from Japan suggest that it, too, is unlikely to meet its stabilization target. In another failure of will, long-standing efforts by the European Union to impose a hybrid carbon/energy tax have so far failed, despite strong support from the European Commission.[15]

Preserving biological diversity is something that all countries have a stake in and that no one country can effectively do alone.

Even if the goal of holding emissions to 1990 levels in 2000 is met, this falls far short of reaching the broader aim of the Rio climate treaty: stabilizing atmospheric concentrations of greenhouse gases, which according to scientists will require bringing carbon emissions 60–80 percent below current levels. As a result, several European countries and the United States have voiced cautious support for strengthening the treaty to promote stronger actions,

though they have not said exactly how.[16]

The first major opportunity to update the climate convention will come in March 1995, when the initial Conference of the Parties to the convention convenes in Berlin. Environmental groups urge that this meeting adopt a target of a 20-percent cut in carbon emissions by 2005. A caucus of small island states has tabled a similar proposal. Prospects are uncertain, but there is a good chance that governments will at least consider goals for emissions levels after 2000, which the current treaty is noticeably silent on. Other possible innovations include stipulating joint actions aimed at revamping policies in critical sectors such as energy, forests, and transport. Requiring that participating countries establish appliance efficiency standards, for example, could make a sizable contribution toward slowing the growth in global carbon emissions.[17]

Work is also slowly getting under way to implement the other major treaty agreed to in Rio—the Convention on Biological Diversity. Signed by 160 countries in Rio, this treaty entered into force on December 29, 1993. As of September 1994, 89 countries had ratified it, including many in both the North and the South. The first Conference of the Parties to the convention was scheduled for November 1994.[18]

As with protecting the atmosphere, preserving biological diversity is something that all countries have a stake in and that no one country can effectively do alone. Ironically, however, one of the convention's most important achievements was its rejection of the notion that biological diversity is the "common heritage of mankind," and—conversely—its recognition that biological resources are the sovereign property of nation-states. The reason: when countries can profit from something, they have an incentive to preserve it.

Genetic diversity is worth a lot. The protection that genetic variability affords crops from pests, diseases, and climatic and soil variations is worth some $1 billion to U.S. agriculture. Overall, the economic benefits from wild species to pharmaceuticals, agriculture, forestry, fisheries, and the chemical industry adds up to more than $87 billion annually—more than 4 percent of the U.S. gross domestic product. Though international pharmaceutical companies have been extracting genes from countries for free for years, the biological diversity convention says that gene-rich countries have a right to charge for access to this valuable resource, and encourages them to pass national legislation to set the terms.[19]

One widely publicized model of this is a 1991 agreement between Merck & Co., the world's largest pharmaceutical company, and Costa Rica's National Institute of Biodiversity (INBio). Merck agreed to pay the Institute $1 million for conservation programs in exchange for access to the country's plants, microbes, and insects. And if a discovery makes its way into a commercialized product, Merck has agreed to pay INBio a share of the royalties. Discussing how to replicate such agreements will likely be a high priority for countries that have signed the convention.[20]

Besides providing a forum for future negotiations, the convention calls for a number of actions by governments to preserve biological wealth, including national plans and strategies for preservation and detailed biological inventories and surveys. Work on strategies has begun in a number of countries, including Canada, Chile, Indonesia, the Netherlands, Norway, Poland, and the United Kingdom; the United States and Costa Rica are in the process of conducting biological surveys. Possible actions in the future include discussions of a protocol on biotechnology, as well as deliberations on international standards for biodiversity prospecting agreements.[21]

The oceans are another natural resource whose protection requires international collaboration. Not only did the Law of the Sea receive sufficient ratifications to enter into force in 1994, but agreement was also reached on modifications to the original agreement that are likely to mean that the United States and other industrial countries will join in. The recent rebirth of this treaty comes just in time for the world's oceans and estuaries, which are suffering from overfishing, oil spills, land-based sources of pollution, and other ills.[22]

The Law of the Sea contains an extensive array of environmental provisions. For instance, though countries are granted sovereignty over waters within 200 miles of their shores (called exclusive economic zones, or EEZs), they also accept an obligation to protect ecological health there. The treaty also serves as an umbrella for scores of existing international agreements covering the oceans, including the London Dumping Convention, the MARPOL agreement regulating shipping, and numerous international fisheries agreements and regionally based initiatives. All countries that are members of the Law of the Sea are obligated to adhere to these various oceans conventions. In addition, the treaty contains pathbreaking compulsory dispute resolution provisions, under which countries are bound to accept the verdict of an international tribunal.[23]

Just as the Law of the Sea is coming into force, however, its rules are already being overtaken by events in one important area—overfishing. In particular, the original treaty failed to resolve the problem of fish stocks that straddle the boundaries of EEZs and of fish species that migrate long distances. The United Nations has convened a series of meetings to discuss possible international action to deal with a situation that has seen seafood catch per person fall 8 percent since 1989. (See Chapter 2.)[24]

The latest addition to the international repertoire of environmental treaties is a convention intended to curb land degradation, adopted in Paris in June 1994 and signed by 87 countries as of October that year. The idea for this came up in Rio, as a response to developing-country concerns that the issues most relevant to them were largely left off the table. According to the U.N. Environment Programme (UNEP), the livelihoods of at least 900 million people in some 100 countries are threatened by such degradation, known to many as desertification, which affects about one quarter of the earth's land area. The degradation—caused by overgrazing, overcropping, poor irrigation practices, and deforestation, and often exacerbated by climatic variations—poses a serious threat to efforts to raise agricultural productivity worldwide.[25]

The desertification treaty supplies a framework for local projects, encourages national action programs, promotes regional and international cooperation on the transfer of needed technologies, and provides for information exchange and research and training. It will also create a global mechanism to coordinate funds from various sources. The convention encourages the creation of national desertification trust funds that incorporate extensive provisions for public participation.

MEETING HUMAN NEEDS

Protecting the environment and combatting poverty are now widely recognized to be interlinked priorities, a reality reflected in the decision to focus UNCED on both environment and development.

Similarly, the Cairo conference looked at the complex interconnections among population growth, deteriorating social conditions, gender inequity, environmental degradation, and a range of other issues. As these landmark international gatherings both underscored, a sustainable future cannot be secured without an aggressive effort to combat poverty and meet basic social needs.

Trends during the last several decades suggest a mixed record on improving human welfare. Though impressive progress has been made in boosting immunization rates, reducing infant mortality, and increasing life expectancy, one in three children remains malnourished, more than 1 billion people lack safe water to drink, and about 1 billion adults cannot read or write. The share of the world's population living in "absolute poverty" has steadily declined, but the actual numbers continue to grow, with more than 1 billion people—a fifth of humanity—consigned to this state. Rather than shrinking, the gap between the rich and the poor is growing: in 1960, the richest 20 percent of the world earned 30 times as much income as the poorest 20 percent; by 1991, the richest fifth was appropriating 61 times as much wealth as the poorest.[26]

A crucial first step toward turning these statistics around was taken in Cairo, when more than 160 countries approved a World Population Plan of Action aimed at keeping human numbers somewhere below 9.8 billion in 2050. It covers a broad range of issues, including the empowerment of women, the role of the family, reproductive rights and health, and migration. The plan calls for expenditures on population programs to more than triple by 2000—from today's $5 billion to some $17 billion. Of the total, $10 billion is intended for family planning programs, $5 billion for reproductive health, $1.3 billion for the prevention of sexually transmitted diseases, and $500 million for research and data collection. Industrial countries are expected to come up with $5.7 billion, with the remainder from domestic resources in the developing world. The action plan also calls for accelerating existing U.N. initiatives aimed at expanding women's literacy and improving their health—though it fails to provide spending targets for doing so.[27]

Vatican opposition to proposed language on abortion rights captured headlines during the Cairo conference, but the real news was the remarkable consensus forged between the industrial and developing worlds and among representatives of population, women's, and human rights groups during two years of preparation for the meeting. Key elements of this include a recognition that slowing population growth and making progress on a range of social fronts are inextricably linked challenges. It follows from the new consensus that reaching population stabilization goals will require a far different approach than in the past. In particular, family planning programs alone will be insufficient to meet the population challenge. Equally important are investments in changing the conditions that generate demand for large families—such as illiteracy and the low status of women. In addition, there was widespread agreement that family planning efforts must be noncoercive and integrated broadly with reproductive health programs.[28]

Cairo provided a vivid demonstration of what U.N. conferences can accomplish when they are skillfully prepared for and when the political climate is ripe for progress. U.S. leadership was widely credited with making the ICPD a success, a factor that has all too often been lacking at past gatherings. These meetings make an important contribution simply as international consciousness-raising events. In addition, they provide a unique forum where countries can share experiences and plot joint strategies on issues of common concern. In one exciting initiative that emerged from the Cairo conference, 10 diverse developing nations representing Muslim, Buddhist, and Christian religious traditions joined together in a program to share their experiences with others. Each has achieved considerable success in recent years in bringing fertility rates down. In Indonesia, for instance, the birth rate dropped from 5.6 births per woman in 1971 to 3.0 in 1991. And in Colombia, it declined from 7.1 children per women to 2.9 over 30 years.[29]

The Social Summit in Copenhagen has a mandate to take on poverty, unemployment, and social integration.

Following quickly on the heels of Cairo, the Social Summit has a mandate to take on poverty, unemployment, and social integration. One prominent issue will be how to make development assistance more effective at combatting these pervasive threats. Overall aid levels have decreased in recent years, as recession-ridden donor nations have found it harder and harder to appropriate funds. Few industrial nations have reached the international target of devoting 0.7 percent of their gross national product to development assistance. And the funds that are spent are often not well targeted. Because bilateral donors have tended to skew their disbursements toward their security interests, the 10 countries that are home to two thirds of the world's poorest people receive just 32 percent of total aid expenditures. The richest 40 percent of the developing world receives twice as much aid per person as the poorest 40 percent.[30]

Aid programs also do not generally

focus on the investments that are most effective at meeting human needs. The U.N. Development Programme (UNDP) has identified these priorities as basic education, primary health care, safe drinking water, adequate sanitation, and family planning and nutrition programs. At present, UNDP estimates that only 7 percent of total bilateral aid allocations and 16 percent of multilateral aid funds these types of programs.[31]

UNDP has put a bold initiative on the Copenhagen agenda—the 20:20 Compact on Human Development. Under this, developing countries would agree to devote 20 percent of their domestic resources to human priorities, and donors would target 20 percent of their aid funds for such purposes. If the Social Summit succeeds in launching the 20:20 Compact, it will be making a major contribution to a more sustainable world.[32]

Additional priorities for the Copenhagen meeting include making progress toward alleviating debt burdens and addressing unfavorable terms of trade for developing countries—two issues largely left off the table in Rio that are critical to ensuring a sustainable future. Though the debt crisis has been eased in absolute terms for some of the largest debtors, such as Brazil and Mexico, it remains very much alive in many of the poorest countries. Indeed, the total external debt of developing countries has grown sevenfold during the past two decades, rising from $247 billion in 1970 to more than $1.7 trillion in 1993. (See Figure 10–3.)[33]

Developing countries paid $160 billion in debt-service payments in 1992— more than two and a half times total official development assistance and $60 billion more than all private capital flows. Though the ratio of debt-service payments to foreign-exchange earnings has been declining globally in recent years, it is still on the rise in sub-Saharan Africa, which spends some 25 percent of

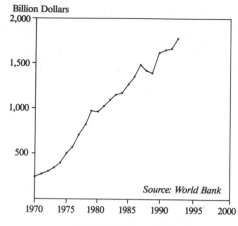

Figure 10-3. External Debt of Developing Countries, 1970–93

export receipts on debt repayments. And for many countries, this number is far higher. In Africa, a particularly large share of total outstanding debt is public rather than private. In 1992, fully 24 percent of the continent's debt was owed to multilateral institutions—primarily to the World Bank.[34]

To generate the hard currency required to pay loans back, the International Monetary Fund (IMF) and others have urged countries to undertake export-promoting reforms, such as devaluing exchange rates, and fiscal reforms to reduce public-sector deficits. Yet the strategy has been only partially successful. A handful of countries in East Asia and Latin America have boosted exports dramatically, but countries with the poorest fifth of humanity have not—they account for only 1 percent of world trade.[35]

Trade barriers to developing-country products continue to be a major impediment to boosting exports; restrictions on trade in textiles and clothing alone are estimated to cost the Third World some $50 billion in lost foreign exchange annually. Though recent negotiations under the General Agreement on Tariffs and Trade (GATT) made modest inroads into the problems, developing countries and the former Eastern bloc are expected to account for only 14–32 percent of the projected global income gains from the revised GATT by 2002. At least in the short term, Africa is actually expected to lose $2.6 billion a year as a result of the agreement, as rising world agricultural prices due to the mandated subsidy cuts will boost its food import bill.[36]

Meanwhile, where the push to expand exports has been successful, the benefits have often been unequally distributed. In Latin America, for instance, economic growth has picked up in recent years, but the share of the population living in poverty is projected to hover near 40 percent through the end of the decade. For some, the strategy is a net loss. For instance, subsistence farmers—frequently women—are often displaced from their land so that it can be devoted to growing crops to please the palates of consumers in distant lands. Indigenous peoples are forced from their homelands as forests are felled for foreign exchange.[37]

The uprising in the Mexican state of Chiapas in early 1994 was a wake-up call to some of the failures of this development model. In terms of resources, Chiapas is rich. It produces 100,000 barrels of oil and 500 billion cubic meters of natural gas daily; its dams supply more than half of the country's hydropower; and it accounts for one third of the nation's coffee production and a sizable share of its cattle, timber, honey, corn, and other products. But the benefit from selling these resources is not flowing to many of the people who live there. Writes Mexican grassroots activist Gustavo Esteva, "Rather than demanding the expansion of the economy, either state-led or market-led, the [Zapatista rebels] seek to expel it from their domain. They are pleading for protection of the 'commons' they have carved out for themselves. . . . The [Zapatistas] have

dared to announce for the world that development as a social experiment has failed miserably in Chiapas." As world leaders gather for the Social Summit, they would do well to heed Esteva's warning that the existing economic orthodoxy needs some fundamental rethinking.[38]

REVAMPING INTERNATIONAL INSTITUTIONS

Achieving sustainable development requires protecting the rights of local people to control their own resources—whether it be forests, fish, or minerals. Yet nations and people everywhere are also discovering that if we are to master today's transnational challenges, a wider role for international institutions is inevitable. It is thus a paradox of our time that effective governance requires control being simultaneously passed down to local communities and up to international institutions.[39]

Nations and people everywhere are discovering that if we are to master today's transnational challenges, a wider role for international institutions is inevitable.

To respond to this need, considerable reforms are needed in the United Nations to prepare it for the world of the future. The U.N. Charter, for instance, was written for a different era. Neither "environment" nor "population" even appear in the document. And though the need for more effective international institutions is clear, people the world over are justifiably worried by the prospect of power being centralized in institutions that are remote from democratic accountability.[40]

Many different U.N. agencies are involved in the quest for sustainable development. To date, the U.N. Environment Programme is the primary environmental organ in the system. (See Table 10–1.) Created after the 1972 U.N. conference in Stockholm, it is charged with catalyzing environmental work throughout the U.N. But many other agencies have active environmental programs: the World Health Organization (WHO), for instance, promulgates air and water pollution guidelines that are considered the international norm, and the World Meteorological Organization has made important contributions to better understanding of the complexities of climate science. The U.N. Food and Agriculture

Organization (FAO) is at the front line of efforts to boost agricultural productivity and protect dwindling fisheries. UNDP launched a Capacity 21 initiative after Rio, which has so far raised $30 million to help countries integrate environmental considerations into their development plans, and has also recently strengthened its natural resources unit.[41]

Numerous agencies contribute to the broader social development agenda. The U.N. Population Fund is instrumental in encouraging family planning programs worldwide, and will play a crucial role in overseeing follow-through on the Cairo conference. And UNICEF has achieved impressive successes in its efforts to improve children's welfare worldwide.

The Bretton Woods institutions— GATT, the IMF, and the World Bank—

Table 10-1. Estimated Expenditures and Staffing of Various U.N. Agencies, 1992–93[1]

Agency	Professional Staff	Expenditure
	(number)	(million dollars)
U.N. Development Programme	1,571	2,235
UNICEF	1,179	1,810
Food and Agriculture Organization	2,659	1,557
World Health Organization	1,833	1,372
Int'l. Labour Organization	1,373	676
UNESCO	1,056	662
Int'l. Atomic Energy Agency	699	535
U.N. Industrial Devel. Organization	660	491
U.N. Population Fund	166	333
U.N. Environment Programme	303	214
World Meteorological Organization	182	145
Int'l. Maritime Organization	122	82

[1]Budget figures are for biennium 1992–93 (which includes both years), but staff size figures are for 1990 except for UNEP (1993) and UNFPA (1994).
SOURCE: Budget figures from United Nations, *Programs and Resources of the United Nations System for the Biennium 1992–1993;* staff sizes from Erskine Childers with Brian Urquhart, "Renewing the United Nations System," *Development Dialogue* (Dag Hammarskjöld Foundation/Ford Foundation), 1994:1, except for U.N. Population Fund (UNFPA) staff from Bikash Shrestha, Administrative Assistant, Personnel Office, UNFPA, New York, private communication, October 18, 1994, and UNEP budget and staff size from Sergei Khromov, communications programme officer, UNEP, Nairobi, private communication, October 31, 1994.

are all also critical players in the sustainable development challenge. GATT, which will be subsumed into a new World Trade Organization once the Uruguay Round of negotiations is ratified, lays down the rules of world trade and procedures for enforcing them. The agreement has been widely criticized as being environmentally insensitive, although governments are now discussing ways to green GATT rules at a newly created Trade and Environment Committee. The World Bank has also come in for heavy criticism in recent years. It has increased its spending on environmental programs as a result, though it continues to have a poor record on enforcing many of its own environmental and social policies. Finally, the IMF is an influential source of macroeconomic policy advice, particularly in the developing world. Unfortunately, it has so far been reluctant to incorporate tools such as natural resource accounting and environmental taxation into its recommendations.[42]

Governments took a number of steps at UNCED to make the United Nations system a stronger force for sustainable development. Perhaps most significant, they created the Commission on Sustainable Development with 53 members of the United Nations to provide an international forum where governments could review progress in implementing Agenda 21, share information about what works and what does not, and discuss impediments such as inadequate financial resources or access to innovative technologies.[43]

To try to improve coordination and cooperation between various U.N. agencies on the sustainable development agenda, governments decided to create an Inter-Agency Committee on Sustainable Development (IACSD), composed of representatives of several relevant U.N. agencies. In addition, an organizational shake-up at the U.N. Secretariat in New York resulted in the creation of a new Department for Policy Coordination and Sustainable Development, headed by Under-Secretary-General Nitin Desai. Among its vast array of responsibilities, this office provides staff support to the CSD and the IACSD, and serves as a high-level focal point for promoting sustainable development throughout the United Nations.[44]

By May 1994, 103 countries had created national commissions charged with implementing Agenda 21.

By mid-1994, the CSD had met twice—with mixed results. On the positive side, it has provided a forum where governments and nongovernmental participants can share information about successes and failures in implementing the Rio accords. Already, there is quite a bit to discuss. Agenda 21 called on all nations to devise national sustainable development strategies. By May 1994, 103 had created national commissions charged with implementing Agenda 21. Beyond this, at least 36 countries have devised strategies based on their deliberations. China, for instance, has recently published a lengthy national Agenda 21 plan designed to reorient both national policies and international assistance. Encouragingly, there is also a growing movement worldwide to create sustainable cities and communities. The Toronto-based International Council for Local Environmental Initiatives is spearheading a campaign to promote the adoption of local Agenda 21s. Cities already participating include Buga, Colombia; Quito, Ecuador; and Lahti, Finland.[45]

Governments are also increasingly using the CSD to exchange views on difficult and sometimes contentious issues related to sustainable development that cut across traditional sectoral lines. For instance, at the May 1994 session the Commission took up the role of trade in sustainable development as well as the controversial question of changing unsustainable production and consumption patterns. Among the issues on its lengthy agenda for the 1995 session are an evaluation of the adequacy of existing international actions to protect biodiversity, forests, and mountains (see Chapter 3) and to combat desertification and drought.[46]

Despite these hopeful signs, the CSD suffers from certain structural defects that impede substantive progress. For one, its mandate is so broad that priorities are often not clear. In addition, the official process for reporting information has not proved altogether satisfactory. The initial suggested format was long and unwieldy, with little concrete guidance on what information is sought. Changes have recently been made to simplify the process. Participation has also been unsatisfactory, with fewer than half the CSD members and only 10 non-CSD members submitting reports for the May 1994 session. Because governments are reporting on their own actions, the documents tend to be long on self-congratulation and short on substantive analysis of remaining challenges.[47]

To overcome these problems, a high-level panel convened by the Interaction Council (an independent group consisting of former heads of government) recommended that instead of relying on national reports, the CSD should request studies by independent experts. In addition, the panel recommended that the secretariat should report directly to governments and the Secretary-General on priority initiatives, rather than the General Assembly and the Economic and Social Council. Other procedural reforms could also help improve the CSD's effectiveness. The U.S.-based National Wildlife Federation, on behalf of a coalition of NGOs, proposes that the ministerial-level segment of the CSD occur before rather than after the regular deliberations, to enable follow-through on initiatives endorsed by the ministers. They also recommend that panel discussions be organized on key subjects on the annual agenda, and that mechanisms be created to ensure follow-up on CSD proposals.[48]

In addition to creating the CSD, the Rio conference gave a shot in the arm to a newcomer on the international stage—the Global Environment Facility (GEF). Countries created this in 1991 to finance investments in preserving the global commons—specifically international waterways, the atmosphere, and biological diversity. Under the joint management of UNDP, UNEP, and the World Bank, the GEF had as of July 1994 committed $742 million in grants—43 percent for biological diversity preservation, 38 percent for global warming–related initiatives, 16 percent to protect international waters, 2 percent for overarching projects, and 1 percent for projects aimed at heading off ozone depletion. After Rio, GEF was designated as the "interim funding mechanism" for the climate and biodiversity treaties.[49]

In March 1994, after months of arduous negotiations, governments agreed to replenish GEF with $2 billion in new resources to be spent over the next three years. They also agreed to make the fund permanent, and to change the way it is governed. For instance, the GEF secretariat will be more independent from the World Bank than it was during the pilot phase. A new and innovative voting system has been devised for GEF: decisions will require two consecutive majorities—the first through a one-nation, one-vote system similar to that used at the United Nations, and the second by a one-dollar, one-vote system comparable to that of the Bretton

Woods institutions. This is intended to make the fund more broadly representative of its members.[50]

These changes were made in response to questions from various quarters about GEF's performance during the pilot phase. Its close association with the Bank had been a source of concern both to developing countries, who resent the fact that donor countries have disproportionate clout there, and to many NGOs, whose long experience with the Bank has made them skeptical that it is the right institution for the job—particularly given its penchant for secrecy and the difficulty it has working closely with local peoples. An independent evaluation of GEF called for by its member-governments in the course of the replenishment negotiations confirmed that there were reasons to worry. Given the recent changes, however, the parties to the climate and biological diversity conventions are likely to make GEF their permanent funding arm.[51]

GEF has a much-needed role to play as a provider of what amounts to venture capital for the global environment, but the far more critical task is to reorient all financial flows to developing countries in support of sustainable development. It should ideally help catalyze broader actions by international funding sources and national governments. At the moment, the good done by a small GEF grant is all too often overwhelmed by larger, poorly conceived World Bank projects. For instance, small loans for solar energy in India, though desirable, pale in significance for the global environment next to massive planned investments in coal-fired power plants there that are expected to become one of the single largest sources of carbon emissions during the next decade.[52]

If the Bank and other donors would develop policies aimed at implementing major environmental conventions such as the climate and biodiversity treaties in their lending programs, it would help avoid such anomalous situations. This would be in keeping with a Bank policy that prevents lending in violation of international treaties. In one small step in this direction, the Bank has initiated a program that will begin to integrate global considerations into some national environmental action plans, country assistance strategies, and other documents. The G7 Summit in 1995 provides an opportunity to push the whole process forward. In addition, governments can promote greater attention to global priorities in multilateral lending through the conventions themselves. Parties to the climate convention, for example, could call for the World Bank to report on the greenhouse gas emissions projected to result from proposed projects.[53]

As the fiftieth anniversary of the U.N. approaches, many ideas are being floated for changes to prepare the world body for the future. Some proposals concern the need to expand membership on the Security Council to make it more broadly representative of today's world. Others focus on the economic and social side of U.N. operations. UNDP, for instance, is advocating an Economic Security Council—a body of 22 members to promote the cause of "sustainable human security" at the highest levels.[54]

While various proposals are debated, one idea merits consideration: the creation of a full-fledged environment agency within the U.N. system.

While these proposals are debated, one other idea merits consideration: the creation of a full-fledged environment agency within the U.N. system. UNEP has contributed a great deal for an organization its size—its limited budget is smaller than that of some private U.S. environmental groups. But it does not enjoy the stature within the U.N. system of a specialized agency. This means it has few operational programs of its own. Though it is charged with coordinating the U.N. response to environmental issues, it has little ability to influence the programs of other agencies with much larger budgets. The fiftieth anniversary of the United Nations is an appropriate time either to upgrade UNEP to specialized agency status or to create a new U.N. environment agency.[55]

Some will disagree with this suggestion, citing the need to integrate environmental policymaking throughout the system rather than isolating it in one, marginalized agency. But such integration is equally important at the national level as well, yet few would dispute the need for strong domestic environmental ministries. What is needed in both cases is a watchdog group.

In considering what the functions of such an organization might be, Dan Esty of Yale University suggests that a Global Environmental Organization (GEO) might develop basic environmental principles analogous to widely recognized trade principles advanced by GATT such as most-favored-nation status and nondiscrimination. High on such a list would be full-cost pricing, the notion that environmental costs should be internalized in the prices of products rather than passed on to taxpayers. Other candidates include the precautionary principle—that decisions to take preventative action sometimes cannot await conclusive scientific proof—and a right to public participation. Governments have already endorsed these ideas and others in the Rio Declaration, but they have not given an organization the task of seeing that they are respected.[56]

In addition, a GEO could play a critical role by serving as an information clearinghouse—as UNEP's Global Environmental Monitoring System already does on a small scale. Such an organization might also serve as the implementing agency for some UNDP-financed projects. For instance, just as WHO and FAO collaborate with UNDP on the ground, a GEO might be a partner in recycling or land reclamation projects. It might also elaborate some common minimum international environmental production standards, particularly for industries such as paper manufacturing, in which pollution control costs are high enough to affect international competitiveness. And it could provide some overarching structure and coordination to the current scattered process of international environmental governance. This could improve the opportunities for bargaining and facilitate access for nongovernmental groups.[57]

A pertinent precedent is provided by the International Labour Organisation (ILO), which constantly modifies and strengthens the hundreds of standards it has issued on concerns such as workplace safety and child labor. The ILO also reviews whether members are complying with its standards. The agency often generates enough pressure in a first, investigatory stage to bring an errant country into line, making its second stage—a public hearing to explain delinquency—unnecessary. Representatives from both management and labor actually form part of the governing body of the ILO, through a unique tripartite system in which they share equal standing with governments. The World Intellectual Property Organization, which has helped rationalize the many complex and often overlapping international agreements in this domain, is another relevant model for a GEO.[58]

Finally, the time has come for governments to create some form of dedicated funding mechanism to finance investments for the transition to a sustainable society—including environmental expenditures, social initiatives, and peacekeeping costs. Among the possibilities for such a fund are a levy on carbon emissions, on international air travel, or perhaps on international flows of money. To discourage destabilizing currency speculation, Nobel-laureate James Tobin has suggested that a 0.5-percent tax be placed on foreign-exchange transactions, which would raise more than $1.5 trillion annually. But even a far smaller levy would raise sizable funds. A tax of just 0.003 percent of current daily currency transactions would raise $8.4 billion—more than four times the recent replenishment of GEF. The Social Summit would be an opportune time to launch such an initiative.[59]

INVOLVING PEOPLE

Even in the best of circumstances, the slow pace of international diplomacy and the rate at which many environmental and social problems are growing worse are difficult to reconcile. The best hope for improving the process of global governance lies with people. Just as national policymaking cannot be considered in isolation from public pressure, so international policymaking increasingly must consider an organized and influential international citizenry.

The most familiar role for NGOs and grassroots groups is within national borders. Around the world, there is an encouraging growth in such activities. In addition to this critical work, citizens' groups are also beginning to make their influence felt in international forums. In Rio, the 20,000 concerned citizens and activists who attended from around the world outnumbered official representatives by at least two to one. Similarly, more than 4,000 NGOs participated in the Cairo conference, where they were widely credited with helping to shape the terms of the debate. Some of the organizations represented at these meetings—such as Friends of the Earth, Greenpeace, the International Planned Parenthood Federation, and the World Wide Fund for Nature—are themselves international, meaning they represent global constituencies rather than parochial national interests. Taken together, all this activity adds up to the creation of a bona fide global environmental movement.[60]

Working through international coalitions such as the Climate Action Network and the Women's Environment and Development Organization, these groups are a powerful force. Daily newsletters produced by citizens' groups, including *Eco* and the *Earth Negotiations Bulletin*, have become mainstays of the international negotiating process. Widely read by official delegates and NGOs alike during international meetings, they reveal key failures in negotiations and prevent the obscure language of international diplomacy from shielding governments from accountability for their actions.[61]

The participation of the international scientific community also is critical. International panels of scientists convened to study both ozone depletion and climate change played instrumental roles in forging the scientific consensus needed to push these political processes forward. The treaties on these two problems created scientific advisory groups that now meet regularly and offer advice on whether the agreements need to be updated in light of new scientific information.

The interests of the business community can also sometimes be harnessed to positive effect. For instance, U.S. industry came to support strongly the Montreal Protocol because it saw U.S. legislation as inevitable and did not want to be at a competitive disadvantage as a result. The Business Council for Sustainable Development, some 50 chief executives from the world's largest corporations, were active in the lead-up to the Earth Summit. Though the Council opposed language in Agenda 21 that would have advocated developing standards to regulate multinational corporations, it argued persuasively in its report *Changing Course* that sound environmental policies and sound business practices go hand in hand. More recently, the U.S.-based Business Council for a Sustainable Energy Future—a coalition of energy efficiency, renewable energy, and natural gas companies that favor taking action to avert global warming—has begun to participate in international climate negotiations, where they counterbalance the lobbying efforts of oil and coal companies.[62]

Despite the impressive contributions they make, citizens' groups working at the global level face formidable obstacles. International law has traditionally functioned as a compact among nations, with no provisions for public participation comparable to those that are virtually taken for granted at the national level in democracies around the world. There is nothing yet resembling an elected parliament in the United Nations or any of its agencies. Though the U.N. has begun to experiment with occasional public hearings on topics of special concern, these continue to be rare events. No formal provisions are made for public review and comment on international treaties, nor is there a mechanism for bringing citizen suits at the World Court. International negotiations are often closed to public participation, and access to documents of critical interest to the public is generally highly restricted.[63]

Agenda 21 encourages the democrati-

zation of international lawmaking by devoting a lengthy section to the important role of "major groups" (including citizens' groups, labor unions, farmers, women, business interests, and others) and by endorsing the need to make information freely and widely available. In an important precedent, the Commission on Sustainable Development has based its rules for NGO participation on the liberal regulations that were in effect for the Rio conference. As a result, more than 500 groups are accredited to observe CSD deliberations and make selective interventions. An international NGO Steering Committee has recently been created to help promote collaboration among these groups from diverse corners of the globe, and to facilitate interaction with the secretariat of the CSD and with governments.[64]

Despite impressive contributions, citizens' groups working at the global level face formidable obstacles.

One interesting NGO initiative at the CSD is Earth Summit Watch, a project of the U.S.-based Natural Resources Defense Council and CAPE 21 (a coalition of U.S. environmental groups). This effort has led to two reports based on in-depth surveys of actions taken to put Agenda 21 and other Rio initiatives into practice around the world. *Four in '94*, prepared for the 1994 CSD session, asked governments to list concrete actions taken in four of the portions of the agenda up for review that year—health, human settlements, fresh water, and toxic chemicals and hazardous waste. Among the findings: 34 of 67 countries surveyed had taken steps to reduce lead exposure by moving toward lead-free gasoline and through other means; 45

reported some initiatives to promote clean water; 61 of the 178 countries at Rio have ratified the Basel convention on trade in hazardous wastes, and 74 have imposed national bans on hazardous waste imports; yet only 10 of 67 countries surveyed have taken steps to protect rivers. For the time being, most countries are simply reporting on actions they were planning to take anyway. But over time, the "peer pressure" process may induce them to move forward on new policies. A *Five in '95* report is planned for this year.[65]

Another way in which NGOs participate in the Rio follow-up process is through their participation in some national sustainable development commissions. These bodies take different forms in different countries. Some are composed only of government representatives; others are "multistakeholder" forums composed of a range of interested parties, including government, NGOs, and the business sector. In 1987, Round Tables on the Environment and the Economy in Canada pioneered the concept of bringing diverse parties to the table. This has since been widely replicated, including by the Philippine Council on Sustainable Development and by the President's Council on Sustainable Development in the United States.[66]

The U.N. Economic and Social Council is currently reviewing the rules for the participation of citizens' groups in the U.N. system at large. Some of those involved in the debate advocate making it easier for groups to be involved, taking the Rio experience as their guide. Others resist this view, worrying about the system being overwhelmed by sheer numbers, or about whom the citizens' groups are accountable to. The outcome of these deliberations remains to be seen, but it seems likely that the UNCED process has set a new standard for participation that the U.N. system will have

difficulty backing away from.[67]

The Bretton Woods institutions pose the greatest challenge when it comes to openness and accountability. To an even greater extent than at the U.N. itself, information and documents at these institutions are a tightly guarded secret, and negotiations between governments are completely closed to observers, with no NGO newsletters offering blow-by-blow accounts of who says what to whom.

GATT has been subject to particularly strong criticism for its secretive procedures. When a national law is challenged as a trade barrier under GATT, the case is heard behind closed doors by a panel of professors and bureaucrats steeped in the intricacies of world trade law, but not in the needs of the planet. Legal briefs and other critical information are generally unavailable to the public, and there is no opportunity for citizens' groups to testify or make submissions. Governments are currently discussing rules on public participation for the Trade and Environment Committee of GATT's successor, the World Trade Organization. Preliminary reports suggest that the fight for public access will be a long and hard-fought battle.[68]

Despite a checkered history regarding openness, the World Bank recently instituted two new policies that others would do well to emulate. Under a new information policy, more Bank documents will be publicly available than before, and an information center has been established to disseminate them. The second change—the creation of an independent inspection panel—will provide an impartial forum where board members or private citizens can raise complaints about projects that violate the Bank's own policies, rules, and procedures. Though both initiatives were watered down in the negotiating process, they nonetheless represent sizable chinks in the World Bank's armor. It will be up to the concerned public to test the limits of these new policies and to press for them to be strengthened—and replicated elsewhere.[69]

Besides access to information, the public needs to become a fuller partner in the development process itself. All too often, "development" has served the purposes of a country's elite, but not its poorest members. A growing body of evidence suggests that for a project to succeed, its planning process must include the people it is supposed to benefit. In other words, aid should be demand-driven rather than imposed from above. Several bilateral aid agencies have developed new ways of fostering widespread participation in the development planning process, and the World Bank has also recently come up with a new strategy along these lines. The challenge, as always, will be moving from words to action.[70]

SECURING THE FUTURE

Just over 25 years ago, photographs of the earth taken from space by Neil Armstrong helped launch the modern environmental movement, indelibly impressing on all who saw them that although the earth is crisscrossed by political boundaries, it is united by ecological systems. Today, we know the condition of the earth and of those who live on it to be more fragile than ever.

Though the planet's health has deteriorated markedly in the last 25 years, the same period has witnessed the rise of an impressive number of international initiatives designed to stabilize ecological support systems. Some of the agreements amounted to just words, but many have led to measurable actions, proving that when the conditions are ripe for it, international collaboration can work. The urgent task now facing the world

community is to accelerate dramatically the international political response to the challenge of ecological deterioration and social disintegration before they become irreversible.

The steps needed to reverse the decline are far too numerous to list here. They involve literally millions of small actions and decisions in villages, farms, businesses, and cities around the world. It is through a diversity of responses, suited to local and regional conditions, that the security of the planet will ultimately be assured. The task for international governance is not to micromanage these actions, which depend on the genius, commitment, and ingenuity of individuals worldwide, but to ensure that the climate is favorable for them.

The task for international governance is not to micromanage actions that depend on the genius, commitment, and ingenuity of individuals worldwide, but to ensure that the climate is favorable for them.

This chapter has made several specific policy recommendations. They include upgrading UNEP to become a full-fledged specialized agency or creating a new Global Environmental Organization, creating a dedicated funding source for environmental and social spending, seizing the opportunity offered by the Social Summit to implement UNDP's proposal for a 20:20 Compact, moving quickly to strengthen and implement the hundreds of international environmental agreements that now exist, putting Agenda 21 and the World Population Plan of Action into practice, and fully opening all parts of the vast United Nations system to public participation.

Surveys indicate that most people would support such changes: a recent groundbreaking Gallup Survey found that public concern about environmental problems is uniformly high around the world—dispelling the myth that only rich countries can afford to care about these issues. In the Philippines, 94 percent of those polled said they cared about environmental problems a "great deal" or a "fair amount"; in Nigeria, 87 percent responded in this way, as did 85 percent of those questioned in the United States and 66 percent of people in Japan. Interestingly, the survey found little inclination toward global finger-pointing. When asked whether rich or poor countries were more responsible for global environmental harm, everyone accepted some share of the blame. Support for international cooperation to solve shared problems was also high: majorities in both industrial and developing countries favor establishing an international agency with a mandate for global environmental protection.[71]

Yet despite public support for far-reaching changes, the international response to the interlinked threat of ecological collapse and social disintegration remains seriously inadequate. Fifty years ago, with large parts of Europe and Asia in ruins in the wake of World War II, the world community pulled together with an impressive period of institution-building that set the tone for the next half-century. The time has come for a similar burst of innovation to forge the new global partnership that will enable the world to confront the daunting challenges that await it in the next millennium.

If the changes called for in this chapter are made, and if the power of public commitment to sustainable development is unleashed, we can head off global ecological collapse and the social disintegration that would be sure to accompany it. But if complacency reigns and international forums generate lots of talk and paper but little action, the future does not look bright. The choice is ours to make.

Notes

Chapter 1. Nature's Limits

1. Number of delegates from "Cairo Conference Adopts 20-Year Program of Action Linking Population, Development and Women's Empowerment," press release, International Conference on Population and Development Secretariat, New York, September 30, 1994; U.N. General Assembly, "Programme of Action of the United Nations International Conference on Population and Development" (draft), New York, September 19, 1994.

2. U.N. General Assembly, op. cit. note 1.

3. Gulhati quoted in Michael Elliot and Christopher Dickey, "Body Politics," *Newsweek*, September 12, 1994.

4. Fish catch from U.N. Food and Agriculture Organization (FAO), *Fishery Statistics: Catches and Landings* (Rome: various years), and from FAO, Rome, private communications, December 20, 1993.

5. Patrick E. Tyler, "China Lacks Water to Meet Its Mighty Thirst," *New York Times*, November 7, 1993; Patrick E. Tyler, "Huge Water Project Would Supply Beijing By 860-Mile Aqueduct," *New York Times*, July 19, 1994.

6. Nigel Collar and P. Andrew, *Birds to Watch, The ICBP World Checklist of Threatened Birds* (Washington D.C.: Smithsonian Institution Press, 1988); Howard Youth, "Birds Are in Decline," in Lester R. Brown, Hal Kane, and David Malin Roodman, *Vital Signs 1994* (New York: W.W. Norton & Company, 1994).

7. Effects of Mount Pinatubo on atmospheric temperatures from "Climate Group Rejects Criticism of Warnings," *Nature*, September 22, 1994.

8. "India Sweltering Through Deadly Heat, Drought," *Los Angeles Times*, May 31, 1994; Michael McCarthy, "USA: New Fires Worry Beleaguered Crews in West," *Reuter Newswire*, August 5, 1994; "Firefighters Battling 33 Major Blazes in the West," *Reuter Newswire*, August 10, 1994.

9. "Japanese Utility to Import Water As Heat Wave Saps Refineries," *Journal of Commerce*, August 17, 1994; Gordon Cramb, "Drought-hit Japan is to Import Water," *Financial Times*, August 18, 1994; Peter Blumberg, "Japan Water Deal Fulfills Alaskan Officials' Dream," *Journal of Commerce*, August 30, 1994; "Heat Wave," *China Daily*, August 3, 1994; "Summer's a Scorcher Across the Atlantic, Melting Old Records," *Wall Street Journal*, August 5, 1994.

10. U.S. Department of Agriculture (USDA), Economic Research Service (ERS), "Production, Supply, and Demand View" (electronic database), Washington, D.C., July 1994.

11. Estimate of 100 million tons from the FAO-sponsored publication, J.A. Gulland, ed., *The Fish Resources of the Ocean* (Surrey, U.K.: Fishing News Ltd., 1971); World Resources Institute, *World Resources 1994–95* (New York: Oxford University Press, 1994); FAO, *Fishery Statistics*, op. cit. note 4, with updates from FAO, private communications, op. cit. note 4.

12. Sandra Postel, *Last Oasis: Facing Water Scarcity* (New York: W.W. Norton & Company, 1992).

13. John Pomfret, "Black Sea, Strangled by Pollution, Is Near Ecological Death," *Washington Post*, June 20, 1994.

14. Conversion figure from FAO, Fishery Information, Data and Statistics Service, "Conversion Factors—Landed Weight to Live Weight," Rome, March 1992; Figure 1–1 from John Jacobs, Maryland Department of Natural Resources, "Eastern Oyster, Fishery Statistics of the United States" (unpublished printout), April 1994, and from Virginia Marine Resource Committee, "Oyster Ground Production" (unpublished printout), Newport News, Va., April 1994.

15. Postel, op. cit. note 12.

16. U.S. situation from Clifford Dickason, "Improved Estimates of Groundwater Mining Acreage," *Journal of Soil and Water Conservation*, May/June 1988, and from Clifford Dickason, USDA, ERS, Washington, D.C. private communication, October 19, 1989; R.P.S. Malik and Paul Faeth, "Rice-Wheat Production in Northwest India," in Paul Faeth, ed., *Agricultural Policy and Sustainability: Case Studies from India, Chile, the Philippines, and the United States* (Washington, D.C.: World Resources Institute, 1993); Population Reference Bureau (PRB), Washington, D.C., private communication, October 5 and October 17, 1994.

17. Timothy Egan, "Las Vegas Stakes Claim in 90's Water War," *New York Times*, April 10, 1994; Tyler, "China Lacks Water," op. cit. note 5.

18. Duane Chapman and Randy Barker, *Resource Depletion, Agricultural Research, and Development* (Ithaca, N.Y.: Cornell University, 1987); Fertilizer Industry Association (IFA), *Fertilizer Consumption Report* (Paris: 1992).

19. IFA, op. cit. note 18; FAO, *Fertilizer Yearbooks* (Rome: various years).

20. IFA, op. cit. note 18; FAO, op. cit. note 19.

21. Figure 1–2 from IFA, op. cit. note 18, from FAO, op. cit. note 19, from USDA, op. cit. note 10, and from U.S. Bureau of the Census projections, published in Francis Urban and Ray Nightingale, *World Population by Country and Region, 1950–1990, with projections to 2050* (Washington, D.C.: USDA, ERS, 1993).

22. Postel, op. cit. note 12; Anne Swardson, "Canada Closes Section of Atlantic to Fishing," *Washington Post*, April 10, 1994; Christopher B. Daly, "Fishermen Beached As Harvest Dries Up," *Washington Post*, March 3, 1994.

23. Beef prices from U.S. Department of Labor, Bureau of Labor Statistics, "Consumer Price Index" (unpublished printout), Washington, D.C., April 21, 1994; Figure 1–3 from FAO, *Fishery Statistics: Trade and Commerce* (Rome: various years), with updates from Adele Crispoldi, Fishery Statistician, Fishery Information, Data and Statistics Service, Fisheries Department, FAO, Rome, unpublished printout, September 12, 1994. World fish price calculated by dividing total global catch by total global value, as opposed to recording prices from one location.

24. "Bluefin Tuna Reported On Brink of Extinction," *Journal of Commerce*, October 11, 1993; Michael Specter, "Pollution Threatens World's Caviar Source," *New York Times*, June 7, 1994.

25. Caroline E. Mayer, "Be Prepared for More Frozen Fish," *Washington Post*, August 14, 1994; Anne Swardson, "Net Losses: Fishing Decimating Oceans' 'Unlimited' Bounty," *Washington Post*, August 14, 1994.

26. FAO, "Time Series for State of Food and Agriculture 1993" (electronic database), Rome, 1993; Steve Coll, "Sub-Saharan Africa's Incredibly Shrinking Economies," *Washington Post*, August 6, 1994.

27. FAO, op. cit. note 26; FAO, *Forest Product Yearbooks* (Rome: various years).

28. Malik and Faeth, op. cit. note 16; PRB, *1994 World Population Data Sheet* (Washington, D.C.: 1994).

29. Tyler, "China Lacks Water," op. cit. note 5.

30. Postel, op. cit. note 12.

31. Rice stocks from USDA, ERS, op. cit. note 10; Asuna Kojima, "Strains of Rice," *Japan Update*, June 1994; rice prices from Chicago Board of Trade, private communication, November 5, 1993.

32. USDA, op. cit. note 10; rice prices from "Futures Market," *Wall Street Journal*, various issues.

33. USDA, op. cit. note 10.

34. FAO, op. cit. note 19.

35. USDA, op. cit. note 10.

36. Figure 1–4 from ibid.; Keith Schneider, "A New Rice Could Raise Yields 20%," *New York Times*, October 24, 1994; PRB, op. cit. note 28.

37. Figure 1–5 from USDA, op. cit. note 10; stocks from ibid., updated October 1994.

38. Idled cropland release from assorted USDA press releases, May-July 1994.

39. Jeremy Warford quoted in "Environmental Damage Robs Countries' Income," *World Bank News*, March 25, 1993.

40. U.N. Development Programme (UNDP), *Human Development Report 1992* (New York: Oxford University Press, 1992); with updates from Worldwatch estimates based on UNDP, *Human Development Report 1993* (New York: Oxford University Press, 1993); Table 1–2 based on World Bank, unpublished printout, February 1992, on gross world product data for 1950 and 1955 from Herbert R. Block, *The Planetary Product for 1980: A Creative Pause?* (Washington, D.C.:

U.S. Department of State, 1981), on U.S. Bureau of the Census, Suitland, Md., private communication, March 26, 1993, and on International Monetary Fund (IMF), *World Economic Outlook: Interim Assessment* (Washington, D.C.: 1993).

41. IMF, *International Financial Statistics Yearbook* (Washington, D.C.: 1994); fish catch from FAO, *Fishery Statistics*, op. cit. note 4; grain harvest from USDA, op. cit. note 10.

42. IMF, *Annual Report 1994* (Washington, D.C.: 1994); World Bank, *World Development Report 1992* (New York: Oxford University Press, 1992).

43. Dickason, "Improved Estimates," op. cit. note 16; Dickason, private communication, op. cit. note 16.

44. "Environmental Scarcities, State Capacities, and Civil Violence," Peace and Conflict Studies Program, University College, University of Toronto, Toronto, Canada.

45. Population from Bureau of the Census, op. cit. note 21; fertility rate from PRB, op. cit. note 28; agricultural statistics from USDA, op. cit. note 10; water situation from Postel, op. cit. note 12.

46. Thomas F. Homer-Dixon, "Environmental Scarcities and Violent Conflict: Evidence from Cases," *International Security*, Summer 1994.

47. Grain-to-fish conversion ratio from Robert Walters, "Aquaculture Catches On," *Mt. Vernon Register News*, July 31, 1987.

48. Intergovernmental Panel on Climate Change, *Climate Change: The IPCC Scientific Assessment* (New York: Cambridge University Press, 1990).

49. U.N. High Commissioner for Refugees (UNHCR) budget from Heather Courtney, public information officer, UNHCR, Washington, D.C., private communication, October 4, 1994; UNDP budget from Ad de

Rad, UNDP, New York, private communication, October 19, 1994.

50. Bureau of the Census, op. cit. note 45; Nicholas D. Kristof and Sheryl WuDunn, *China Wakes* (New York: Random House, 1994).

51. PRB, op. cit. note 28; income rises from Kristof and WuDunn, op. cit. note 50.

52. USDA, op. cit. note 10; population from PRB, op. cit. note 28.

53. Population projection from Bureau of the Census, op. cit. note 21; economic expansion from International Monetary Fund, *International Financial Statistics* (Washington, D.C.: October 1994).

54. Use of grain for animal feed from USDA, op. cit. note 10; grain-to-beef conversion ratio based on Allen Baker, Feed Situation and Outlook Staff, ERS, USDA, Washington, D.C., private communication, April 21, 1992; grain-to-pork conversion ratio from Leland Southard, Livestock and Poultry Situation and Outlook Staff, ERS, USDA, Washington, D.C., private communication, April 27, 1992; feed-to-poultry conversion ratio derived from data in Robert V. Bishop et al., *The World Poultry Market—Government Intervention and Multilateral Policy Reform* (Washington, D.C.: USDA, 1990), from Linda Bailey, Livestock and Poultry Situation Staff, ERS, USDA, Washington, D.C., private communication, April 21, 1992, and from various issues of *Feedstuffs*.

55. FAO, *FAO Production Yearbook 1991* (Rome: 1992); USDA, *Dairy, Livestock and Poultry: World Livestock Situation*, Washington, D.C., October 1993.

56. USDA, op. cit. note 55; grain-to-beer conversion from Jack McCabe, Brew Master, Chicago, Ill., private communication, June 10, 1994, and from Virginia Brewers Association, private communication, June 12, 1994.

57. USDA, op. cit. note 10.

58. Ibid.

59. Patrick E. Tyler, "China Planning People's Car to Put Masses Behind Wheel," *New York Times*, September 22, 1994; Kristof and WuDunn, op. cit. note 50.

60. Niu quoted in Tyler, "China Lacks Water," op. cit. note 5.

61. Schneider, op. cit. note 36; Figure 1–6 from USDA, op. cit. note 10.

62. USDA, op. cit. note 10.

63. Ibid.

64. Figure 1–7 from ibid.

65. FAO, *FAO Production Yearbook 1990* (Rome: 1991); Figure 1–8 Worldwatch projections based on ibid., on USDA, "Grain Situation and Outlook Report," Washington, D.C., July 12, 1994, and on population projections in Bureau of the Census, op. cit. note 21.

66. Zhou quoted in Patrick E. Tyler, "The Dynamic New China Still Races Against Time," *New York Times*, January 2, 1994.

67. "US Deficit With China May Widen, CIA Reports," *Journal of Commerce*, July 25, 1994.

68. USDA, "World Grain Situation Outlook Report," Washington, D.C., July 12, 1994.

69. Projected demands from Lester Brown and Hal Kane, *Full House: Reassessing the Earth's Population Carrying Capacity* (New York: W.W. Norton & Company, 1994).

Chapter 2. Protecting Oceanic Fisheries and Jobs

1. Based on statistical data in the U.N. Food and Agriculture Organization (FAO) fisheries database, FISHSTAT-PC, FAO Fisheries Statistics Division, Rome, 1994. The catch in the Antarctic is 356,000 tons, down from a peak of 653,000 tons in 1982, primarily because of reduced interest in krill; the catch in the Arctic is zero.

2. In this chapter, the term "catch" refers to wild catch only, although FAO "catch" statistics include aquaculture yields as well; Figure 2–1 based on growth rates from FAO, *Marine Fisheries and the Law of the Sea: A Decade of Change*, Fisheries Circular No. 853 (Rome: 1993), on 1984–91 aquaculture, inland wild, and marine wild data from Maurizio Perotti, Fishery Information, Data and Statistics Service (FIDI), FAO, Rome, unpublished printout, November 3, 1993, on 1950–91 world catch, marine catch, and inland catch data from FAO, *Yearbook of Fishery Statistics: Catches and Landings* (Rome: 1967–91), for before 1984, on estimates based on 1975 aquaculture production estimate from National Research Council, *Aquaculture in the United States: Constraints and Opportunities* (Washington, D.C.: National Academy of Sciences, 1978), and on country estimates in Conner Bailey and Mike Skladeny, "Aquacultural Development in Tropical Asia," *Natural Resources Forum*, February 1991; reliance on fish for animal protein from Lennox Hinds, "World Marine Fisheries," *Marine Policy*, September 1992, from Edmondo Laureti, *Fish and Fishery Products: World Apparent Consumption Statistics Based on Food Balance Sheets (1961–1990)* (Rome: FAO Fisheries Department, 1992), and from FAO, *Marine Fisheries*, op. cit. in this note.

3. FAO, *Marine Fisheries*, op. cit. note 2; marine fish supply from Laureti, op. cit. note 2. At approximately 70 million tons per year and 52 million tons per year, respectively, pork and beef production are second and third to marine fish production of 80 million tons per year, from Lester R. Brown et al., *Vital Signs 1993* (New York: W.W. Norton & Company, 1993). Availability varies from country to country. A number of species are not readily available fresh, such as halibut from Alaska and rockfish from the Chesapeake. Fresh salmon and catfish caught in the wild are not easily available in Washington, D.C., although farmed species are, based on an informal survey of Washington, D.C. supermarkets, June 24, 1994.

4. Depleted species from John Caddy, FAO Fisheries Division, Rome, private communication, March 23, 1994; depleted coastal waters from FAO, *Marine Fisheries*, op. cit. note 2.

5. Estimate of 100 million tons from FAO-sponsored publication, J.A. Gulland, ed., *The Fish Resources of the Ocean* (Surrey, U.K.: Fishing News Ltd., 1971). This estimate is meant to include traditional bony fish ranging from commonly eaten species such as cod and haddock to the small shoaling species such as the Peruvian anchovy. Similar results are found in M.A. Robinson, *Trends and Prospects in World Fisheries*, Fisheries Circular No. 772 (Rome: FAO, 1984), cited in World Resources Institute (WRI), *World Resources 1992–93* (New York: Oxford University Press, 1992). Qualitative discussion of limits in FAO, *Marine Fisheries*, op. cit. note 2.

6. For a detailed discussion of environmental degradation of marine fisheries, see Peter Weber, *Net Loss: Fish, Jobs, and the Marine Environment*, Worldwatch Paper 120 (Washington, D.C.: Worldwatch Institute, July 1994), as well as Peter Weber, *Abandoned Seas: Reversing the Decline of the Oceans*, Worldwatch Paper 116 (Washington, D.C.: Worldwatch Institute, November 1993). No systematic global estimates for loss due to pollution and habitat destruction exist because of the difficulty of attributing cause. Nonetheless, we know that salmon losses total at least 500,000 tons per year; losses in such semienclosed seas and estuaries as the Baltic, the Chesapeake, and the Yellow, Black, Azov, and Aral Seas indicate that other losses are at least on the order of 500,000 tons per year. Coastal wetland loss may have reduced productivity on the order of 4 million tons per year, and coral reef destruction, another 500,000 tons per year, based on various sources included in text. With half the world's mangrove forests destroyed, coastal fishers may have lost on the order of 4.7 million tons of potential annual fish catch, including 1.5 million tons per year of shrimp. Total and mangrove wetland loss from WRI,

op. cit. note 5. With 5–10 percent of the world's coral reefs destroyed, the potential productivity of this resoure could be down on the order of 250,000–500,000 tons per year. Coral reef loss from Clive R. Wilkinson, "Coral Reefs are Facing Widespread Extinctions: Can We Prevent These Through Sustainable Management Practices?" presented at the Seventh International Coral Reef Symposium, Guam, 1992.

7. Canada has lost some 30,000–50,000 fishing jobs; New England is likely to lose around 20,000 jobs, from Elizabeth Ross, "Hard-Hit New England Fishermen Receive Financial Aid," *Christian Science Monitor*, March 23, 1994; U.S. Pacific salmon fisheries have lost on the order of 60,000 jobs, from Mark Trumbull, "Pacific Northwest Fisheries Shrink, Taking Thousands of Jobs Along," *Christian Science Monitor*, March 28, 1994; China's leading fishing province, Guangdong, has lost 14,000 jobs, from Fan Zhijie and R.P. Côté, "Population, Development and Marine Pollution in China," *Marine Policy*, May 1991. In addition, European nations have lost at least several thousand fishing jobs, and the disbanding of the Soviet Union has put an uncounted number of fishers out of work, as have the decline of the Black Sea fisheries and the closure of the Azov Sea fisheries; the environmental collapse of the Aral Sea put 60,000 people out of work since the sixties. The potential for future job loss is discussed later in this chapter.

8. Southeast Asia from Mohd Ibrahim Hj Mohamed, "National Management of Malaysian Fisheries" *Marine Policy*, January 1991, pp. 2–14; Leslie Crawford, "Chile No Longer has Plenty More Fish in the Sea," *Financial Times*, July 19, 1991; Gylfi Gautur Pétursson and Kristján Skarphéðinsson, "Restructuring the Fishing Industry in Iceland," Ministry of Fisheries in Iceland, Reykjavk, 1992; 200 million from Hinds, op. cit. note 2.

9. Boat numbers from Susan Pollack, "No More Fish Stories," *The Amicus Journal*, Spring 1994; Chris Newton, FAO Fisheries Division, Rome, private communication, March 25, 1994.

10. Norway and Europe from Carl-Christian Schmidt, "The Net Effects of Over-fishing," *The OECD Observer*, October/November 1993.

11. Bonnie McCay et al., "Privatization in Fisheries: Lessons from Experiences in the U.S., Canada, and Norway," presented at Symposium of the Ocean Governance Study Group, "Moving Ahead on Ocean Governance: Practical Applications Guided by Long-Range Visions," Lewes, Del., April 9–13, revised March 31, 1994.

12. Bill Shapiro, "The Most Dangerous Job in America," *Fortune*, May 31, 1993.

13. Global and European subsidies from FAO, *Marine Fisheries*, op. cit. note 2; Malaysia policy from James Clad, "The Fish Catches It," *Far Eastern Economic Review*, June 21, 1984; Malaysia exchange rate of M$2.2 per U.S. dollar from International Monetary Fund (IMF), *International Financial Statistics Yearbook* (Washington, D.C.: 1993).

14. Taiwan from Julian Baum, "Drifting Downstream," *Far Eastern Economic Review*, August 29, 1991; Russia from Newton, op. cit. note 9; estimate for the United States from Mike Weber, fisheries consultant, Washington, D.C., private communication, June 1, 1994.

15. John Kurien and T.R. Thankappan Achari, "Overfishing Along Kerala Coast: Causes and Consequences," *Economic and Political Weekly*, September 1–8, 1990.

16. Eduardo A. Loayza and Lucian M. Sprague, *A Strategy for Fisheries Development*, World Bank Discussion Papers, Fisheries Series No. 135 (Washington, D.C.: World Bank, 1992); Alfredo Sfeir-Younis and Graham Donaldson, *Fishery Sector Policy Paper* (Washington, D.C.: World Bank, December 1982).

17. Kurien and Achari, op. cit. note 15.

18. Ibid.

19. Fishers in Japan and China from Adele Crispoldi, Fishery Statistician, FIDI, FAO, Rome, private communication, April 8, 1994.

20. Table 2–2 adapted from Conner Bailey, "Optimal Development of Third World Fisheries" in Michael A. Morris, ed., *North-South Perspectives on Marine Policy* (Boulder, Colo.: Westview Press, 1988); employment data from FAO, *Marine Fisheries*, op. cit. note 2, with additional estimates for small-scale fishers from International Center for Living Aquatic Resources Management, *ICLARM 1992 Report* (Manila: Philippines, 1993), from R.S. Pomeroy and A. Cruz-Trinidad, "Socio-economic Aspects of Artisanal Fisheries in Asia" in S.S. de Silva, ed., *Asian Fisheries Society Commemorative Volume* (Manila, Philippines: Asian Fishery Society, in press), and from H. Josupeit, *The Economic and Social Effects of the Fishing Industry: A Comparative Study*, FAO Fisheries Circular No. 314 (Rome: 1981); income, fuel consumption, investment figures, and catch estimates from FAO, *Marine Fisheries*, op. cit. note 2. Fishers are categorized according to the FAO boat survey described in *Marine Fisheries*, op. cit. note 2; large-scale fishers are those who crew boats over 500 gross registered tons; medium-scale refers to 100–500 gross registered tons, and small-scale means under 100 gross registered tons, including traditional boats and canoes. Estimates of small-scale fishers range widely partially because these individuals often make a living from various activities.

21. Income estimates from FAO, *Marine Fisheries*, op. cit. note 2; Newfoundland from Peter R. Sinclair, "Introduction," in Peter R. Sinclair, ed., *A Question of Survival* (St. Johns, Newfoundland: Institute of Social and Economic Research, 1988); Asia and India figures from Pomeroy and Cruz-Trinidad, op. cit. note 20.

22. Mediterranean and Persian Gulf examples from Caddy, op. cit. note 4.

23. Based on projected limits of the oceans, current overcapacity estimates and current employment, all cited above.

24. Population growth rate and Mexican population from Population Reference Bureau, *1993 World Population Data Sheet* (Washington, D.C.: 1993); population projections from United Nations, Department for Economic and Social Information and Policy Analysis, *World Population Prospects: The 1992 Revision* (New York: 1993). The necessary increases are calculated on the basis of the fish supply that goes for human consumption, 70 million tons in 1990, excluding the portion that goes to animal feed. Maintaining the status quo for animal feed would require even greater increases, which are not likely for the species currently used for this purpose.

25. Rehabilitation from FAO, *Marine Fisheries*, op. cit. note 2; aquaculture growth from Perotti, op. cite note 2. Projecting future growth rates is virtually impossible for the nascent aquaculture industry. No prediction is intended by the figures given; this is only one possible scenario.

26. Laureti, op. cit. note 2.

27. Protein figures from ibid. and from FAO, *FAO Yearbook of Fishery Statistics: Production* (Rome: 1993).

28. In Figure 2–2, beef, pork, and chicken prices from FAO, *FAO Yearbook of Production: Trade and Commerce* (Rome: various years), and fish prices from FAO, *FAO Yearbook of Fishery Statistics: Commodities* (Rome: various years). See also price discussion in FAO, *Marine Fisheries*, op. cit. note 2.

29. Kurien and Achari, op. cit. note 15; conversion to U.S. dollars based on 1961 and 1981 exchange rates, 4.765 and 10.591 rupees per dollar respectively, from IMF, *International Financial Statistics Yearbook* (Washington, D.C.: 1990).

30. Trade data from FAO, *Commodities*, op. cit. note 28; "Vietnam to Improve Quality of

Its Seafood," *Journal of Commerce*, March 18, 1994.

31. James R. McGoodwin, *Crisis in the World's Fisheries* (Stanford, Calif.: Stanford University Press, 1990).

32. FAO, *Marine Fisheries*, op. cit. note 2; European Parliament, Directorate General for Research, *European Community Fisheries Agreements with Third Countries and Participation in International Fisheries Agreements* (Luxembourg: 1993); percentage catch from FISH-STAT-PC, op. cit. note 1.

33. FAO, *Yearbook of Fisheries Statistics: Commodities* (Rome: 1991). In 1991, these countries accounted for a total of $36.6 million worth of world fisheries imports.

34. Ibid.; Olav Schram Stokke, "Transnational Fishing: Japan's Changing Strategy," *Marine Policy*, July 1991.

35. United Nations, op. cit. note 24; Laureti, op. cit. note 2.

36. FAO, op. cit. note 33; FAO, *Yearbook of Fishery Statistics: Catches and Landings* (Rome: 1991).

37. Chile from John F. Kearney, "Restoring the Common Wealth of Ocean Fisheries," A Discussion Paper Oriented Toward Enlarging the Concept of Sustainability in the Deliberations Leading to the UN Conference On Straddling and Highly Migratory Fish Stocks, prepared for The Conservation Council of New Brunswick, June 1993.

38. United Nations, op. cit. note 24; Laureti, op. cit. note 2.

39. FISHSTAT-PC, op. cit. note 1; Perotti, op. cit. note 2.

40. FAO, *Marine Fisheries*, op. cit. note 2.

41. Wolfgang Hannig, "Innovation and Tenant Survival: Brackish Pond Culture in Java," *NAGA, The ICLARM Quarterly*, April 1988.

42. Chris Wille, "The Shrimp Trade Boils Over," *International Wildlife*, November/December 1993.

43. See, for example, J. Honculada Primavera, "A Critical Review of Shrimp Pond Culture in the Philippines," *Reviews in Fisheries Science*, Vol. 1, No. 2, 1993; *Wild Salmon: Present and Future*, proceedings of international conference, Sherkin Island Marine Station, Sherkin Island, Ireland, September 16–17, 1988; and overview from Hal Kane, "Growing Fish in Fields," *World Watch*, September/October 1993.

44. C. Kwei Lin and Christopher Lee, "Production of Freshwater Prawns in the Mekong Delta," *NAGA, The ICLARM Quarterly*, April 1992; photosection, *NAGA, The ICLARM Quarterly*, April-July 1993; "Shrimp Farming in Indonesia," Bulletin No. 20, Appropriate Technology International, Washington, D.C., November 1989.

45. Taiwan from Baum, op. cit. note 14; Malaysia from Robert Birsel, "Malaysian Fishermen Under Threat," *Pakistan & Gulf Economist*, August 1–7, 1987, and from Mohamed, op. cit. note 8; Europe from Commission of the European Communities, "Report 1991 from the Commission to the Council and the European Parliament on the Common Fisheries Policy," Brussels, December 18, 1991; Iceland from Schmidt, op. cit. note 10; Canada from McCay et al., op. cit. note 11.

46. McCay et al., op. cit. note 11.

47. Ibid. Note that McCay et al. did not use the term "windfall."

48. New Zealand example from Mark Feldman, "Fishing Boom, Fishing Bust, a Cautionary Tale," *Forest & Bird*, May 1990, and from Mark Bellingham, "A Better Deal for Life in the Sea?" *Forest & Bird*, February 1993.

49. Linda Binken, Alaska Longline Fishermen's Association, Sitka, Alaska, private communication, April 2, 1994.

50. *The Law of the Sea: United Nations Convention on the Law of the Sea* (New York: United Nations, 1983); Judith Fenwick, *International Profiles on Marine Scientific Research* (Woods

Hole, Mass.: Woods Hole Oceanographic Institution, 1992).

51. Canada example from Colin Nickerson, "Pirates Plunder Fisheries," *Boston Globe*, April 17, 1994.

52. Ibid. For more information on regional fishing agreements, see Michael J. Savini, *Summary Information on the Role of International Fishery Bodies with Regard to the Conservation and Management of Living Resources of the High Seas*, Fisheries Circular No. 835, Revision 1 (Rome: FAO, 1991).

53. "Bluefin Tuna Reported on Brink of Extinction," *Journal of Commerce*, November 10, 1993; Carl Safina, "Bluefin Tuna in the West Atlantic: Negligent Management and the Making of an Endangered Species," *Conservation Biology*, June 1993.

54. Restriction on catch from Debora MacKenzie, "Too Little Too Late to Save Atlantic Bluefin," *New Scientist*, November 20, 1993; non-ICCAT vessels from Newton, op. cit. note 9.

55. Development of the split from David E. Pitt, "U.N. Talks Combat Threat to Fishery," *New York Times*, July 25, 1993, and from Andy Palmer, American Oceans Campaign, Seattle, Wash., private communication, September 27, 1993. Additional information on the U.N. Conference on Straddling and Highly Migratory Fish Stocks is available in *Earth Negotiations Bulletin*, December 21, 1993, and *ECO*, March 1994 issues, published by Greenpeace, Washington, D.C.

56. FAO, *Marine Fisheries*, op. cit. note 2.

57. Discussion of traditional management, from which the tenets of fishery management come, in Gary A. Klee, "Oceania," in Gary A. Klee, ed., *World Systems of Traditional Resource Management* (New York: John Wiley & Sons, 1980); R.E. Johannes, CSIRO Marine Laboratories, Australia, "Small-Scale Fisheries: A Storehouse of Knowledge for Managing Coastal Marine Resources," presented at Ocean Management Symposium, Smithsonian Institution, Washington, D.C., November 20, 1991; Conner Bailey and Charles Zerner, "Role of Traditional Fisheries Resource Management Systems for Sustainable Resource Utilization," presented at Perikanan Dalam Pembangunan Jangka Panjang Tahap II: Tantangan dan Peluang, Sukabumi, West Java, June 18–21, 1991; example of boats as wide as long from Sinclair, op. cit. note 21.

58. James M. Acheson, "The Lobster Fiefs Revisited: Economic and Ecological Effects of Territoriality in Maine Lobster Fishing," in Bonnie J. McCay and James M. Acheson, eds., *The Question of the Commons: The Culture and Ecology of Communal Resources* (Tucson: University of Arizona Press, 1987).

59. Kenneth Ruddle, "The Continuity of Traditional Management Practices: The Case of Japanese Coastal Fisheries," in Kenneth Ruddle and R.E. Johannes, eds., *The Traditional Knowledge and Management of Coastal Systems in Asia and the Pacific* (Jakarta Pusat, Indonesia: UNESCO, 1985).

60. Ibid.

61. Charles Zerner, "Imagining Marine Resource Management Institutions in the Maluka Islands, Indonesia 1870–1992," Case Study No. 6, prepared for the Liz Claiborne and Art Ortenberg Foundation Community Based Conservation Workshop, Airlie, Va., October 18–22, 1993.

62. Philippine example from Don Hinrichsen, presentation at Worldwatch Institute, July 16, 1993; see also Don Hinrichsen, "Philippine Mangroves: Bounty in the Brine," *International Wildlife*, May/June 1992, and Don Hinrichsen, "Managing Mangroves in the Philippines," *People* (International Planned Parenthood Federation), November 3, 1991.

63. J.M. Vakily, "Assessing and Managing the Marine Fish Resources of Sierra Leone, West Africa," *NAGA, The ICLARM Quarterly*, January 1992.

64. Australia rents from FAO, *Marine Fisheries*, op. cit. note 2; quota system percentage

from "Fish: The Tragedy of the Oceans," *The Economist*, March 19, 1994, and from public information brochure, New South Wales Fisheries, Pyrmont, Australia.

65. A discussion of U.S. fishery law can be found in John P. Wise, *Federal Conservation & Management of Marine Fisheries in the United States* (Washington, D.C.: Center for Marine Conservation, 1991).

66. Vlad Kaczynski, School of Marine Affairs, University of Washington, Seattle, private communication, April 14, 1994.

67. Ross, op. cit. note 7.

Chapter 3. Sustaining Mountain Peoples and Environments

1. James Hilton, *Lost Horizon* (New York: William Morrow & Co., 1934).

2. One fifth of the landscape and one tenth of humanity from Jack Ives, "Preface," in Peter B. Stone, ed., *State of the World's Mountains: A Global Report* (London: Zed Books Ltd., 1992); number of people living downstream from "Managing Fragile Ecosystems: Sustainable Mountain Development," Chapter 13 in United Nations, *Agenda 21: The United Nations Program of Action From Rio* (New York: U.N. Publications, 1992); Norman Myers, "Threatened Biotas: 'Hot Spots' in Tropical Forests," *The Environmentalist*, Vol. 8, No. 3, 1988; Norman Myers, "The Biodiversity Challenge: Expanded Hot-Spots Analysis," *The Environmentalist*, Vol. 10, No. 4, 1990; Yuri Badenkov et al., "Mountains of the former Soviet Union: Value, Diversity, Uncertainty," in Stone, op. cit. in this note.

3. Area of mountains and high plateaus is Worldwatch estimate, based on proportion of land surface that is mountains and high plateaus from H. Louis, "Neugefasstes Höhendiagramm der Erde," *Bayer. Akad. Wiss.* (Math.-Naturwiss. Klasse), cited in Roger G. Barry, *Mountain Climate and Weather* (New York: Routledge, 1992), and on earth's total land surface from *The Times Atlas of the*

World (London: Times Books, 1993); number of mountain people in mid-1994 is Worldwatch estimate, based on proportion of world population in mountains from Ives, op. cit. note 2, and on world population from Population Reference Bureau, *1994 World Population Data Sheet* (Washington, D.C.: 1994); two fifths of mountain people in Andes, Himalaya-Hindu Kush, and African mountains is Worldwatch estimate. Table 3–1 based on Stone, op. cit. note 2, and the following: Tibetan Plateau figures from John Ackerly, director, International Campaign for Tibet, Washington, D.C., private communication, November 1, 1994; U.S. area figures from Robert G. Bailey, "Description of the Ecoregions of the United States," U.S. Forest Service, U.S. Department of Agriculture (USDA), Washington, D.C., 1994; U.S. population figures based on 1990 U.S. Census from Greg Alward, economist, Ecosystem Management, U.S. Forest Service, USDA, Fort Collins, Colo., unpublished printout, September 20, 1994; population of Alps from Werner Bätzing, professor of geography, Institute of Geography, University of Bern, Switzerland, private communication, August 8, 1994; Brazilian figures from José Pedro de Oliveira Costa, Assessor, Andean Group, World Conservation Union (IUCN)–Brazil, São Paulo, Brazil, unpublished printout and private communication, October 6, 1994; area of Antarctica from Robert G. Bailey, "Ecoregions Map of the Continents" and "Explanatory Supplement to Ecoregions Map of the Continents," *Environmental Conservation*, Winter 1989; Canadian area and population from Harry Hirvonan, Science Advisor, State of the Environment Reporting, Environment Canada, Ottawa, private communications and unpublished printouts, September 22 and 27, 1994; population densities from "Papua New Guinea Highlands," in Stone, op. cit. note 2; Francis F. Ojany, "Mount Kenya and its Environs: A Review of the Interaction between Mountains and People in an Equatorial Setting," *Mountain Research and Development*, August 1993; Elizabeth A. Byers, "Heterogeneity of Hydrologic

Response in Four Mountainous Watersheds in Northwestern Rwanda," *Mountain Research and Development*, November 1991.

4. *Webster's Ninth New Collegiate Dictionary* (Springfield, Mass.: Merriam-Webster, 1991).

5. Larry W. Price, *Mountains and Man: A Study of Process and Environment* (Berkeley: University of California Press, 1990); Bruno Messerli, "Stability and Instability of Mountain Ecosystems," *Mountain Research and Development*, May 1983.

6. Carl Troll, "High Mountain Belts between the Polar Caps and the Equator: Their Definition and Lower Limit," *Arctic and Alpine Research*, Vol. 5, No. 3, 1973; Worldwatch Institute estimate, based on Bailey, "Ecoregions Map," op. cit. note 3.

7. Jayanta Bandyopadhyay, "On the Perceptions of Mountain Characteristics," *World Mountain Network Newsletter*, November 1992; Elizabeth Byers and Meeta Sainju, "Mountain Ecosystems and Women: Opportunities for Sustainable Development and Conservation," *Mountain Research and Development*, August 1994.

8. Martin Price, "The Highlands: Environmental Problems and Management Conflicts," in "Tundra and Insularity," *Biosfera* (Barcelona, Spain: *Enciclopedia Catalana*), Vol. 9, forthcoming; Sumitra M. Gurung, "Human Perceptions of Mountain Hazards in the Kakani-Kathmandu Area: Experiences from the Middle Mountains of Nepal," *Mountain Research and Development*, November 1989; "Natural Hazards," in Mountain Agenda 1992, *Appeal for the Mountains* (Berne, Switzerland: Institute of Geography, University of Berne, 1992).

9. Molly Moore, "World's Wettest Place Suffers Drought-Like Conditions," *Washington Post*, October 8, 1994; Jack D. Ives et al., "The Andes: Geoecology of the Andes," in Stone, op. cit. note 2; Barry, op. cit. note 3; Peter Whiteman, "The Mountain Environment: An Agronomist's Perspective with a Case Study from Jumla, Nepal," *Mountain Research and Development*, May 1985; Michael A. Little, ed., "A General Prospectus on the Andean Region," *Mountain Research and Development*, February 1981.

10. Jayanta Bandyopadhyay and Dipak Gyawali, "Himalayan Water Resources: Ecological and Political Aspects of Management," *Mountain Research and Development*, February 1994; California from Sandra Postel, *Last Oasis: Facing Water Scarcity* (New York: W.W. Norton & Company, 1992), and from Bureau of the Census, "Resident Population of the States," press release, U.S. Department of Commerce, Washington, D.C., July 1, 1993; reliance on mountain water is Worldwatch estimate, based on "Managing Fragile Ecosystems," op. cit. note 2, and on Ives, op. cit. note 2.

11. "Water Towers of Mankind," in Mountain Agenda 1992, op. cit. note 8.

12. Byers and Sainju, op. cit. note 7; Karl S. Zimmerer, "The Loss and Maintenance of Native Crops in Mountain Agriculture," *GeoJournal*, May 1992; Jack D. Ives, "The Future of the Mountains," in Jack D. Ives (consulting ed.), *Mountains: The Illustrated Library of the Earth* (Emmaus, Pa.: Rodale Press, 1994); "Biodiversity: Future Wealth," in Mountain Agenda 1992, op. cit. note 8.

13. Ojany, op. cit. note 3; Adam Kotarba, ed., "Special Issue on Environmental Transformation and Human Impact in the Polish Tatra Mountains," *Mountain Research and Development*, February 1992; Mount Kinabalu from "Biodiversity: Future Wealth," in Mountain Agenda 1992, op. cit. note 8; U.S. flowering plant species from World Conservation Monitoring Centre, *Global Biodiversity: Status of the Earth's Living Resources* (New York: Chapman & Hall, 1992); "Southern Appalachian Ecoregion: Amid Hills and Hollows," *Sierra*, March/April 1994.

14. Reed F. Noss and Allen Y. Cooperrider, *Saving Nature's Legacy: Protecting and Restoring Biodiversity* (Washington, D.C.: Island

Press, 1994); C.J. Bibby et al., *Putting Biodiversity on the Map: Priority Areas for Global Conservation* (Cambridge: International Council for Bird Preservation, 1992); number of mountainous endemic bird areas (EBAs) from geographic information system analysis of digitized information, derived from comparison of BirdLife's maps of EBAs with Bailey's map of continent's ecoregions, op. cit. note 3; Simon Blyth, GIS technician, Habitats Department, World Conservation Monitoring Centre, Cambridge, United Kingdom, unpublished printout and map, November 1, 1994; Andes from Blyth, ibid., and from Adrian J. Long, "Restricted Range and Threatened Bird Species in Tropical Montane Cloud Forests," in Lawrence S. Hamilton, James O. Juvik, and Fred N. Scatena, *Tropical Montane Cloud Forest: Proceedings of an International Symposium at San Juan, Puerto Rico, 31 May–5 June, 1993* (Honolulu: East-West Center, 1993).

15. Noss and Cooperrider, op. cit. note 14; "Biodiversity: Future Wealth," op. cit. note 12; range of tropical mountain ecosystems from Lawrence S. Hamilton, "Mountain Chronicle: Status and Current Developments in Mountain Protected Areas," *Mountain Research and Development*, August 1993; David Tilman and John A. Downing, "Biodiversity and Stability in Grasslands," *Nature*, January 27, 1994; John C. Ryan, *Life Support: Conserving Biological Diversity*, Worldwatch Paper 108 (Washington, D.C.: Worldwatch Institute, April 1992); John C. Ryan, *State of the Northwest*, NEW Report No. 1 (Seattle, Wash.: Northwest Environment Watch, 1994).

16. "Cultural Diversity," in Mountain Agenda 1992, op. cit. note 8; Byers and Sainju, op. cit. note 7; Suresh Chand Rai, Eklabya Sharma, and Rakesh Chandra Sundriyal, "Conservation in the Sikkim Himalaya: Traditional Knowledge and Land-use of the Mamlay Watershed," *Environmental Conservation*, Spring 1994.

17. Agarwal from Centre for Science and Environment, *State of India's Environment, A Citizen's Report: Floods, Flood Plains, and Envi-ronmental Myths* (New Delhi: 1991); throughout this chapter, indigenous, native, and tribal are terms used interchangeably to describe the people and cultures that originally inhabited the land before colonization or conversion occurred; for a discussion of the various definitions of "indigenous peoples," and for number of Quechua, see Alan Thein Durning, *Guardians of the Land: Indigenous Peoples and the Health of the Land*, Worldwatch Paper 112 (Washington, D.C.: Worldwatch Institute, December 1992); Art Davidson, *Endangered Peoples* (San Francisco: Sierra Club Books, 1993); Robert W. Kates, B.L. Turner, and William C. Clark, "The Great Transformation," in B.L. Turner et al., eds., *The Earth as Transformed by Human Action: Global and Regional Changes in the Biosphere over the Last 300 Years* (New York: Cambridge University Press, 1990); Badenkov et al., op. cit. note 2.

18. Rural Andeans from Hugo Li Pun, International Development Research Centre, "Sustainable Andean Development: Project Summary," Ottawa, Canada, 1992, and from George Psacharopoulos and Harry A. Patrinos, "Indigenous People and Poverty In Latin America," *Finance and Development*, March 1994; the World Bank defined absolute poverty in China by taking 2,150 calories per day of food energy and then adding a sum for nonfood commodities and services based on the average expenditure pattern of the poor, and having the poverty line measure welfare against the ability to buy the predetermined bundle of commodities and services, according to World Bank, *China: Poverty Reduction Strategies for the 1990s* (Washington, D.C.: 1992); majority of poor Chinese being ethnic minorities in mountains from Jack D. Ives, *Children and Poverty in Mountains* (New York: UNICEF Environment Section, forthcoming); Appalachian poverty from D. Schnelling et al., "The Appalachians of North America: Marginal in the Midst of Plenty," in Stone, op. cit. note 2.

19. Major armed conflicts (involving more than 1,000 deaths) from Stockholm International Peace Research Institute, *SIPRI Year-*

book 1994 (New York: Oxford University Press, 1994), with number based in mountains being a Worldwatch estimate; Ives, "The Future of the Mountains," op. cit. note 12.

20. Byers and Sainju, op. cit. note 7; Edwin Bernbaum, *Sacred Mountains of the World* (San Francisco: Sierra Club Books, 1990); H. Byron Earhart, "Sacred Mountains in Japan: Shugendo as 'Mountain Religion'," in Michael Charles Tobias and Harold Drasdo, eds., *The Mountain Spirit* (Woodstock, N.Y.: Overlook Press, 1979).

21. A. John De Boer, "Sustainable Approaches to Hillside Agricultural Development," in H. Jeffrey Leonard et al., *Environment and the Poor: Development Strategies for a Common Agenda* (New Brunswick, N.J.: Transaction Books, for Overseas Development Council, 1989); Alan B. Durning, *Poverty and the Environment: Reversing the Downward Spiral*, Worldwatch Paper 92 (Worldwatch Institute, November 1989); Bryan Carson, *Erosion and Sedimentation Processes in the Nepalese Himalaya*, Occasional Paper No. 1 (Kathmandu, Nepal: International Centre for Integrated Mountain Development (ICIMOD), 1985); Bryan Carson, *The Land, the Farmer, and the Future: A Soil Fertility Management Strategy for Nepal*, Occasional Paper No. 25 (Kathmandu, Nepal: ICIMOD, 1992); Lawrence S. Hamilton, "The Protective Role of Mountain Forests," *GeoJournal*, May 1992.

22. Leonard Berry, Laurence A. Lewis, and Cara Williams, "East African Highlands," in Turner et al., op. cit. note 17; Rwandan arable land from U.N. Food and Agriculture Organization (FAO), *Production Yearbook 1993* (Rome: 1994); Jack D. Ives and Bruno Messerli, *The Himalayan Dilemma: Reconciling Conservation and Development* (New York: Routledge and the United Nations University, 1989); Nepal from N.S. Jodha, M. Banskota, and Tej Partap, "Strategies for the Sustainable Development of Mountain Agriculture: An Overview," in N.S. Jodha, M. Banskota, and Tej Partap, *Sustainable Mountain Agriculture: Perspectives and Issues*,

Vol. 1 (Kathmandu and New York: ICIMOD and Intermediate Technology Publications, 1992).

23. Erik P. Eckholm, *Losing Ground: Environmental Stress and World Food Prospects* (New York: W.W. Norton & Company, 1976); Lawrence S. Hamilton, "What Are the Impacts of Himalayan Deforestation on the Ganges-Brahmaputra Lowlands and Delta? Assumptions and Facts," *Mountain Research and Development*, August 1987; D.A. Gilmour, "Not Seeing the Trees for the Forest: A Re-Appraisal of the Deforestation Crisis in Two Hill Districts of Nepal," *Mountain Research and Development*, November 1988; Ives and Messerli, op. cit. note 22; J.S. Rawat and M.S. Rawat, "The Nana Kosi Watershed, Central Himalaya, India. Part II: Human Impacts on Stream Runoff," *Mountain Research and Development*, August 1994.

24. Kenneth Hewitt, "Mountain Hazards," *GeoJournal*, May 1992; Bertil Lintner, "Opium War," *Far Eastern Economic Review*, January 20, 1994; Salamat Ali, "Opiate of the Frontier," *Far Eastern Economic Review*, May 27, 1993; Victor Mallett, " 'Golden Quadrangle' United by a Desire to Make Money," *Financial Times*, March 3, 1994; "Drugs War High in the Andes," *The Economist*, February 13, 1993; James McGregor, "The Opium War: Burma Road Heroin Breeds Addicts, AIDS along China's Border," *Wall Street Journal*, September 29, 1992; Peru coca deforestation from Marc Dourojeanni, Senior Environmental Adviser, World Bank, private communication, October 1989, cited in "Latin America: Resource Environment Overview," in World Resources Institute, *World Resources 1990/91* (New York: Oxford University Press, 1990).

25. Byers and Sainju, op. cit. note 7.

26. Reed F. Noss, "Cows and Conservation Biology," and Thomas L. Fleischner, "Ecological Costs of Livestock Grazing in Western North America," both in *Conservation Biology*, September 1994; Alan B. Durning and Holly B. Brough, *Taking Stock: Animal Farming and the Environment*, Worldwatch

Paper 103 (Washington, D.C.: Worldwatch Institute, July 1991).

27. Commission on Development and Environment, *Amazonia Without Myths* (Washington, D.C.: InterAmerican Development Bank, U.N. Development Programme (UNDP), and Amazon Cooperation Treaty, 1992), cited in Bruce Cabarle, Manuel Huaya Panduro, and Oswaldo Manihuari Murayari, "Ecofarming in the Peruvian Amazon: the Integrated Family and Communal Gardening Project (HIFCO)," prepared for the Liz Claiborne and Art Ortenberg Foundation Community Based Conservation Workshop, Airlie, Va., October 18–22, 1993.

28. FAO, *Forest Resources Assessment 1990: Tropical Countries*, Forestry Paper 112 (Rome: 1993).

29. Noss and Cooperrider, op. cit. note 14; Price, op. cit. note 8.

30. David J. Fox, "Mining and Damming," in Ives, *Mountains*, op. cit. note 12.

31. Nicholas Lenssen, *Empowering Development: The New Energy Equation*, Worldwatch Paper 111 (Washington, D.C.: Worldwatch Institute, November 1992); Robert Goodland, "Environmental Sustainability in the Power Sector" (incomplete draft), World Bank, Washington, D.C., August 23, 1994; Kieran Cooke, "Daring Vision or Time Bomb?" *Financial Times*, May 30, 1994.

32. World Bank, *Nepal Arun III Hydroelectric Project, Credit and Project Summary of Staff Appraisal Report*, unpublished internal document, 1994; Goodland, op. cit. note 31; King Mahendra Trust for Nature Conservation, Consultant to the World Bank for the Arun III: Management of Basinwide Environmental Impacts Study, *Environmental Management and Sustainable Development in the Arun Basin, Volume 1: Summary and Synthesis* (Washington, D.C.: World Bank, UNDP, and His Majesty's Government of Nepal, 1991).

33. Eduardo Lachica, "Environmentalists Are Opposing Plans of World Bank to Build Dam in Nepal," *Wall Street Journal*, September 12, 1994; Juliette Majot, "Bank Stalled on Arun III, Japan Reluctant to Commit Funds to Nepali Dam," *Bank Check*, September 1994; Binod Hattarai, "Arun III, Nepal's Reluctant Narmada," *Himal*, March/April 1993; Environmental Defense Fund, "The World Bank's Dam Project in Nepal: Environmental Quagmire and Economic Folly?" Washington, D.C., September 13, 1994; Janet Bell, "Hydrodollars in the Himalaya," *The Ecologist*, May/June 1994; "Seeking Alternatives to Arun III," *World Rivers Review*, Second Quarter 1993; Godfrey Cromwell, "What Makes Technology Transfer? Small-Scale Hydropower in Nepal's Public and Private Sectors," *World Development*, Vol. 20, No. 7, 1992; Jane Pratt, President and CEO, Woodlands: The Mountain Institute, Franklin, W. Va., private communication, October 19, 1994.

34. John E. Young, *Mining the Earth*, Worldwatch Paper 109 (Washington, D.C.: Worldwatch Institute, July 1992); Julio Díaz Palacios, "Environmental Destruction in Southern Peru," *Earth Island Journal*, Summer 1989, cited in Young, ibid.; Abhinandan Bhardwaj and Sunil Dhar, Centre for Advanced Study of Geology, Panjab University, Chandigarh, India, private communication, September 2, 1993.

35. James Brooke, "For U.S. Miners, the Rush is on to Latin America," *New York Times*, April 17, 1994; Thomas J. Hilliard, "Stibnite—The Next Summitville?" *Clementine*, Autumn 1993; EPA cleanup estimate from Rick Young and Dan Noyes, "The Road to Summitville, Gold Mining Debacle," *New York Times*, August 14, 1994.

36. Minewatch, "Ok Tedi: The Environmental and Sociological Impacts of Mining on Mount Fublian," London, October 1990; Minewatch, "Ok Tedi," Minewatch Briefing No. 13, London, June 1991; "BHP Faces Huge Damages Claim," *Mining Journal*, May 6, 1994; "Ok Tedi Writ Shelved," *Mining Journal*, September 30, 1994.

37. John Muir, *John of the Mountains* (Madison: University of Wisconsin Press, 1975).

38. Ray Rasker and Dennis Glick, "Footloose Entrepreneurs: Pioneers of the New West?" *illahee* (Institute of Environmental Studies, University of Washington, Seattle), Spring 1994; Ray Rasker, Norma Tirrell, and Deanne Kloepfer, *The Wealth of Nature: New Economic Realities in the Yellowstone Region* (Washington, D.C.: The Wilderness Society, 1992).

39. Figure 3–1 from Kenneth E. Hornback, Chief, Socio-economic Studies, National Park Service, Fort Collins, Colo., unpublished printout and private communication, August 26, 1994; Yu-fai Leung and Jeffrey L. Marion, "Trail Degradation as Influenced by Environmental Factors: A State of the Knowledge Review," *Journal of Soil and Water Conservation*, forthcoming; Machu Picchu from Dennis G. Hanson, "Look to the Mountains," in Ives, *Mountains*, op. cit. note 12; Gangotri from Edwin Bernbaum, Commission on National Parks and Protected Areas (CNPPA), "Recommendations for Using Cultural Resources to Enhance the Gangotri Conservation Project in the Indian Himalaya," IUCN, Gland, Switzerland, September 1994.

40. International Commission for the Protection of the Alps, press release, cited in "Seven-nation Convention to Protect Alps Expected to Come into Force by End of Year," *International Environment Reporter*, September 21, 1994; number of jobs from Christian Pfister and Paul Messerli, "Switzerland," in Turner et al., op. cit. note 17; "Alp Action: Corporate Environmental Partnership," *Newsweek*, special advertising section, January 31, 1994; Alan Riding, "Swiss Give New Meaning to Roadblock," *New York Times*, February 28, 1994.

41. Alpine golf courses from "Seven-nation Convention to Protect Alps," op. cit. note 40; Anne E. Platt, "The Trouble with Golf," *World Watch*, May/June 1994; Larry Hamilton, Vice Chair for Mountains, CNPPA, IUCN, private communication, July 23, 1994; Jack Ives, professor of geoecology, Division of Environmental Studies, College of Agricultural and Environmental Sciences, University of California at Davis, private communication, September 28, 1994.

42. Jack D. Ives, "Mountains North and South," in Stone, op. cit. note 2; "Alpine Skiing: The Dangers of Overdevelopment," in Ives, *Mountains*, op. cit. note 12; Shawn Emery, "Helicology," *Summit*, Spring 1994; D.J. Herda and L.A. Pifer, "Fast and Loose on the Slopes," *Washington Post*, November 14, 1993; Elizabeth Ross, "Slippery Slope for Snowmaking: Vermont Conservationists Take the Lead in Trying to Limit Ski Resorts' Use of River Water," *Christian Science Monitor*, November 22, 1993; Alex Markels, "Moving to the Mountains," *Snow Country*, July/August 1994; Kenneth Labich, "The Geography of an Emerging America," *Fortune*, June 27, 1994; Raymond Rasker, "A New Look at Old Vistas: The Economic Role of Environmental Quality in Western Public Lands," *University of Colorado Law Review*, Vol. 65, Issue 2, 1994.

43. Increases since 1950 from Pfister and Messerli, op. cit. note 40; Kotarba, op. cit. note 13; Rodolphe Schlaepfer, ed., *Long-term Implications of Climate Change and Air Pollution in Forest Ecosystems: Progress Report of the IUFRO Task Force, "Forest, Climate Change and Air Pollution,"* World Series Vol. 4 (Vienna: International Union of Forestry Research Organizations' Secretariat, 1993).

44. Robert L. Peters and Thomas E. Lovejoy, eds., *Global Warming and Biological Diversity* (New Haven, Conn.: Yale University Press, 1992); Executive Summary, "Draft Summary for Policymakers of the 1994 Working Group I Report on Radiative Forcing of Climate Change," Intergovernmental Panel on Climate Change, Maastricht, The Netherlands, September 15, 1994; Noss and Cooperrider, op. cit. note 14.

45. Georg Grabherr, Micheal Gottfried, and Harald Pauli, "Climate Effects on Mountain Plants," *Nature*, June 9, 1994.

46. Zhang Xinshi, "A Vegetation-climate Classification System for Global Change Studies in China," *Quaternary Sciences*, No. 2,

1993; Patrick N. Halpin, "GIS Analysis of the Potential Impacts of Climate Change on Mountain Ecosystems and Protected Areas," in Martin F. Price and D. Ian Heywood, *Mountain Environments and Geographic Information Systems* (London: Taylor and Francis, 1994); Noss and Cooperrider, op. cit. note 14; David Tilman et al., "Habitat Destruction and the Extinction Debt," *Nature*, September 1, 1994.

47. Tongariro Mountains from P.H.C. Lucas, "History and Rationale for Mountain Parks as Exemplified by Four Mountain Areas of Aotearoa (New Zealand)," in Lawrence S. Hamilton, Daniel P. Bauer, and Helen F. Takeuchi, eds., *Parks, Peaks and People: A Collection of Papers Arising from an International Consultation on Protected Areas in Mountain Environments, Held In Hawaii Volcanoes National Park, October 26-November 2, 1991* (Honolulu: East-West Center Program on the Environment, 1993); Larry Hamilton, "Mountain Protected Areas," in Stone, op. cit. note 2. Table 3–3 includes protected areas over 10,-000 hectares with a minimum of 1,500 meters of relative relief in IUCN's classes I-IV of management classification (Strict Nature Preserve, National Park, National Monument/ Natural Landmark, Wildlife Sanctuary); does not include production-oriented areas such as timber reserves or national forests; may include Biosphere Reserves or World Heritage Sites; if Greenland National Park (97 million hectares) were excluded, the area of mountain protected areas would be equivalent to the area of Alaska alone.

48. Noss and Cooperrider, op. cit. note 14; James W. Thorsell and Jeremy Harrison, "National Parks and Nature Reserves in Mountain Environments of the World," *GeoJournal*, May 1992; Duncan Poore, ed., *Guidelines for Mountain Protected Areas*, CNPPA, IUCN Protected Area Programme Series No. 2 (Gland, Switzerland: IUCN, 1992); U.S. Congress, Office of Technology Assessment, *Harmful Non-Indigenous Species in the United States* (Washington, D.C.: U.S. Government Printing Office, 1993); Kevin O'Connor,

" 'Invaders': Plant and Animal Invasions of Mountain Ecosystems and Implications for Protected Area Management," in Hamilton, Bauer, and Takeuchi, op. cit. note 47; Lawrence S. Hamilton, James O. Juvik, and Fred N. Scatena, "The Puerto Rico Tropical Cloud Forest Symposium: Introduction and Workshop Synthesis" in Hamilton, Juvik, and Scatena, op. cit. note 14; James O. Juvik, Sonia P. Juvik, and Lawrence S. Hamilton, "Altitudinal Resource Zonation Versus Vertical Control: Land-use Conflict on Two Hawaiian Mountains," *Mountain Research and Development*, August 1992.

49. James E. Enote and Alisa A. Mallari, "Indigenous Cultures and Sustainable Development: Two Years After the UNCED Conference," Working Group Paper Indigenous Issues, 1994. Table 3–4 from Woodlands Mountain Institute, *Nepal's Newest National Park: Makalu-Barun National Park and Conservation Area, Annual Report 1992* (Franklin, W. Va.: 1993); Task Force, *Makalu-Barun Conservation Project Management Plan* (Kathmandu, Nepal, and Franklin, W. Va.: 1991); Alton Byers, senior conservationist and protected area specialist, Woodlands: The Mountain Institute, Franklin, W. Va., private communication, October 17, 1994; Roman Haug, "A Bold New Program in the Hindelang," in "Alp Action: Corporate Environmental Partnership," op. cit. note 40; Richard Covington, "Worth Saving: Moving Mountains with the Prince," *Travel & Leisure*, October 1993; "Tuenjai Deetes, Asia winner," in "Detailed Background Information on the 1994 Fifth Annual Goldman Environmental Prize Winners," Goldman Environmental Foundation, San Francisco, April 18, 1994; Juan Mayr Maldonado, executive director, Fundación Pro-Sierra Nevada de Santa Marta, Bogota, Colombia, private communication, October 31, 1994; Ladakh Project, *Ecological Steps Towards a Sustainable Future* (Berkeley, Calif.: 1991); Helena Norberg-Hodge, *Ancient Futures: Learning from Ladakh* (San Francisco: Sierra Club Books, 1991); Mattole from Peter Berg, "Putting

'Bio' in front of 'Regional'," *Landscape Architecture*, April 1994; World Neighbors, *Beyond Cairo: The Integration of Population and Environment in Baudha-Bahunipati, Nepal* (Oklahoma City, Okla.: 1994); Cabarle, Panduro, and Murayari, op. cit. note 27.

50. Basnet quote from Don Hinrichsen, "Rescuing the Himalaya," *Scanorama*, forthcoming.

51. John L. Hough and Mingma Norbu Sherpa, "Bottom Up vs. Basic Needs: Integrating Conservation and Development in the Annapurna and Michiru Mountain Conservation Areas of Nepal and Malawi," *Ambio*, Vol. 18, No. 8, 1989; Michael Wells and Katrina Brandon, *People and Parks: Linking Protected Area Management with Local Communities* (Washington, D.C.: World Bank, World Wildlife Fund, and U.S. Agency for International Development, 1992); Michael P. Wells, "A Profile and Interim Assessment of the Annapurna Conservation Area Project, Nepal," prepared for the Claiborne-Ortenberg Foundation Workshop, op. cit. note 27; Chandra P. Gurung, "Linking Biodiversity Conservation to Community Development: Annapurna Conservation Area Project Approach to Protected Area Management," presented at Regional Seminar on Community Development and Conservation of Biodiversity through Community Forestry, Kasetsart University, Bangkok, Thailand, October 26–28, 1994.

52. Wells and Brandon, op. cit. note 51; Hough and Sherpa, op. cit. note 51; "The Annapurna Conservation Area Project, Nepal: A Case Study," Annex B, in Michael Brown and Barbara Wyckoff-Baird, *Designing Integrated Conservation and Development Projects* (Washington, D.C.: Biodiversity Support Program, 1992); Gurteng, op. Cit. note 51.

53. The Nature Conservancy, *Parks In Peril: A Conservation Partnership for the Americas* (Arlington, Va.: 1991).

54. Miriam Torres, Project Coordinator, Fundación Peruana para la Conservación de la Naturaleza (FPCN), Lima, Peru, private communication, July 23, 1994; FPCN, "FPCN/WWF-UK Manu Biosphere Reserve Project," *El Condor Pasa*, January-April 1993.

55. Pueblo of Zuni, Zuni Conservation Project, "Zuni Sustainable Resource Development," Zuni, N.M., 1993; James Enote, Project Leader, Pueblo of Zuni, Zuni Conservation Project, Zuni, N.M., private communication, July 25, 1994.

56. Stanford Lalio, geographic information systems coordinator, Pueblo of Zuni, Zuni Conservation Project, Zuni, N.M., private communication, October 14, 1994; Pueblo of Zuni, op. cit. note 55; James Enote, "Saving the Land and Preserving the Culture: Environmentalism at the Pueblo Zuni," in Barbara R. Johnson, ed., *Who Pays the Price?: Examining the Sociocultural Context of Environmental Crisis* (Oklahoma City, Okla.: Society for Applied Anthropology, 1993).

57. Wells and Brandon, op. cit. note 51; Claire Kremen, Adina M. Merenlender, and Dennis Murphy, "Ecological Monitoring: A Vital Need for Integrated Conservation and Development Programs in the Tropics," *Conservation Biology*, June 1994.

58. Woodlands: The Mountain Institute, *Report on the NGO Workshop on the Mountain Agenda, Spruce Knob, West Virginia, July 22–26, 1994* (Franklin, W. Va.: 1994); Jack D. Ives, "Editorial," *Mountain Research and Development*, August 1994.

59. Woodlands: The Mountain Institute, op. cit. note 58; Ives, op. cit. note 58; ICIMOD, "Regional Conference on Sustainable Mountain Development of Fragile Mountain Areas of Asia," Kathmandu, Nepal, December 13–15, 1994; potential date of conference from Tagé Michaelsen, Senior Officer, Forest Conservation, Forestry Department, FAO, Rome, private communication, October 20, 1994.

60. Ryan, *Life Support*, op. cit. note 15; Durning, op. cit. note 17.

61. Derek Denniston, "Defending the Land with Maps," *World Watch*, January/February 1994; Durning, op. cit. note 17; Goldman Environmental Foundation, "1991 Goldman Environmental Prize Winners," press release, San Francisco, April 22, 1991.

62. Figure of at least half reduction does not include significant reductions available through more-efficient building construction (see Chapter 6); from Table 5–4 in Sandra Postel and John C. Ryan, "Reforming Forestry," in Lester R. Brown et al., *State of the World 1991* (New York: W.W. Norton & Company, 1991); John E. Young and Aaron Sachs, *The Next Efficiency Revolution: Creating a Sustainable Materials Economy*, Worldwatch Paper 121 (Washington, D.C.: Worldwatch Institute, September 1994).

63. Young, op. cit. note 34; Durning, op. cit. note 17; Goodland, op. cit. note 31.

64. Sandra Postel and Christopher Flavin, "Reshaping the Global Economy," in Brown et al., op. cit. note 62; "Community Enterprise Unlimited," *Down to Earth*, March 15, 1994.

65. Sunder Lal Bahuguna, "A Practical Step Towards a Sustainable Society: Development Re-defined," Save Himalaya Movement, Ganga-Himalaya Kuti, 1994; Sunder Lal Bahuguna, "Strategies for Sound Development in the Himalaya," in Tej Vir Singh and Jagdish Kaur, eds., *Studies in Himalayan Ecology and Development Strategies* (New Delhi: Himalayan Books, 1989).

66. Noss and Cooperrider, op. cit. note 14; Joel T. Heinen and Pralad B. Yonzon, "A Review of Conservation Issues and Programs in Nepal: From a Single Species Focus toward Biodiversity Protection," *Mountain Research and Development*, February 1994; Maximo Libermann, "Sustainable Use and Conservation of Andean Mountains," advance notice for Conference to be held in Huaranilla, Bolivia, April 2–14, 1995; Larry Hamilton, Vice-Chair (Mountains), CNPPA, IUCN, "Mountain Protected Area Update,"

Islands and Highlands, Hinesburg, Vt., September 28, 1994; Dave Foreman et al., "The Wildlands Project," *Earth Island Journal*, Spring 1993; Dave Foreman, "NREPA and the Evolving Wilderness Model," and Marcia Cary and Rod Mondt, "The Wildlands Project Update," both in *Wild Earth*, Winter 1993/94; Leslie Ann Duncan, "Feinstein Victorious on Desert Bill; Colo. Only Other Measure Enacted," in Environmental and Energy Study Institute, *Environment, Energy and Natural Resources Status Report for the 103rd Congress* (Washington, D.C.: 1994).

67. Daniel Taylor-Ide, Alton C. Byers, and Gabriel J. Campbell, "Mountains, Nations, Parks, and Conservation," *GeoJournal*, May 1992; area of reserves from Nepal National Conservation Strategy Implementation Programme, National Planning Commission, His Majesty's Government of Nepal and IUCN, *Background Papers to the National Conservation Strategy for Nepal, Vol. II* (Kathmandu, Nepal, and Gland, Switzerland: 1991); Mount Everest Ecosystem Program, *Qomolangma Nature Preserve Project, Annual Report 1992* (Franklin, W. Va.: Woodlands: The Mountain Institute, 1993); Task Force for the Makalu-Barun Conservation Project, *The Makalu-Barun National Park and Conservation Area Management Plan* (Kathmandu, Nepal, and Franklin, W. Va.: Department of National Parks and Wildlife Conservation, His Majesty's Government of Nepal, and Woodlands: The Mountain Institute, 1990); Bob Davis, Senior Program Officer, Woodlands: The Mountain Institute, Franklin, W. Va., private communication, October 19, 1994; migratory corridors from Rodney Jackson, Wang Zhongyi, and Lu Xuedong, "Mountain Protected Areas and Snow Leopards: The Role of an Indicator Species in Reserve Design and Management," in *Proceedings of the First Conference of East Asian Protected Areas*, sponsored by CNPPA-IUCN and Chinese Academy of Sciences, September 12–16, 1993, Beijing, forthcoming.

68. Jack D. Ives, "The Mountain Malaise," in Tej Vir Singh and Jagdish Kaur, *Integrated*

Mountain Development (New Delhi: Himalayan Books, 1985); Ives, "The Future of the Mountains," op. cit. note 12; Swiss program from Bruno Messerli, "Mountain Environments—A Reaction," *GeoJournal*, September 1994; Andes from Li Pun, op. cit. note 18; African Mountain Association, Mount Kenya Ecological Programme, Annex I, Third International AMA Workshop Proceedings, Nairobi, Kenya, 1993; Ojany, op. cit. note 3; Francis F. Ojany, President of African Mountain Association and Professor of Geography, University of Nairobi, Kenya, private communication, July 27, 1994; Stone, op. cit. note 2.

69. "Seven-nation Convention to Protect Alps," op. cit. note 40.

70. ICIMOD, *Proceedings of the Tenth Anniversary Symposium of International Centre for Integrated Mountain Development (ICIMOD)* (Kathmandu, Nepal: 1994); Egbert Pelinck, Director-General, ICIMOD, Kathmandu, Nepal, private communication, September 23, 1994.

71. Figures for total World Bank lending from World Bank, *Annual Report* (Washington, D.C.: various years); another five mountain projects totalling $2.19 billion were for hydroelectric power projects, from Information Services Division, Operation Policy Department, World Bank, unpublished printout of internal project summaries, Washington, D.C., June 1994; records of other institutions from Jane Pratt, President and CEO, Woodlands: The Mountain Institute, Franklin, W. Va., private communications, September 27 and October 19, 1994.

72. International Fund for Agricultural Development, *1993 Annual Report* (Rome: 1994); Nessim Ahmad, Environment Adviser, International Fund for Agricultural Development, Rome, in Minutes of "Ad-Hoc Inter-Agency Meeting on UNCED Agenda 21, Chapter 13, *Managing Fragile Ecosystems: Sustainable Mountain Development*," FAO, Rome, March 21–22, 1994.

73. Mohammed T. El-Ashry, "The New Global Environment Facility," *Finance & Development*, June 1994; The World Bank, "Facing the Global Environment Challenge: A Progress Report on World Bank Global Environment Operations," March-May 1994; Russell A. Mittermeier and Ian A. Bowles, *The GEF and Biodiversity Conservation: Lessons to Date and Recommendations for Future Action*, Conservation International Policy Papers 1 (Washington, D.C.: Conservation International, May 1993); Frederik van Bolhuis, senior economist, Global Environment Facility, World Bank, Washington, D.C., private communication, September 28, 1994.

74. John Clark, *Democratizing Development* (West Hartford, Conn.: Kumarian Press, 1991); UNDP, *Human Development Report 1994* (New York: Oxford University Press, 1994).

75. Derek Denniston, "Saving the Himalaya," *World Watch*, November/December 1994; "Credit as a Human Right," *Far Eastern Economic Review*, March 18, 1993; Mahbub Hossain, *Credit for Alleviation of Rural Poverty: The Grameen Bank in Bangladesh*, Research Report 65 (Washington, D.C.: International Food Policy Research Institute, 1988); Kenneth H. Bacon, "Clinton Looks to a Bank in Bangladesh for Model to Help U.S. Poor Get Loans," *Wall Street Journal*, August 27, 1993; "Credit Solutions Are Not Simple," *IFAD Update*, April 1993; Manjari Mehta, *Cash Crops and the Changing Context of Women's Work and Status: A Case Study from Tehri Garwhal, India*, ICIMOD Mountain Population and Employment Series No. 2 (Kathmandu, Nepal: ICIMOD, 1993); Jodi L. Jacobson, *Gender Bias: Roadblock to Sustainable Development*, Worldwatch Paper 110 (Washington, D.C.: Worldwatch Institute, September 1992); Byers and Sainju, op. cit. note 7.

Chapter 4. Harnessing the Sun and the Wind

1. Summit story from David Schwartzbok, Natural Resources Defense Council, Wash-

ington, D.C., private communication, August 18, 1994.

2. See *The Solar Letter* and *Windpower Monthly*, various issues.

3. Neelakant Patri and Darryl D'Monte, "High-Profile U.S.-India Meetings Leading to Prominent Agreements," *The Solar Letter*, July 22, 1994.

4. Solar resource figure from Denis Hayes, *Rays of Hope: The Transition to a Post-Petroleum World* (New York: W.W. Norton & Company, 1977).

5. Figure 4–1 based on Paul Gipe, Gipe and Associates, Tehachapi, Calif., private communication and printout, April 6, 1994; Birger Madsen, BTM Consult ApS, "Technological Development of Commercial Wind Turbines and Business Opportunities," presented to Seminar on Wind Energy in Southern Europe, Cádiz, Spain, November 11–13, 1993, and Birger Madsen, BTM Consult ApS, Ringkoeping, Denmark, private communication to René Karottki, Forum for Energy and Development, Copenhagen, March 21, 1994.

6. Susan Hock, Robert Thresher, and Tom Williams, "The Future of Utility-Scale Wind Power," in Karl W. Boer, *Advances in Solar Energy: An Annual Review of Research and Development*, Vol. 7 (Boulder, Colo.: American Solar Energy Society, 1992).

7. R. Lynette, "Assessment of Wind Power Station Performance and Reliability," EPRI Report GS-6256, Electric Power Research Institute (EPRI), Palo Alto, Calif., 1989; R. Davidson, "Performance Up and Costs Down," *Windpower Monthly*, November 1991.

8. J.C. Chapman, *European Wind Technology* (Palo Alto, Calif.: EPRI, 1993); Hock, Thresher, and Williams, op. cit. note 6; David Milborrow, "Variable Speed Comes of Age," *Windpower Monthly*, December 1993; Ros Davidson, "Texas Order for Trans Atlantic Alliance," *Windpower Monthly*, October 1994.

9. California plans for 1,500 megawatts of nameplate capacity figure from Jeff Schlichting, Hansen, McQuat and Hamrin, Inc, San Francisco, Calif., private communication, June 30, 1994; California capacity from Ros Davidson, "Five Hundred Megawatt Agreement Signed," *Windpower Monthly*, April 1994; Sam McMurtrie, American Wind Energy Association (AWEA), Washington, D.C., private communication and printout, February 25, 1994.

10. Chapman, op. cit. note 8.

11. David Milborrow, "Europe in the Nineties: Entering the Age of Cheap Wind Power," *Windpower Monthly*, October 1994; "The Quixotic Technology," *The Economist*, November 14, 1992; Lyn Harrison, "Europe Gets Clean Away," *Windpower Monthly*, September 1992.

12. "Dynamic Market Rapidly Unfolds," *Windpower Monthly*, September 1994; S. Gopikrishna Warrier, "Wind Power Projects Push Land Cost Sky-High," *Down to Earth*, April, 15, 1993.

13. Robin Bromby, "U.S. Windpower, Wing Merrill to Build N.Z.'s First Wind Farm," *The Solar Letter*, August 6, 1993; "Mexico and Chile Follow Suit," *Windpower Monthly*, October 1993; Tom Gray, "Hydro-Quebec Looks at Wind," *Wind Energy Weekly*, September 6, 1994; Jeff Pelline, "Bay Firm to Supply Windmills to Speed Chernobyl Closure," *San Francisco Chronicle*, February 19, 1993; "Ukraine Addition," *Windpower Monthly*, October 1994; "Argentina Announces Huge Wind Development Project," *Windpower Monthly*, October 1993.

14. Less than 0.1 percent is a Worldwatch estimate based on United Nations (UN), *1991 Energy Statistics Yearbook* (New York: 1993), and on Paul Gipe, Gipe and Associates, Tehachapi, Calif., private communication and printout, January 28, 1994; Jon G. McGowan, "Tilting Toward Windmills," *Technology Review*, July 1993; U.S. Depart-

ment of Energy (DOE), "Technology Evolution for Wind Energy Technology," unpublished draft, June 7, 1993; Leslie Lamarre, "A Growth Market in Wind Power," *EPRI Journal*, December 1992.

15. Michael J. Grubb and Niels I. Meyer, "Wind Energy: Resources, Systems and Regional Strategies," in Thomas B. Johansson et al., eds., *Renewable Energy: Sources for Fuels and Electricity* (Washington, D.C.: Island Press, 1993); D.L. Elliott, L.L. Windell, and G.L. Gower, *An Assessment of the Available Windy Land Area and Wind Energy Potential in the Contiguous United States* (Richland, Wash.: Pacific Northwest Laboratory, 1991); these figures are for Class 3 wind areas and above, which includes area with a wind power density at a height of 50 meters of 300–400 watts per square meter and an average annual wind speed of at least 6.4 meters per second (14 miles per hour).

16. Grubb and Meyer, op. cit. note 15.

17. Elliott, Windell, and Gower, op. cit. note 15; William Babbitt, Associated Appraisers, Cheyenne, Wyo., private communication, October 11, 1990; Paul Gipe, "Wind Energy Comes of Age," Paul Gipe and Associates, Tehachapi, Calif., May 13, 1990.

18. "UK Wind Power Expansion: The Good, the Bad, and the Ugly?" *Renewable Energy Report*, Supplement to the *European Energy Report*, December 10, 1993; "A New Way to Rape the Countryside," *The Economist*, January 22, 1994; "Wind Energy and the Landscape," *Landscape Architecture*, November 1993.

19. California Energy Commission, "Avian Mortality at Large Wind Energy Facilities in California: Identification of a Problem," Sacramento, Calif., August 1989; Anthony Luke, with Alicia Watts Hosmer and Lyn Harrison, "Bird Deaths Prompt Rethink on Wind Farming in Spain," *Windpower Monthly*, February 1994; Ros Davidson, "Environmentalists Say Stop," *Windpower Monthly*, October 1993.

20. Resource geography is from Elliott, Windell, and Gower, op. cit. note 15; J. Douglas, "The Delivery System of the Future," *EPRI Journal*, October/November 1992; "Revolutionary News on Superconductivity," *Energy Economist*, September 1994.

21. Richard Stone, "Polarized Debate: EMFs and Cancer," *Science*, December 11, 1992.

22. Alfred J. Cavallo, "Wind Energy: Current Status and Future Prospects," in *Science and Global Security*, Vol. 4, 1993, pp. 1–45.

23. Ken Butti and John Perlin, *A Golden Thread: 2500 Years of Solar Architecture and Technology* (Palo Alto, Calif.: Cheshire Books, 1980).

24. François Pharabod and Cédric Philibert, *LUZ Solar Power Plants: Success in California and Worldwide Prospects* (Paris: Agency for the Control of Energy and the Department of the Environment, 1991).

25. Pat De Laquil III et al., "Solar-Thermal Electric Technology," in Johansson et al., op. cit. note 15; David Kearney, KJC Operating Company, Kramer Junction, Calif., private communication, July 30, 1993; Peggy Sheldon, Luz International Limited, Los Angeles, Calif., private communication and printout, August 28, 1990; Don Logan, Luz International Limited, Los Angeles, Calif., private communication, September 26, 1990; Bureau of the Census, U.S. Department of Commerce, *Statistical Abstract of the United States 1990* (Washington, D.C.: U.S. Government Printing Office (GPO), 1990); number of plants and capacity from David Mills and Bill Keepin, "Baseload Solar Power: Near-term Prospects for Load Following Solar Thermal Electricity," *Energy Policy*, August 1993; export ranking from Michael Lotker, "Barriers to Commercialization of Large-Scale Solar Electricity: Lessons for the LUZ Experience," Sandia National Laboratories, Albuquerque, N.M., November 1991.

26. Newton Becker, "The Demise of Luz: A Case Study," *Solar Today*, January/February 1992; Gabi Kennen, Solel, Jerusalem, private communication and printout, June 24, 1993; David Mills, University of Sydney, private communication and printout, April 5, 1994.

27. Mills, op. cit. note 26; Mills and Keepin, op. cit note 25.

28. Idaho National Engineering Laboratory et al., *The Potential of Renewable Energy: An Interlaboratory White Paper*, prepared for the Office of Policy, Planning and Analysis, DOE, in support of the National Energy Strategy (Golden, Colo.: Solar Energy Research Institute, 1990); Charles Bensinger, "Solar Thermal Repowering: A Technical and Economic Pre-Feasibility Study," The Energy Foundation, San Francisco, Calif., draft, revised version 2.0, 1993.

29. DOE, Office of Solar Energy Conversion, "Solar Thermal Electric Technology Rationale," Washington, D.C., August 1990; Stephen Kaneff, "Mass Utilization of Solar Thermal Energy," Energy Research Centre, Australian National University, Canberra, September 1992; Stephen Kaneff, Australian National University, Canberra, private communication, August 4, 1993; Ian Anderson, "Sunny Days for Solar Power," *New Scientist*, July 2, 1994.

30. Isoroku Kubo, Cummins Power Generation, Inc., "Cummins Power Generation Dish-Stirling Program," presented at Soltech '93, Washington, D.C., April 27, 1993; Bensinger, op. cit. note 28.

31. De Laquil et al., op. cit. note 25.

32. James E. Cavanagh, John H. Clarke, and Roger Price, "Ocean Energy Systems," in Johansson et al., op. cit. note 15; William J. Broad, "Ocean Pioneer Mines Energy that is Cool, Clean and Free," *New York Times*, July 13, 1993.

33. Kulsum Ahmed, *Renewable Energy Technologies: A Review of the Status and Costs of Selected Technologies* (Washington, D.C.: World Bank, 1994); Dennis Anderson and Kulsum Ahmed, "The Case for a Solar Initiative," World Bank, Washington, D.C., draft, September 1994.

34. Bensinger, op. cit. note 28; De Laquil et al., op. cit. note 25.

35. Figure of one quarter is Worldwatch estimate based on John P. Holdren, "The Transition to Costlier Energy," prologue, in Lee Schipper and Steven Meyers, *Energy Efficiency and Human Activity: Past Trends and Future Prospects* (New York: Cambridge University Press, 1992) for solar resource, on James J. MacKenzie, Roger C. Dower, and Donald D.T. Chen, *The Going Rate: What It Really Costs to Drive* (Washington, D.C.: World Resources Institute, 1992) for U.S. paved area (which is doubled for a conservative estimate of global paved area), and on British Petroleum (BP), *BP Statistical Review of World Energy* (London: 1993), and D.O. Hall, King's College, London, private communication and printout, March 7, 1994, for global primary energy consumption; for pricing, see DOE, op. cit. note 29, Mills and Keepin, op. cit. note 25, and David Mills, University of Sydney, private communication and printout, April 14, 1994.

36. Figure of more than 2 billion from Derek Lovejoy, "Electrification of Rural Areas by Solar PV," *Natural Resources Forum*, May 1992.

37. For the history of PV development, see Christopher Flavin, *Electricity from Sunlight: The Future of Photovoltaics*, Worldwatch Paper 52 (Washington, D.C.: Worldwatch Institute, December 1982), and Butti and Perlin, op. cit. note 23.

38. Figure 4–2 is based on Paul Maycock, Photovoltaic Energy Systems, Inc., Casanova, Va., private communications and printouts, December 20, 1993, and March 23, 1994; for history of cost reductions, see Ken Zweibel, *Harnessing Solar Power: The Photovoltaics Challenge* (New York: Plenum Publishing,

1990); worldwide shipments are from Paul D. Maycock, "1993 World Module Shipments," *Photovoltaic News*, February 1994; Victoria Griffith, "Twilight Hour," *Financial Times*, November 26, 1993.

39. Japanese sales from Maycock, "1993 World Module Shipments," op. cit. note 38.

40. Figure of 200,000 homes is from Neville Williams, Solar Electric Light Fund (SELF), Washington, D.C., private communication, January 14, 1994; Mark Hankins, *Solar Rural Electrification in the Developing World* (Washington, D.C.: SELF, 1993).

41. Richard Hansen, Enersol Associates, Inc., Somerville, Mass., private communication and printout, December 6, 1993.

42. Hankins, op. cit. note 40; Williams, op. cit. note 40; solar lantern from "India's Photovoltaics Program Accelerates on All Fronts," *PV News*, July 1993.

43. Gerald Foley, *Electricity for Rural People* (London: Panos Institute, 1990); Hankins, op. cit. note 40; Robert van der Plas, "Solar Energy Answer to Rural Power in Africa," *Lessons* (World Bank, Washington, D.C.), April 1994.

44. Neville Williams, SELF, Washington, D.C., private communication, December 17, 1993; Charles Feinstein, World Bank, Washington, D.C., private communication and printout, December 20, 1993.

45. Anil Cabraal, World Bank, Washington, D.C., private communication, December 8, 1993; Williams, op. cit. note 44.

46. EPRI, *Technical Assessment Guide, Vol. 1: Electric Supply* (Palo Alto, Calif.: 1986); Mary Beth Regan, "The Sun Shines Brighter on Alternative Energy," *Business Week*, November 8, 1993; 500-watt system from Doug Pratt, Real Goods, Ukiah, Calif., private communication, March 1, 1994; Steven J. Strong, "An Overview of Worldwide Development Activity in Building-integrated Photovoltaics," Solar Design Associates, Inc., Harvard, Mass., undated.

47. Carlotta Collette, "Remote Possibilities," *Northwest Energy News*, July/August 1993; Roger Taylor, National Renewable Energy Laboratory, Golden, Colo., private communication, December 16, 1993.

48. Worldwatch estimate, based on UN, *1990 Energy Statistics Yearbook* (New York: 1992), on Edison Electric Institute, *Statistical Yearbook of the Electric Utility Industry/1991* (Washington, D.C.: 1992), and on UN, op. cit. note 14.

49. Donald Osborn, Solar Program, Sacramento Municipal Utility District, Sacramento, Calif., private communication, February 22, 1994; Southern California Edison, "Southern California Edison and Texas Instruments Develop a Low Cost Solar Cell," Rosemead, Calif., undated; "Photovoltaic Bidders Please SMUD with Lower Prices," *The Solar Letter*, June 24, 1994.

50. Zweibel, op. cit. note 38; "PV Efficiencies to Rise Sharply, Costs to Crumble by 2010: Maycock," *The Solar Letter*, July 23, 1993; Maycock, "1993 World Module Shipments," op. cit. note 38; "New Silicon Cell Can Halve Cost of Solar Energy," *Wall Street Journal*, January 19, 1994; "USSC Panel Tests at Stable 10.3%; Production Line Running in Spring 1995," *The Solar Letter*, January 21, 1994.

51. Ken Zweibel, "Thin-Film Photovoltaic Cells," *American Scientist*, July/August 1993; Paul Maycock, "Exciting Times for Photovoltaics," *PV News*, June 1994; Ian Anderson, "Sunny Days for Solar Power," *New Scientist*, July 2, 1994; Enron Emerging Technologies Inc., Houston, Tex., "Draft Summary Report of the Responses to the Request for Expressions of Interest," presented to Task Force Meeting, July 30, 1994.

52. Henry Kelly and Carl J. Weinberg, "Utility Strategies for Using Renewables," in Johansson et al., op. cit. note 15.

53. Ibid.; Carl Weinberg, Weinberg and Associates, Walnut Creek, Calif., private communication, April 13, 1994.

54. Christopher Hocker, "The Miniboom in Pumped Storage," *Independent Energy*, March 1990; Rod Boucher and Paul Rodzianko, "Advanced Pumped Storage: The New Competitive Edge," *The Electricity Journal*, July/August 1994; Leslie Lamarre, "Alabama Cooperative Generates Power from Air," *EPRI Journal*, December 1991; Mills and Keepin, op. cit. note 25; "Revolutionary News on Superconductivity," op. cit. note 20; Steven Ashley, "Flywheels Put a New Spin on Electric Vehicles," *Mechanical Engineering*, October 1993.

55. Electricity as a percentage of final energy demand is Worldwatch estimates, based on Organisation for Economic Co-operation and Development, International Energy Agency, *Energy Statistics and Balances of Non-OECD Countries 1990–1991* (Paris: 1993), and on Hall, op. cit. note 35.

56. Verne reference from Peter Hoffmann, *The Forever Fuel: The Story of Hydrogen* (Boulder, Colo.: Westview Press, 1981).

57. Joan M. Ogden and Joachim Nitsch, "Solar Hydrogen," in Johansson, et al., op. cit. note 15; 1-percent figure is a Worldwatch estimate, based on DOE, Energy Information Administration (EIA), *Monthly Energy Review March 1994* (Washington, D.C.: GPO, 1994); on DOE, EIA, *State Energy Data Report 1991: Consumption Estimates* (Washington, D.C.: GPO, 1993), and on Wayne B. Solley et al., *Estimated Use of Water in the United States in 1990* (Washington, D.C.: GPO, 1993).

58. Derek P. Gregory, "The Hydrogen Economy," *Scientific American*, January 1973; Joan M. Ogden and Robert H. Williams, *Solar Hydrogen: Moving Beyond Fossil Fuels* (Washington, D.C.: World Resources Institute, 1989).

59. Ogden and Williams, op. cit. note 58.

60. Ogden and Nitsch, op. cit. note 57.

61. Fuel Cell Commercialization Group, "What Is a Fuel Cell?" Washington, D.C., 1992; Philip H. Abelson, "Applications of Fuel Cells" (editorial), *Science*, June 22, 1990.

62. Ogden and Nitsch, op. cit. note 57; loss of 3–5 percent is a Worldwatch estimate, based on Hydro Quebec's operating experience with both alternating and direct current long-distance power transmission lines, from Raymond Elsliger, Hydro Quebec, Montreal, private communication, May 24, 1994.

63. Oil reserves from BP, op. cit. note 35.

64. Land area calculations based on Keith Lee Kozloff and Roger C. Dower, *A New Power Base: Renewable Energy Policies for the Nineties and Beyond* (Washington, D.C.: World Resources Institute, 1993), on Paul Gipe, Gipe and Associates, Tehachapi, Calif., private communication and printout, March 29, 1994, and on David Mills, University of Sydney, Australia, private communication and printout, March 25, 1994.

65. United Nations, Report of the Intergovernmental Negotiating Committee for a Framework Convention on Climate Change, Fifth session, Second part, New York, April 30–May 9, 1992.

66. Interim Secretariat of the United Nations Framework Convention on Climate Change, "Status of Ratification of the United Nations Framework Convention on Climate Change" (electronic bulletin board posting), April 15, 1994.

67. Carl J. Weinberg and Robert H. Williams, "Energy from the Sun," *Scientific American*, September 1990.

68. Learning curve is Boston Consulting Group research, cited in Robert H. Williams and Gregory Terzian, "A Benefit/Cost Analysis of Accelerated Development of Photovoltaic Technology," Center for Energy and Environmental Studies, Princeton University, Princeton, N.J., October 1993.

69. Wind turbine output is a Worldwatch estimate based on Gipe, op. cit. note 5; John Trocciola, International Fuel Cells, South Windsor, Conn., private communication,

April 15, 1994; photovoltaic prices from Maycock, private communications and printouts, op. cit. note 38, and from Maycock, "1993 World Module Shipments," op. cit. note 38.

70. "DOE, Industry to Set Up Task Force for Solar Enterprise Zone Action Plan," *The Solar Letter*, April 15, 1994; "Nevada SEZ Should Have Positive Global Implications," *The Solar Letter*, October 14, 1994.

71. Utility PhotoVoltaic Group, "Electric Utilities Serving 40% of U.S. Consumers Propose $513 Million Program to Accelerate Use of Solar Photovoltaics," Washington, D.C., September 27, 1993; Anderson and Ahmed, op. cit. note 33.

Chapter 5. Creating a Sustainable Materials Economy

1. David Riggle, "Creating Markets Close to Home," *BioCycle*, July 1994.

2. Jennifer Seymour Whitaker, *Salvaging the Land of Plenty: Garbage and the American Dream* (New York: William Morrow, 1994); Paul Hawken, *The Ecology of Commerce* (New York: HarperBusiness, 1993); Friedrich Schmidt-Bleek, "Toward Universal Ecology Disturbance Measures," unpublished paper, Wuppertal Institute, Wuppertal, Germany, 1992; Friedrich Schmidt-Bleek, "MIPS and the Ecological Safety Factor of 10 Revisited," unpublished paper, Wuppertal Institute, Wuppertal, Germany, 1993.

3. Population share from Population Reference Bureau (PRB), *1994 World Population Data Sheet* (Washington, D.C.: 1994); consumption shares from Alan Thein Durning, *How Much Is Enough? The Consumer Society and the Future of the Earth* (New York: W.W. Norton & Company, 1992).

4. Primary production toxic emissions from U.S. Environmental Protection Agency (EPA), Office of Pollution Prevention and Toxics (OPPT), *1992 Toxics Release Inventory Public Data Release* (Washington, D.C.: 1994);

Alan Thein Durning, *Guardians of the Land: Indigenous Peoples and the Health of the Earth*, Worldwatch Paper 112 (Washington, D.C.: Worldwatch Institute, December 1992).

5. Soil and rock from John E. Young, *Mining the Earth*, Worldwatch Paper 109 (Washington, D.C.: Worldwatch Institute, July 1992); the annual sediment load of the world's rivers is estimated at 16.5 billion tons, according to J.D. Milliman and R.H. Meade, cited in Brian J. Skinner, "Resources in the 21st Century: Can Supplies Meet Needs?" *Episodes*, December 1989; Superfund sites from Van Housman, Office of Solid Waste, EPA, Washington, D.C., private communication, August 26, 1994; see also Johnnie N. Moore and Samuel N. Luoma, "Large-Scale Environmental Impacts: Mining's Hazardous Waste," *Clementine* (Mineral Policy Center, Washington, D.C.), Spring 1991.

6. Forest clearing from Alan Thein Durning, *Saving the Forests: What Will It Take?* Worldwatch Paper 117 (Washington, D.C.: Worldwatch Institute, December 1993); industrial logging from Nancy Chege, "Roundwood Production Unabated," in Lester Brown, Hal Kane, and David Malin Roodman, *Vital Signs 1994* (New York: W.W. Norton & Company, 1994); farmland contamination from Robin Clarke, *Water: The International Crisis* (Cambridge, Mass.: The MIT Press, 1993).

7. U.S. manufacturing energy use from Durning, op. cit. note 3.

8. Figure 5–1 and U.S. population and consumption of paper, minerals, metals, plastics, and overall materials from Donald G. Rogich, U.S. Department of Interior (DOI), Bureau of Mines (BOM), "Changing Minerals and Material Use Patterns," presented at the Annual General Meeting of the Academia Europaea, Parma, Italy, June 23–25, 1994.

9. See, for example, Marc H. Ross and Robert H. Williams, *Our Energy: Regaining Control* (New York: McGraw-Hill, 1981), Eric

D. Larson et al., "Materials, Affluence, and Industrial Energy Use," *Annual Review of Energy, Vol. 12* (Palo Alto, Calif.: 1987), Peter F. Drucker, "The Changed World Economy," *Foreign Affairs*, Spring 1986, Robert U. Ayres, "Industrial Metabolism," and Robert Herman et al., "Dematerialization," in Jesse H. Ausubel and Hedy E. Sladovich, eds., *Technology and Environment* (Washington, D.C.: National Academy Press, 1989), DOI, BOM, *The New Materials Society, Vol. 3: Materials Shifts in the New Society* (Washington, D.C.: 1991), and Rogich, op. cit. note 8.

10. Figure 5–2 from Rogich, op. cit. note 8.

11. World Resources Institute, *World Resources 1994–95* (New York: Oxford University Press, 1994).

12. U.S. House of Representatives, Committee on Natural Resources, "Taking From the Taxpayer: Public Subsidies for Natural Resource Development" (majority staff report), Washington, D.C., 1994.

13. For further discussion of this subject, see Young, op. cit. note 5, and Alan B. Durning, *Poverty and the Environment: Reversing the Downward Spiral*, Worldwatch Paper 92 (Washington, D.C.: Worldwatch Institute, November 1989).

14. The preamble of the Resource Conservation and Recovery Act lists a hierarchy of waste management options, with waste reduction at the top, followed by reuse, recycling, incineration, and landfilling; EPA, *Characterization of Municipal Solid Waste in the United States, 1992 Update* (Washington, D.C.: 1992); the national recycling rate was probably considerably higher than 10 percent during World War II, and then it probably plunged after the war, but data before 1960 are not available.

15. Organisation for Economic Co-operation and Development, *OECD Environmental Data, Compendium 1993* (Paris: 1993); U.S. Congress, Office of Technology Assessment, *Background Paper: Managing Industrial Solid Wastes* (Washington, D.C.: U.S. Government Printing Office (GPO), 1992).

16. Energy savings from recycling is a Worldwatch estimate, based on estimates of energy savings per ton of various materials in Jeffrey Morris and Diana Canzoneri, *Recycling Versus Incineration: An Energy Conservation Analysis* (Seattle, Wash.: Sound Resource Management Group, 1992), on tonnages of materials in U.S. solid waste from EPA, op. cit. note 14, and on energy conversion factors in U.S. Department of Energy (DOE), Energy Information Administration (EIA), *Monthly Energy Review March 1994* (Washington, D.C.: GPO, 1994).

17. For discussion of green taxes, see Commission of the European Communities, *Growth, Competitiveness, Employment: The Challenges and Ways Forward into the 21st Century (A White Paper)* (Luxembourg: 1993), and Robert Repetto et al., *Green Fees: How a Tax Shift Can Work for the Environment and the Economy* (Washington, D.C.: World Resources Institute, 1992).

18. Bette K. Fishbein, *Germany, Garbage, and the Green Dot: Challenging the Throwaway Society* (New York: INFORM, 1994); Megan Ryan, "Packaging a Revolution," *World Watch*, September/October 1993.

19. Geoffrey Lomax, "Many Happy Returns: the Environmental and Economic Effects of Refillable Beverage Packaging," National Environmental Law Center, Boston, Mass., 1992.

20. William Rathje and Cullen Murphy, *Rubbish!: The Archaeology of Garbage* (New York: HarperCollins, 1992).

21. Christopher Flavin and Nicholas Lenssen, *Power Surge: Guide to the Coming Energy Revolution* (New York: W.W. Norton & Company, 1994).

22. Sandra Postel and John C. Ryan, "Reforming Forestry," in Lester R. Brown et al.,

State of the World 1991 (New York: W.W. Norton & Company, 1991).

23. National Audubon Society and Croxton Collaborative, Architects, *Audubon House: Building the Environmentally Responsible, Energy-Efficient Office* (New York: John Wiley & Sons, 1994).

24. Amory B. Lovins, "Energy-Efficient Buildings: Institutional Barriers and Opportunities," Strategic Issues Paper, E SOURCE, Inc., Boulder, Colo., 1992.

25. Ibid.

26. Peter Weber, "Green Seals of Approval Heading to Market," *World Watch*, July/August 1990.

27. Construction Specifications Institute, *Services and Publications Catalog* (Alexandria, Va.: 1993).

28. For more on the U.K. initiative, see Building Research Establishment, "BREEAM/New Offices," Version 1/93, Garston, Watford, U.K.; Michael Scholand, "Buildings for the Future," *World Watch*, November/December 1993.

29. Rogich, op. cit. note 8; DOI, BOM, op. cit. note 9; Donald Rogich, Division of Mineral Commodities, DOI, BOM, Washington, D.C., private communication, August 3, 1994. DOE's 1991 Manufacturing Energy Consumption Survey will break down energy use by narrower industrial categories than previous surveys; final results are expected to be available in late 1994; DOE, EIA, *Monthly Energy Review September 1993* (Washington, D.C.: GPO, 1993).

30. EPA, OPPT, op. cit. note 4; Cameron Keyes and Christine Ervin, "Environmental Review of U.S. Industrial Facilities: A Survey of Information Tools" (draft), World Wildlife Fund, Washington, D.C., 1991.

31. Robert Steuteville, "The State of Garbage in America, Part I," *BioCycle*, April 1994; David Riggle, *BioCycle*, Emmaus, Pa.,

private communication, August 29, 1994; PRB, op. cit. note 3; Fishbein, op. cit. note 18; Arnold O. Tanner, "Materials Recycling 1992," annual report, DOI, BOM, Washington, D.C., 1994.

32. Robert F. Stone and Nicholas A. Ashford, *Package Deal: The Economic Impacts of Recycling Standards for Packaging in Massachusetts* (Cambridge, Mass.: Center for Technology, Policy, and Industrial Development, Massachusetts Institute of Technology, 1991).

33. White House Office of the Press Secretary, "Executive Order: Federal Acquisition, Recycling, and Waste Prevention," Washington, D.C., 1993; federal paper consumption from Robert Steuteville, "The State of Garbage in America, Part II," *BioCycle*, May 1994.

34. Steuteville, op. cit. note 33; newsprint recycling facilities from Michael Alexander, "Developing Markets for Old Newspapers," *Resource Recycling*, July 1994.

35. Kenneth Gooding, "Recycled Aluminum Contract Looks Like a Winner," *Financial Times*, October 2, 1992; Recycling Advisory Council, "Fact Sheet: Chicago Board of Trade Recovered Materials Demonstration Project," Washington, D.C., 1993; Curtis Ravenel, National Recycling Coalition, Washington, D.C., private communication, August 25, 1994.

36. Neal R. Peirce et al., "Market Standards, Community Dividends: Economically Targeted Investments for the '90s," National Academy of Public Administration, Washington, D.C., 1994.

37. Ravenel, op. cit. note 35; Jeanne Wirka, *Financing Small Recovered Material Enterprises in California: Strategies for Private and Public Action—The First Report of the Financing Working Group of the Materials for the Future Foundation* (Oakland, Calif.: Materials for the Future Foundation and Californians Against Waste Foundation, 1993).

38. Stone and Ashford, op. cit. note 32; see also Environmental Defense Fund, *Developing Markets for Recycled Materials* (Washington, D.C.: 1988), and Northeast Recycling Council, *Value Added to Recyclable Materials in the Northeast* (Brattleboro, Vt.: 1994).

39. Durning, op. cit. note 6.

40. U.S. Bureau of the Census, *Statistical Abstract of the United States 1993* (Washington, D.C.: 1993); International Labour Office, *Year Book of Labour Statistics, 1993* (Geneva: 1993).

41. Dr. Thomas Michael Power, *Not All That Glitters: An Evaluation of the Impact of Reform of the 1872 Mining Law on the Economy of the American West* (Washington, D.C.: Mineral Policy Center and the National Wildlife Federation, 1993).

42. Bureau of the Census, op. cit. note 40.

43. Iron foundries from Steve Apotheker, "A Marriage Made in Iron," *Resource Recycling*, March 1994.

44. Tire retreading from Center for Neighborhood Technology, *Beyond Recycling: Materials Reprocessing in Chicago's Economy* (Chicago: 1993).

45. Martin Medina, "Collecting Recyclables in Metro Manila," *BioCycle*, June 1993.

46. Gulf Coast Recycling, Gulfport, Miss., private communiction, August 10, 1994.

47. Smith study from Center for Neighborhood Technology, op. cit. note 44; inks from Nora Goldstein, "Recycled Paper with a Side of Soy," *In Business*, May/June 1992, and from Conservatree Information Services, Environmentally Sound Information, "Everything You Need to Know About the Environmental Impact of Inks," San Francisco, 1991.

48. Scott Bernstein, "Environment, Distributive Equity and Energy Savings: Capturing the Benefits Where They Are Needed" (draft), Center for Neighborhood Technology, Chicago, 1994.

49. For an extensive discussion of the implications of a more populous world consuming at the levels now prevalent in industrial nations, see Durning, op. cit. note 3.

50. Herman Daly, *Steady State Economics* (Washington, D.C.: Island Press, rev. ed., 1991).

Chapter 6. Making Better Buildings

1. Figure of 90 percent from U.S. Environmental Protection Agency (EPA), Office of Air and Radiation (OAR), *Report to Congress on Indoor Air Quality, Volume II: Assessment and Control of Indoor Air Pollution* (Washington, D.C.: 1989).

2. Share of global economy is a Worldwatch estimate, based on U.S. data from Richard G. Stein, *Architecture and Energy: Conserving Energy Through Rational Design* (New York: Anchor Press, 1977), and from U.S. Bureau of the Census, *Statistical Abstract of the United States 1993* (Washington, D.C.: 1993).

3. Internationale Nederlanden (ING) Bank, "Building with a Difference: ING Bank Head Office," Amsterdam, undated; Bill Holdsworth, "Organic Services," *Building Services*, March 1989; Rob Vonk, ING Bank, Amsterdam, private communication, March 25, 1994.

4. Worldwatch estimate, based on National Audubon Society and Croxton Collaborative, Architects, *Audubon House: Building the Environmentally Responsible, Energy-Efficient Office* (New York: John Wiley & Sons, 1994), and on Organisation for Economic Co-operation and Development (OECD), International Energy Agency (IEA), *Energy Statistics and Balances of Non-OECD Countries 1991– 1992* (Paris: 1994).

5. Figure of 40 percent is an extrapolation from U.S. data based on Donald G. Rogich, U.S. Department of the Interior (DOI), Bureau of Mines (BOM), "Changing Minerals and Material Use Patterns," presented at the Annual General Meeting of the Academia

Europaea, Parma, Italy, June 23–25, 1994, and on Bill Kelleher, National Stone Association, Silver Spring, Md., private communication, July 13, 1994; Rogich, op. cit. in this note; John E. Young, *Mining the Earth*, Worldwatch Paper 109 (Washington, D.C.: Worldwatch Institute, July 1992).

6. Daniel Edelstein, DOI, BOM, Washington, D.C., private communication, July 19, 1994; share of copper recycled excludes "new scrap," waste metal that factories send back to the copper mills for recycling, never having reached the consumer, and is based on ibid.; Young, op. cit. note 5.

7. Sandra Kraemer, "Material Changes in the Building and Construction Industry: Piping Applications," in DOI, BOM, *The New Materials Society: Materials Shifts in the New Society*, *Vol. 3* (Washington, D.C.: 1991); Nadav Malin and Alex Wilson, "Should We Phase Out PVC?" *Environmental Building News*, January/February 1994; Keith Schneider, "E.P.A. Moves to Reduce Health Risks from Dioxin," *New York Times*, September 14, 1994; German position on PVC is from Lisa Finaldi, Greenpeace International, "PVC Debate Continues" (letter to the editor), *Environmental Building News*, November/December 1993; Rich Gilbert, American Public Health Association, Washington, D.C., private communication, August 15, 1994.

8. Sandra Postel and John Ryan, "Reforming Forestry," in Lester Brown et al., *State of the World 1991* (New York: W.W. Norton & Company, 1991); Steve Loken, "Materials for a Sustainable Building Industry," *Solar Today*, November/December 1991; Lee Schipper, Stephen Meyers, and Henry Kelly, *Coming in From the Cold: Energy-Wise Housing in Sweden* (Cabin John, Md.: Seven Locks Press, 1985); International Tropical Timber Association (ITTO), *Annual Review and Assessment of the World Tropical Timber Situation, 1990–1991* (Yokohama, Japan: 1992); Nancy Chege, "Roundwood Production Unabated," in Lester R. Brown, Hal Kane, and David Malin Roodman, *Vital Signs 1994* (New

York: W.W. Norton & Company, 1994); D.O. Hall, King's College London, private communication and printout, March 7, 1994.

9. Alan Thein Durning, *Saving the Forests: What Will It Take?* Worldwatch Paper 117 (Washington, D.C.: Worldwatch Institute, December 1993); ITTO, op. cit. note 8.

10. Worldwatch estimates, based on OECD, IEA, *Energy Balances of OECD Countries 1960–79* (Paris: 1991), on OECD, *World Energy Statistics and Balances 1971–1987*, (Paris: 1989), and on OECD, op. cit. note 4, with biomass estimates for developing countries from Hall, op. cit. note 8, and from U.S. Congress, Office of Technology Assessment (OTA), *Energy in Developing Countries* (Washington, D.C.: U.S. Government Printing Office (GPO), 1991).

11. Brenda Vale and Robert Vale, *Green Architecture: Design for an Energy-conscious Future* (Boston: Bulfinch Press, 1991); U.S. Department of Energy (DOE), Energy Information Administration (EIA), *Annual Energy Review 1993* (Washington, D.C.: GPO, 1994); 45 percent figure is a Worldwatch estimate, based on ibid., on National Audubon Society and Croxton Collaborative, op. cit. note 4, and on Kelleher, op. cit. note 5.

12. Worldwatch estimates, based on OECD, op. cit. note 4.

13. Building's share of world water use is a Worldwatch estimate, based on Peter H. Gleick, "Water and Energy," in Peter H. Gleick, ed., *Water in Crisis: A Guide to the World's Fresh Water Resources* (New York: Oxford University Press, 1993), on OECD, op. cit. note 4, and on World Resources Institute, *World Resources 1994–95* (New York: Oxford University Press, 1994), and excludes the impacts of electricity production for manufacturing and transporting building materials; Sandra Postel, *Last Oasis: Facing Water Scarcity* (New York: W.W. Norton & Company, 1992).

14. Figure of 150 tons is a Worldwatch estimate, based on the minerals content of a

typical U.S. home, from Aldo F. Barsotti, DOI, BOM, Washington, D.C., private communication and printout, July 13, 1994; refuse figure is from Stephen D. Cosper, William H. Hallenbeck, and Gary R. Brenniman, "Construction and Demolition Waste: Generation, Regulation, Practices, Processing, and Policies," Office of Solid Waste Management, University of Illinois, Chicago, 1993; Jane Maynard, Bureau of the Census, Suitland, Md., private communication, August 5, 1994; Erik K. Lauritzen and Niels Jørn Hahn, "Building Waste—Generation and Recycling," *International Solid Wastes & Public Cleansing Association Yearbook 1991–1992* (London: Associated Publishing Group plc, undated); OECD, *OECD Environmental Data: Compendium 1993* (Paris: 1993).

15. Figure of 30 percent is from a 1984 World Health Organization committee report, cited in EPA, OAR, "Indoor Air Facts No. 4: Sick Building Syndrome," Washington, D.C., 1991; EPA, Office of Acid Deposition, Environmental Monitoring and Quality Assurance, *Indoor Air Quality in Public Buildings: Vol. I* (Washington, D.C.: 1988).

16. David Mudarri, EPA, Indoor Air Division, private communication, Washington, D.C., July 15, 1994; William Fisk, Lawrence Berkeley Laboratory (LBL), Berkeley, Calif., private communication, July 15, 1994; Kirk R. Smith and Youcheng Liu, "Indoor Air Pollution in Developing Countries," in Jonathan M. Samet, ed., *Epidemiology of Lung Cancer* (New York: Marcel Dekker, Inc., 1994).

17. Amory B. Lovins, "Energy-Efficient Buildings: Institutional Barriers and Opportunities," Strategic Issues Paper, E SOURCE, Inc., Boulder, Colo., 1992; James Howard Kunstler, *The Geography of Nowhere* (New York: Simon & Schuster, 1993); Peter Blake, *Form Follows Fiasco: Why Modern Architecture Hasn't Worked* (Boston: Little, Brown and Company, 1977).

18. Figure 6–1 is from Lee Schipper and Stephen Meyers, *Energy Efficiency and Human Activity: Past Trends and Future Prospects* (Cambridge: Cambridge University Press, 1992), and from L. Schipper and C. Sheinbaum, "Recent Trends in Household Energy Use Efficiency in OECD Countries: Stagnation or Improvement," in *Proceedings of 1994 ACEEE Summer Study on Energy Efficiency in Buildings* (Washington, D.C.: American Council for an Energy-Efficient Economy (ACEEE), 1994); Durning, op. cit. note 9; Ahluwalia is from Mitchell Owens, "Building Small . . . Thinking Big," *New York Times*, July 21, 1994; Japan from ITTO, op. cit. note 8, and from United Nations, *World Population Prospects: The 1992 Revision* (New York: 1993).

19. Leon Krier and Japan from Stewart Brand, *How Buildings Learn: What Happens After They're Built* (New York: Viking Penguin, 1994).

20. Ibid.

21. Erik Toxvaerd Nielsen, Toftegård, Herlev, Denmark, private communication, April 20, 1994; National Audubon Society and Croxton Collaborative, op. cit. note 4.

22. Worldwatch estimate, based on Population Reference Bureau, *1994 World Population Data Sheet* (Washington, D.C.: 1994).

23. Loken, op. cit. note 8; Carl Weinberg, Weinberg and Associates, Walnut Creek, Calif., private communication, April 23, 1993.

24. Nigel Howard, Davis Langdon Consultancy, London, private communication and printout, September 20, 1994; OTA, *Green Products by Design: Choices for a Cleaner Environment* (Washington, D.C.: GPO, 1992); "Developments to Watch," *Business Week*, September 13, 1993.

25. Vale and Vale, op. cit. note 11; Mark Wachle, Recycled Materials Company, Colorado Springs, Colo., private communication, August 11, 1994; Sydney from "Bulletin Board," *NCS Bulletin* (IUCN Pakistan), Karachi, September 1992.

26. Carole Douglis, "Making Houses Out of Trash," *World Watch*, November/Decem-

ber 1993; Robert Noble, Gridcore Systems International, Carlsbad, Calif., private communications, July 8 and July 29, 1994.

27. Michael Moquin, "Adobe, Rammed Earth, & Mud: Ancient Solutions for Future Sustainability," *Earthword*, No. 5, 1994; European history from Brenda Vale, University of Nottingham, U.K., private communication, July 29, 1994; Marina Trappeniers, Craterre, Grenoble, France, private communication, September 6, 1994.

28. Koshy Cherail, "Mud Housing is the Key," *Down to Earth*, October 15, 1992; John Norton and Peter Tunley, "Doing Away With Wood," *Down to Earth*, December 15, 1993.

29. Michael Langley, Terra Verde, Austin, Tex., private communication, August 3, 1994; ecological cost is a Worldwatch estimate, based on ibid., on Tina King, Featherlite Building Products, Round Rock, Tex., private communication, October 7, 1994, and on Howard, op. cit. note 24.

30. Brent C. Brolin, *The Failure of Modern Architecture* (New York: Van Nostrand Reinhold Company, 1976).

31. Two thirds figure is a Worldwatch estimate, based on U.S. data from DOE, op. cit. note 11, from DOE, EIA, *Monthly Energy Review September 1993* (Washington, D.C.: GPO, 1993), from DOE, EIA, *Annual Energy Outlook 1994* (Washington, D.C.: GPO, 1994), and from Mohammad Adra, DOE, EIA, Washington, D.C., private communication, March 7, 1994; Steven Ternoey et al., *The Design of Energy-Responsive Commercial Buildings* (New York: John Wiley & Sons, 1985).

32. Residential energy use statistics are based on energy use per degree day per square meter of home area, and are from Schipper and Meyers, op. cit. note 18, and from Schipper and Sheinbaum, op. cit. note 18.

33. David Olivier, "The House that Came in from the Cold," *New Scientist*, March 9, 1991.

34. Figure 6–2 considers windows to be "advanced" if they include low-E coating or argon fill, and is based on K. Frost, D. Arasteh, and J. Eto, "Savings from Energy Efficient Windows: Current and Future Savings from New Fenestration Technologies in the Residential Market," LBL, Berkeley, Calif., April 1993.

35. Ibid.; Joan Gregerson et al., *Space Heating Technology Atlas* (Boulder, Colo.: E SOURCE, Inc., 1993); Tim Mayo, "Canada's Advanced Houses Program," in A.H. Fanney et al., eds., *U.S. Green Buildings Conference–1994* (Washington, D.C.: GPO, 1994).

36. Ken Butti and John Perlin, *Golden Thread: 2500 Years of Solar Architecture and Technology* (Palo Alto, Calif.: Cheshire Books, 1980).

37. Ken Yeang, *Bioclimatic Skyscrapers* (London: Artemis, 1994); LBL and Sacramento Municipal Utility District, "Peak Power and Cooling Energy Savings of Shade Trees and White Surfaces: Year 2," LBL, Berkeley, Calif., April 27, 1993; Karen L. George, "Highly Reflective Roof Surfaces Reduce Cooling Energy Use and Peak Demand," Tech Update, E SOURCE, Inc., Boulder, Colo., December 1993.

38. Vale and Vale, op. cit. note 11; Steven Ternoey, LightForms, Boulder, Colo., private communication, March 29, 1994; Alicia Ravetto, "Daylighting Schools in North Carolina," *Solar Today*, March/April 1994; Larry Hatfield, Draper and Kramer, Inc., Chicago, Ill., private communication, August 9, 1994; Lindsay Audin et al., *Lighting Technology Atlas* (Boulder, Colo.: E SOURCE, Inc., 1994).

39. Butti and Perlin, op. cit. note 36; Helena Norberg-Hodge, *Ancient Futures: Learning from Ladakh* (San Francisco: Sierra Club Books, 1991).

40. Doug Balcomb, National Renewable Energy Laboratory (NREL), Golden, Colo., private communication and printout, June 2, 1993; Cecile M. Liboef and Craig Christensen, "The Minimum Energy House,"

Solar Today, January/February 1991; Vale and Vale, op. cit. note 11.

41. Yeang, op. cit. note 37.

42. David A. Jump and Mark Modera, "Energy Impacts of Attic Duct Retrofits in Sacramento Houses," in *Proceedings of ACEEE 1994 Summer Study*, op. cit. note 18; James Woods, Virginia Polytechnic Institute and State University, Blacksburg, Va., private communication, August 9, 1994; stories of waste in commercial buildings from Frank Kensill, Institute for Human Development, Philadelphia, Pa., private communication, October 1991, and from Lee Eng Lock, Supersymmetry Services Pte. Ltd., Singapore, private communication, August 11, 1994.

43. Robert van der Plas and A.B. de Graaff, "A Comparison of Lamps for Domestic Lighting in Developing Countries," World Bank, Washington, 1988; M.D. Levine et al., "Electricity End-Use Efficiency: Experience with Technologies, Markets, and Policies Throughout the World," ACEEE, Washington, D.C, 1992; Evan Mills, LBL, Berkeley, Calif., private communication, February 3, 1993; Nils Borg, National Board for Industrial and Technical Development, Stockholm, Sweden, private communication, March 14, 1994; market share is a Worldwatch estimate, taking into account that compact fluorescents last 10 times as long as incandescents, based on Mills, op. cit. this note, and on Borg, op. cit. this note; $40 figure is a Worldwatch estimate of the net present value of the payback from replacing a 60-watt, 1,000-hour incandescent bulb with a 15-watt 10,000-hour CFL, using a 5-percent annual rate of return on five-year savings, a price of 75¢ for incandescent bulbs, and an electricity price from OECD, IEA, *Energy Prices and Taxes, Third Quarter, 1992* (Paris: 1992); 80 percent figure is from Leslie Lamarre, "Shedding Light on the Compact Fluorescent," *EPRI Journal*, March 1993.

44. Brooke Stauffer, Association of Home Appliance Manufacturers, Washington, D.C.,

private communication, December 9, 1993; David Goldstein, Natural Resources Defense Council, San Francisco, Calif., private communication, June 20, 1993; Steven Nadel et al., "Emerging Technologies in the Residential & Commercial Sectors," ACEEE, Washington, D.C., 1993; Amy Vickers, "The Energy Policy Act: Assessing Its Impact on Utilities," *Journal of the American Water Works Association*, August 1993.

45. Amory B. Lovins, "Designing Buildings for Greater Profit," presentation at the National Association of Homebuilders, Washington, D.C., March 2, 1994.

46. Butti and Perlin, op. cit. note 36; Josef Nowarski, Division of Research and Development, Ministry of Energy and Infrastructure, Jerusalem, private communication, January 19, 1994; Eddie Bet Hazavdi, Energy Conservation Division, Ministry of Energy and Infrastructure, Jerusalem, private communication and printout, January 26, 1994; Solar System Development Association, "The Status of Solar Energy Systems in Japan," Tokyo, 1993; Botswana from Chris Neme, Memorandum to Mark Levine, LBL, Berkeley, Calif., March 28, 1992; Mario Calderón and Paolo Lugari, Centro Las Gaviotas, Bogota, Colombia, private communication, April 13, 1992; Kenya from Christopher Hurst, "Establishing New Markets for Mature Energy Equipment in Developing Countries; Experience with Windmills, Hydro-Powered Mills and Solar Water Heaters," *World Development*, Vol. 18, No. 4, 1990.

47. Joachim Brenemann, "Energy Active Façades: Technology and Possibilities of Photovoltaic Integration into Buildings," Flachglas Solartechnik, Köln, Germany, undated; "Reference List," Flagsol, Flachglas Solartechnik Gmbh, Köln, Germany, January 14, 1994; Steven Strong, "An Overview of Worldwide Development Activity in Building-Integrated Photovoltaics," Solar Design Associates, Harvard, Mass., undated; western Germany from W.H. Bloss et al., "Grid-Connected Solar Houses," in *Proceedings of the*

10th EC Photovoltaics Solar Energy Conference (Dordrecht: Kluwer Academic Publishing, 1991); R. Hill, N.M. Pearsall, and P. Claiden, *The Potential Generating Capacity of PV-Clad Buildings in the UK*, Vol. 1 (London: Department for Trade and Industry, 1992); OECD, IEA, *Energy Policies of IEA Countries: 1991 Review* (Paris: 1992); glazing examples assume a 25-percent capacity factor for photovoltaics.

48. Weinberg, op. cit. note 23.

49. Mayo, op. cit. note 35.

50. *Health and Environment Digest* (Freshwater Foundation, Wayzata, Minn.), May 1993; Woods, op. cit. note 42.

51. Netherlands Agency for Energy and the Environment (NOVEM), "Ecolonia: Demonstration Project for Energy-Saving and Environmentally-aware Building and Living," Sittard, The Netherlands, undated.

52. Marlise Simons, "Earth-Friendly Dutch Homes Use Sod and Science," *New York Times*, March 7, 1994.

53. Worldwatch estimate, based on labor-to-energy cost comparison in text, and on ING Bank in Joseph J. Romm and William D. Browning, "Greening the Building and the Bottom Line: Increasing Productivity Through Energy-Efficient Design," in *Proceedings of 1994 ACEEE Summer Study*, op. cit. note 18.

54. Ibid.

55. Lovins, op. cit. note 17.

56. OTA, *Energy Efficiency Technologies for Central and Eastern Europe* (Washington, D.C.: GPO, 1993); Yu Joe Huang, "Potential for and Barriers to Building Energy Conservation in China," *Contemporary Policy Issues* (California State University, Long Beach), July 1990.

57. Vale and Vale, op. cit. note 11; National Audubon Society and Croxton Collaborative, op. cit. note 4.

58. John Picard, Environmental Enterprises, Inc., Marina del Rey, Calif., private communication, July 26, 1994; Japan from John Bennett, *International Construction Project Management: General Theory and Practice* (Oxford: Butterworth Heinemann, 1991).

59. S.P. Halliday, *Environmental Code of Practice for Buildings and Their Services* (Bracknell, U.K.: Building Services Research and Information Association (BSRIA), May 1994); Zoe Crawford, BSRIA, Bracknell, U.K., private communication, July 25, 1994; Harry T. Gordon, "The American Institute of Architects Committee on the Environment," in Fanney et al., op. cit. note 35.

60. Vonk, op. cit. note 3.

61. The White House, Office on Environmental Policy (OEP), "The Greening of the White House: Phase I Action Plan," Washington, D.C., March 11, 1994; Brian Johnson, The White House, OEP, Washington, D.C., private communication, August 18, 1994; Soontorn Boonyatikarn, Chulalongkorn University, Bangkok, private communication, August 26, 1994.

62. James Woods, Virginia Polytechnic Institute and State University, Blacksburg, Va., private communication, August 25, 1994; indoor air quality regulations were proposed in U.S. Department of Labor, Occupational Safety and Health Administration, *Federal Register*, April 5, 1994; Mexico from Postel, op. cit. note 13; Thailand from Boonyatikarn, op. cit. note 61.

63. Siwei Lang and Yu Joe Huang, "Energy Conservation Standard for Space Heating in Chinese Urban Residential Buildings," *Energy—The International Journal*, August 1993; Yu Joe Huang, LBL, Berkeley, Calif., private communication, September 26, 1994; "Non-Compliance Widespread in Washington, Oregon," *Conservation Monitor*, August 1992.

64. Randolph R. Croxton, "Foreword," in National Audubon Society and Croxton Collaborative, op. cit. note 4; Amory B. Lovins,

"Negawatts for Development," Energy Efficiency Roundtable, World Bank, Washington, D.C., September 14, 1994.

65. Cynthia Cocchi, The Bigelow Group, Inc., Palatine, Ill., private communication, March 29, 1994; Brenda Vale and Robert Vale, University of Nottingham, U.K., private communication, September 15, 1994.

66. Building Research Establishment (BRE), "BREEAM/New Offices," Version 1/93, Garston, Watford, U.K.; John Doggart, ECD Partnership, London, private communication, July 28, 1994; BRE, "BREEAM/New Homes," Version 3/91, Garston, Watford, U.K.; BRE, "BREEAM/ Existing Offices," Version 4/93, Garston, Watford, U.K.; Michael Scholand, "Buildings for the Future," *World Watch*, November/December 1993.

67. Doggart, op. cit. note 66; Roger Baldwin, BRE, Garston, Watford, U.K., private communication, August 15, 1994; Raymond Cole, University of British Columbia, "Building Environmental Performance Assessment Criteria (BEPAC)," in Fanney et al., op. cit. note 35; U.S. Green Building Council, "Building Rating System," Staff Draft Issue Paper, for discussion at March 7, 1994, executive, public, and task force briefings; W. Lawrence Doxsey, "The City of Austin Green Builder Program," in Fanney et al., op. cit. note 35.

68. Gary Sharp, Post Harvest Developments, Inc., Ottawa, private communication, July 20, 1994.

69. Ibid.

70. Sweden from Schipper, Meyers, and Kelly, op. cit. note 8, and from Lee Schipper, LBL, Berkeley, Calif., private communication, April 1, 1994; Barbara Farhar and Jan Eckert, "Energy-Efficient Mortgages and Home Energy Rating Systems: A Report on the Nation's Progress," NREL, Golden, Colo., September 1993.

71. The World Bank, *Annual Report 1993* (Washington, D.C.: 1993); Michael Cohen, senior advisor to the vice-president, Environmentally Sustainable Development, World Bank, Washington, D.C., private communication, September 9, 1994.

72. David Malin Roodman, "Power Brokers: Managing Demand for Electricity," *World Watch*, November/December 1993; "R-2000 Reaches New Milestone," *R-2000 News Communiqué*, Energy, Mines, and Resources Canada, Ottawa, February 1993; David Grafstein, Ontario Hydro, Toronto, private communication, April 6, 1994; Gary Sharp, Post Harvest Developments, Inc., Ottawa, private communication, March 31, 1994.

73. Schipper, Meyers, and Kelly, op. cit. note 8.

74. Robert Kwartin, EPA, Washington, D.C., private communication, September 13, 1994; EPA, OAR, "Introducing . . . The Energy Star Buildings Program," Washington, D.C., November 1993; Chris O'Brien, EPA, Washington, D.C., private communication, March 9, 1994.

75. Ministry of Housing, Spatial Planning and the Environment (VROM), *The Netherlands' National Environmental Policy Plan 2* (The Hague: 1994); VROM, "Working with the Construction Sector," Environmental Policy in Action No. 2, The Hague, March 1994.

76. Gonda van Hal, VIBA, Den Bosch, The Netherlands, private communication, July 28, 1994; NOVEM, op. cit. note 51; VROM, "Working with the Construction Sector," op. cit. note 75; VROM, *National Environmental Policy Plan*, op. cit. note 75.

77. VROM, *National Environmental Policy Plan*, op. cit. 75.

78. Ernst U. Von Weizsäcker and Jochen Jesinghaus, *Ecological Tax Reform: A Policy Proposal for Sustainable Development* (London: Zed Books, 1992).

Chapter 7. Facing China's Limits

1. Mary Evelyn Tucker, "Ecological Themes in Taoism and Confucianism," in Tu Wei Ming et al., eds., *Worldviews & Ecology* (Lewisberg, Pa.: Bucknell University Press, 1993).

2. Population data from U.S. Bureau of the Census, Center for International Research, Suitland, Md., private communication and database, May 11, 1994; Orville Schell, "To Get Rich Is Glorious," *The New Yorker*, July 25, 1994; Worldwatch estimate based on coal production trends for 1983–93, in British Petroleum (BP), *BP Statistical Review of World Energy* (London: 1994); grain projection from Lester Brown, "Who Will Feed China?" *World Watch*, September/October 1994.

3. Gross domestic product growth calculated from World Bank, *World Development Report 1994* (New York: Oxford University Press, 1994).

4. Costa Rica example from Jack Freeman, "Taking the Lead on Sustainability," *The Earth Times*, October 15, 1994; Kerala example in Alan B. Durning, *Poverty and the Environment: Reversing the Downward Spiral*, Worldwatch Paper 92 (Washington, D.C.: Worldwatch Institute, November 1989).

5. Population Reference Bureau (PRB), *1994 World Population Data Sheet* (Washington, D.C.: 1994); Bureau of the Census, op. cit. note 2.

6. PRB, op. cit. note 5; Bureau of the Census, op. cit. note 2; historical population data and Mao quote from Vaclav Smil, *China's Environmental Crisis: An Inquiry into the Limits of National Development* (New York: M.E. Sharpe, 1993).

7. Judith Banister, *China's Changing Population* (Palo Alto, Calif.: Stanford University Press, 1987); PRB, op. cit. note 5; fertility data from Bureau of the Census, op. cit. note 2; 1.38 billion is the mid–range projection in Population Division, Department for Economic and Social Information and Policy Analysis, *World Population Prospects: The 1994 Revision* (New York: United Nations, forthcoming).

8. Minorities from World Bank, *China: Strategies for Reducing Poverty in the 1990s* (Washington, D.C.: 1992).

9. U.N. Development Programme (UNDP), *Human Development Report 1994* (New York: Oxford University Press, 1994); Nicholas D. Kristof and Sheryl WuDunn, *China Wakes: The Struggle for the Soul of a Rising Power* (New York: Times Books, 1994).

10. For examples of conspicuous consumption, see Kristof and WuDunn, op. cit. note 9; economic data from Kam Wing Chan, "Economic Development in China in the Reform Era: Environmental Implications," *Chinese Environment and Development*, Vol. 4, 1993.

11. Kam, op. cit. note 10; UNDP, op. cit. note 9.

12. Xiao-huang Yin, "China's Gilded Age," *Atlantic Monthly*, April 1994; State Statistical Bureau, *China Statistical Yearbook* (Beijing: 1993).

13. David Moberg, "Playing Favorites," *In These Times*, May 2, 1994; Kam, op. cit. note 10; information on growth in special economic zones in Sally Stewart, Michael Tow Cheung, and David W. K. Yeung, "The Latest Asian Newly Industrialized Economy Emerges: The South China Economic Community," *The Columbia Journal of World Business*, Summer 1992; in addition to offically recognized special economic zones, there are more than 1,000 that the government recently ordered shut, as documented in Nicholas D. Kristof, "Beijing Restricts Land Speculation," *New York Times*, August 15, 1993.

14. Worldwatch estimate based on International Monetary Fund, *International Financial Statistics Yearbook* (Washington D.C.: 1994); exports in 1993 equalled $90.97 bil-

lion, and imports (cif) totalled $103.1 billion (market exchange rate in 1993 of 5.7620 yuan to the dollar); World Bank estimate from Tom Tsui, China and Mongolia Department, World Bank, Washington, D.C., personal communication, October 14, 1994; P.T. Bangsberg, "Export Surge for China's Foreign-Backed Textiles," *Journal of Commerce*, August 29, 1994; "By the Numbers: A Statistical Look at China," *Wall Street Journal*, December 10, 1993; "You've Won, America: Let China Join the World Trade Organization," *Asiaweek*, August 31, 1994; Stewart, Cheung, and Yeung, op. cit. note 13.

15. Paul J. Smith, "China's Reforms Go Awry As Peasants Surge to Cities," *Christian Science Monitor*, March 9, 1994; World Bank, op. cit. note 8; Kristof and WuDunn, op. cit. note 9; "Top Chinese Judge Warns of Serious Crime Problem in Rural Areas," *New York Times*, May 23, 1994.

16. Kristof and Wudunn, op. cit. note 9; comparative gross national product (GNP) projections are based on comparable international prices, using purchasing power parity in World Bank, *International Economic Insights*, May-June 1993; quote from Lee in Kristof and WuDunn, op. cit. note 9.

17. Daniel Hillel, "Lash of the Dragon," *Natural History*, August 1991; Patrick Tyler, "Huge Water Project Would Supply Beijing By 860-Mile Aqueduct," *New York Times*, July 19, 1994.

18. Percentage of world's water from World Resources Institute (WRI), *World Resources 1994–95* (New York: Oxford Universtiy Press, 1994); current water use and total irrigated grain percentage from Tsui, op. cit. note 14; U.S. percentage is Worldwatch estimate based on U.S. Department of Agriculture (USDA), Economic Research Service (ERS), *1992 Agricultural Statistics* (Washington, D.C.: U.S. Government Printing Office (GPO), 1992); China water use increase from He Bochuan, *China on the Edge: The Crisis of Ecology and Development* (San Francisco: China Books and Periodicals, Inc., 1991); agricul-

tural water use percentage from WRI, op. cit. in this note; increased irrigated area from U.N. Food and Agriculture Organization (FAO), *Production Yearbooks* (Rome: various years), and USDA, ERS, "China: Situation and Outlook Series," Washington, D.C., July 1993.

19. Sectoral breakdown from WRI, op. cit. note 18; Minister quoted in Patrick E. Tyler, "China Lacks Water to Meet Its Mighty Thirst," *New York Times*, November 7, 1993; lost economic output from Tyler, op. cit. note 17; Academy of Social Sciences projection in Tony Walker, "China Faces Mass Migration from Countryside to Cities," *Financial Times*, August 26, 1994; Tyler, op. cit. note 17.

20. National Environmental Protection Agency and State Planning Commission, People's Republic of China, *National Environmental Action Plan 1991–2000* (Beijing: 1994); "Experts Report on Guangdong Water Resources," (Hong Kong) *Zhongguo Tongxun She*, March 22, 1994, as reprinted in *JPRS Report: Environmental Issues*, April 15, 1994; percentage of treated wastewater from Smil, op. cit. note 6; "Study Blasts Township Firms for Pollution," *China Environment News* (NEPA), March 1994.

21. Dong Shi, "Water Crisis in Northern China and Counter-Measures," *Beijing Review*, April 2–8, 1990; Tyler, op. cit. note 17.

22. Length from Tsui, op. cit. note 14; quote from Tyler, op. cit. note 17.

23. Steel from Smil, op. cit. note 6; newsprint from Dong, op. cit. note 21; G.D. McRae, M. Greenfield, and W. Pelz, "Current Initiatives in Water Demand Management in Dalian, Province of Liaoning, P.R.C.," in *Proceedings from the International Workshop on Urban Water Conservation*, April 22–26; national average for wastewater recycling from Smil, op. cit. note 6.

24. Smil, op. cit. note 6; worldwide, irrigation efficiency averages less than 40 percent, according to Sandra Postel, *Last Oasis: Facing*

Water Scarcity (New York: W.W. Norton & Company, 1992); Dong, op. cit. note 21.

25. Smil, op. cit. note 6; "Proceedings," op. cit. note 23.

26. China had the highest yield per hectare for any large area in the world before 1800, according to Caroline Blunden and Mark Elvin, *Cultural Atlas of China* (New York: Facts on File, Inc, 1983); Daniel Southerland, "Repression's Higher Toll: New Evidence Shows Famine, Violence Spared Few," *Washington Post*, July 17, 1994.

27. Figure 7–2 from USDA, ERS, "Production, Supply, and Demand View" (electronic database), Washington, D.C., July 1994; 1965 per capita calories from FAO, "Time Series for State of Food and Agriculture '93" (electronic database), Rome, 1993; 1990 per capita calories from UNDP, op. cit. note 9; comparison to Japan from Smil, op. cit. note 6; malnutrition from World Bank, op. cit. note 8; grain as a total percentage of calories from Smil, op. cit. note 6.

28. USDA, op cit. note 27; water shortages in Smil, op. cit. note 6; Fertilizer Industry Association, *Fertilizer Consumption Report* (Paris: 1992).

29. Smil, op. cit. note 6; cropland from FAO, *Production Yearbooks* (Rome: various years); France and Italy comparison from Smil, op. cit. note 6; Sun Shangwu, "Building Eats up Farmland as More Mouths Need More Food," *China Daily*, July 18, 1994; Singapore land area from PRB, op. cit. note 5.

30. Smil, op. cit. note 6; World Bank, *China: Urban Land Management in an Emerging Market Economy* (Washington, D.C.: 1993); farmer quoted in Philip Shenon, "Good Earth is Squandered. Who'll Feed China?" *New York Times*, September 21, 1994.

31. Smil, op. cit. note 6; Northeast China plain from World Bank, *China Environmental Strategy Paper Vol. 1: Main Report* (Washington, D.C., 1992); Loess Plateau from Sandra Postel, "China Revives Lost Land," *World Watch*, March/April 1989; Smil, op. cit. note 6.

32. USDA, op. cit. note 27; and Brown, op. cit. note 2.

33. Projected grain deficit calculated using consumption figures from USDA, op. cit. note 27, and population figures from Population Division, op. cit. note 7; global grain exports from USDA, op. cit. note 27.

34. Wang Yonghong, "Pilot Zones to Pursue Sustainable Farming," *China Daily*, July 23, 1994.

35. Efforts to prevent land conversion from Smil, op. cit. note 6.

36. Alan B. Durning and Holly B. Brough, *Taking Stock: Animal Farming and the Environment*, Worldwatch Paper 103 (Washington, D.C.: Worldwatch Institute, July 1991); FAO, *1989 Yearbook of Fishery Statistics: Catches and Landings* (Rome: 1991); 1992 data from Maurizio Perotti, Fishery Statistician, Fishery Information Data and Statistics Service, Fisheries Department, FAO, Rome, personal communication, November 11, 1993; fishing fleet expansion in Stanley D.H. Wang and Bing-yi Zhan, "Marine Fishery Resource Management in PR China," *Marine Policy*, May 1992; 1993 data in Wang Yonghong, "China's Fish Output Increases This Year," *China Daily*, December 30, 1993; Victoria Griffith, "Troubled Waters," *Financial Times*, July 27, 1994; aquaculture land area from Xiangke Lu, Fishery Resources and Environment Division, *Fishery Management Approaches in Small Reservoirs in China* (Rome: FAO, 1992); Japan's cropland from WRI, op. cit. note 18.

37. Historical information from S.D. Richardson, *Forests and Forestry in China: Changing Patterns of Resource Development* (Washington, D.C.: Island Press, 1990); Vaclav Smil, "Deforestation in China," *Ambio*, Vol. 12, No. 5, 1983.

38. Smil, op. cit. note 6; Li Yongzeng, "Chinese Forestry: Crisis and Options,"

Liaowang (Outlook) Vol. 12, 1989, pp. 9–10; Wu Yunhe, "China's Dependence on Foreign Timber to Grow," *China Daily*, February 15, 1993; timber import figures and paper production from FAO, *Forest Products: 1980–1991* (Rome: 1993); Leena Paavilainen, "A Potential Fibre Source," *Paper*, June 1993; Ed Ayres, "Making Paper Without Trees," *World Watch*, September/October 1993.

39. Smil, op. cit. note 6; Peru comparison from PRB, op. cit. note 5; Fred Langan, "Forest Plantations in China Receive Canada Funding," *Christian Science Monitor*, June 8, 1994.

40. "Great Green Wall Dampens Gobi Dust Storms," *Science News*, June 25, 1994; length from Liu Dizhong, "'Greening of Motherland' Campaign Bears Fruit," *China Daily*, June 29, 1985; Wang Yonghong, "Forests Greening, But Mature Stands Few," *China Daily*, December 15, 1993; Smil, op. cit note 6; Wang Yonghong, "Government Urges Better Protection of Forests," *China Daily*, June 3, 1994.

41. FAO, op. cit. note 38; Smil, op. cit. note 6; Wu, op. cit. note 38.

42. Megadiversity countries in Russell A. Mittermeier, "Primate Diversity and the Tropical Forest: Case Studies from Brazil and Madagascar and the Importance of Megadiversity Countries," in E.O. Wilson, *Biodiversity* (Washington, D.C.: National Academy Press, 1988); species data from "Conservation of Biodiversity," *China's Agenda 21, White Paper on China's Population, Environment and Development in the 21st Century*, English translation on diskette from China Database Services, Arlington, Va.; share of higher plants Worldwatch estimate based on WRI, op. cit. note 18.

43. Mark Collins et al., eds., *The Conservation Atlas of Tropical Forests: Asia and the Pacific* (New York: Simon & Schuster, 1991); He, op. cit. 18; threatened or endangered data from *China's Agenda 21*, op. cit note 42.

44. Collins, op. cit. note 43; *China's Agenda 21*, op. cit. note 42; WRI, op. cit. note 18; Stephen J. O'Brien, Pan Wenshi, and Lu Zhi, "Pandas, People and Policy," *China Environment News* (NEPA), August 1994; poaching and CITES from Collins, op. cit. note 43.

45. Michael Moquin, "Ancient Solutions for Future Sustainability, Building with Adobe, Rammed Earth, and Mud," *Adobe Journal*, Issue 10; Paavilainen, op. cit. note 38.

46. Coal as a share of primary energy in Japan from BP, op. cit. note 2; Jonathan E. Sinton, ed., *China Energy Data Book* (Berkeley, Calif.: Lawrence Berkeley Laboratory, 1992).

47. Sinton, op. cit. note 46; Robert Taylor, Senior Energy Economist, Industry and Energy Operations Division, China and Mongolia Department, World Bank, speech at Resources for the Future, Washington, D.C., September 13, 1994.

48. "China," in WRI, op. cit. note 18; Zhaoyi Xu et al., "The Health Effect of Air Pollution on Citizens in Liaoning Cities," presented at the International Conference on the Environmental Impact of Air Pollution: The Challenge for China, Beijing, April 1991; Hilary F. French, *Clearing the Air: A Global Agenda*, Worldwatch Paper 94 (Washington, D.C.: Worldwatch Institute, January 1990); Bronwen Maddox, "It Will Get Worse," *Financial Times*, November 18, 1993; H. Keith Florig, "The Benefits of Air Pollution Reduction" (draft), Resources for the Future, Washington, D.C., November 1993.

49. "China," op. cit. note 48; P.T. Bangsberg, "US, China Reportedly Team Up To Build Clean-Coal Power Plant," *Journal of Commerce*, January 5, 1994.

50. Jessica Hamburger, "Linking Energy and Environmental Policy in China" (draft), Battelle Pacific Northwest Laboratory, Washington, D.C., May 5, 1994; Florig, op. cit. note 48; Smil, op. cit. note 6.

51. Worldwatch estimate based on 1988 figure of 300 million, plus China's annual bi-

cycle production of 30–40 million bicycles in 1988–93, from Marcia D. Lowe, "Bicycle Production Rises Again," in Lester R. Brown, Hal Kane, and David Malin Roodman, *Vital Signs 1994* (New York: W.W. Norton & Company, 1994); road comparison in Smil, op. cit. note 6; Motor Vehicle Manufacturers Association (MVMA), *Facts & Figures '92* (Detroit, Mich.: 1992); MVMA, *Facts & Figures '72* (Detroit, Mich.: 1972); "Private Motor Vehicles in China," *East Gate China Marketing News*, May 1994; Patrick Tyler, "China Planning People's Car to Put Masses Behind Wheel," *New York Times*, September 22, 1994.

52. Hamburger, op. cit. note 50; inefficient trucks and buses in Yingzhong Lu, *Fueling One Billion: An Insiders Story of Chinese Energy Policy Development* (Washington, D.C.: The Washington Institute, 1993).

53. Figure 7–3 from BP, op. cit. note 2; 1994 data are a Worldwatch estimate based on Robert J. Beck, "Economic Growth Lifts Oil Demand Projections for 1994," *Oil and Gas Journal*, July 25, 1994; Li quote from P.T. Bangsberg, "China Expects Oil Imports to Soar in Next 20 Years," *Journal of Commerce*, October 4, 1994.

54. Figure 7–4 from Thomas A. Boden, Oak Ridge National Laboratory, private communcation and printout, September 20, 1993; 1992 and 1993 data are Worldwatch estimates based on ibid. and on BP, op. cit. note 2; Sheryl WuDunn, "Difficult Algebra for China: Coal=Growth=Pollution," *New York Times*, May 25, 1992.

55. Greenpeace International, *The Climate Time Bomb* (Amsterdam: 1994); "Typhoon Kills 700 in China; Damage is Put at $1.6 Billion," *New York Times*, August 24, 1994.

56. "United Nations Framework Convention on Climate Change," *International Environment Reporter*, January 26, 1994; Environmental Information Center, *Energy Demand Forecast and Environmental Impact in China* (Tokyo: 1994); Nicholas Anderson, China and Mongolia Department, World Bank, Washington, D.C., private communication, October 19, 1994.

57. "Coal," *Energy Economist*, July 1994; Sinton, op. cit. note 46.

58. The three paths concept is from Amulya Reddy, International Energy Initiative, Bangalore, India, private communication, September 21, 1994.

59. Mark Levine et al., *Energy Efficiency, Developing Nations, and Eastern Europe, A Report to the U.S. Working Group on Global Energy Efficiency* (Washington, D.C.: International Institute for Energy Conservation, 1991); Steve Nadel, deputy director, American Council for an Energy-Efficient Economy, Washington, D.C., October 7, 1994.

60. Robert A. Hefner III, "Onshore Natural Gas in China," presented at the World Bank Energy Roundtable Discussion on Gas Development in Less Developed Countries, Paris, March 25–26, 1985; "Electricity," *Energy Economist*, July 1994.

61. "SELF Signs Joint Venture to Make Household PV Systems for China," *The Solar Letter*, March 4, 1994; Kulsum Ahmed and Dennis Anderson, *Renewable Energy Technologies: A Review of the Status and Costs of Selected Technologies* (Washington, D.C.: World Bank, 1994); Christopher Flavin and Nicholas Lenssen, *Power Surge: Guide to the Coming Energy Revolution* (New York: W.W. Norton & Company, 1994).

62. Gao Jin, "Blueprint Drawn for Switch to New Energy," *China Daily*, October 8, 1994; "New World Enters China Venture, Signs Deals for Two Projects," press release, New World Power, Lime Rock, Conn., July 13, 1994.

63. World Bank, op. cit. note 8.

64. Ibid. The World Bank defines absolute poverty by taking consumption of 2,150 calories a day and then adding a sum for nonfood commodities and services based on the average expenditure pattern of the poor, and

having the poverty line measure welfare against the ability to buy the predetermined bundle of commodities and services, according to World Bank, op. cit. note 8.

65. UNDP, op. cit. note 9; Kristof and WuDunn, op. cit. note 9.

66. World Bank, op. cit note 8.

67. Ibid.; "China to Start Imposing a Fee For Privilege of Living in Beijing," *Journal of Commerce*, September 27, 1994.

68. In Shanghai, 9.9 out of every 1,000 infants die in their first year of life. In New York City, the infant mortality rate is 10.2 per 1,000, from Kristof and WuDunn, op. cit. note 9; Tibet estimate in Banister, op. cit. note 7.

69. Sheila Hillier and Xiang Zheng, "Rural Health Care in China: Past, Present and Future," in Denis Dwyer, ed., *China: The Next Decades* (New York: John Wiley & Sons, Inc., 1994); Banister, op. cit. note 7; UNDP, op. cit. note 9; World Bank, *World Tables 1992* (Baltimore, Md.: Johns Hopkins University Press, 1992).

70. Hillier and Xiang, op. cit. note 69.

71. World Bank, op. cit. note 8; Kristof and WuDunn, op. cit. note 9.

72. World Bank, op. cit. note 8; Kristof and WuDunn, op. cit. note 9.

73. U.N. General Assembly, "Programme of Action of the United Nations International Conference on Population and Development" (draft), New York, September 19, 1994.

74. Kristof and WuDunn, op. cit. note 9; Lena H. Sun, "A Great Leap Back: Chinese Women Losing Jobs, Status as Ancient Ways Subvert Socialist Ideal," *Washington Post*, February 2, 1993; "Chinese Women Take Great Leap Backward," *IPPF Open File* (International Planned Parenthood Federation, London), June 1994.

75. Kristof and WuDunn, op. cit. note 9; Nicholas D. Kristof, "A U.N. Agency May Leave China Over Coercive Population Control," *New York Times*, May 15, 1993.; Lena H. Sun, "China Lowers Birth Rate to Levels in West," *Washington Post*, April 22, 1993; Nicholas D. Kristof, "China's Crackdown on Births: A Stunning, and Harsh, Success: Draconian Steps Cut Fertility Rate to Lowest Ever," *New York Times*, April 25, 1993; Sheryl WuDunn, "Births Punished by Fire, Beating or Ruined Home," *New York Times*, April 25, 1993.

76. Amnesty International, *Amnesty International Report 1994* (New York: 1994); U.S. Department of State, *Country Reports on Human Rights Practices for 1993: Report Submitted to the Committee on Foreign Affairs, U.S. House of Representatives, and the Committee on Foreign Relations, U.S. Senate* (Washington: GPO, 1994).

77. G.M. Bankobeza, Ozone Secretariat, United Nations Environment Programme, Nairobi, private communication, September 27, 1994.

78. Albert P. Blaustein and Gilbert H. Flanz, eds., *Constitutions of the Countries of the World* (Dobbs Ferry, N.Y.: Oceana Publications, 1992); *China's Agenda 21*, op. cit. note 42; number of projects from "Environmental Technology Exports to China to Be Discussed," *Aftenposten*, August 24, 1994, as reprinted in *JPRS Report: Environmental Issues*, September 20, 1994.

79. Michael E. Porter, *The Comparative Advantage of Nations* (New York: The Free Press, 1990).

80. China's environmental expenditure as percent of GNP and World Bank's recommendation in Xu Chengshi and Zhong Bu, "Vitriolic Fallout From China's Economic Boom," *Panoscope*, April 1994; pollution's cost to China in "China Totes Up Pollution Costs," *Wall Street Journal*, September 20, 1994; U.S. and Japan's expenditures in Or-

ganisation for Economic Co-operation and Development, *Environmental Data Compendium 1993* (Paris: 1993).

81. You Qin Li, "Chinese Researchers Told to Fend for Themselves," *Nature*, November 5, 1992.

82. Size of flood area from Sheila Tefft, "Despite Controversy, China Pushes Ahead on Colossal Dam," *Christian Science Monitor*, May 11, 1994; size of Hong Kong from PRB, op. cit. note 5; cost figure from "Appendix E: Some Issues Regarding the Preliminary Design of the Three Gorges Project," in Dai Qing, *Yangtze! Yangtze!* (London: Earthscan, 1994).

83. "Continued Economic Growth Linked To Pollution Control, Bank Official Says," *International Environment Reporter*, May 19, 1994.

84. Katherine Sierra, Chief, China and Mongolia Department, World Bank, Washington, D.C., personal communication, October 6, 1994.

85. Alan B. Durning, *Action at the Grassroots: Fighting Poverty and Environmental Decline*, Worldwatch Paper 88 (Washington, D.C.: Worldwatch Institute, January 1989); Wang Rong, "China's NGOs Must Enter Global Network," *China Daily*, December 16, 1993; Todd Lapin, "Can Green Mix With Red?" *Nation*, February 14, 1994.

Chapter 8. Leaving Home

1. Aaron Segal, *An Atlas of International Migration* (London: Hans Zell Publishers, 1993).

2. Ibid.; Colin McEvedy and Richard Jones, *Atlas of World Population History* (New York: Penguin, 1978).

3. U.S. Committee for Refugees (USCR), *World Refugee Survey 1994* (Washington, D.C.: 1994); Segal, op. cit. note 1.

4. Figure 8–1 is based on United Nations High Commissioner for Refugees (UNHCR), *The State of the World's Refugees 1993: The Challenge of Protection* (London: Penguin, 1993), with Worldwatch estimates based on press reports.

5. Gil Loescher, *Beyond Charity* (Oxford: Oxford University Press, 1993).

6. USCR, op. cit. note 3.

7. Worldwatch estimate based on Hania Zlotnik, Population Division, United Nations, private communication, October 3, 1994, on Michael S. Teitelbaum, Sloan Foundation, private communication, October 3, 1993, and on Segal, op. cit. note 1.

8. Migrant figure is a Worldwatch estimate based on United Nations, "International Migration Stock, Trends In Total Migrant Stock" (electronic database), United Nations, New York, 1994, on Sharon Stanton Russell and Michael S. Teitelbaum, "International Migration and International Trade," *World Bank Discussion Paper 160* (Washington, D.C.: World Bank, 1992), on Teitelbaum, op. cit. note 7, on Zlotnik, op. cit. note 7, and on Segal, op. cit. note 1; Chinese migrants from World Bank, *China: Strategies for Reducing Poverty in the 1990s* (Washington, D.C.: World Bank, 1992).

9. Paul Theroux, "Going to See the Dragon," *Harpers*, October 1993.

10. William G. Rosenberg and Marilyn B. Young, *Transforming Russia and China: Revolutionary Struggle in the Twentieth Century* (New York: Oxford University Presss, 1982); Myron Weiner, "Rejected Peoples and Unwanted Migrants in South Asia," *Economic and Political Weekly*, August 21, 1993.

11. USCR, op. cit. note 3; Morton Abramowitz, "Exodus: The World Refugee Crisis," *Foreign Policy*, Summer 1994.

12. Abramowitz, op. cit. note 11; refugees admitted to United States during Reagan years from Loescher, op. cit. note 5.

13. Deborah Sontag, "Illegal Aliens Put Uneven Load on States, Study Says," *New York Times*, September 15, 1994; William Drozdiak, "Rolling Up a Worn-Out Welcome Mat," *Washington Post*, July 13, 1993.

14. Jeffrey S. Passel and Michael Fix, "Myths About Immigrants," *Foreign Policy*, Summer 1994.

15. Ibid.

16. Mike Edwards, "Chornobyl: Living With the Monster," *National Geographic*, August 1994.

17. *Bangladesh Flood Action Plan Newsletter* (National Audubon Society, New York), March 1993.

18. Department of Information and International Relations, Central Tibetan Administration of His Holiness the XIV Dalai Lama, "Tibet: Environment and Development Issues 1992," Dharamsala, India, 1992; International Campaign for Tibet, "The Long March: Chinese Settlers and Chinese Policies in Eastern Tibet, Results of a Fact Finding Mission in Tibet," Dharamsala, India, September 1991.

19. Machiavelli quote from Christa Meindsma, quoted in "UN Recognizes Population Transfer as a Violation of Human Rights," *Tibet Press Watch*, December 1992; Dalai Lama quoted in "Dalai Lama: U.S. Must Help Stop Chinese Population Influx into Tibet," *Tibet Press Watch*, May 1993.

20. Iraqi exodus cited in Raymond Bonner, "Trail of Suffering as Rwandan Exodus Continues," *New York Times*, July 16, 1994.

21. USCR, op. cit. note 3.

22. Josef Vavrousek and Colleagues, Department of the Environment, State Commission for Science, Technology, and Investments, *The Environment in Czechoslovakia* (Prague: Institute of Technical, Economic, and Ecological Information, 1990).

23. Joseph A. Tainter, *The Collapse of Complex Societies* (Cambridge: Cambridge University Press, 1988); Victor Mallet, "Vietnamese Settlers in Cambodia Flee Attacks," *Financial Times*, March 31, 1993.

24. Robin Wright and Doyle McManus, *Flashpoints: Promise and Peril in a New World* (New York: Alfred A. Knopf, 1991).

25. World Bank Environment Department, *Resettlement and Development: The Bankwide Review of Projects Involving Involuntary Resettlement 1986–1993* (Washington, D.C.: 1994).

26. Bruce Rich, *Mortgaging the Earth* (Boston: Beacon Press, 1994).

27. Norman Myers, "Environmental Refugees in a Globally Warmed World," *Bioscience*, December 1993.

28. Population figures from U.S. Bureau of the Census, published in Francis Urban and Ray Nightingale, *World Population by Country and Region, 1950–90 and Projections to 2050* (Washington, D.C.: U.S. Department of Agriculture (USDA), Economic Research Service, 1993).

29. Number in fifties from Ruth Leger Sivard, *World Military and Social Expenditures 1993* (Washington, D.C.: World Priorities, 1993); number of major wars in the nineties from Birger Heldt, Peter Wallensteen, and Kjell-Ake Nordquist, "Major Armed Conflicts in 1991," in Stockholm International Peace Research Institute (SIPRI), *SIPRI Yearbook 1992: World Armaments and Disarmament* (New York: Oxford University Press, 1992), and from Peter Wallensteen and Karin Axell, "Major Armed Conflicts," in SIPRI, *SIPRI Yearbook 1994* (New York: Oxford University Press, 1994).

30. Thomas L. Friedman, *From Beirut to Jerusalem* (New York: Anchor Books, 1989).

31. Ibid.

32. Population Reference Bureau (PRB), *1994 World Population Data Sheet* (Washington, D.C.: 1994); USDA, "Production, Supply, and Demand View" (electronic

database), Washington, D.C., November 1993.

33. USCR, op. cit. note 3; Bureau of the Census, op. cit. note 28; USDA, op. cit. note 32.

34. Bruce Byers, "Roots of Somalia's Crisis," *Christian Science Monitor*, December 24, 1992.

35. Kenyan cropland scarcity from United Nations, *Report on the World Social Situation 1993* (New York: 1993); Keith B. Richburg, "Kenya's Ethnic Conflict Drives Farmers Off Land," *Washington Post*, March 17, 1994; Leslie Crawford, "Suffering the Politics of Drought," *Financial Times*, March 17, 1994; Tribal Clashes Resettlement Volunteer Service, "Politically Motivated Tribal Clashes in Kenya," Nairobi, Kenya: undated; doubling time from PRB, op. cit. note 32.

36. Number of refugees from U.S. Agency for International Development, "Consolidated Rwanda Report, Update #10," August 30–September 8, 1994.

37. Tina Malone, Catholic Relief Services, Baltimore, Md., private communication, September 22, 1994.

38. Population density from PRB, op. cit. note 32; "Rwanda: A Case of Successful Adaptation," in World Bank, *Sub-Saharan Africa: From Crisis to Sustainable Growth* (Washington, D.C.: 1989); farm size from Centro Internacional de Agricultura Tropical, "Rwanda Civil War Disrupts Key African Food Program," *CIAT On-Line: News on Research Progress, Impact, and Achievement*, July 1994.

39. Benoit Bosquet, Africa Department, World Bank, Washington, D.C., private communication, July 19, 1994; Malone, op. cit. note 37.

40. Malone, op. cit. note 37; PRB, op. cit. note 32.

41. Gillian Tett, "Elegant Exorcism of Central Bogeymen" (review of *The Resurgence of Central Asia—Islam or Nationalism?*), *Financial Times*, July 28, 1994; Raymond Bonner, "Asian Republic Still Caught in Web of Communism," *New York Times*, October 13, 1993; number of Tajik refugees from USCR, op. cit. note 3.

42. "Refugees On Move In Azerbaijan War," *New York Times*, August 16, 1993; Mark A. Uhlig, "The Karabakh War," *World Policy Journal*, Winter 1993; USCR, op. cit. note 3.

43. Ian Steele, "Countries Prepare for War While People Die of Hunger, Disease," *Depthnews Asia*, June, 1994; United Nations Development Programme (UNDP), *Human Development Report 1994* (New York: Oxford University Press, 1994).

44. Robert D. Kaplan, "The Coming Anarchy," *The Atlantic Monthly*, February 1994.

45. Jaques Attali, "An Age of Yugoslavias," *Harpers Magazine*, January 1993 (reprinted from *New Perspectives Quarterly*, Fall 1992).

46. Segal, op. cit. note 1.

47. Russell and Teitelbaum, op. cit. note 8.

48. UNDP, op. cit. note 43; Emma Tucker, "Global Pressures are Getting Worse," *Financial Times*, January 31, 1994.

49. Kaplan, op. cit. note 44; PRB, op. cit. note 32.

50. United Nations, *Prospects of World Urbanization 1988* (New York: 1989); Jane Pryer and Nigel Crook, *Cities of Hunger: Urban Malnutrition in Developing Countries* (Oxford: Oxfam, 1988).

51. Jorge E. Hardoy and David Satterthwaite, *Squatter Citizen* (London: Earthscan, 1989); Segal, op. cit. note 1; Roberto Suro, "Chinese Smuggling Grows, Forcing U.S. Resentment," *Washington Post*, June 2, 1994; Ashley Dunn, "Golden Venture, Then a New Ordeal," *New York Times*, June 5, 1994.

52. "Latin American Speedup Leaves Poor Behind," *New York Times*, September 7,

1994; Thomas Kamm, "Epidemic of Slums Afflicts Latin America," *Wall Street Journal*, August 30, 1994; United Nations, *World Urbanization Prospects, The 1992 Revision* (New York: United Nations, 1993).

53. World Bank, op. cit. note 8; Tony Walker, "China's Golden Era 'To Last Well Into Next Century,' " *Financial Times*, August 26, 1994; National Academy findings from "China's Next Revolution," *Financial Times*, August 26, 1994.

54. Helene Cooper, "Sub-Saharan Africa is Seen as Big Loser in GATT's New World Trade Accord," *Wall Street Journal*, August 15, 1994; brain drain from John Darnton, " 'Lost Decade' Drains Africa's Vitality," *New York Times*, June 19, 1994.

55. "International Migration and Trade," *HRO Dissemination Notes: Human Resources Development and Operations Policy*, World Bank, Washington, D.C., June 20, 1994; Irish politician from Barbara K. Rodes and Rice Odell, compilers, *A Dictionary of Environmental Quotations* (New York: Simon & Schuster, 1992).

56. International Monetary Fund (IMF), *International Financial Statistics* (Washington, D.C.: various years); Ralph Hakkert and Franklin W. Goza, "The Demographic Consequences of Austerity in Latin America," in William L. Canak (ed.), *Lost Promises: Debt, Austerity, and Development in Latin America* (Boulder, Colo.: Westview Press, 1989).

57. IMF, op. cit. note 56; Hakkert and Goza, op. cit. note 56.

58. "Expert Group Meeting on Population Distribution and Migration," *Population Bulletin of the United Nations*, Nos. 34/35, 1993 (summary findings of The Expert Group Meeting held in Santa Cruz, Bolivia, 18–22 January 1993); Wright and McManus, op. cit. note 24.

59. Wilfredo Cruz and Robert Repetto, *The Environmental Effects of Stabilization and Structural Adjustment Programs: The Philippines Case* (Washington, D.C.: World Resources Institute, 1992); Hakkert and Goza, op. cit. note 56.

60. Sharon Stanton Russell, review of *Labour Migration to the Middle East: From Sri Lanka to the Gulf*, *Population and Development Review*, September 1993.

61. Bradley Graham, "Pentagon Officials Worry Aid Missions Will Sap Military Strength," *Washington Post*, July 29, 1994; Jane Perlez, "Aid Agencies Hope to Enlist Military Allies In the Future," *New York Times*, August 21, 1994.

62. Wealthiest-country development assistance from Organisation for Economic Co-operation and Development, "Sharp Changes in the Structure of Financial Flows to Developing Countries and Countries in Transition," press release, Paris, June 20, 1994; U.N. development and peacekeeping spending from Erskine Childers with Brian Urquhart, "Renewing the United Nations System," *Development Dialogue* (Dag Hammarskjöld Foundation/Ford Foundation), 1994:1; UNHCR budget from Heather Courtney, public information officer, UNHCR, Washington, D.C., private communication, October 4, 1994; UNDP budget from Ad de Rad, UNDP, New York, private communication, October 19, 1994.

63. Ian Steele, "Peacekeeping Gives UN Serious Money Troubles," *Depthnews Asia*, June 1994; UNDP, op. cit. note 43; Oscar-Jean N'Galamulume, "Arms Embargo, Food Aid Could Stay Zaire's Crisis," *Christian Science Monitor*, March 16, 1994.

64. Jennifer Parmelee, "U.S. Aims to Head Off Threat of an African Famine," *Washington Post*, May 31, 1994.

65. U.N. General Assembly, "Draft Programme of Action of the International Conference on Population and Development," New York, September 19, 1994; UNICEF and World Health Organization, New York and Geneva, private communications, February 17, 1994; Andreas Fuglesang and Dale Chandler, *Participation As Process: What We Can*

Learn from Grameen Bank, Bangladesh (Dhaka, Bangladesh: Grameen Bank, 1988).

66. Amartya Sen, "The Economics of Life and Death," *Scientific American*, May 1993; Harald Muller, Director, Frankfurt Peace Research Institute, private communication, February 1991.

Chapter 9. Budgeting for Disarmament

1. United Nations Development Programme (UNDP), *Human Development Report 1994* (New York: Oxford University Press, 1994).

2. Development of global military spending from UNDP, op. cit. note 1, and from Michael Renner, "Military Expenditures Falling," in Lester R. Brown, Christopher Flavin, and Hal Kane, *Vital Signs 1992* (New York: W.W. Norton & Company, 1992).

3. Herbert Wulf, "Conversion as an Investment: Costs and Benefits," paper prepared for the Monterey Institute of International Studies, May 1993; Middle Eastern prospects from Julian Ozanne and Roger Matthews, "Ploughed Back Into Swords," *Financial Times*, September 9, 1994.

4. Number of major wars from Birger Heldt, Peter Wallensteen, and Kjell-Åke Nordquist, "Major Armed Conflicts in 1991," in Stockholm International Peace Research Institute (SIPRI), *SIPRI Yearbook 1992: World Armaments and Disarmament* (New York: Oxford University Press, 1992), and from Peter Wallensteen and Karin Axell, "Major Armed Conflicts," in SIPRI, *SIPRI Yearbook 1994* (New York: Oxford University Press, 1994); trend in number of all wars from "Anzahl der pro Jahr geführten und der neu begonnenen Kriege," *Frieden 2000*, February 1993, and from Ruth Leger Sivard, *World Military and Social Expenditures 1993* (Washington, D.C.: World Priorities, 1993).

5. Cumulative military spending from Renner, op. cit. note 2; Malaysia from UNDP, op. cit. note 1.

6. For a discussion of some of these issues and cost estimates, see Michael Renner, "Assessing the Military's War on the Environment," in Lester R. Brown et al., *State of the World 1991* (New York: W.W. Norton & Company, 1991), and Michael Renner, "Cleaning Up After the Arms Race," in Lester R. Brown et al., *State of the World 1994* (New York: W.W. Norton & Company, 1994). Comprehensive analyses of the costs of the war system are rare; a notable exception is Michael Cranna, ed., *The True Cost of Conflict* (London: Earthscan, 1994).

7. U.N. High Commissioner for Refugees (UNHCR) budget from Dutch Ministry of Foreign Affairs, *Humanitarian Aid Between Conflict and Development* (The Hague: 1993); amount and rise in consolidated appeals from Secretary-General of the United Nations, *Report on the Work of the Organization from the Forty-Seventh to the Forty-Eighth Session of the General Assembly* (New York: United Nations, 1993), and from U.N. Department of Humanitarian Affairs, "Secretary-General Reports to Economic and Social Council on Strengthening Coordination of Emergency Humanitarian Assistance," Briefing Note, New York, July 5, 1994; European Union from "ECHO Becomes Important Relief Fund," *D+C—Development and Cooperation*, No. 4, 1994.

8. Paul Lewis, "U.S. Forces U.N. to Put Off Plan to Send 5,500 Troops to Rwanda," *New York Times*, May 17, 1994; Michael R. Gordon, "U.N.'s Rwanda Deployment Slowed by Lack of Vehicles," *New York Times*, June 9, 1994; Douglas Jehl, "Officials Told to Avoid Calling Rwanda Killings Genocide," *New York Times*, June 10, 1994; United Nations Daily Highlights Press Release, August 19, 1994; Milton Leitenberg, "Anatomy of a Massacre" (op ed), *New York Times*, July 31, 1994; projected six-month peacekeeping force costs from United Nations, "Report of the Secretary-General on the Situation in Rwanda," New York, May 13, 1994.

9. United Nations, "Secretary-General Addresses Opening of Inter-Agency Appeal in Aid of Persons Affected By Rwandese Crisis," press release, New York, July 22, 1994; White House, Office of the Press Secretary, "Statement by the President," press release, Washington, D.C., July 29, 1994.

10. Failure to assist reconstitution of government and national institutions from Donatella Lorch, "In Rwanda, Government Goes Hungry," *New York Times*, September 18, 1994.

11. Refugee Policy Group, "Challenges of Demobilization and Reintegration–A Discussion Paper," prepared for a working meeting sponsored by U.N. Department for Humanitarian Affairs, New York, June 7, 1994.

12. Ibid.; World Bank, *Demobilization and Reintegration of Military Personnel in Africa: The Evidence from Seven Country Case Studies*, Discussion Paper, Africa Regional Series (Washington, D.C.: 1993); Nat J. Colletta and Nicole Ball, "War to Peace Transition in Uganda," *Finance & Development*, June 1993; Nicole Ball, Director, Program on Enhancing Security and Development, Overseas Development Council, Washington, D.C., private communication, October 11, 1994; United Nations, "Sixth Progress Report of the Secretary-General on the United Nations Observer Mission in Liberia," Security Council Document S/1994/1006, August 26, 1994; World Food Programme, "Renewed Fighting Cuts Off Vast Areas of Liberia from Humanitarian Aid; New Exodus of Refugees Recorded," press release, Rome, September 29, 1994; Mozambique from United Nations, Daily Highlights Press Releases, August 17, 1994, and August 24, 1994, and from *International Security Digest*, July 1994.

13. Refugee Policy Group, op. cit. note 11; World Bank, op. cit. note 12; Colletta and Ball, op. cit. note 12.

14. World Bank, op. cit. note 12.

15. Table 9–3 from World Bank, op. cit. note 12, from Humberto Ortega Saavedra,

"The Role of International Financial Institutions in the Democratization and Demilitarization Processes," in Francisco José Aguilar Urbina, ed., *Demobilization, Demilitarization, and Democratization in Central America* (San José, Costa Rica: Arias Foundation for Peace and Human Progress, Centre for Peace and Reconciliation, 1994).

16. Number of mine victims from James P. Grant, Executive Director, United Nations Children's Fund, Statement before Hearing on the Global Landmine Crisis, Subcommittee on Foreign Operations, Appropriations Committee, U.S. Senate, Washington, D.C., May 13, 1994; percentage of civilian victims from Cyrus R. Vance and Herbert A. Okun, Statement before Landmine Hearing, op. cit. in this note; number of mines scattered from Human Rights Watch/Arms Project and Physicians for Human Rights (HRW and PHR), *Landmines: A Deadly Legacy* (New York: Human Rights Watch, 1993); mines-to-people ratio in countries with extremely severe situation is a Worldwatch calculation based on U.S. Department of State, *Hidden Killers: The Global Problem with Uncleared Landmines* (Washington, D.C.: 1993), and on Population Reference Bureau, *1993 World Population Data Sheet* (Washington, D.C.: 1993); production during past 25 years from Kenneth Anderson, Director, The Arms Project of Human Rights Watch, Statement before Landmine Hearing, op. cit. in this note; annual production estimate from United Nations, "UNHCR Calls for International Ban on Land-Mines," press release, May 26, 1994.

17. HRW and PHR, op. cit. note 16; Donovan Webster, "One Leg, One Life at a Time," *New York Times Magazine*, January 23, 1994; U.N. Department of Humanitarian Affairs, op. cit. note 7.

18. Inadequacy of available funds from HRW and PHR, op. cit. note 16; Kuwait from Paul Lewis, "Red Cross to Urge U.N. to Adopt a Complete Ban on Land Mines," *New York Times*, February 28, 1994; peace-

keeping-related demining spending from Patrick Blagden, United Nations Department of Peace-Keeping Operations, New York, private communication, May 3, 1994, and from Patrick M. Blagden, Statement before Landmine Hearings, op. cit. note 16; total U.N. spending from David Gowdey, U.N. Department of Humanitarian Affairs, New York, private communication, September 1, 1994.

19. Afghanistan from U.N. Department of Humanitarian Affairs, *DHA News*, September-December 1993; Cambodia from HRW and PHR, op. cit. note 16.

20. John Darnton, "U.N. Faces Refugee Crisis That Never Ends," *New York Times*, August 8, 1994; Hal Kane, "Refugee Flows Swelling," in Lester R. Brown, Hal Kane, and David Malin Roodman, *Vital Signs 1994* (New York: W.W. Norton & Company, 1994).

21. Figure for 1988 from reports issued by United Nations, General Assembly, Executive Committee of the High Commissioner's Programme, "Overview of UNHCR Activities—Report for 1988–1989," August 25, 1989, and "Voluntary Funds Administered by the UNHCR. Accounts for the Year 1988 and Report of the Board of Auditors Thereon," July 18, 1989; figure for 1993 from Heather Courtney, Public Information Assistant, UNHCR, U.S. Branch Office, Washington, D.C., private communication, May 25, 1994; figure for 1994 projection and Jessen-Petersen quote from Paul Lewis, "Agency Hopes for Fall in Number of Refugees," *New York Times*, March 20, 1994.

22. Table 9–4 based on Alvaro de Soto and Graciana del Castillo, "Obstacles to Peacebuilding," *Foreign Policy*, Number 94, Spring 1994, for overview; Guatemala from "FONAPAZ 1993 Annual Report," "FONAPAZ: The Reason for its Existence," and "FONAPAZ and the Communities: Building Peace" (information brochures), Fondo Nacional para la Paz, Presidency of the Republic of Guatemala, undated; El Salvador from Gabriel Aguilera, "Problems of Military Demo-

bilization in Central America," *Cuadernos de Trabajo*, No. 14, Arias Foundation for Peace and Human Progress, San José, Costa Rica, July 1993, from United Nations, "Report of the Secretary-General on the United Nations Observer Mission in El Salvador," 11 May 1994, and from U.S. General Accounting Office (GAO), *El Salvador: Status of Reconstruction Activities One Year After the Peace Agreement* (Gaithersburg, Md.: 1993); Haiti from United Nations, Daily Highlights Press Release, September 21, 1994, and from Larry Rohter, "After the Homecoming, the Hard Part," *New York Times*, October 16, 1994; Mozambique from United Nations, "Report of the Secretary-General on the United Nations Operation in Mozambique," July 7, 1994, and from Mark C. Chona and Jeffrey I. Herbst, "Southern Africa," in Anthony Lake et al., *After the Wars: Reconstruction in Afghanistan, Indochina, Central America, Southern Africa, and the Horn of Africa* (New Brunswick, N.J.: Transaction Books for Overseas Development Council, 1990); Palestine from Thomas L. Friedman, "Agency Offering an Aid Blueprint for Palestinians," *New York Times*, May 3, 1994, from Youssef M. Ibrahim, "P.L.O. Pleads for Faster Disbursement of Foreign Aid Money," *New York Times*, June 10, 1994, from Alan Riding, "Palestinians Given Pledges For More Aid," *New York Times*, June 11, 1994, from Youssef M. Ibrahim, "Israeli-P.L.O. Squabble Delays Aid for Arabs," *New York Times*, September 10, 1994, and from "UNRWA: Supporting the Peace," *Palestine Refugees Today*, January 1994; Kuwait from GAO, *Persian Gulf: U.S. Business Participation in the Reconstruction of Kuwait* (Gaithersburg, Md.: 1992), and from Cory Wright, U.S. Department of Commerce, Washington, D.C., private communication, August 9, 1994; Bosnia from United Nations, "Pledging Conference to Raise Funds for Restoration of Essential Services to Sarajevo, to be Held in New York on 29 June," press release, New York, June 24, 1994; Oscar Arias S., "Peace and Security in Central America," in Aguilar Urbina, op. cit. note 15.

23. Jennifer Tufts, Delegation of the European Communities, Washington, D.C., private communication, August 22, 1994.

24. World Bank, op. cit. note 12; Jürgen Brauer and Domenick Bertelli, "Passing the Buck: International Banks and Aid for Conversion," *CEP Research Report*, January 1994; Nat Colletta, Population and Human Resources Division, East Africa Department, World Bank, Washington, D.C., private communication, August 29, 1994.

25. De Soto and del Castillo, op. cit. note 22; Liisa L. North, "The Challenge of Demobilization: The Construction of Peace and Regional Security," in Aguilar Urbina, op. cit. note 15.

26. Anthony Lake, "After the Wars— What *Kind* of Peace?" in Lake et al., op. cit. note 22.

27. START II does not take effect before START I enters into force, which the Clinton Aministration hopes will have happened by the end of 1994; Presidents Clinton and Yeltsin agreed in September 1994 to speed up the implementation of START II, see R.W. Apple Jr., "U.S. and Russia to Speed Disarmament," *New York Times*, September 29, 1994; potential savings from U.S. Congress, Congressional Budget Office (CBO), *The START Treaty and Beyond* (Washington, D.C.: 1991), and from CBO, *Implementing START II*, CBO Papers (Washington, D.C.: 1993); $5 trillion estimate from William Arkin and Robert S. Norris, "The Nuclear Follies, Post-Cold War," in Sivard, op. cit. note 4.

28. Submarine decommissioning from Captain F.G. Leeder, Deputy Chief of Information, Department of the Navy, Office of Information, Washington, D.C., private communication, May 6, 1994; Air Force costs are a Worldwatch calculation based on Major Cindy Scott-Johnson, Air Force Public Affairs, Media Relations Division, Washington, D.C., private communication, September 30, 1994, and on Institute for Defense and Disarmament Studies (IDDS), *Arms Control Reporter*

1993 (Cambridge, Mass.: 1993); warhead dismantlement cost estimate from U.S. Congress, Office of Technology Assessment (OTA), *Dismantling the Bomb and Managing the Nuclear Materials* (Washington, D.C.: U.S. Government Printing Office, 1993); storage costs from David Rohde, "Disposal of Warhead Plutonium Awaits Federal Study of Options," *Christian Science Monitor*, June 14, 1994.

29. Russian costs from Alexei Arbatov, ed., *Implications of the START II Treaty for US-Russian Relations*, Report No. 9 (Washington, D.C.: Henry L. Stimson Center, October 1993); Ukraine from IDDS, *Arms Control Reporter 1994* (Cambridge, Mass.: 1994), sheet 611.E-3.94; Kazakhstan from IDDS, op. cit. note 28, sheet 611.B.820.

30. Initial plans from Frances Williams, "Hopes High for International Chemical Weapons Treaty," *Financial Times*, August 26, 1992; reduced staff size from Anil Wadhwa, "The Preparatory Phase of Setting up the Organisation for the Prohibition of Chemical Weapons," *Disarmament. A Periodic Review by the United Nations*, Vol. 16, No. 3, 1993; 1994 budget from Serguei B. Batsanov, Director for External Relations, Preparatory Commission for the Organisation for the Prohibition of Chemical Weapons, Provisional Technical Secretariat, The Hague, Netherlands, private communication, April 7, 1994; limits to OPCW's capability from "Editor's Note," *The CWC Chronicle* (Henry L. Stimson Center), January 1994.

31. Destruction-to-production cost ratio from J.P. Perry Robinson, Thomas Stock, and Ronald G. Sutherland, "The Chemical Weapons Convention: The Success of Chemical Disarmament Negotiations," in SIPRI, *SIPRI Yearbook 1993: World Armaments and Disarmament* (New York: Oxford University Press, 1993); U.S. cost estimate, Russian foreign aid need, and 1997 starting date from Thomas Stock and Anna De Geer, "Chemical Weapon Developments," in SIPRI 1994, op. cit. note 4, and from U.S. Department of the

Army, Non-Stockpile Chemical Materiel Program, "Survey and Analysis Report," U.S. Army Chemical Materiel Destruction Agency, Program Manager for Non-Stockpile Chemical Materiel, Aberdeen Proving Ground, Md., November 1993; annual funding from Marilyn Tischbin, Chief, Public Affairs Office, U.S. Army Chemical Materiel Destruction Agency, Aberdeen Proving Ground, Md., private communications, January 4 and 24, 1994; cost estimates from IDDS, op. cit. note 28, sheet 704.E-2.96, and from Thomas Stock, "Chemical and Biological Weapons: Developments and Proliferation," in SIPRI 1993, op cit. in this note; recent cost estimate from Serguei Kisselev, Deputy Head of the Delegation of the Russian Federation to the Preparatory Commission for the Organization for the Prohibition of Chemical Weapons, Embassy of the Russian Federation, The Hague, Netherlands, private communication, July 10, 1994 (his estimate does not include the cost of destroying production facilities).

32. German spending (actual expenditures for 1991–93 and appropriations for 1994) from *Bundeshaushaltsplan, Einzelplan 14, Geschäftsbereich des Bundesministeriums der Verteidigung*, Kapitel 1409 (Rüstungskontrolle und Abrüstung), Titel 55302 (Bonn, Germany, 1994, 1992, and 1991 editions), and from "Stand der Bewirtschaftung HH-Einnahmen/-Ausgaben, Endergebnis des BMF," Haushaltsjahr 1993, Kapitel 1409, computer printout, German Ministry of Finance, February 16, 1994, as provided by the Press Office of the German Defense Ministry, Bonn, July 20, 1994; U.S. spending from GAO, *Conventional Arms Control: Former Warsaw Pact Nations' Treaty Compliance and U.S. Cost Control* (Gaithersburg, Md.: 1993); other countries from private communications with Andrew Duncan, Assistant Director for Information, International Institute for Strategic Studies, London, December 14, 1993, and others.

33. GAO, op. cit. note 32; IDDS, op. cit. note 29, sheets 407.B.505, B.506, and B.508;

Directorate for Press, Information and Public Relations of the Ministry of Defense of the Czech Republic, *1994 Army of the Czech Republic* (Prague: 1994); Russian preference from Steven Miller, Editor, *International Security*, Cambridge, Mass., private communication, August 15, 1994.

34. Global disposal market estimate from Adam Bryant, "Venture Hopes to Cash in on Military Cutbacks," *New York Times*, June 23, 1992; tonnage demilitarized from "Army Looks for Ways to Reuse, Recycle Munitions," *Environmental Update. A Quarterly Publication of Army Environmental News*, October 1993; expenditures from John McCoy, U.S. Army Materiel Command, Alexandria, Va., private communication, August 26, 1994; ammunition production capacity funding requests from GAO, *1994 Defense Budget: Potential Reductions to Ammunition Programs* (Gaithersburg, Md.: 1993), and from Thomas E. Ricks, "A Post-Cold War Defense Plan Maps a Smaller But Ready Force," *Wall Street Journal*, February 28, 1994; ammunition procurement appropriations from relevant sections of Department of Defense Appropriations Acts, 1990–94.

35. Herbert Wulf, "The Demobilization of Military Personnel as a Problem and a Potential for Human Development," in Aguilar Urbina, op. cit. note 15; Wulf, op. cit. note 3.

36. Previous closures from Tyrus W. Cobb, "Close the Bases—Now," *Washington Post*, June 1, 1994; projected costs and savings from U.S. Department of Defense, "FY 1995 Budget Estimates: DoD Base Realignment and Closure. Justification Data Submitted to Congress," Washington, D.C., February 1994; U.S. overseas base closures from "US to Cut Military Facilities in Europe," *Financial Times*, June 17, 1994.

37. Herbert Wulf, "Arms Industry Limited: The Turning-Point in the 1990s," in Herbert Wulf, ed., *Arms Industry Limited* (New York: Oxford University Press, 1993).

38. Wulf, op. cit. note 3.

39. Early funding from Michael Oden, "Dual-Use or Doublespeak?," *Positive Alternatives*, Winter 1994, and from Maggie Bierwirth, "Capitol Hill and Conversion: A Summary of Recent Congressional Action," in Kevin J. Cassidy and Gregory A. Bischak, eds., *Real Security. Converting the Defense Economy and Building Peace* (Albany: State University of New York Press, 1993); 1994–97 figures from "Defense Reinvestment and Conversion," *The New Economy*, Winter 1994; portion of civilian-oriented dual-use funds from Greg Bischak, Executive Director, National Commission for Economic Conversion and Disarmament, Washington, D.C., private communication, August 11, 1994.

40. Lack of conversion budget in Germany from Johann Peter, Arbeitsstab des Bevollmächtigten des Ministerpräsidenten für die Westgruppe der Streitkräfte und Konversion, Land Brandenburg, Potsdam, Germany, private communication, August 2, 1994, in Spain from Vicenç Fisas Armengol, Centre UNESCO de Catalunya, Barcelona, Spain, private communication, July 14, 1994, and in Britain from Adrian Kendry, "The Defense Budget and Defense Employment in the UK: Iceberg Effect for the Supply Chain," *The New Economy*, Spring 1994; Italy from Mario Pianta, National Research Council, Rome, Italy, private communication, August 1, 1994, and from John Simkins, "Italy Announces Plan to Reshape and Boost State Defence Industry," *Financial Times*, March 11, 1994; France from Ian Anthony et al., "Arms Production and Arms Trade," in SIPRI 1994, op. cit. note 4.

41. "European Commission Addresses Conversion," *The New Economy*, Summer 1993; Les Verts au Parlement Européen, Groupe de Travail "Paix et Disarmament," *Vers une Nouvelle Politique de Sécurité, Non-Prolifération, Essais Nucléaires, Industries d'Armements, Commerce des Armes, Objection de Conscience, Ex-Yugoslavie* (Brussels, undated); Herbert Wulf, Bonn International Center for Conversion, private communication, October 14, 1994.

42. Liu Yumin, "Conversion in China," *Press for Conversion!* May 1994; Nicole Ball et al., "World Military Expenditure," in SIPRI 1994, op. cit. note 4.

43. Yudit [sic] Kiss, "The Pains of Defense Industry Conversion in East Central Europe," *The New Economy*, Spring 1994; Oldrich Cechak, Jan Selesovsky, and Milan Stembera, "Czechoslovakia: Reductions in Arms Production in a Time of Economic and Political Transformation," in Wulf, op. cit. note 37.

44. Unfulfilled conversion plans from David W. McFadden, "Post-Soviet Conversion: Problems and Prospects," in Cassidy and Bischak, op. cit. note 39; Russian conversion cost estimates from Alexei Izyumov, "The Soviet Union: Arms Control and Conversion—Plan and Reality," in Wulf, op. cit. note 37.

45. Ksenia Gonchar, IMEMO Institute, Moscow, private communications, July 18 and September 19, 1994; Julian Cooper, Director, Centre for Russian and East European Studies, University of Birmingham, United Kingdom, private communication, October 4, 1994; re-emerging arms export emphasis from Ball et al., op. cit. note 42.

46. Number of troops and dependents from Stephen Kinzer, "Russian Troops Bid 'Wiedersehen' to Germany," *New York Times*, September 1, 1994; Grachev from Ball et al., op. cit. note 42; German payments from "Leistungen nach dem Überleitungsabkommen, Stand Februar 1994," unpublished printout, as provided by Mr. Reim, German Federal Finance Ministry, Bonn, Germany, private communication, August 23, 1994; the 1991–95 total is composed of actual expenditures (1991–93), budget appropriations (1994), and projections (1995).

47. Nuclear disarmament aid from IDDS, op. cit. note 28, and from IDDS, *Arms Control Reporter 1992* (Cambridge, Mass.: 1992), section 611.E-3; chemical disarmament from GAO, *Arms Control: Status of U.S.-Russian*

Agreements and the Chemical Weapons Convention (Gaithersburg, Md.: 1994), and from IDDS, op. cit. note 28, sheet 704.E-2.107.

48. Nunn-Lugar program from "U.S. Helps Former Soviet Union Reduce Threat," news release, U.S. Department of Defense, Office of Assistant Secretary of Defense (Public Affairs), Washington, D.C., March 15, 1994, from "Semi-Annual Report on Program Activities to Facilitate Weapons Destruction and Nonproliferation in the Former Soviet Union," Washington, D.C., April 30, 1994, submitted by U.S. Secretary of Defense to Speaker of the House of Representatives and President of the Senate, May 14, 1994, and from U.S. Department of Defense, Defense Nuclear Agency, private communication, August 8, 1994.

49. Worth of deal from IDDS, op. cit. note 29, sheet 611.E-3.90; annual revenues are a Worldwatch estimate based on this source.

50. Worldwatch calculations based on Organisation for Economic Co-operation and Development (OECD), Centre for Co-Operation with Economies in Transition (CCET), "CCET Register Projects in the Defence Conversion Sector," CCET Register Report #0071, Paris (as of February 22, 1994). A request for an updated version of the register was denied: officially, access is restricted to governments and multilateral institutions; OECD might allow nongovernmental organizations, universities, and private-sector access in the future, but as of August 1994 no such decision was imminent. Jean Gomm, Principal Administrator, CCET, Paris, private communication, August 8, 1994.

51. Perry quote from "Semi-Annual Report," op. cit. note 48; conversion-related funds from the Technical Assistance Program to the Commonwealth of Independent States (TACIS) from Christina Thormählen, European Commission, Directorate General I, External Economic Relations, TACIS Information Office, Brussels, Belgium, private communication, August 3, 1994; European Bank from Brauer and Bertelli, op. cit. note

24, and from European Bank for Reconstruction and Development, "Russia: Military Conversion Programme," Presentation to the European Parliament Committee on Military Conversion, April 28/29, 1993; fees to Western consultants from Brooks Tigner, "Europeans Push Conversion in Russia," *Press for Conversion!* May 1994, and from Domenick Bertelli, Council on Economic Priorities, "DoD to review conversion aid to NI. Shakeup in Russian aid program may be on the way," February 16, 1994, as posted on igc:econ.conversion on Econet, based on a preliminary study ordered by Graham Allison, U.S. Assistant Secretary of Defense for Policy and Plans.

52. Oscar Arias S., "A Global Demilitarization Fund," special contribution to UNDP, op. cit. note 1. The proposals discussed in this section have in part been developed in a series of informal consultations in January and February 1994 with staff at the Center for Peace and Reconciliation, Arias Foundation for Peace and Human Progress in San José, Costa Rica.

53. Arias, op. cit. note 52.

54. In the context of reforming multilateral and bilateral lending conditionalities to include military budget considerations, there is a growing discussion over how to define "excessive" military spending. See Nicole Ball, *Pressing for Peace: Can Aid Induce Reform?* (Washington, D.C.: Overseas Development Council, 1992), and Joan M. Nelson and Stephanie J. Eglinton, *Global Goals, Contentious Means: Issues of Multiple Aid Conditionality* (Washington, D.C.: Overseas Development Council, 1993). This discussion is equally relevant to establishing eligibility criteria for a Demilitarization Fund.

55. Ball, op. cit. note 12.

Chapter 10. Forging a New Global Partnership

1. Don Hinrichsen, "The Earth Summit," *The Amicus Journal*, Winter 1992; United Na-

tions, *Agenda 21: The United Nations Program of Action From Rio* (New York: U.N. Publications, 1992); United Nations Framework Convention on Climate Change and Convention on Biological Diversity included in Lakshman D. Guruswamy, Sir Geoffrey W. R. Palmer and Burns H. Weston, *International Environmental Law and World Order* (A Problem-Oriented Coursebook), Supplement of Basic Document (St. Paul, Minn.: West Publishing Co., 1994).

2. Call for a global partnership is in Article 7 of the Rio Declaration on Environment and Development, included in Guruswamy, Palmer, and Weston, op. cit. note 1.

3. "Lack of Concrete Action at Talks Decried by NGOs but Backed by Industry as Not Needed," *International Environment Reporter*, September 7, 1994; David E. Pitt, "Biological Pact Passes Into Law," *New York Times*, January 2, 1994; United Nations Non-Governmental Liaison Service (UN–NGLS), *E & D File*, Briefings on UNCED follow-up, June 1994; Boyce Rensberger, "Cairo Conference Ends With Broad Consensus for Plan to Curb Growth," *Washington Post*, September 14, 1994.

4. Lester R. Brown, Hal Kane, and David Malin Roodman, *Vital Signs 1994* (New York: W.W. Norton & Company, 1994); United Nations Development Programme (UNDP), *Human Development Report 1994* (New York: Oxford University Press, 1994); poverty trends from World Bank, *Implementing the World Bank's Strategy to Reduce Poverty: Progress and Challenges* (Washington, D.C.: 1993).

5. "United Nations World Summit for Social Development," Fact Sheet, New York, May 1994; "Draft Platform for Action," Fourth World Conference on Women, undated.

6. "50," The Newsletter of the 50th Anniversary of the United Nations, New York, Summer 1994; "'Our Global Neighbourhood': Commission Report Nears Comple-

tion," *Update*, Commission on Global Governance, Geneva, September 1994; "Summit Communique," Naples, Italy, July 9, 1994.

7. Quote from D.C. Browning, *Dictionary of Quotations and Proverbs* (London: Cathay Books, 1989).

8. Figure 10–1 based on U.N. Environment Programme (UNEP), *Register of International Treaties and Other Agreements in the Field of the Environment 1993* (Nairobi: 1993) and on Mark Labelle, legal assistant, Treaty Office, United Nations, New York, private communication, October 17, 1994; figure of 800 from Edith Brown Weiss, Paul Szasz, and Daniel Magraw, *International Environment Law: Basic Instruments and References* (Transnational Publishers, Inc., 1992); "Climate Change Treaty Comes Into Force," *International Environment Reporter*, March 23, 1994; Pitt, op. cit. note 3; Anthony Goodman, "UN's Law of the Sea to Take Effect Next Year," *Journal of Commerce*, December 8, 1993; Information Program on Sustainable Development, "Legal Agreement to Curb Desertification is Concluded," Press Release, United Nations, New York, July 1994.

9. Marc Levy, "European Acid Rain: The Power of Tote-Board Diplomacy," *Institutions for the Earth: Sources of Effective International Environmental Protection* (Cambridge, Mass.: MIT Press, 1993); Megan Ryan, "CFC Production Continues to Drop," in Brown, Kane, and Roodman, op. cit. note 4; "Africa's Elephants Could Soon Be Under the Gun Again," *Christian Science Monitor*, February 2, 1992; Gareth Porter and Janet Welsh Brown, *Global Environmental Politics* (Boulder, Colo.: Westview Press, 1991).

10. Hilary F. French, "Making Environmental Treaties Work," *Scientific American*, December 1994; U.S. General Accounting Office, *International Environment: International Agreements Are Not Well Monitored* (Washington D.C.: 1992).

11. Montreal Protocol and subsequent amendments from Guruswamy, Palmer, and

Weston, op. cit. note 1; UNEP, "Copenhagen Amendment on Ozone Layer to Enter Into Force," Press Release, Nairobi, March 22, 1994.

12. As of August 30, 1994, 140 countries had ratified the Montreal Protocol, from Valery Smirnov, Program Officer, Multilateral Fund for the Implementation of the Montreal Protocol, Montreal, Canada, private communication, October 6, 1994; UNEP, op. cit. note 11; Figure 10–2 from Ryan, op. cit. note 9, based on data from Michael Prather and Mack McFarland, E.I. Du Pont de Nemours; UNEP, World Meteorological Organization, U.S. National Aeronautics and Space Administration, and National Oceanic and Atmospheric Administration, "Scientific Assessment of Ozone Depletion: 1994," Executive Summary, Washington, D.C., August 19, 1994; "Synthesis of the Reports of the Ozone Scientific Assessment Panel, Environmental Effects Assessment Panel, Technology and Economic Assessment Panel," Prepared by the Assessment Chairs for the Parties to the Montreal Protocol, November 1991.

13. "Climate Change Treaty," op. cit. note 8.

14. Organisation for Economic Co-operation and Development (OECD), International Energy Agency, *Climate Change Policy Initiatives—1994 Update, Vol. 1, OECD Countries* (Paris: 1994); "IEA Reviews Energy Policies in Germany, UK, and Denmark," *Energy, Economics, and Climate Change*, August 1994.

15. Climate Action Network, *Independent NGO Evaluations of National Plans for Climate Change Mitigation* (Brussels: 1994); John H. Cushman, "Clinton Wants to Strengthen Global Pact on Air Pollution," *New York Times*, August 16, 1994; "Japan Will Substantially Overshoot Year 2000 CO_2 Emissions Target, Report Says," *International Environment Reporter*, August 10, 1994; "EU Ratifies Climate Convention Without Carbon/Energy Tax," *Energy, Economics, and Climate Change*, December 1993.

16. Robert Evans, "UN Conference Says New Cuts in Emissions are Needed," *Journal of Commerce*, February 22, 1994; Executive Summary, "Draft Summary for Policymakers of the 1994 Working Group I Report on Radiative Forcing of Climate Change," Intergovernmental Panel on Climate Change (IPCC), Maastricht, The Netherlands, September 15, 1994; IPCC, *Climate Change: The IPCC Scientific Assessment* (New York: Cambridge University Press, 1990); John H. Cushman, Jr., "Clinton Wants to Strengthen Global Pact on Air Pollution," *New York Times*, August 16, 1994; "Lack of Concrete Action at Talks Decried by NGOs," op. cit. note 3.

17. U.S. Climate Action Network, Letter to the Hon. Timothy E. Wirth, U.S. Undersecretary of State for Global Affairs, July 28, 1994; "Small Island Nations Protocol Proposes 20 Percent CO_2 Cut for Developed Nations," *International Environment Reporter*, October 5, 1994; The Hon. Timothy F. Wirth, U.S. Undersecretary of State for Global Affairs, "Next Steps on International Climate Policy," speech to Next Steps on Climate Change: A Public Consultation, U.S. Department of State, Washington, D.C., August 3, 1994.

18. Pitt, op. cit. note 3; ratifications from Mark Labelle, legal assistant, Treaty Office, United Nations, New York, private communication, September 27, 1994.

19. Walter Reid, vice president, World Resources Institute, Hearings on Convention on Biological Diversity, Committee on Foreign Relations, U.S. Senate, Washington, D.C., April 12, 1992; World Resources Institute, World Conservation Union, and UNEP, "Global Biodiversity Strategy: Policy-makers' Guide," Washington, D.C., 1992.

20. Walter V. Reid et al., eds., *Biodiversity Prospecting: Using Genetic Resources for Sustainable Development* (Washington, D.C.: World Resources Institute, 1993).

21. Steven M. Lanou, World Resources Institute, "National Biodiversity Planning Activities: Overview," unpublished matrix, Washington, D.C., June 7, 1994; World Resources Institute, *World Resources 1994–95* (New York: Oxford University Press, 1994); "Parties to Biodiversity Treaty to Discuss Possible Protocol on Biotechnology Safety," *International Environment Reporter*, July 13, 1994; Reid et al., op. cit. note 20.

22. Canute James, "Oceans Set to Yield Up Their Treasures," *Financial Times*, July 7, 1994; Rebecca Fowler, "Law of the Sea: An Odyssey to U.S. Acceptance," *Washington Post*, July 29, 1994.

23. Peter Weber, *Abandoned Seas: Reversing the Decline of the Oceans*, Worldwatch Paper 116 (Washington, D.C.: Worldwatch Institute, November 1993); *The Law of the Sea: United Nations Convention on the Law of the Sea* (New York: United Nations, 1983).

24. "Summary of the Third Session of the UN Conference on Straddling Fish Stocks and Highly Migratory Fish Stocks 15–26 August 1994," *Earth Negotiations Bulletin*, August 29, 1994; fish catch from U.N. Food and Agriculture Organization (FAO), *Fishery Statistics: Catches and Landings* (Rome: various years), and from FAO, Rome, private communications, December 20, 1993.

25. UNEP estimate from Information Program on Sustainable Development, op. cit. note 8; "Summary of the Fifth Session of the INC for the Elaboration of an International Convention to Combat Desertification 6–17 June 1994," *Earth Negotiations Bulletin*, June 20, 1994; Mark Labelle, legal assistant, Treaty Office, United Nations, New York, private communication, October 20, 1994.

26. UNDP, op. cit. note 4; UNDP, *Human Development Report 1991* (New York: Oxford University Press, 1991).

27. U.N. General Assembly, "Programme of Action of the United Nations International Conference on Population and Development" (draft), New York, September 19, 1994; Alan Cowell, "The Hidden Population Issue: Money," *New York Times*, September 12, 1994.

28. John Bongaarts, "Population Policy Options in the Developing World," *Science*, February 11, 1994; U.N. General Assembly, op. cit. note 27.

29. The countries are Bangladesh, Colombia, Egypt, Indonesia, Kenya, Mexico, Morocco, Thailand, Tunisia, and Zimbabwe; Barbara Crossette, "A Third-World Effort on Family Planning," *New York Times*, September 7, 1994.

30. "United Nations World Summit for Social Development," op. cit. note 5; UNDP, op. cit. note 4.

31. UNDP, op. cit. note 4.

32. Ibid.; UNDP, UNFPA, and UNICEF, "The 20/20 Initiative: Achieving Universal Access to Basic Social Services for Sustainable Human Development," New York, undated.

33. Figure 10–3 from World Bank, unpublished printouts, and from Manuel Trucco, debt specialist, World Bank, private communication, October 17, 1994 (1993 number).

34. UNDP, op. cit. note 4; Jonathan E. Sanford, "African Debt: Recent Initiatives and Policy Options for Multilateral Bank Debt," Congressional Research Service (CRS), U.S. Library of Congress, Washington, D.C. July 9, 1993; updated figure provided by Jonathan Sanford, CRS, U.S. Library of Congress, Washington, D.C., private communication, October 20, 1994.

35. UNDP, op. cit. note 4.

36. Ibid.; OECD, "Assessing the Effects of the Uruguay Round," *Trade Policy Issues*, No. 2, Paris, 1993; Helene Cooper, "Sub-Saharan Africa is Seen as Big Loser in GATT's New World Trade Accord," *Wall Street Journal*, August 15, 1994.

37. Nathaniel C. Nash, "Latin Economic Speedup Leaves Poor in the Dust," *New York*

Times, September 7, 1994; Jodi L. Jacobson, *Gender Bias: Roadblock to Sustainable Development*, Worldwatch Paper 110 (Washington, D.C.: Worldwatch Institute, September 1992); Lori Ann Thrupp, "Challenges in Latin America's Recent Agroexport Boom," *Issues in Development*, World Resources Institute, Washington, D.C., February 1994; Alan Thein Durning, *Guardians of the Land: Indigenous Peoples and the Health of the Earth*, Worldwatch Paper 112 (Washington, D.C.: Worldwatch Institute, December 1992).

38. Gustavo Esteva, "Mexican Indians Say No to Development," *People-Centered Development Forum* (New York), May 20, 1994; Andrew Reding, "Chiapas is Mexico: The Imperative of Political Reform," *World Policy Journal*, Spring 1994.

39. David C. Korten, "Sustainable Development," *World Policy Journal*, Winter 1991–92; Robin Broad and John Cavanagh, "Beyond the Myths of Rio: A New American Agenda for the Environment," *World Policy Journal*, Spring 1993; Nicholas Colchester, "Goodbye, Nation-State. Hello . . . What?" *New York Times*, July 17, 1994.

40. Office of Public Information, "Charter of the United Nations and Statute of the International Court of Justice," United Nations, New York.

41. Peter H. Sand, "International Cooperation: The Environmental Experience," in Jessica Tuchman Mathews, ed., *Preserving the Global Environment: The Challenge of Shared Leadership* (New York: W.W. Norton & Company, 1991); UNDP, "Capacity 21: Management Report on the First Year of Operation," New York, undated.

42. Hilary F. French, "GATT: Global Menace or Potential Ally?" *World Watch*, September/October 1993; "Decision on Trade and Environment," General Agreement on Tariffs and Trade, Marrakesh, Morocco, April 15, 1994; Hilary F. French, "Rebuilding the World Bank," in Lester R. Brown et al., *State of the World 1994* (New York: W.W.

Norton & Company, 1994); World Bank, *Making Development Sustainable: The World Bank Group and the Environment, Fiscal 1994 Report* (Washington, D.C.: 1994); David Reed, ed., *Structural Adjustment and the Environment* (Boulder, Colo.: Westview Press, 1992); Wilfredo Cruz and Robert Repetto, *The Environmental Effects of Stabilization and Structural Adjustment Programs: The Philippines Case* (Washington, D.C.: World Resources Institute, 1992).

43. Lee A. Kimball, "International Institutional Developments," in *Yearbook of International Law 1993* (Oxford: Oxford University Press, 1994); Lee A. Kimball, "International Institutional Developments: The U.N. Conference on Environment and Development," *Yearbook of International Law 1992* (Boston/Dordrecht: Graham & Trotman/Martinus Nijhoff, 1993); Kathryn G. Sessions, "Institutionalizing the Earth Summit," UNA-USA Occasional Paper, United Nations Association of the United States of America (UNA-USA), Washington, D.C., October 1992.

44. Kimball, *1993 Yearbook*, op. cit. note 43; Kimball, *1992 Yearbook*, op. cit. note 43.

45. Earth Council, Natural Resources Defense Council (NRDC), and World Resources Institute, "Directory of National Commissions on Sustainable Development," Washington, D.C., May 1994; Earth Summit Watch, *Four in '94. Assessing National Actions to Implement Agenda 21: A Country-by-Country Report* (Washington, D.C.: 1994); "Formulating and Implementing China's Agenda 21," Capacity 21 Program information sheet, UNDP, undated; Kathleen Gildred and Sheila Kelly, Citizens Network for Sustainable Development, "Sustainable Communities Working Group Paper," unpublished, July 21, 1994; "Local Agenda 21 Network News," International Council for Local Environmental Initiatives, Toronto, June 1994.

46. Martin Khor, "CSD Still Alive, But Not Yet Kicking Into Action," *Third World Economics*, June 1–15, 1994; "Summary of the Sec-

ond Session of the Commission on Sustainable Development 16–27 May 1994," *Earth Negotiations Bulletin*, May 30, 1994; UN-NGLS, op. cit. note 3.

47. Interaction Council, Report on the Conclusions and Recommendations by a High-level Group on "The Future Role of the Global Multilateral Organizations," The Hague, Netherlands, May 7–8, 1994; "Reporting System on Environmental Progress Needs Simplification, Groups Tell CSD Session," *International Environment Reporter*, June 1, 1994.

48. Interaction Council, op. cit. note 47; CAPE 21/Citizens Network for Sustainable Development, Procedural Recommendations to Klaus Töpfer, Chairman of the Commission on Sustainable Development, October 1994; Barbara Bramble, "CSD Needs a Better Structure," Newsletter of the Citizens Network for Sustainable Development, Bolinas, Calif., Summer 1994.

49. Global Environment Facility (GEF), brochure, Washington, D.C., December 1991; GEF, "Quarterly Operational Report," Washington, D.C., August 1994.

50. "Agreement Reached on Funding GEF; Program to Receive More than $2 Billion," *International Environment Reporter*, March 23, 1994; GEF, "Instrument for the Establishment of the Restructured Global Environment Facility," Report of the GEF Participants Meeting, Geneva, Switzerland, March 14–16, 1994.

51. UNDP, UNEP, and World Bank, *Global Environment Facility: Independent Evaluation of the Pilot Phase* (Washington, D.C.: World Bank, 1994).

52. Indian renewables project described in World Bank, *The World Bank and the Environment, Fiscal 1993 Report* (Washington, D.C.: 1993); "Memorandum: IBRD NTPC Loan Global Warming Implications," Environmental Defense Fund, Washington, D.C., June 1993.

53. Global Environment Operations, World Bank, "Business Plan. Fiscal Year 1995," Washington, D.C., 1994; Jens Rosebrock, World Bank, Washington, D.C., private communication, October 20, 1994; Greenpeace International, "Lending for the Climate: MDBs and the Climate Convention," Prepared for the 10th Session of the Intergovernmental Negotiating Committee for a Framework Convention on Climate Change," Geneva, Switzerland, August 22-September 2, 1994; Liz Barratt-Brown, Kando Velasco, and Scott Hajost, "Financial Reform and the Climate Convention," *Eco* (NGO Newsletter at the Intergovernmental Negotiating Committee), September 2, 1994.

54. Barbara Crossette, "At the U.N., a Drive for Diversity," *New York Times*, October 24, 1994; UNDP, op. cit. note 4; for a number of recommendations on needed reforms, see Erskine Childers with Brian Urquhart, "Renewing the United Nations System," *Development Dialogue* (Dag Hammarskjöld Foundation/Ford Foundation), 1994:1.

55. On the achievements of UNEP see, for instance, Richard Elliot Benedick, *Ozone Diplomacy* (Cambridge, Mass.: Harvard University Press, 1991); budgets from Sergei Khromov, communications program officer, UNEP, Nairobi, private communication, October 31, 1994, and from National Wildlife Federation, *1993 Annual Report,* Washington, D.C., 1993; Pamela Leonard and Walter Hoffman, *Effective Global Environmental Protection: World Federalist Proposals to Strengthen the Role of the United Nations* (Washington, D.C.: World Federalist Association, 1990).

56. Daniel C. Esty, "GATTing the Greens," *Foreign Affairs*, November/December 1993; Daniel C. Esty, "The Case for a Global Environmental Organization," in Peter B. Kenen, ed., *Managing the World Economy: Fifty Years After Bretton Woods* (Washington, D.C.: Institute for International Economics, 1994).

57. Branislav Gosovic, *The Quest for World Environmental Cooperation* (London and New

York: Routledge, 1992); UNDP, "Heading for Change: UNDP 1993 Annual Report," New York, undated; Gareth Porter, "Multilateral Agreement on Minimum Standards for Manufacturing and Processing Industries," Environmental and Energy Study Institute, Washington, D.C., July 1994; French, op. cit. note 10.

58. James Avery Joyce, *World Labor Rights and Their Protection* (London: Croom Helm, 1980); Esty, "Case for a Global Environmental Organization," op. cit. note 56.

59. UNDP, op. cit. note 4; Martin Walker, "Global Taxation: Paying for Peace," *World Policy Journal*, Summer 1993; Childers with Urquhart, op. cit. note 54.

60. Lester M. Salamon, "The Rise of the Nonprofit Sector," *Foreign Affairs*, July/August 1994; Julie Fisher, *The Road from Rio: Sustainable Development and the Nongovernmental Movement in the Third World* (Westport, Conn.: Praeger, 1993); Hinrichsen, op. cit. note 1; Kate Randolph, Coordinator, NGO Planning Committee for ICPD, private communication, October 18, 1994; Michael Clough, "Grass-Roots Policymaking: Say Good-Bye to the 'Wise Men'," *Foreign Affairs*, January/February 1994.

61. *Eco* is produced regularly by NGOs at major international negotiations. The *Earth Negotiations Bulletin* is published by the International Institute for Sustainable Development of Winnipeg, Manitoba.

62. Benedick, op. cit. note 55; Greenpeace International, *Beyond UNCED* (Amsterdam: 1992); John Zarocostas, "Earth Summit Nations at Odds Over Issue of Multinationals," *Journal of Commerce*, April 6, 1992; Stephan Schmidheiny with the Business Council for Sustainable Development, *Changing Course* (Cambridge, Mass.: The MIT Press, 1992); "Constructive Industry Hits INC 10," *ECO*, Climate Negotiations, Geneva, August 26, 1994.

63. David A. Wirth, "A Matchmaker's Challenge: Marrying International Law and American Environmental Law," *Virginia Journal of International Law*, Winter 1992; Daniel J. Shepard, "UN Seeks Experts' Testimony in Series of Extraordinary Hearings on Development," *Earth Times*, June 15, 1994; Leonard and Hoffman, op. cit. note 55.

64. United Nations, op. cit. note 1; Kathryn G. Sessions, "Options for NGO Participation in the Commission on Sustainable Development," UNA-USA Background Paper, UNA-USA, Washington, D.C., May 1993; Ferita Ayoub, Chief of NGO Section, Department of Policy Coordination and Sustainable Development, United Nations, New York, private communication, August 24, 1994; "The NGO Steering Committee to the Commission on Sustainable Development," memorandum, New York, June 5, 1994.

65. Earth Summit Watch, *One Year After Rio: Special First Edition* (New York: NRDC, June 1993); Earth Summit Watch, op. cit. note 45.

66. Earth Summit Watch, op. cit. note 45; Earth Council, NRDC, and World Resources Institute, op. cit. note 45.

67. Yolanda Kakabadse N. with Sarah Burns, "Movers and Shapers: NGOs in International Affairs," *International Perspectives on Sustainability*, World Resources Institute, Washington, D.C., May 1994; The Stanley Foundation, "The UN System and NGOs: New Relationships for a New Era?" Report of the Twenty-Fifth United Nations Issues Conference, Harriman, N.Y., February 18–20, 1994.

68. For a discussion of the GATT dispute resolution procedure, see Steve Charnovitz, "Dolphins and Tuna: An Analysis of the Second GATT Panel Report," *Environmental Law Reporter*, October 1994; John Zarocostas, "Environmental Proposal for WTO Met Coolly," *Journal of Commerce*, September 19, 1994.

69. "The World Bank Policy on Disclosure of Information," World Bank, Washing-

ton, D.C., March 1994; "Operations Inspection Function: Objectives, Mandate and Operating Procedures for an Independent Inspection Panel," World Bank, 1993; David Hunter and Lori Udall, "The World Bank's New Inspection Panel: Will It Increase the Bank's Accountability?" Center for International Environmental Law, Brief No. 1, Washington, D.C., April 1994; Barbara Bramble, "World Bank Reforms: The Beginnings of Accountability," Newsletter of the Citizens Network for Sustainable Development, Bolinas, Calif., October/November 1993.

70. Importance of participatory approaches to project success from Operations Evaluation Department, *Evaluation Results for 1991* (Washington, D.C.: World Bank, 1993), and from Bhuvan Bhatnagar and Aubrey C. Williams, eds., *Participatory Development and the World Bank: Potential Directions for Change* (Washington, D.C.: World Bank Discussion Papers, 1992); Nancy Alexander, Bread for the World Institute, private communication, October 20, 1994; "The World Bank and Participation," Report to the Board of the World Bank, August 25, 1994, including NGO Addendum; Jo Marie Griesgraber, ed., *Rethinking Bretton Woods: Toward Equitable, Sustainable, and Participatory Development* (Washington, D.C.: Center of Concern, 1994).

71. Riley E. Dunlop, George H. Gallup, Jr., and Alec M. Gallup, "Of Global Concern: Results of the Health of the Planet Survey," *Environment*, November 1993.

Index